LUTHER'S WORKS

American Edition

VOLUME 32

Published by Concordia Publishing House

and Muhlenberg Press in 55 volumes.

General Editors are Jaroslav Pelikan (for vols. 1-30)

and Helmut T. Lehmann (for vols. 31-55)

LUTHER'S WORKS

VOLUME 32

Career of the Reformer II

EDITED BY

GEORGE W. FORELL

GENERAL EDITOR

HELMUT T. LEHMANN

MUHLENBERG PRESS / PHILADELPHIA

GENERAL EDITORS' PREFACE

The first editions of Luther's collected works appeared in the sixteenth century, and so did the first efforts to make him "speak English." In America serious attempts in these directions were made for the first time in the nineteenth century. The Saint Louis edition of Luther was the first endeavor on American soil to publish a collected edition of his works, and the Henkel Press in New Market, Virginia, was the first to publish some of Luther's writings in an English translation. During the first decade of the twentieth century, J. N. Lenker produced translations of Luther's sermons and commentaries in thirteen volumes. A few years later the first of the six volumes in the Philadelphia (or Holman) edition of the *Works of Martin Luther* appeared. But a growing recognition of the need for more of Luther's works in English has resulted in this American edition of Luther's works.

The edition is intended primarily for the reader whose knowledge of late medieval Latin and sixteenth-century German is too small to permit him to work with Luther in the original languages. Those who can will continue to read Luther in his original words as these have been assembled in the monumental Weimar edition (*D. Martin Luthers Werke.* Kritische Gesamtausgabe; Weimar, 1883–). Its texts and helps have formed a basis for this edition, though in certain places we have felt constrained to depart from its readings and findings. We have tried throughout to translate Luther as he thought translating should be done. That is, we have striven for faithfulness on the basis of the best lexicographical materials available. But where literal accuracy and clarity have conflicted, it is clarity that we have preferred, so that sometimes paraphrase seemed more faithful than literal fidelity. We have proceeded in a similar way in the matter of Bible versions, translating Luther's translations. Where this could be done by the use of an existing

English version—King James, Douay, or Revised Standard—we have done so. Where it could not, we have supplied our own. To indicate this in each specific instance would have been pedantic; to adopt a uniform procedure would have been artificial—especially in view of Luther's own inconsistency in this regard. In each volume the translator will be responsible primarily for matters of text and language, while the responsibility of the editor will extend principally to the historical and theological matters reflected in the introductions and notes.

Although the edition as planned will include fifty-five volumes, Luther's writings are not being translated in their entirety. Nor should they be. As he was the first to insist, much of what he wrote and said was not that important. Thus the edition is a selection of works that have proved their importance for the faith, life, and history of the Christian church. The first thirty volumes contain Luther's expositions of various biblical books, while the remaining volumes include what are usually called his "Reformation writings" and other occasional pieces. The final volume of the set will be an index volume; in addition to an index of quotations, proper names, and topics, and a list of corrections and changes, it will contain a glossary of many of the technical terms that recur in Luther's works and that cannot be defined each time they appear. Obviously Luther cannot be forced into any neat set of rubrics. He can provide his reader with bits of autobiography or with political observations as he expounds a psalm, and he can speak tenderly about the meaning of the faith in the midst of polemics against his opponents. It is the hope of publishers, editors, and translators that through this edition the message of Luther's faith will speak more clearly to the modern church.

J. P.
H. T. L.

CONTENTS

General Editors' Preface   v

Abbreviations   VIII

Introduction to Volume 32   IX

Defense and Explanation of All the Articles, 1521   3
    Translated by Charles M. Jacobs
    Revised by George W. Forell

Luther at the Diet of Worms, 1521   101
    Translated by Roger A. Hornsby

Against Latomus, 1521   133
    Translated by George Lindbeck

The Burning of Brother Henry, 1525   261
    Translated by A. T. W. Steinhäuser
    Revised by George W. Forell

Indexes   287

C. R.	— *Corpus Reformatorum,* edited by C. G. Bretschneider and H. E. Bindseil (Halle, 1834-1860).
CL	— *Luthers Werke in Auswahl,* edited by Otto Clemen *et al.* (Bonn, 1912-1933; Berlin, 1955-1956).
EA	— *D. Martin Luthers sämmtliche Werke* (Frankfurt and Erlangen, 1826-1857).
LW	— American edition of *Luther's Works* (Philadelphia and St. Louis, 1955-).
MA³	— *Martin Luther.* Ausgewählte Werke (München, 1948-).
Migne	— *Patrologiae, Series Latina,* 221 vols. in 222 (Paris, 1844-1904), J. P. Migne, editor.
PE	— *Works of Martin Luther* (Philadelphia, 1915-1943).
St. L.	— *D. Martin Luthers sämmtliche Schriften,* edited by Johann Georg Walch. Edited and published in modern German, 23 vols. in 25 (St. Louis, 1880-1910).
WA	— *D. Martin Luthers Werke.* Kritische Gesamtausgabe (Weimar, 1883-).
WA, Br	— *D. Martin Luthers Werke.* Briefwechsel (Weimar, 1930-1948).
WA, TR	— *D. Martin Luthers Werke.* Tischreden (Weimar, 1912-1921).
WA, DB	— *D. Martin Luthers Werke.* Deutsche Bibel (Weimar, 1906-).

INTRODUCTION TO VOLUME 32

The writings of Luther in this volume show the response of the reformer to the manifold attacks which were leveled against him when it became clear that the movement which he led was much more than a "monkish quarrel." They show him to be fully aware of the seriousness and the scope of the conflict, trying to defend his cause and to articulate his position in very different situations.

After the Leipzig Debate of 1519 Luther found himself attacked from many diverse directions. He had to defend the cause of the Reformation against the papacy, the emperor, the learned theological faculties of many universities, and even in the face of doubts from his own supporters. This volume offers writings which illustrate his efforts to find the answer to all these challenges.

The attack from the papacy came first. Initially the pope had hesitated to become involved in what appeared to him to be one of the many jealousy-inspired controversies between the representatives of hostile monastic orders, or perhaps an academic dispute between enemies and friends of the new classical learning which was sweeping the universities. When the pope realized that this view of the situation was too superficial, he took the necessary steps which, according to canon law, would in due time lead to Luther's excommunication, should he prove recalcitrant.

In this process Dr. Johann Eck of Ingolstadt, Luther's opponent at the Leipzig Debate, proved to be the papacy's main source of information concerning the controversy. For Eck had gone to Rome to place his expert knowledge at the Curia's disposal. And it was he who, together with Cardinal Cajetan and Sylvester Cardinal Prierias, was largely responsible for the bull, *Exsurge Domine*, of June 15, 1520. This papal pronouncement condemned forty-one of Luther's statements made in previous writings as "poisonous, offensive, misleading for godly and simple minds, uncharitable, counter to all reverence for the Holy Roman Church, the mother of the faithful and the mistress of faith." [1]

---

[1] *EA Var. Arg.* 4, 280.

Eck himself reported in a letter of May 3, 1520 to Johann Fabri, "It was indeed fortunate and most necessary that I came to Rome at this time, otherwise only a few would have known Luther's erroneous and misleading teaching." And he stated further that in the preparation of the condemnation, "His Holiness the pope, two cardinals, a theologian from Spain and I spent almost five hours together." [2]

The result was the well-known document which called dramatically upon Christ, the Apostle Peter, the Apostle Paul, and the entire communion of saints to take action against Luther and his teachings: "Bishop Leo, the servant of all servants of God. Arise, O Lord [Ps. 7:6], judge thy cause; remember how fools scoff at thee all day [Ps. 74:22]. Incline thy ear to our prayer [Ps. 88:2]. For foxes have come to spoil the vineyard [Song of Sol. 2:15] whose wine press thou alone hast trodden [Isa. 63:3]. And when thou didst desire to ascend to the Father into heaven thou didst commit the care, government, and administration of this vineyard to Peter as the head and thy vicar and to his successors as the church triumphant. Now a wild boar from the forest threatens to ravage this vineyard, indeed, a wild animal threatens to pluck its fruit [Ps. 80:12-13]." [3]

The document continued in this somewhat pompous style with an abundance of scriptural passages but without much concern for the context in which they originally appeared. Then the bull listed the forty-one statements of Luther, chosen also without special regard for the context, for explicit condemnation. Anyone who held or defended these views, were he clergyman or layman, peasant or prince, was condemned. Luther himself received sixty days, from the proclamation of the bull, to return as "the prodigal son to the bosom of the church." In the meantime he was ordered to keep silent and his books were to be burned.

Defense and Explanation of All the Articles, the first work presented in this volume, was Luther's reply. It is a clear-cut statement, showing how Luther intended to defend himself against the charges of the papacy.

As far as Luther was concerned the pope and his bull did not speak for the true church. Rather the bull made it plain that the

---

[2] *Ibid.*, pp. 256-257.
[3] *Ibid.*, p. 263.

men in Rome were "tyrants," and their condemnation of obvious Christian truth would now reveal their tyranny to everybody. In his struggle with the papacy, Luther made, by this time, no effort to compromise the issues. On the contrary, he went out of his way to show that the differences were even greater than the bull might have suggested.

His reply to the condemnation of his statement, "Indulgences are a pious fraud practiced upon Christians; they are remissions of good works and belong to the things that are permitted but not necessary," [4] is very significant. He stated his willingness to recant this proposition, because he now considered it far too mild. Luther was now prepared to say, "The indulgences are not a pious fraud, but an infernal, diabolical, antichristian fraud, larceny and robbery, whereby the Roman Nimrod and teacher of sin peddles sin and hell to the whole world and sucks and entices away everybody's money as the price of this unspeakable harm." [5] And he added, sarcastically, "If this recantation is not enough, I will improve on it some other time."

He dealt similarly with the thirtieth article. Here the bull had condemned his statement, "Certain articles of John Huss, condemned at Constance, are most Christian, most true and altogether evangelical, and these all Christendom together could not condemn." [6] He was now prepared to say, "As a matter of fact, on this point I have greatly erred. . . . Now I say, not only certain articles, but all the articles of John Huss, condemned at Constance, are altogether Christian." [7]

As far as his conflict with Rome was concerned Luther appeared to be utterly sure of himself. In fact, the violent opposition from the papacy became for him a vindication of the truth of his cause. Looking at the history of Israel he said, "God never made prophets out of the high priests or others of lofty station, but usually he raised up lowly and despised persons, even at last the shepherd, Amos. . . . The dear saints have always had to preach against and chide those in high places, to rebuke kings, princes, priests, and scholars, and to risk and sometimes lose their necks." And he

---

[4] Cf. p. 64.
[5] Cf. p. 64.
[6] Cf. p. 82.
[7] Cf. p. 82.

continued, "In those days, too, the bigwigs gave the holy prophets no other answer than to say, 'We are the authorities and you must obey us and not those lowly and despised prophets.' . . . Today they act the same way." [8]

And Luther made the source of his confidence very clear. He said, "I am sure the Word of God is with me and not with them, for I have the Scriptures on my side and they have only their own doctrine. This gives me courage, so that the more they despise and persecute me, the less I fear them." [9]

In his struggle with Rome Luther was confident that he had Scripture to back him up. This enabled him to discard the accusations and condemnations of the papacy with a shocking lack of concern. "Scripture alone," Luther said, "is the lord and master of all writings and doctrine on earth." [10] Since the bull and its condemnations were not founded on Scripture, they meant nothing to him.

It was this same complete trust in the power of the Word which he expressed in a letter to his friend, Spalatin, accompanying the Latin version of *Defense and Explanation of All the Articles*. Referring to Ulrich von Hutten's war-like plans to defend the cause of the gospel by force of arms he wrote, "You can see what Hutten has in mind. I do not want the gospel to be contested by force and the shedding of blood. . . . Through the Word the world was overcome, through the Word the church was maintained, and through the Word she will again be restored." [11] It was on this power that Luther relied in the struggle with the papacy.

But how did Luther respond to the accusations that were leveled against him from the highest political authority of his time, the emperor? The second work selected for this volume is a record of some of the proceedings concerning Luther at the Diet of Worms in 1521, *Luther at the Diet of Worms*. It offers at least a partial answer to the question about Luther's response to political pressure.

Luther's appearance at Worms was based upon somewhat obscure negotiations. At first neither his friends nor his enemies had wanted it. His friends, remembering John Huss, feared for his

---

[8] Cf. p. 9.

[9] Cf. p. 9.

[10] Cf. p. 11.

[11] WA, Br 2, 249 (No. 368, Wittenberg, Jan. 16, 1521).

safety. His enemies were afraid that his appearance at Worms would add greatly to his prestige. It was not in accord with the wishes of the Curia and its representatives at the imperial court to have an excommunicated heretic appear publicly at a diet of the empire. Even in the sixteenth century it was the desire of the popes and their most ardent supporters that the slogan, *Roma locuta, causa finita,*[12] should be universally accepted. By the time Luther appeared in Worms, Rome had spoken twice, in the above-mentioned bull, *Exsurge Domine,* and again in a bull of excommunication issued on January 3, 1521, *Decet Pontificem.* Under these circumstances, the only action proper for the emperor, in the eyes of the papacy's supporters, was to enforce the excommunication through the imperial ban.[13]

There can be little doubt that Charles V's own inclinations were to support the papacy to the hilt in a matter essentially theological. As the emperor stated later before the diet, he was convinced that, "It is certain that a single friar errs in his opinion which is against all of Christendom and according to which all of Christianity will be and will always have been in error, both in the past thousand years and even more in the present." And he continued, "I regret having so long delayed to proceed against this Luther and his false doctrine." [14]

But while this was an expression of the emperor's true sentiments, he had cited Luther to Worms both as a favor to Elector Frederick the Wise and in the hope of giving the greatest possible publicity to a potential recantation. Furthermore he and his advisers thought that, should Luther refuse to recant, the enforcement of the ban against him would be far easier if he had first appeared at the diet. In that case, the emperor felt, nobody would be able to doubt that all legal remedies had been exhausted.

All this explains Charles' letter to Frederick of November 28, 1520, stating that since the elector wished Luther to be examined before he be condemned, he should bring him to the diet, where

---

[12] "Rome has spoken, the case is closed."
[13] Cf. C. Mirbt, *Quellen zur Geschichte des Papsttums und des römischen Katholizimus* (4th ed., Tübingen, 1924), p. 186, where the agreement of Frederick II of Nov. 22, 1220, is quoted which imposes the punishment of the empire on the heretics.
[14] Cf. p. 114 n. 9.

he could then be questioned. The emperor was prepared to guarantee his safety.[15]

Even though this invitation was later temporarily withdrawn, since it was completely unacceptable to the papal party at the imperial court, it was eventually renewed. On March 6, 1521, Luther was formally cited by the emperor to appear within twenty-one days in Worms for an investigation. A letter of safe conduct accompanied this document.[16]

Luther's own attitude in all these diplomatic negotiations was clearly shown in a letter to Spalatin of March 19, 1521. "I have received the articles which I am to recant," he wrote, "but never doubt that I shall recant anything, for I see that their only basis for such a demand is that I wrote against their fictitious 'custom' and 'usage of the church.' I shall answer Emperor Charles that if I have been cited only in order to recant, I shall not appear. For then the trip is useless. If recanting is all that is to be done, I could recant here. But if he then wants to cite me in order that I might be killed and if he considers me an enemy of the empire because of my reply, I shall offer to come anyway. For if Christ grants me his grace I shall not flee and desert the Word in the midst of the battle. But I am quite sure that these bloodthirsty people will not rest until they have killed me. Were it in my power I would only wish that none but the papists would be accountable for my death. We have again become altogether pagan, as we were in the days before Christ, since this cunning Antichrist holds the kingdoms and this world captive." [17]

Here it is apparent that Luther's attitude toward the emperor and the princes was just as intransigent as was his attitude toward the pope. The one difference was that he did not blame the political authorities for their actions against him. He felt rather that they were being used as a screen by the false leaders of the church. He was firmly convinced that the secular authorities and the common people, if they opposed him, opposed him against their own true interests. It was on behalf of all of them that he had to remain firm. In his speech before the diet he made this quite clear by saying, "If, therefore, I should have retracted these writings,

---

[15] St. L. 15, 1697, 1698.

[16] WA, Br 2, 278-281 (No. 383, Worms, March 6, 1521).

[17] WA, Br 2, 289 (No. 389, Wittenberg, March 19, 1521).

I should have done nothing other than to have added strength to this [papal] tyranny, and I should have opened not only windows but doors to this great godlessness. It would rage farther and more freely than ever it has dared until this time." [18]

Luther believed that if he should recant he would be personally responsible for a strengthening of the oppression of the Word. It would be, as he had written to Spalatin, a "desertion of the Word in the midst of the battle." And so he continued, "Yes, from the proof of such a revocation on my part, their wholly lawless and unrestrained kingdom of wickedness would become still more intolerable for the already wretched people; and their rule would be further strengthened and established, especially if it should be reported that this evil deed had been done by me by virtue of the authority of your most serene majesty and of the whole Roman Empire." [19] Luther was prepared to claim nothing for himself, personally. He was ready to say that he was "the lowest scum and able to do nothing except err." [20] But as far as he was concerned, the controversy was not about his person or his opinions but rather whether the Word or the ecclesiastical dignitaries in Rome should be the final authority in the church.

To others this alternative might have appeared far less simple; to Luther it was utterly clear. And thus in spite of, or perhaps because of, a well-developed sense of respect for emperor and empire, he would not recant. For to him such a retraction would have meant the betrayal of both church and empire for the sake of his personal safety.

But his speech at Worms reveals also that his attitude toward the secular authorities was far more tolerant than that toward the spiritual authorities. It appeared to Luther that the emperor was to be excused since he did not know any better. But the pope and the theologians in Rome were supposed to know, and were therefore without excuse. This is the reason why he hoped that should he be killed, as he had every reason to expect, only the papists should be held accountable before God for his death.

The third work of Luther presented in this volume, *Against Latomus,* shows the manner in which the reformer dealt with the

[18] Cf. p. 110.
[19] Cf. p. 110.
[20] Cf. p. 111.

attacks from his professorial enemies on the theological faculties of many European universities. If the keynote in his conflict with the papacy was his confidence in the power of the Word, and if in his appearance before the empire it was his concern for the truth which his recantation might have obliterated, then the keynote in his controversy with the professors at the University of Louvain was his disdain for their ignorance of the true sources of all theological discourse.

During his enforced sojourn at the Wartburg Luther received a copy of the work of a certain Latomus who was a member of the theological faculty at Louvain. In it the author defended the condemnation of Luther's teachings by that faculty. Luther was annoyed. In order to answer the man, whom he considered a simpleton, he had to tear himself away from his work on the translation of the Bible.[21]

On May 26, 1521, he wrote to Melanchthon, "I answer the book of Jacob Latomus reluctantly since my mind is now concentrated on quiet studies. Yet I see that it is necessary that I reply myself. But it is annoying to have to read such an aimless and poorly written work." [22] His dedicatory letter to Justus Jonas revealed the same frame of mind. He wrote, "Truly, it won't be easy for you to believe how unwillingly I have torn myself away from the peace-giving words of Christ, with which I have been occupied on this my Patmos, in order to waste my time reading the nonsense of this prickly and thorny sophist." [23] Luther felt that the attack against him as developed by the universities was essentially "sophistical." They attacked him without trying to meet his arguments and their reasoning seemed to him captious and specious.

This explains the mood of his reply to Latomus. For example, Latomus had suggested that in dealing with any possible weakness in the pope three steps were open: first, not to criticize the papacy

---

[21] It appears that Luther later changed his mind in regard to Latomus' competence. In a table talk, reported by Veit Dietrich (February 1, 1533), he said that Latomus had been the ablest of all those who had written against him. Lauterbach records a similar remark (November, 1538). Here Luther elaborates by saying that Latomus had a plausible, if erroneous, basic argument, namely, whatever the church has accepted should not be rejected. WA, TR 1, 202 (No. 463) and 4, 145 (No. 4119).

[22] WA, Br 2, 347 (No. 413, Wartburg, May 26, 1521).

[23] Cf. p. 138.

but for the cities and princes to refrain from such acts as they objected to in the pope; second, to pray; and third, to be patient.[24]

To Luther this approach seemed nothing but the most obvious kind of flattery. It was merely a pious exhortation to everyone to keep quiet in the face of evil, error, and injustice. "I grant," Luther wrote, "One ought to respect superiors, but not to the extent of offending against the Word of God—which is God himself." [25] And he continued, "Thrice cursed be the man who does the Lord's work fraudulently, who flatters the pope, who winks at and plays along with hell's wolf, and who has no pity on the many souls of his brethren, purchased by Christ's blood, but now perishing miserably." [26]

As Luther saw it, it was the task of the theologians to speak up for the Word against its enemies. He was convinced that the "sophists" were betraying it out of a mixture of ignorance, cowardice, and conceit.

As far as the discussion of specific articles of faith was concerned, Luther accused Latomus of constantly begging the question. He said, "Latomus' entire book equivocates by begging the question, which is the very worst way of arguing. The perpetual foolishness of the sophists is to seize upon that which must first of all be proved and demonstrated, and assume that it is an infallible rule of faith." [27] It was Luther's claim that Latomus tried to win the argument by assuming the soundness of an opinion which he had not even tried to demonstrate from the Scriptures.

And this led Luther to a detailed and fairly technical discussion of the way in which Scripture must be used in theological discourse. He insisted, calling upon Augustine as his witness, that "figurative language proves nothing." [28] He said, "In no writings, least of all the divine, is it right in mere whimsy to grasp at figurative meanings. These ought to be shunned, and the pure, simple, original sense should be sought, unless the context or an evident absurdity forces one to recognize a figurative expression." [29] In later years Luther

---

[24] Cf. p. 143.
[25] Cf. p. 146.
[26] Cf. p. 146.
[27] Cf. p. 157.
[28] Cf. p. 167.
[29] Cf. p. 167.

stated that, "Faith is built on history," [30] while understanding history as the holy and eventful record of God's dealing with men. It seems evident that he had developed this crucial insight in the struggle for a sound exegesis against men like Latomus.

However, as far as the argument with Latomus was concerned, it was doomed from the start. Luther's presuppositions, his confidence in the Word as a final and sufficient authority for the proclamation of the church, combined with his lack of reverence for the accepted scholastic theologians, made him incomprehensible to most of his professorial colleagues. How could Latomus understand a statement like this: "Thomas [Aquinas] wrote a great deal of heresy and is responsible for the rule of Aristotle, the destroyer of godly doctrine. What do I care that the bishop of bulls [pope] has canonized him?" [31] Of Latomus and his colleagues Luther said, "He, together with his sophists, has never recognized what grace and sin, law and gospel, Christ and man are." [32] And he asserted that his opponents' arguments were worthless, "For he proves everything from human writings. Neither Gregory [whom Latomus had quoted] nor any angel has the right to set forth or teach in the church something which cannot be demonstrated from Scripture." [33]

The tone of Luther's reply to Latomus was disdainful and impatient. It showed that no real meeting of minds could be expected from further theological discussions with the scholastic professors. The reason, which had become ever more apparent, was that Luther and these opponents no longer spoke the same theological language.

The final work presented in this volume, *The Burning of Brother Henry*, was written four years after *Against Latomus*, early in 1525. It shows the reformer in a completely different mood. He is describing the events which led to the death of Henry of Zütphen, one of the first martyrs of the Reformation. The book was designed to comfort his friends and to call his murderers to repentance.

Here Luther was not dealing with pope or emperor, theologians or lawyers, but with a simple Christian congregation grieved by the loss of its pastor, and he was also thinking of the individual members

---

[30] WA 31II, 242 (*Lectures on Isaiah*, 1527-1530).
[31] Cf. p. 258.
[32] Cf. p. 257.
[33] Cf. p. 257.

of the drunken mob which had committed the murder, who might now be ready to repent their evil deed. To the Christians he said that they should not grieve nor speak ill of the murderers, but rather be glad and thank God for the opportunity to see the wonders of His grace. As far as the murderers were concerned Luther hoped and prayed, "that not the murderers alone but the whole land of Dithmarschen may be converted and come to the knowledge of the truth." [34]

It is Martin Luther, the pastor, who pleads with the Christians in Bremen in these words, "I ask you, for God's sake, take care of the people of Dithmarschen. Comfort and help them as friends so that they may join us . . . God has kindled a good spark. It will spread and become a great fire if you act in the spirit of friendship and kindness so that it is not extinguished." [35]

In this situation Luther showed his compassion not only for the bereaved congregation, but also for the repentant murderers. Gone is the tough assurance which expressed itself in his response to pope and emperor, but gone is also the impatient disdain that he showed in his argument with Latomus. When dealing with people in trouble, whether they were sad over the loss of a beloved pastor or horrified and repentant because of their share in his death, Luther showed himself tender and patient. It is perhaps significant that at least a few of the chief perpetrators of the murder of Henry of Zütphen did repent and become staunch supporters of the Reformation.[36]

The volume here presented offers four quite different "occasional writings" of Luther. They were his responses to situations largely not of his own making. They reflect the heat of battle, for it was his destiny to have to produce his theology basically in response to conditions which he had not been allowed to choose. Yet in spite of the vast differences in the occasions which produced them a study of the documents here offered seems to show that in all these very different situations Luther wrote as he did because he firmly believed: "Through the Word the world was overcome, through the Word the church was maintained, through the Word she will be restored." [37]

---

[34] Cf. p. 267.
[35] Cf. p. 272.
[36] Cf. pp. 278 n. 20; 279 n. 21.
[37] Cf. p. xii.

In the preparation of this volume the editor was supported by Professor George Lindbeck of Yale Divinity School, New Haven, Connecticut, who translated *Against Latomus,* and Professor Roger Hornsby of the classics department of the State University of Iowa, who translated *Luther at the Diet of Worms.* He was assisted in the editorial tasks by the Rev. Linwood Fredricksen of Iowa City, Iowa, and by Miss Sandra Levinson, who typed parts of the manuscript. The text of *Defense and Explanation of All the Articles* is a revision of the translation of Professor Charles M. Jacobs for the Philadelphia Edition and *The Burning of Brother Henry* is a revision of the translation of the Rev. A. T. W. Steinhäuser for the same edition. The indexes were prepared by Miss Elizabeth S. Reed.

G.W.F.

LUTHER'S WORKS

VOLUME 32

DEFENSE AND EXPLANATION
OF ALL THE ARTICLES

1521

Translated by Charles M. Jacobs

Revised by George W. Forell

INTRODUCTION

The work here presented was one of Luther's four answers to the bull, *Exsurge Domine*, issued by Pope Leo X on June 15, 1520, which had been published in Germany in September, 1520. The papal bull did not excommunicate Luther but rather condemned forty-one theses taken from Luther's writings as either "heretical or scandalous or false, or offensive to pious ears, or dangerous to simple minds, or subversive of catholic truth." Luther was asked to recant these errors within sixty days or face excommunication.

In order to focus public attention on this condemnation of Luther's writings, the men in charge of the bull's publication, especially Aleander and Eck, Luther's opponent at Leipzig, saw to it that the offending books were ceremoniously burned.

Luther retaliated by burning the papal bull outside the gates of Wittenberg on December 10, 1520, thus demonstrating that, since books are combustible, both sides could play that game. He then proceeded to defend the condemned propositions in two Latin and two German works, *Adversus execrabilem Antichristi bullam* (November, 1520); *Wider die Bulle des Endchrists* (November, 1520); *Assertio omnium articulorum M. Lutheri per bullam Leonis X. novissimam damnatorum* (December, 1520); *Grund und Ursach aller Artikel D. Martin Luthers so durch römische Bulle unrechtlich verdammt sind* (March, 1521).

Our translation is based upon the last of these four replies, which was in Luther's own opinion "smoother and simpler" than the preceding efforts.* Since Luther's own manuscript of this work has been preserved and is published, together with the first printed edition, in WA 7, 308-357, we were able to use both texts for our translation and revision. All significant differences between the two texts are noted in the footnotes.

The English translation here is a revision of the translation by Dr. C. M. Jacobs in the Philadelphia edition of Luther's works.

---

* *Luther's Correspondence and Other Contemporary Letters,* trans. and ed. by P. Smith and C. M. Jacobs (2 vols.; Philadelphia, 1913-1918), I, 442-443.

DEFENSE AND EXPLANATION
OF ALL THE ARTICLES

Defense and Explanation of All the
Articles of Dr. Martin Luther
which were Unjustly Condemned by the Roman Bull

JESUS. Grace and peace from God to all good Christians who will read this book or hear it read. Amen.

Blessed and praised be God, the Father of our Lord Jesus Christ, who in these days has enlightened so many hearts and has given Christian understanding also to the laity. Thus all over the world people are beginning to distinguish rightly between the counterfeit and hypocritical church or church leadership, and the true, basically sound church. This true church has been hidden so long beneath sacred vestments, ritual, works, and similar outward pretensions and man-made laws that we have finally been taught that we can be saved through the contribution of money rather than through faith. Now God's divine goodness can and will no longer let such abominations and errors rage in his church. This we are beginning to see and for this result we should hope and pray. Amen. Amen.

It is not the smallest sign of his divine goodness that God has lately made some of these tyrants of Christendom so blind and confounded them with such a spirit of confusion [Isa. 19:14] that, to their great shame and irretrievable downfall, they have issued a bull in which they have even neglected the very thing that up to now has helped them to deceive and fool the world, namely, the outward appearance of decency and fairness. Indeed, they have condemned such evident truth that even stone and wood should cry out against them. Never has a bull been received with such scorn, contempt, and derision.

May God, who has begun this good work perfect it according to

7

his mercy [Phil. 1:6] and give us grace to know this his grace, to thank him for it, and to pray earnestly for a blessed outcome so that poor souls may no longer be so sadly led astray by such deceit and trickery. Amen. Amen

Therefore, I, Dr. Martin Luther by name, have with a joyful heart undertaken to demonstrate from Scripture the truth of all the articles [condemned by the pope's bull], for your further instruction, and to expose the pretense of this false church, so that everyone may be able to defend himself against the blind feints these swindlers like to use. Someday, perhaps, even they will sober up and consent to exchange their hypocrisy for truth, their trickery for sincerity, and their pretensions for proofs. First, however, I must defend myself against some of the charges they bring against me.

First of all, I shall ignore the charge that I am caustic and impatient. I shall not apologize very much for that, for I have not been caustic or impatient in those books that have treated of Christian doctrine, but only in controversies, silly arguments about the papacy, indulgences, and similar foolishness. I was forced into these arguments and they were not worth all this discussion, let alone kindly and peaceful words.

They accuse me of claiming that I alone am everybody's teacher. My answer is that I have not done this, since I am always inclined to crawl into a corner. But my enemies have dragged me into the open through cunning and force to win glory and honor at my expense. Now that the game is going against them, they consider me guilty of vainglory. And even if it were true that I had set myself up all alone, that would be no excuse for their conduct. Who knows? God may have called me and raised me up [to be everybody's teacher]. They ought to be afraid lest they despise God in me.

Do we not read in the Old Testament that God generally raised up only one prophet at a time? Moses was alone during the exodus from Egypt. Elijah was alone in King Ahab's day. After him, Elisha stood alone. Isaiah was alone in Jerusalem, Hosea alone in Israel, Jeremiah alone in Judea, Ezekiel alone in Babylon, and so it went. Even though they had many disciples called "children of the prophets," God never allowed more than one man alone to preach and rebuke the people.

8

Moreover, God never made prophets out of the high priests or others of lofty station, but usually he raised up lowly and despised persons, even at last the shepherd, Amos [Amos 1:1]. King David was the one exception, but even he came at first from lowly rank [I Sam. 16:6-13]. The dear saints have always had to preach against and chide those in high places, to rebuke kings, princes, priests, and scholars, and to risk and sometimes lose their necks. In those days, too, the bigwigs gave the holy prophets no other answer than to say, "We are the authorities and you must obey us and not those lowly and despised prophets," as Jer. 18 [:18] reports. Today they act the same way. Everything that does not please the pope, the bishops, and the scholars, is supposed to be wrong. We are supposed to listen to them, no matter what they say.

Even in the New Testament, have not the true bishops and teachers been rare indeed? St. Ambrose[1] was alone in his day; after him, St. Jerome[2] and St. Augustine. Furthermore, God did not choose many eminent and great bishops for this work. St. Augustine was bishop in one little unimportant city,[3] but did he not accomplish more than all the Roman popes with all their fellow-bishops? They cannot hold a candle to him. Moreover, it is a fact that all heresies have been started, or at least have been encouraged, by bishops and scholars. If they were unreliable at a time when they were better, more learned, and more diligent, why shall we trust them now when they no longer even serve the church and have become secular lords? Do we insist on being blind?

I do not claim to be a prophet, but I do say that the more they scorn me and the higher they regard themselves, the more reason they have to fear that I may be a prophet. God is marvelous in his works and judgments. He pays attention neither to numbers, greatness, cunning, or power. As Ps. 138 [:6] says: "The haughty he knows from afar." And even if I am not a prophet, as far as I am concerned I am sure that the Word of God is with me and not with them, for I have the Scriptures on my side and they have only their own doctrine. This gives me courage, so that the more they despise

---

[1] Bishop of Milan (374-397).

[2] Living as a hermit near Bethlehem (386-420), St. Jerome defended the orthodox faith.

[3] Bishop of Hippo in North Africa (395-430).

and persecute me, the less I fear them. There were many asses in the world in the days of Balaam, but God spoke only through Balaam's ass [Num. 22:28]. He says in Ps. 14 [:6] to these same prominent men: "You have confounded the sound doctrine of the poor preacher because he trusted in God," as if to say that because he is not great and high and mighty, his doctrine must be false in your eyes.

They say also that I propose new ideas and it is not to be expected that everybody else should have been so long in error. That, too, the ancient prophets had to hear. If length of time were sufficient proof, the Jews would have had the strongest kind of case against Christ on that ground. His doctrine was different from any they had heard for a thousand years. The Gentiles, too, would have been justified in regarding the apostles with contempt, since their ancestors for more than three thousand years held to a different faith. There have been murderers, adulterers, and thieves since the beginning of the world, and will be to its end. Does that make their actions right? I preach nothing new, but I say that all Christian things have perished among the very people who ought to have preserved them, namely, the bishops and scholars. But I have no doubt that the truth has been retained in some hearts to this day, if only in the hearts of infants in their cradles. In Old Testament times also, the spiritual understanding of the law was retained among some of the common people, though it was lost by the high priests and the learned who ought to have preserved it. Thus Jeremiah says [Jer. 5:4f.] that he has found less understanding and justice among the leaders than among the laity and the common folk. Likewise today, poor peasants and children understand Christ better than pope, bishops, and doctors. Everything is topsy-turvy.

Now, if that is the way they want it, well and good. Let them make me out a heathen. But what would their answer be, or how should we present our case, if a Turk were to ask us to give reasons for our faith? He doesn't care how long we have believed a certain way or how many or how eminent the people are who have believed this or that. We would have to be silent about all these things and direct him to the holy Scriptures as the basis for our faith. It would be absurd and ridiculous if we were to say: look here, so many

10

priests, bishops, kings, princes, lands, and peoples have believed this and that ever so long.

Let them now treat me the same way. Let us see what our reasons and resources are. Let us examine them, if only for our own reassurance and attention. Shall we have such good reasons and not know them? Shall we keep them hidden when it is the will of Christ that they shall be generally known to all men? He says in Matt. 5 [:15], "Nor do men light a lamp and put it under a bushel, but on a stand, and it gives light to all in the house." Christ allowed his hands, his feet, his sides to be touched so that the disciples might be sure that it was he, himself [John 20:27]. Why, then, should we not touch and examine the Scriptures—which are in truth the spiritual body of Christ—to make sure whether we believe in them or not? For all other writings are treacherous; they may be spirits in the air [cf. Eph. 2:2] which have no flesh or bone, as Christ had.

This is my answer to those also who accuse me of rejecting all the holy teachers of the church. I do not reject them. But everyone, indeed, knows that at times they have erred, as men will; therefore, I am ready to trust them only when they give me evidence for their opinions from Scripture, which has never erred. This St. Paul bids me to do in I Thess. 5:21, where he says, "Test everything; hold fast what is good." St. Augustine writes to St. Jerome to the same effect, "I have learned to do only those books that are called the holy Scriptures the honor of believing firmly that none of their writers has ever erred. All others I so read as not to hold what they say to be the truth unless they prove it to me by holy Scripture or clear reason." [4]

Holy Scripture must necessarily be clearer, simpler, and more reliable than any other writings. Especially since all teachers verify their own statements through the Scriptures as clearer and more reliable writings, and desire their own writings to be confirmed and explained by them. But nobody can ever substantiate an obscure saying by one that is more obscure; therefore, necessity forces us to run to the Bible with the writings of all teachers, and to obtain there a verdict and judgment upon them. Scripture alone is the

---

[4] Letter 82 (to St. Jerome). Migne 33, 286-287.

true lord and master of all writings and doctrine on earth. If that is not granted, what is Scripture good for? The more we reject it, the more we become satisfied with men's books and human teachers.

That many of the bigwigs hate and persecute me for this reason does not frighten me at all. It rather comforts and strengthens me since it is clearly revealed in the Scriptures that the persecutors and haters have usually been wrong and the persecuted have usually been right. The lie has always had the greater following, the truth the smaller. Indeed, I know if only a few insignificant men were attacking me, then what I have taught and written were not yet from God. St. Paul caused a great uproar with his teaching, as we read in Acts [17:5, 18; 18:12; 19:23-41], but that did not prove his teaching false. Truth has always caused disturbance and false teachers have always said, "Peace, peace!" as Isaiah [Ezekiel] and Jeremiah tell us [Ezek. 13:10, 16; Jer. 6:14; 8:11].

Therefore, without regard to the pope and his great following, I will gladly come to the rescue and defense of the articles condemned in the bull, as God gives me grace. I trust, by God's grace, to protect them against the wrong that has been done them. In the face of force, nothing more is here than one poor body; that I commend to God and his holy truth which the pope has condemned. Amen.

THE FIRST ARTICLE

It is heresy to hold that the sacraments give grace to all who do not put an obstacle in the way.[5]

In order to understand this article, it should be noted that my opponents have taught that the holy sacraments give grace to anyone, even if he does not repent his sin and has no intention to do good. They claim it is enough that he not "put an obstacle in the way," that is, that he be without wanton intention to sin. My article is stated in view of this teaching and I continue to hold and insist that this doctrine is un-Christian, misleading, and heretical. Besides the removal of the obstacle, that is, the evil intention, the reception

---

[5] This statement occurs in the Seventh of Luther's *Explanations of the Ninety-Five Theses* (1518), LW 31, 106-107.

of the sacrament requires not only genuine repentance for sin, but the worthy reception of the sacraments also requires that there be a firm faith within the heart.

Christ proved this in Matt. 9 [:2] when, in healing the paralytic, he first said to him, "Believe,[6] my son, and thy sins are forgiven." If faith had not been necessary for the forgiveness of his sins, why should Christ have demanded it? Again, we read that Christ did no signs nor ever helped anyone unless he found faith that the person could and would do it. Thus St. John writes,[7] "In his own country, he could do no signs because of their unbelief."

Furthermore, in Mark 11 [:24], where he teaches his disciples to pray, he says, "I tell you, whatever you ask in prayer, believe that you receive it, and you will." But what else does it mean to receive the sacraments, except to have a desire for divine grace, and what is a desire for divine grace but a true, heartfelt prayer? How, then, can it be anything else than un-Christian to teach that the sacraments and God's grace are to be received without such a desire, without faith, indeed without repentance for sin, and without any intention to do good? Is it not pathetic to hear such teachings in Christendom? But because this article is the main article and all the others are derived from it, we must substantiate it and explain it still further; perhaps it will do some good.

St. James in James 1 [:5ff.] says, "If any of you lacks wisdom, let him ask God who gives to all men generously and without reproaching, and it will be given him. But let him ask in faith, with no doubting, for he who doubts is like a wave of the sea that is driven and tossed by the wind. For that person must not suppose that a double-minded man, unstable in all his ways, will receive anything from the Lord." Does not that say clearly enough that the man who prays and does not firmly believe that he will receive what he asks, cannot receive anything from God? How much less can he receive anything who does not pray, does not believe, does not repent, has no intention to do good, but only, as they teach, "removes the obstacle of an evil design." How can the sacraments give grace to hearts that are without faith and desire, unrepentant, and unkind? May God protect all his Christians against such an

---

[6] The Vulgate's *confide* may be translated "believe."
[7] Luther refers to Matt. 13:58; perhaps also to John 4:44.

13

un-Christian error as taught by this deceitful bull and leaders of the same sort. Its like has never been heard since the beginning of the world.

Furthermore, St. Paul says in Rom. 14 [:23], "Whatever does not proceed from faith is sin." How, then, can the sacraments give grace to unbelievers who in all their works and ways do nothing else than sin so long as they do not believe. Indeed, how can they remove the obstacle if they remain in that unbelief which makes all that they do sin, as St. Paul here states? Yet they teach that faith is not necessary in order to receive the sacraments and grace and, condemning me, they condemn these clear passages of Scripture.

For the same reason, St. Paul quotes in Rom. 1 [:17] and Heb. 10 [:38] the saying of the prophet Habakkuk as one of the chief articles in all Christian teaching when he says, "The righteous shall live by his faith" [Hab. 2:4]. He does not say that the righteous shall live by the sacraments, but by his faith, for not the sacraments, but faith in the sacraments, gives life and righteousness. Many receive the sacraments and obtain from them neither life nor godliness, but he that believes is godly and will live.

That is also the meaning of Christ's saying in the last chapter of Mark [16:16], "He who believes and is baptized will be saved." He puts faith before baptism for where there is no faith, baptism does no good. As he himself afterwards says, "He who does not believe will be condemned," even though he is baptized, for it is not baptism, but faith in baptism, that saves. For this reason, we read in Acts 8 [:36f.] that St. Philip would not baptize the eunuch until he had asked him whether he believed. And we can see every day that wherever in the whole world baptism is administered, the question is put to the child, or the sponsors in his stead, whether he believes, and on the basis of this faith and confession, the sacrament of baptism is administered.

Why, then, does this heretical, blasphemous bull presume to teach against all of Scripture and against the faith and practice of Christians everywhere that one need not believe or repent, or intend to do good? This is so grossly un-Christian that if it were not for the bull, no one would believe that anybody even held such an absurd doctrine. I hope they will be sincerely ashamed

14

of this bull. They would not like to have the laity read it in German.[8]

Moreover, St. Paul says (Rom. 10 [:10]) that, "A man believes with his heart and so is justified." He does not say that it is necessary that he receive the sacraments, for one can become righteous by faith without the bodily reception of the sacraments (so long as one does not despise them). But without faith, no sacrament is of any use, indeed, it is altogether deadly and pernicious. For this reason, he writes in Rom. 4 [:3] that, "Abraham believed, or trusted, God, and it was reckoned to him as righteousness" or godliness. This Moses had previously written in Gen. 15 [:6] and it was set down in order that we might know that nothing makes us good and righteous except faith. Without faith, no one can have any dealings with God, nor receive his grace.

All this is also verified by reason and the common sense of mankind. When one deals with words and promises, one needs faith even between men here on earth. No business or community could last very long if no one were prepared to trust another's word or signature. Now, as we can plainly see, God deals with us in no other way than by his holy word and sacraments, which are like signs or seals of his words. The very first thing necessary, then, is faith in these words and signs, for when God speaks and gives signs, man must firmly and wholeheartedly believe that what he says and signifies is true, so that we do not consider him a liar or juggler, but trust him to be faithful and true. This faith pleases God above all things and does him the highest honor because it believes him to be true and a righteous God. Therefore, he in turn considers this faith as godliness, good and sufficient unto salvation.

Since every sacrament contains a divine word and promise in which God offers and pledges us his grace, it is truly not enough to "put away the obstacle," as they call it, but there must be an unwavering, unshaken faith in the heart which receives the promise and sign and does not doubt that what God promises and signifies is indeed so. Then the grace which the sign or sacrament promises and indicates is certainly granted to faith. But if faith is absent, then the "putting away of the obstacle" is lost labor and God,

---

[8] A German translation of the bull was published toward the end of 1520. Whether this was done upon the initiative of one of Luther's opponents (MA[8] 2, 419) or one of his friends (WA 7, 371) does not seem to be certain.

moreover, is utterly blasphemed and dishonored as though he were a liar and foolish juggler. In this case, the sacraments not only fail to grant grace to those who "put away the obstacle," but they confer disgrace, wrath, and misfortune, so that it is better, if faith is not present, to stay far away from these words and signs which are the sacraments of God.

The sacrament of baptism is a divine sign or seal given by virtue of the promise and word of Christ in the last chapter of Mark [16:16], "He who believes and is baptized will be saved." For this reason, he who is baptized must hold these words to be true and must believe that he will certainly be saved if he is baptized as these words say and the sign signifies. But if he does not believe, then these words and signs of God are in vain and God is despised in this very act. Unbelief makes him into a fool and a liar. Such a serious, un-Christian, horrible, terrible sin is unbelief or distrust of the sacraments. And into such wickedness this blasphemous, damnable bull would drive us. It makes faith a heresy and blasphemy a Christian truth. God preserve us from the desolating sacrilege standing in the holy place! [Matt. 24:15; cf. Dan. 9:27; 11:31; 12:11].

The divine sign or sacrament of penance[9] is given by virtue of Christ's word and promise (Matt. 16 [:19]), "Whatever you loose on earth shall be loosed in heaven," etc. Therefore, he who goes to confession and does penance must remember before everything else to hold fast to the truth of this word and firmly believe that he is loosed before God in heaven when he is absolved on earth. If he doubts and does not believe this, then God must seem to him a liar and by this unbelief or doubt, he denies Him. What good, then, is this "putting away of the obstacle," this laying aside of evil intention, if he keeps the greatest obstacle, the worst intention, namely, unbelief, doubt, and denial of God?

It is the same with the sacrament of the altar. Because it is given by virtue of Christ's words in Matt. 26 [:26], "Take, eat; this is my body which is given for you," he who goes to the sacrament must firmly believe that what the words of Christ say is really true,

---

[9] The translators have followed here the reproduction of Luther's handwritten text, rather than the printer's edition, which contains an error in word order. Compare WA 7, 325 with WA 7, 324.

that His body is given for him and His blood shed for him. If he does not believe this or if he believes that it is given not for him but for others, Christ is again made a liar and His words and signs come to nothing. O the innumerable abominable sins which are committed these days as a result of this unbelief and abuse of the sacraments because faith is nowhere taught! And now this faith is condemned by this bull! All we are taught is to "put away the obstacle," to repent and go to confession. If they preach about faith, all they say is that Christ is truly present and that bread is not present, but only the form of bread. But what Christ does, or why he is there, we hear neither preached nor rightly taught by anybody.

From all this, I think it is clear that faith is necessary for the sacrament, a faith which does not doubt that it receives everything which the words declare and the sacraments signify. Their twaddle about the "putting away of the obstacle" is profitless, indeed it is heretical to claim that with the mere "putting away of the obstacle" without faith, grace is granted by the sacrament. This saying, taken from the teachings of St. Augustine, holds true, "Not the sacrament but the faith in the sacrament makes righteous and saves." [10] And in his commentary on the Gospel according to St. John, St. Augustine says of baptism, "The word is added to the element, and there results a sacrament," and again, "The water touches the body, yet purifies the soul, not because of the work or the pouring, but because of faith." [11]

Against these strong arguments in defense of this Christian article, my opponents have not produced a tittle of Scripture or a spark of reason for their opinion and the "putting away of the obstacle." Their entire view is a naked, baseless, human fabrication and dream. I would like to hear their refutation. Is it not a shame, even if it were not heresy, that they dare to teach doctrines of their own invention in the church where nothing should be taught except God's Word?

They have one lone argument with which they support their view and it goes as follows: If the sacraments of the New Testament

---

[10] Cf. Augustine, *On the Gospel of John* [John 15:3] (*In Ioannis Evangelium*). Migne 35, 1840; also *LW* 31, 193 n. 69.
[11] *Ibid.*

do not grant grace to those who "put away the obstacle" even though they have no faith, then there would be no difference between them and the sacraments of the Old Testament. The Old Testament sacrament also had the power to give grace to those who believed and the New Testament sacraments must be more powerful and better than those of the Old Testament. For this reason, they must give grace to those also who do not yet believe, to whom the Old Testament sacraments did not give grace. This is a vast subject and much could be said about it. To put it briefly, their whole argument rests on a false and erroneous conception. Actually, there is no difference between the sacraments of the Old and New Testaments. Neither the one nor the other grants the grace of God, but, as has been said, it is nothing but faith in God's Word and signs which gave grace then and gives it now. The ancients, therefore, obtained grace through the same faith as we. Thus St. Peter says in Acts 15 [:11], "We believe that we shall be saved through the grace of the Lord Jesus, just as they will." And in II Cor. 4 [:13] St. Paul says, "We have the same spirit of faith as they had." And in I Cor. 10 [:3f.], "Our fathers ate the same spiritual food and all drank the same spiritual drink which we eat and drink." This means they believed as we do.

It is indeed true that the symbols of the Old Testament granted no grace, but these symbols are not sacraments, as they claim. For in these symbols, there is no word or promise of God, as there must be in every sacrament. They were merely symbols or signs such as we have now. Bodily adornments and finery are mere symbols and signs containing no word or promise from God that he who possesses them shall have this or that divine gift. They include no such promise as we observe in baptism, namely that he who believes and is baptized shall be saved. Whatever promises of God, in which men believed, were given in the Old Testament were in all respects equal to our sacraments, except that they had many of them and of different kinds while we have few and all of one kind. And ours are the common property of all men in the whole world.

On the other hand, the symbols and signs which we have and which are not sacraments and not accompanied by a word of God, are like the Old Testament symbols. So, for instance, a bishop's vestments are just as much a symbol as was the dress of Aaron, and neither bestows any grace. Therefore, they ought not to confuse the sacraments and the symbols and mistake the one for the other; then they would not have fallen into the error of making a distinction between the sacraments of the Old and of the New Testaments, for they cannot separate the Old and the New Testament faith.

Now, if this article is thoroughly grasped and understood, all the rest will be easy and the whole bull will be openly put to shame, for, since it deals with faith, this is by far the most important article.

THE SECOND ARTICLE

He who denies that after baptism sin remains in every child tramples upon Christ and St. Paul.[12]

In Rom. 7 [:7] St. Paul says, "I should not have known that evil lust and covetousness are sin, if God's commandment had not said, 'You shall not covet.'" Now the Apostle was not only baptized, but he was a saint when he wrote this of his own covetousness and of the covetousness of all saints. But where did it come from after baptism? There is no other explanation but that it remained after baptism.

Again, in Gal. 5 [:17], he writes to baptized people and to saints in these words, "The desires of the flesh are against the spirit, and the desires of the spirit are against the flesh; for these are opposed to each other, to prevent you from doing what you would." What can anyone say in reply to this plain passage? It says clearly that they have flesh and spirit within themselves, two contradictory desires or lusts which are so deep-rooted that although they would wish to be without the desires of the flesh, they cannot achieve this. Where does such evil lust come from in people who are baptized and saints? No doubt from their physical birth, when this original sin of evil desire is born with them; and it lasts until death and battles and resists our spirit as long as we live.

Similarly, we read in Rom. 7 [:18], "For I know that nothing good dwells within me, that is, in my flesh. I can will what is right, but I cannot do it. For I do not do the good I want, but the evil I do not want is what I do." What else does St. Paul mean here

---

[12] Cf. Thesis 2 in *The Leipzig Debate* (1519). LW 31, 317.

except that although according to the spirit he would like to do good, that is, be without evil desires and inclinations, the flesh is nevertheless so evil and full of lusts that he does not do what he wants to do and cannot be without these lusts? For this reason he does the evil according to his flesh which according to his spirit he does not wish to do. All this means that he has evil desires, although he fights against them so that they may not get the better of him and be expressed in works. This he also teaches others to do in Rom. 6 [:12], "Let not sin reign in your mortal bodies, to make you obey their passions," as if to say, "Sin and evil lusts are in your body, but see to it that you subdue them and consent not to them nor follow after them."

God makes this struggle between our flesh and spirit, with their contradictory desires, the task of all whom he causes to be baptized and called. This is announced in Gen. 3 [:15] when he says to the serpent, "I will put enmity between you and the woman, and between your seed and her seed; she shall crush your head and you shall lie in wait for her foot." [13] This means that spirit and flesh strive against one another, but the spirit shall prevail, though only with difficulty and hard work, and shall put down the disobedient flesh, as St. Paul says in Gal. 5 [:24], "All who are Christians or belong to Christ crucify the flesh with its lusts and vices." And St. Peter says, "Beloved brethren, abstain from the passions of the flesh that wage war against your soul" [I Pet. 2:11].

From all this it is evident that sin remains in the baptized and the saints as long as they are flesh and blood and live on earth and that the condemnation of this article in the bull is most un-Christian. But let us add further evidence. St. Paul says in Rom. 7 [:22], "I delight in the law of God, in my inmost self, but I see in my members another law at war with the law of my mind and making me captive to the law of sin which dwells in my members." St. Paul confesses here that he finds a good law and will in his spirit, and also an evil law and will in his members. How is it then possible to deny that sin remains in a holy baptized man? If it is not sin which is at war with the good spirit and the law of God, then I should like to be told what sin is. What is the cause of

---

[13] Luther quotes freely from the Vulgate.

this strife of the evil against the good within us, if not our physical birth as children of Adam? This remains even after the good Spirit has begun [his work] in baptism and repentance until it is overcome by the grace of God and the resistance and growth of the Spirit and at last strangled by death and driven out.

Moreover, St. Paul adds even more plainly in the same passage [Rom. 7:25], "I myself serve the law of God with my spirit, but with my flesh I serve the law of sin." Does not that make it abundantly clear that one and the same man finds in himself two things? Through the spirit, he wills the good and serves the law of God and is godly. He even takes pleasure and delight in this service. But with the rebellious flesh, he wills evil, and takes pleasure and delight in the service of evil. And since flesh and spirit are one man, he is held accountable for both aspects of his nature, work, love, and desire, even though they contradict each other. Because of the spirit, this man is godly; because of the flesh, he is a sinner, as St. Paul says in Rom. 6 [8:10], "The spirit is alive in the sight of God because of its righteousness but the flesh is dead before him because of its sin." And since the noblest, best and most important part of man, the spirit, remains by faith godly and righteous, God does not charge the sin which remains in the lesser part, the flesh, toward his condemnation.

Surely I, and everyone else, have the right to be amazed that this article is not considered the most certain, the best known, the most evident truth; not to mention that anyone should condemn it. For what do we read in the lives of all the saints? What is it that they confess and demonstrate with all their works, prayers, fastings, labors, and various exercises but that, through all these efforts, they are fighting their own flesh, to chastise it, make it subject to the spirit and quench its evil lusts and desires? This is what St. Paul writes to the Colossians [Col. 3:5]: "Put to death, therefore, your members which are upon the earth; fornication, uncleanness, evil concupiscence and avarice." And again in Rom. 8 [:13]: "For if you live according to the flesh you will die, but if by the Spirit you put to death the deeds of the body, you will live." And to the Philippians [I Cor. 9:27]: "I chastise my body, and bring it into subjection. Lest perhaps when I have preached to others, I myself should become a castaway." And so I could continue. Is there a saint who does not sigh, groan, lament, and cry out about his own flesh and his evil desires?

How often does St. Jerome lament that evil desire rages in his flesh, not only after baptism, but even when he had fasted, watched, and labored unto weariness and was most saintly? St. Cyprian, in a sermon on the sickness unto death finds here his comfort when thinking of his sins and says,[14] "Ceaselessly, we must fight against avarice, unchastity, anger, and ambition. Steadfastly and with toil and sorrow we must wrestle with carnal desires and the enticements of the world. The mind of man, surrounded and besieged by the assaults of the devil, can scarcely meet or resist them all. If avarice is prostrated, unchastity springs up. If lust is overcome, ambition takes its place. If ambition is despised, then anger is provoked, pride puffs up, drunkenness takes the offensive, hatred breaks the bonds of unity, jealousy breaks up friendship. You are constrained to curse, though God has forbidden it; you are compelled to swear, though it is not becoming. The spirit of man must suffer many persecutions and the heart must expect many perils. Should he nevertheless desire to abide in this world faced by the devil's swords? Should we not rather desire and pray that the swift help of death may bring us soon to Christ?"

Since, then, the lives and confessions of these and all other saints substantiate the saying of St. Paul in Rom. 7 [:22], "I delight in the law of God in spirit, yet find in my members a contrary law of sin," no one can deny that sin is still present in all the baptized and holy men on earth, and that they must fight against it. What, then, does this miserable bull mean by condemning all this? Must the Scriptures and all the saints be regarded as liars in its eyes? Let anyone try it for himself and find out! Let him fast, watch, labor even unto death, and be as holy as he possibly can. Then let him tell whether he still finds in himself evil desires and inclinations toward unchastity, wrath, hatred, pride, or the like. For it is not unchastity alone, but all evil lust and desires which are expressed in the flesh that are included in the "desires of the flesh," as St. Paul tells us in Gal. 5 [:19].

Indeed, I would say that by condemning this article, the bull

---

[14] Luther seems to quote from memory the treatise, *On Mortality*, of Cyprian (Bishop of Carthage, 248-258). Migne 4, 607.

calls God a liar and blasphemes him. For the Apostle John says in I John 1 [:8], "If we say that we have no sin, we deceive ourselves and the truth is not in us; but if we confess our sins, he is faithful and just to forgive us our sins and to cleanse us from all unrighteousness; if we say that we have not sinned, we make him a liar and his word is not in us." Is it not quite clear from this passage that we are still to be cleansed and still are sinners? In the same vein, St. Paul says to the Hebrews [Heb. 12:1], "Let us lay aside every weight, and sin which clings so closely, etc." Here the Apostle includes himself, and confesses that there is in him not only sin, but "sin which clings closely," that is, the wilful evil lust that does not cease so long as we live, but always sticks to us and wars against the spirit, putting a burden and a weight upon it. The Apostle commands us to lay both aside.

Again, in John 13,[15] Christ said to his disciples, "You are clean by the word which I have spoken to you." But he says afterward, in chapter 15, "I am the vine, you are my branches and my Father is the vinedresser. Every branch that does bear fruit he prunes that it may bear more fruit." Here we see that the branches that are fruitful, that is, godly and holy, are nevertheless still unclean and in need of further pruning. Similarly, David, though already godly and clean, said in Ps. 51 [:10], "Create in me a clean heart, O Lord, and put a new and right spirit within me." And in Ps. 19 [:12] he says, "O Lord, who can discern all of his sins? Cleanse thou me from secret, hidden sins."

Let us understand this properly! A man cannot pray against sin and about sin, or have such a desire to be free from sin, unless he is already godly. Only the Spirit who has just begun his work and incipient grace are so constituted that they work against the sin which remains. He would like to be altogether godly, but cannot achieve this because of the resistance of the flesh. But those who have never begun to be godly do not struggle or lament or pray against their flesh and sin. They feel no resistance, but go on and follow where the flesh leads. St. Paul describes them in Eph. 4 [:19], where he says that they have gone so far that "they have become callous and have given themselves to licentiousness, greed, etc."

---

[15] This quotation occurs in John 15:3 and the next quotation is actually found earlier, in John 15:1ff.

At this point, the parables of the gospel shed light on the problem. First, the one about the Samaritan [Luke 10:29-37] who placed the half-dead man on his beast, poured wine and oil into his wounds, and asked the groom[16] to take care of him. He did not straightway cure him altogether. Similarly, we too are not entirely cured by baptism or repentance, but a beginning is made in us and the bandage of the first grace binds our wounds so that our healing may proceed from day to day until we are cured. For this reason, St. James says in James 1 [:18], "God has given us birth through his word, out of his sheer gracious will, without our merit, that we should be a first fruit of his work or creatures." This is as if to say, "So long as we live here on earth, believing in his word, we are a work that God has begun, but not yet completed; but after death we shall be perfect, a divine work without sin or fault."

The second parable is written in Matt. 13 [:33]. It tells of the leaven which the woman mixes in three measures of meal until it is thoroughly leavened. The new leaven is the faith and grace of the Spirit. It does not leaven the whole lump at once but gently, and gradually, we become like this new leaven and eventually, a bread of God. This life, therefore, is not godliness but the process of becoming godly, not health but getting well, not being but becoming, not rest but exercise. We are not now what we shall be, but we are on the way. The process is not yet finished, but it is actively going on. This is not the goal but it is the right road. At present, everything does not gleam and sparkle, but everything is being cleansed.

To bring the matter to a conclusion, the Lord's Prayer alone is enough to show that all of us are still sinners, for all the saints must also pray, "Hallowed be thy name, thy will be done, thy kingdom come," etc. Here they actually confess that they do not now adequately hallow God's name; nevertheless they could not even offer this prayer if the Spirit had not already begun to hallow this name. Thus they confess that they do not yet fulfil the will of God and yet they could not pray this petition had they not already begun to fulfil it. For those who have not made a beginning care nothing about the name and will of God, pray for nothing, and

---

[16] Where the parable speaks of the innkeeper, Luther refers in this instance to the *Stalknecht*.

24

show no interest. Nor can it be said that in these petitions the saints pray only over their past sins and not their present and remaining sins. For there is a special petition in the Lord's Prayer that deals with past sins which says, "Forgive us our debts as we forgive our debtors." These other petitions, however, obviously refer to the other sins which are now present. For this reason, they ask that in the future God's name be honored, the divine will be obeyed, and the kingdom of God be attained. These are the prayers of men who are still partly in the kingdom of the devil, partly disobedient, and partly guilty of dishonoring the name of God.

I know, of course, what my opponents like to say to all this. They claim that this evil which remains after baptism is not sin and they invent a new name for it. They call it penalty and not guilt, claiming it to be a defect or weakness, rather than sin. My answer is that all this is arbitrarily fabricated without any basis or reason in Scripture. Indeed, it is contrary to Scripture, for St. Paul does not say, "I find in me a defect," but expressly, "With my flesh I serve the law of sin" [Rom. 7:25], and again, "The sin which dwells within me" [Rom. 7:20] does the evil. And St. John says not, "If we say that we have no defect," but, "If we say we have not sinned" [I John 1:10].

It is an outrage that cannot be tolerated that men should do such violence to God's Word and call that a defect which God calls sin. The whole Scripture could be enfeebled by saying that the word, "sin," wherever it occurs means, "defect." Then nothing would be sin anymore, but merely a defect or a weakness. Who would then prevent anyone from saying that adultery, murder, and robbery are only "defects" and "weaknesses," but not sin? To be sure, they are defects and weaknesses, but they are sinful defects and weaknesses, which must be healed through grace.[17] Anger, evil lust, and the inclination to all sorts of iniquity are defects, but are they not also sins? Are they not against commandments of God, who said, "Thou shalt not have evil desires," "Thou shalt not be angry"? What will they call sin if not that which is against God's commandments? Indeed, St. Paul brought God's commandment into the very text in which he speaks of the sin of those who are

---

[17] Luther's handwritten manuscript reads, "God's grace." WA 7, 338.

baptized when he said: "I would not have known that evil desire is sin if the commandment had not said, 'Thou shalt not have evil desire'" [Rom. 7:7], as if to say, "This desire which remains in me and in all who are baptized, is not simply a defect, but it is the sin which is contrary to this commandment of God and forbidden by it."

Such tricks and evasions, used to distort the Scriptures, St. Paul describes in Eph. 4 [:14] with the Greek words, *kybeia* and *panourgia*, which mean "sleight of hand," "gamblers' tricks," "double dealing." Here people toss the Word of God around as gamblers throw their dice and because, like impersonators who put on a new nose and change their whole appearance, they take from the Scripture its single, simple, and stable meaning, they blind our eyes, so that we stagger about and retain no reliable interpretation. We are like men bewitched or tricked while they play with us as gamblers with their dice.

This is how they handle this clear text and the little word, "sin." They say "sin" does not mean "sin" but "defect" or "weakness," and they play their tricks on us until we no longer see what is plainly before our eyes, just as he [St. Paul] writes to the Galatians: "O foolish Galatians, who has bewitched you and tricked you that you cannot hear the truth?" [Gal. 3:1].

If we permitted them to distort God's word in this fashion, they might eventually claim that a tree should be called a stone and a horse, a cow. Sad to say, they have done this and are still doing it with the words, "faith," "love," "hope," "righteousness," "good works," "sin," "law," "grace of God," and many others. These words I have taken an oath to preserve and I am ready to prove that the men who in the last four hundred years have written on the *Sentences*[18] have never understood these words but have in their ignorance played and juggled with them until the meaning of Scripture has been lost. In its place we have been taught fables and fairy tales. But let nobody go astray because of such human insolence and fiction. What God expressly calls sin, we ought to accept and believe is sin indeed. God does not lie, while man does (Num. 24 [23:19]). He does not play and juggle with words, as do men, but his words are sure and trustworthy (Pss. 119 [:86]; 111 [:7]).

---

[18] The textbooks in theology were chiefly commentaries on a famous work of Peter Lombard (*ca.* 1100-1160) called *Sententiae.*

What tricks they would have played with the Scriptures had the Apostle quoted one of the great commandments against idolatry from Moses' first table, which these pretentious spirits do not fully understand, if they try their tricks with this lesser commandment against evil desires! Everyone knows that evil desires are against God's commandment, and yet they are not willing to let sin be sin. St. Paul, doubtlessly, cited this lesser commandment to stop every mouth and convict and convince us by our own experience so that no one would be able to contradict him. But it did not help. In spite of everything they invent tricks to fight the plain truth and their own experience.

But let us listen to their reasons and why they refuse to admit that sin remains after baptism. They say it would be an insult and disgrace to baptism to grant that sin remains. For we believe that in baptism all sins are forgiven and man is born again, pure and new. But if all sins are forgiven, then that which remains is not sin.

This is the way human reason works when, without divine illumination, it interferes with God's Word and works and tries to calculate and measure them according to its own power. What can I reply except repeat the answer which St. Augustine gave to his Pelagians who also tried to pierce him with their spears of straw? "Certain sins," he says, "such as actual sins, pass away as works, but remain as guilt, for a murder is quickly done and over with, but guilt remains until the murderer repents. On the other hand, this original sin, born in the flesh, passes away in baptism as guilt, but remains as work; although it is forgiven, nevertheless it lives, twists, turns, raves, and assails us until our physical death, and only then is it destroyed." [19]

I would not believe St. Augustine if St. Paul did not support him when he says in Rom. 8 [:1], "Those who believe in Christ have nothing damnable in them, because they do not obey the flesh." He does not say, "They have nothing sinful in them," but, "nothing damnable," for he has said previously that there is sin in the members and the flesh which is at war with the spirit. But since the spirit fights against this sin and does not obey it, it does no harm, and God judges a man not according to the sin which assails

---

[19] Cf. Augustine, *On Marriage and Concupiscence*, and *Against Julian*. Migne 44, 430, 852, 858.

27

him in the flesh, but according to the spirit which is at war against sin, and is thereby like the will of God, which hates and fights against sin. It is one thing, then, to say that sins are forgiven and another to say that there is no sin present. After baptism and repentance, all sins are forgiven, but sin remains present until death. But because of God's forgiveness, this sin does not impair our salvation, provided we fight against it and do not surrender. Therefore our opponents should not deny that sin remains after baptism, as though we needed grace no longer to drive out sin. Rather, they should deny the assertion that not all sins are forgiven. Then they and I would be unanimous in our denial.

For this is the abundant grace of the New Testament and the surpassing mercy of the Heavenly Father that, through baptism and repentance, we begin to become godly and pure. God does not hold against us whatever sin is still to be driven out, because of the beginning that we have made in godliness and because of our steady battle against sin which we continue to expel. He chooses not to charge this sin against us, though, until we become perfectly pure, he might justly do so. For this reason, he has given us a bishop, namely Christ, who is without sin and who is to be our representative until we too become entirely pure like him [Heb. 7:26; Rom. 8:34]. Meanwhile, the righteousness of Christ must be our cover. His perfect godliness must be our shield and defense. For his sake, the sin that remains in those who believe in him, may not be charged against them, as St. Paul so masterfully describes it in Rom. 3 [:24-26].

Let us now conclude the discussion of this article—almost the best and most important of them all—with the beautiful saying of St. Augustine, "Sin is forgiven in baptism; not that it is no longer present, but it is not imputed." [20] Here we see plainly that sin remains, but it is not imputed. The two reasons were mentioned above. First, because we believe in Christ, who, through faith, takes our place and covers our sin with his innocence; second, because we battle unceasingly against sin, to destroy it. Where these two reasons are not present, sin is imputed, is not forgiven, and condemns us eternally. The joy, the comfort, and the blessing

---

[20] Augustine, *On Marriage and Concupiscence.* Migne 44, 430.

28

of the New Testament is this: We learn the benefits Christ offers us and why we need him. Out of this root grow love and delight, praise and thanksgiving to Christ and to the Father of all mercy. This makes for free, joyful, and brave Christians, whose love causes them to fight against sin, and gladly repent. But those who would hide our sin from us and make it out to be merely a weakness, lull us into a false security, make us lazy and sullen, take Christ from us, and allow us to go on without fear and without care concerning the eradication of our sin. If we become callous in such horrible presumption we shall relish neither Christ nor God. God preserve us from this presumption and save all those now caught in it. Amen.

THE THIRD ARTICLE

The tinder of original sin, even without actual sin, bars the entrance to the kingdom of heaven.[21]

The sin remaining after baptism, of which we spoke in the preceding article, is called "tinder" because, just as tinder easily catches fire, it is easily inflamed and excited to evil love, lust, and works, as everyone knows from his own experience. Up till now, I held this article only as an opinion and theory, not as a settled and certain truth that ought to be taught. It was, therefore, not necessary to condemn it. But my opponents produce no better argument against it than the single word, "disapproved." Since I am not interested in what they like or do not like, and, in the meantime, have given the matter more thought, I am now ready to assert this article as a settled and true doctrine. I am willing to confess and defend it and I defy them to overthrow it with Scripture or with reason. My proof follows.

St. Peter says in the last chapter of II Pet. [3:13], that at the last day God will create a new heaven and a new earth in which

---

[21] This proposition refers to the Twenty-fourth of Luther's *Explanations of the Ninety-Five Theses* (1518). *LW* 31, 153. The Latin word here translated as "tinder" is *fomes*. The Roman church teaches, "that in the one baptized there remains concupiscence or an inclination to sin (*concupiscentiam vel fomitem*). . . . This concupiscence, which the Apostle sometimes calls sin, the holy council declares the Catholic Church has never understood to be called sin in the sense that it is truly and properly sin in those born again, but in the sense that it is of sin and inclines to sin." H. J. Schroeder (trans.), *Canons and Decrees of the Council of Trent* (St. Louis, Mo., and London, 1941), Fifth Session, p. 23.

no sin shall dwell, as in this world, but only righteousness. It has been demonstrated in the preceding article that the "tinder" is sin. It now stands to reason that no one will enter heaven who has not laid aside this sin. Certainly they will not take sin with them into heaven. But although this truth is so evident that there is really no need to demonstrate it—since no one is so foolish as to hold that a man can enter heaven with his sin—nevertheless, because this bull is so mad and they are so foolish or so impudent as to claim this publicly, I will cite another passage.

St. Paul says in Eph. 5 [:26, 27] that Christ cleanses his church through the baptism of water and the gospel, that he may lead home a bride, the glorious church, "without spot or wrinkle or any such thing." Here, I think, St. Paul teaches plainly that no sin can go with us to heaven, since no spot or wrinkle or any other blemish shall enter.

Even if this "tinder" we have been talking about were, as they mistakenly think, not sin but only a disease or weakness, everyone nevertheless realizes, I would think, that this weakness would also bar the entrance to heaven. For every disease and weakness, all spots, all wrinkles, and all such deficiencies must first be laid aside, as St. Paul says, if we are to enter into heaven. Then the symbol in Exod. 13 [:18] will be fulfilled, where we read that the children of Israel went out of Egypt not only strong and well, but also "armed." Of this exodus David sings in Ps. 105 [:37], "There was not one among them who was sick or feeble." Obviously, all weakness must be completely put away when we journey into the real promised land of heaven out of the real Egypt of this world.

But perhaps the pope is jesting with his followers in this bull. He may be talking about the "heaven" that is prepared in the abyss of hell with Lucifer and his angels, for him and all his supporters who, with him, blaspheme and persecute the truth of God. Into his "heaven" will go not only the tinder but the fire of all sin and woe. I cannot imagine what other kind of "heaven" he may have, where sin and disease do not bar the entrance. The entrance to our heaven, where God dwells, is obstructed by the very smallest sin and weakness, and all who are to enter must "shine like the sun" [Matt. 13:43], as Scripture says. Or it may be that the pope and his papists want to build themselves a heaven of their own, like those the jugglers build themselves out of linen cloth at the Shrove Tuesday carnival.[22] Is it not disgusting that we have to read such foolish and childish things in papal bulls? And yet they command us to accept these things as solemn Christian articles of faith!

THE FOURTH ARTICLE

A dying man's imperfect love for God brings with it, beyond doubt, great fear. This of itself might be a purgatory and bar the entrance to heaven.[23]

It has been said and demonstrated that nothing deficient can enter heaven. Everything must be according to its own measure, perfect, sinless, and without deficiency. While the saints will not all be alike in heaven, each of them will be in his own way fully pure and perfect. But since imperfect love is a deficiency and sinful in proportion to the extent of this deficiency, I take it to be evident that imperfect love bars the entrance to heaven.

For the assertion that imperfect love is accompanied by fear, I will let St. John take the responsibility. He says in I John 4 [:18], "Where fear is, love is not perfect, for perfect love drives out fear." As for the man who does not believe these words, I do not ask him to believe me. But since this bull condemns these words, I should be sorry if it did not also condemn my article which is based on these words of St. John.

The question whether this great fear is a purgatory, I have left undecided, not knowing how to prove or disprove it; we shall learn from our own experience. Besides, our lack of knowledge on this point makes no difference. Nevertheless, I think Scripture shows that the pains of hell (which all of them identify with purgatory) are fear, terror, horror, the desire to flee, and despair. This is shown in Ps. 2 [:5], "He will speak to them in his wrath, and terrify them in his fury," and in Ps. 6 [:2f.], "All my bones are terrified, and my soul is exceedingly terrified," and in Prov. 26 [28:1], "The wicked flee when no one pursues," and also in Deut. 28 [:65], "God will give you a fearful, despairing heart."

---

[22] The canopy over the stage where the jugglers performed their tricks was known as "heaven." Cf. WA 14, 428, 758.
[23] From Thesis 14 of the *Ninety-Five Theses* (1517). LW 31, 26.

And we see daily what great punishment these horrible terrors are. As a result some suddenly die, others go mad and in an instant become like different beings. We must admit that there is no punishment which equals this true and awful terror. For this reason, we read of the righteous man in Ps. 112 [:7], "He shall not be afraid of evil tidings which terrify all the wicked." Such fear and terror is the result of nothing but a bad conscience, which lacks love and faith. For this reason I consider this article sufficiently acceptable, though if anyone does not want to believe it, he may leave the question open. But the bull and its masters know nothing about it.

THE FIFTH ARTICLE

There is no basis in Scripture or in the holy teachers of ancient times for the doctrine that penance has three parts: contrition, confession, and satisfaction.[24]

Here it is to be noted that I have never denied that God at times punishes sin, as we read of Moses, Aaron, David, and many others. I have said, however, that the satisfaction which the pope pretends to remit by means of indulgences means nothing, and is not based on Scripture but has grown out of the laws of men. This I will prove.

First of all we can prove it from their own words. For they say correctly that contrition might possibly be so great that satisfaction would be unnecessary. But if satisfaction were based on Scripture it would always be necessary, regardless of the profundity of the contrition or the purity of the confession. For whatever is commanded in Scripture cannot be remitted because of anything else, since Christ has said, "Not a letter or a dot shall pass away; it must all be fulfilled" [Matt. 5:18]. Therefore it is obvious from their own words that they are biting their own tongue and condemning their own teaching.

Secondly, Christ absolved the adulteress without satisfaction (John 8 [:11]), and forgave the sin of the paralytic also without satisfaction (Matt. 9 [:2]). This Christ would not have done if

---

[24] From the *Sermon on Indulgence and Grace* (1518). WA 1, 243.

satisfaction were based on Scripture, for he said, "I have not come to abolish the law, but to fulfil it" [Matt. 5:17]. But when the example of Christ contradicts any doctrine, that doctrine is undoubtedly neither right nor founded on Scripture. It does not help their case to cite as a conflicting example concerning satisfaction Mary Magdalene, who washed Christ's feet with tears.[25] It is easy to show that this was not satisfaction. For obviously many works that have been done and can be done are not "satisfaction." Yet no remission of satisfaction can mean anything but remission of satisfaction; if, therefore, satisfaction is remitted, it demonstrates that satisfaction is not commanded in Scripture. On the other hand, the mere fact that a work is done is no proof that a satisfaction is commanded.

Again, when God punishes sin, whether it is satisfaction or not, nobody can remit this penalty, as he says in Ps. 89 [:32], "I will punish their transgression with the rod and with scourges," through the hands of men. These words must also be fulfilled to the letter and the dot, for the pope cannot remit the penalty for sin because he cannot abolish Scripture and God's Word. True, a man may anticipate God's punishment and punish himself or let somebody else punish him in order that God might withhold the rod, as St. Paul says in I Cor. 11 [:31], "If we would punish ourselves, we should not be punished by God." And so it may happen that contrition is so great that God demands no further penalty.

In this manner the holy fathers in ancient times established the canons of repentance for sin.[26] They were called "satisfaction" because they anticipated God's punishment, and we punished ourselves. For sin must be punished either by ourselves or by others who act in God's stead. It is for this reason that I have said in the past[27] and continue to say now that the pope's indulgences are nothing but lies and deceit. If God demands that sin be punished (and this is the truth and the teaching of Scripture), then the pope cannot remit it, and overthrow Scripture. By claiming this power, he cheats the people. But if there is no penalty (as is the case when

---

[25] Luther is referring to Luke 7:36-50, though Mary Magdalene is not mentioned in this passage.
[26] The canons, or decrees of the church, have the force of law. Here Luther refers to the penitential canons. Cf. *LW* 31, 26 n. 5, 32, 33, *passim.*
[27] In his *Babylonian Captivity of the Church* (1520). WA 6, 497; PE 2, 171.

contrition is great enough or when we inflict the penalty upon ourselves), then the pope remits nothing, and again he cheats the people.

It is for this reason that I have said that the three parts of penance are not based on Scripture. I do not reject contrition, confession, and penalty, but I declare the indulgences invalid because they give the illusion of remitting satisfaction, the third part of penance, which is simply not true. I have clearly shown that the satisfaction which is remitted, or alleged to be remitted, by the indulgences is nowhere mentioned in Scripture. By saying this, I have not denied that there is such a thing as punishment or satisfaction for sin; I only insist that it cannot be remitted. That which is remitted has been invented by men without any basis in Scripture. Therefore, I hate this word "satisfaction" and wish it had never come into use. The Scripture calls it "penalty" and "chastisement" for sin. No one can make satisfaction to God for one of his venial sins, but he can be punished for all his sins, according to grace in time or wrath in eternity.

This article must therefore stand. Penance does not have three parts as the pope and his followers babble and lie, claiming that the third part is in the pope's power and that he can remit it by means of indulgences. According to divine holy Scripture it has three parts, of which the third is sometimes omitted because of great contrition or self-punishment. But no sin ever goes unpunished, as St. Augustine says, "No evil goes unpunished," [28] and the proverb has it, "When man does not punish, God does." The pope, therefore, has as little power to remit the penalty of sin as he has to remit contrition or confession. Penance is a sacrament[29] and not his property. He cannot change any part of it.

THE SIXTH ARTICLE

The contrition which is produced by the discovery, contemplation, and hatred of sin—as when a sinner with bitterness of heart considers his life, and ponders the greatness, the number, and the foulness of his sins, his loss of eternal

---

[28] Augustine, *Sermons* (19). Migne 38, 133, 139.
[29] Luther later changed his view on this subject. Cf. *PE* 2, 291-292.

life, and his gain of eternal damnation—this contrition makes a man a hypocrite and a greater sinner.[30]

"Whatever does not proceed from faith is sin," says St. Paul in Rom. 14 [:23]. And all my opponents say also that true contrition for sin must be the fruit of love, otherwise it is not true contrition. That is the very doctrine I have taught in this article, yet they condemn their own doctrine just because I also teach it. Even though one contemplates his own sin, and all the harm that sin has done, without faith and love it does not help him before God. For the devil and all the damned show this sort of contrition, which we call in German, "Judas contrition" or "gallows contrition."

It is this way. Because men are without grace and have not the Spirit of God, it is impossible for them to love righteousness. And even if they are fearfully and painfully forced to think upon their sins, compelled by the commandment of the church or by the anguish of death, nevertheless their hearts are in such a state that if there were no hell, or if they could do it without fear and shame, they would prefer to have nothing to do with the contrition, confession, and satisfaction. They cannot possibly change their hearts by the power of their own nature without the grace of God, for, of himself, man can do nothing good, but only evil, as I shall prove in Article 26. Even though he may go through the motions of doing good, these acts are nothing but lies, deceit, and hypocrisy.

For this reason I have taught that each one should first search his own heart and see whether he hates sin thoroughly and of his own will and desire. If he discovers that this is not the case, let him despise his contrition and first fall on his knees and pray to his Lord, and have prayers offered in his behalf, that this contrition become real and sincere. This is what the church does when it prays, "Grant us a penitent heart." [31] Then let him meditate upon his sins. A contrite heart is rare indeed and an eminent gift of grace.

---

[30] From Luther's *Sermon on Repentance* (1518). WA 1, 319.
[31] This is a reference to a hymn in the breviary:
> "Da tempus acceptabile
> Et poenitens cor tribue,
> Convertat ut benignitas
> Quos longa suffert pietas."

H. A. Daniel, *Thesaurus Hymnologicus* (1841), I, 235, CCXIV.

It is not attained by contemplating sin and hell, but only by receiving the "inpouring" of the Holy Spirit. Otherwise, Judas' contrition would have been the best, for he thought of his sin with great sorrow. And a forced and imagined contrition is very popular, as experience shows, for many confessions are made in Lent and yet there is little improvement in men's lives.

St. Paul foretold the coming of these false teachers of a hypocritical and false contrition in I Tim. 4 [:1]: "There shall come teachers who follow deceitful spirits, and with hypocrisy and good outward appearance they shall teach lies, and shall have scars branded on their conscience." Is it not "teaching lies" when men are taught to consider that contrition good which only appears to be good, but is without faith, love, desire and willingness (which are given only by the grace of God)? They "brand a scar on their consciences." Such a scar is not congenital, nor does it grow gradually, but it is branded [upon the animal] by force. Even so, their qualms of conscience are not the fruit of grace but have rather been forced upon them and brought about by false and fictitious notions. Thus they feign a contrition which is not real.

Such a deceitful conscience and contrition make a man not only a hypocrite, but a greater sinner than he was before. This is what St. Jerome says, "Pretended godliness is double wickedness." [32] "Double" because in the first place, there is no real, true godliness present, but rather a heart that has no desire or love for righteousness. In the second place, this real wickedness is concealed with forced notions and a pretended contrition while it feigns true contrition and godliness, trying to lie to God and deceive him. It is against this insincere contrition which the pope and his liars teach in all their books to be the true contrition that I have placed this article, and I am prepared to stand by it.

It also happens that while meditating upon their sins, these false penitents feel again (though deep in their hearts) the flames and sparks of desire for the repetition of past sins or wicked inclinations toward former hatred and envy. Thus, in their very contrition, they acquire a real desire to commit sins which they

---

[32] This is a reference to Jerome's *Commentary on Isaiah;* however, Luther's quotation is not quite accurate. Cf. Migne 24, 240.

would perhaps have forgotten had they not meditated upon them. For everything that does not spring from the gracious activity of God is utterly useless. For this reason, St. Paul says that sins only increase when they are recognized and considered without the grace of God (Rom. 5 [:13]; Gal. 3 [:21]; I Cor. 15 [:56]). But these branded leaders of the blind still try to deceive us. They represent acts which cause us to stumble and which increase our sin as true contrition and try to persuade us to accept this view.

It is true indeed that, by the imposition of penalties and by this sort of compulsory repentance, hardened sinners are temporarily kept from committing their evil deeds in the sight of men. But this does not make their hearts godly in the sight of God. They refrain from their wickedness only so long as they are obliged to respect and fear men. But it has been the aim of my teaching to diminish the number of these hypocrites and "branded consciences"—which the pope and his followers daily increase by means of their diabolic doctrine—and to make a sincere contrition, rich in grace, more common. Only then will we no longer increase the anger of Almighty God by our false doctrines and "contritions" in addition to what we have already done by our sins. To these men He will apply the words of Matt. 21 [:31], "Harlots and knaves shall enter the kingdom of God before you." For He is more embittered by hypocritical and deceitful penitents and by this forced godliness than by open sin and open sinners.

Let me show this even more clearly. In the first article[33] I showed conclusively that even the saints, who live in God's grace, must work and labor hard to love righteousness and to resist their fleshly lusts and sins. If these men, then, cannot hate their sin sufficiently, what are they to do who are not in grace and who wage no warfare against sin? What is the carnal man to do against sin, without the help of the Spirit and of grace, when he contends for sin and against God even when the Spirit is present? Can anything be more foolish than to say that nature must of its own accord repent and hate and avoid sin, without God's grace and before it receives God's grace? We see that it loves, seeks, and desires sin and fights and rages against grace even after grace has laid hold

---

[33] His reference is actually to the second article. Cf. above, pp. 19-29.

of this nature. And this is the lament of all the saints. To say that nature shall do of its own accord what the grace of God, with ceaseless striving, is not able to bring it to do, is the same thing as to say that a great tree, which all my power cannot bend, will bend by itself, if I only let it alone. It is the same thing as to say that a stream of water, which I cannot restrain with any dam or weir, will stop of its own accord, if only I'll let it go. So pope and papists teach us that grace is insufficient to suppress sin, but without grace, sin suppresses and checks itself. Forget about such preachers! [34]

To teach, therefore, that repentance is to be achieved by merely meditating upon sin and its consequences is simply lying, stinking, and seducing hypocrisy. First of all, we ought to look into the wounds of Christ and see in them his love for us and our ingratitude toward him and thus with sincere affection for Christ and rejection of self, meditate upon our sin. This is true contrition and fruitful repentance. Contrition must precede meditation upon sin. Such meditation must develop out of contrition and be its result and not the other way around. There must be contrition before there can be any meditation upon sin, just as there must be love and desire before there can be any good works or any meditation upon them. Meditation is the fruit of contrition, contrition is the tree. In our country, fruit grows on trees and from trees, and meditation upon sin grows from contrition. But in the holy land of pope and papists, trees may grow on fruits, contrition from sins; people walk on their ears, and everything is upside down.

THE SEVENTH ARTICLE

This proverb is true and better than all the doctrines of contrition which they have taught up till now, which says, "To sin no more is the highest form of repentance," and, "A new life is the best repentance"; that is to say, "To turn from evil ways is best." [35]

If to sin no more is not the highest form of repentance, as everybody

---

[34] The literal translation would read: "To the dog days with such preachers." For Luther's use of the phrase, "dog days," cf. Grimm's *Deutsches Wörterbuch*, Vol. IV, 2, p. 1941.
[35] From Luther's *Sermon on Repentance* (1518). WA 1, 321.

rightly says, then what is the highest form of repentance? Speak up, O holy father pope, we are ready to listen! O you wolf in Christendom, is it not true that to sin no more is not only true contrition for sin but involves a change in the whole life? Why, then, is it not the highest and best form of repentance? Where, through God's grace, contrition has truly started, there the whole man is at the same time transformed into another man with another heart, another disposition, another mind, and another life. This I call "sinning no more" and "a new life."

Now, since the pope denies that "to sin no more is the highest form of repentance," let us see what it is in his opinion. Surely, he will not say that to keep on sinning is the best repentance, though, in fact, this is the way he and his followers do repent. The first letter of "never" is too much for them, and out of "never sinning" they do make "ever sinning." No wonder he says that "Judas repentance" or "gallows repentance" is the best repentance. For this is brought about entirely by the power of man's nature, without divine grace. It is utterly false, does not create a new life, and does not even stop from sinning as a result of any serious and heartfelt intention. It has been shown above that without grace there is nothing good in man, and even those who are living in grace must struggle against sin and evil within.

The dear pope, however, is thinking of that word of Christ, where he says, "Whatever you loose on earth shall be loosed in heaven" [Matt. 16:19].

He figures, maybe, if to sin no more were the highest form of repentance, a man could become godly at home and would not need to run or write to Rome. That would do away entirely with the Roman junk shop, where they sell and barter keys, letters, seals, sin, grace, God, hell, and everything else. Therefore, he must tie the best form of repentance to his own purse and coffers at Rome.

However, we shall demonstrate the truth of our article from the Scriptures. St. Paul says in Gal. 6 [:15] that among Christians neither circumcision nor uncircumcision counts for anything, but only "a new creation." Dear pope, why don't you condemn this apostle too, for he says clearly that nothing except "a new creation" counts for anything in Christendom. Now this "Judas contrition" without grace is surely not a "new creation," but hypocrisy;

therefore, it certainly counts for nothing. How, then, can it be the best form of repentance?

To be sure, the "new creation" and the entry of grace begin with a profound assault and terror attacking the conscience or with some other great suffering and misfortune. Revelation 3 [:20] calls this "God's knocking" or "visitation" and this gives so much pain that man wants to die and thinks that he must perish. But at the same time God pours grace and strength into him so that he does not despair. At this point a "new creation" and an intention to do good has its beginnings. This is the true and good contrition similar to the conversion of St. Paul who, at the very time when he was surrounded by a light from heaven and terror-stricken, received grace, and said "Lord, what shall I do?" [Acts 9:6]. It is during such storms of adversity that God pours his grace into us, as it is written in Isa. 41 [:3], "God pursues them and turns peacefully toward them." And the prophet Nahum says in the first chapter, "God is a Lord whose ways are all thunder and lightning and storm, and his footsteps are like thick clouds of dust" (Nah. 1 [:3]), as if to say, "Him on whom God wishes to bestow his grace, he assails by bringing upon him all sorts of misfortune, inward and outward, until he thinks that he must perish because of the greatness of the storm and the assault."

Those who do not accept these works and ways of God drive away his grace. They cannot greet God when he meets them, nor understand or return his greeting. This greeting is awful in the beginning but comforting in the end. The angel Gabriel terrified Mary with his salutation, but at the end,[36] he comforted her most sweetly [Luke 1:26-37]. Therefore, a repentance which is preoccupied with thoughts of peace is hypocrisy. It must express a great earnestness and deep pain if the old man is to be put off. Similarly, when lightning strikes a tree or a man it does two things at the same time; it rends the tree and swiftly slays the man, but it also turns the face of the dead man and the broken tree toward heaven. So the grace of God terrifies, pursues, and drives a man and turns him toward God. But about this work of contrition and

---

[36] "At the end" (Zculetzt) is found only in Luther's handwritten manuscript. WA 7, 364.

of grace my dear pope knows less than does a log on the ground. Yet he wants to decide and judge these matters.

In ancient times, there used to be heretics called Donatists,[37] who taught that nobody could receive baptism or the sacrament that was valid unless the priest or bishop who administered it was holy. St. Augustine vanquished them and showed that the sacraments belong not to man but to God only, who can administer them through good and bad servants. Now that this heresy has been suppressed, the pope's heresy takes its place. He teaches that, though he who administers the sacraments need not be godly, he must be high and mighty. What those heretics ascribed to human holiness, the pope ascribes to human might and greatness. Even though God may give to another man the faith of the gospel, the Spirit of God, and all holiness, the pope wants the sacraments to be administered only by him or on his authority. The very sacraments which in the past could not be bound to holiness are now bound to power and are pasted to red [cardinals'] hats and golden [papal] crowns and [bishops'] miters, like sea shells on the felt hats and cloaks of the pilgrims to St. James [of Compostella].[38]

Not satisfied with this, the pope goes on to ascribe such authority to his keys that if somebody comes along who has neither faith nor contrition, and hardly even that superficial repentance which they call "attrition," [39] he can, by the power of the keys, turn this superficial repentance into good, genuine, salutary contrition, if only the man himself does not put an obstacle in the way. Of this we spoke under the first article. Thus the pope can now create grace and contrition within us, even though we are unbelievers, heathen, and Jews, and have no contrition at all. Now the sacraments depend not merely on the holiness of the priests, as the Donatists said, but on the power and the rank of men, and so faith is obliterated and forgotten. Indeed, in order that the pope may not

---

[37] The Donatists received their name from the fourth-century bishop of Carthage, Donatus, who made the validity of the sacraments dependent upon the worthiness of the administrant.

[38] Shells sewed to the hats and cloaks of the pilgrims to the shrine of Santiago de Compostella in Spain as signs of the sea voyage.

[39] "Attrition" is sorrow for sin having fear as its motive, as distinct from "contrition," which must be motivated by love. For the official Roman Catholic position, cf. Schroeder, *op. cit.*, Fourteenth Session (On Penance), chap. 4.

lose this heretical and fictitious power, which enables him to manufacture the best sort of repentance at will, he must deny that "to sin no more is the best form of repentance."

Beware of the Antichrist, the pope! Rest assured that the sacraments do not depend on sanctity, rank, power, riches, hats, gloves, pope, bishops, priests, or monks. They depend on your faith, that no matter whether he who gives you absolution is holy or unholy, high or low, poor or rich, pope or priest, you believe that through him God is absolving you, and you are absolved. If the sacraments do not depend on holiness, how much less shall they depend on rank, power, greatness, honor, and riches? For holiness is the greatest thing in all the world. This is the meaning of the words of Christ, when he says, "Whatever you loose on earth shall be loosed in heaven" [Matt. 16:19].

In these words Christ does not confer authority, but rather he moves every Christian heart to faith so that when a man is absolved by the priest he may be sure that he is absolved by God. The power of the keys accomplishes no more than you believe and not as much as the pope and his followers choose. Nevertheless, we must suffer their mad and usurped sacrilegious power and authority. But, remember, you must hold to the true faith and believe that no one can give you either more or less than your faith permits and it is a lie to assert that, by the power of the keys, the pope and his followers can create contrition within you apart from faith.

THE EIGHTH ARTICLE

Do not try to confess all your venial sins, nor even all your mortal sins, for no one can know all his mortal sins, and in ancient times, only public, mortal sins of which one was aware were confessed.[40]

They themselves teach that it is not necessary to confess venial sins, but now, because I say it, it must be heresy. I think, if I said that there is a God and then confessed all the articles of the faith, all of it would immediately be heresy, merely because I said it. This is

---

[40] From Luther's *Sermon on Repentance* (1518). WA 1, 322.

the goodness and sincerity which the pope and his followers show toward me.

But it is the clear teaching of Scripture that not all mortal sins can be either confessed or known. In Ps. 19 [:12] we read, "Lord, who can discern all his sins? Cleanse thou me from secret sins." Here, the prophet teaches us that we cannot confess our secret sins, for God alone knows them, and we are to obtain remission by prayer. Futhermore, Ps. 143 [:2] testifies that these sins are mortal sins, "Lord enter not into judgment with thy servant; for no man living is righteous before thee." If the dear saints, God's servants (whom we regard as sinless), have such sins that they cannot be justified in God's sight, how dare you, wretched pope, justify before God those who have neither faith nor true contrition and who bring to penance only their accursed "gallows contrition"? Sins which make it impossible for the saints to be justified in God's sight must surely be mortal. Indeed, anything that prevents justification is mortal sin and vice versa.

It is for this reason that I have taught the people, and everybody ought to teach it, that they should fear God, and after they have diligently confessed, say to him with David, "Behold, dear Lord, I have confessed this sin and that, but thy judgments are secret and terrible; if thou wilt enter into judgment with me I shall never stand, no matter what I do. For who can know all his sins? Therefore, I flee from thy judgment to thy grace and pray that thou wilt cleanse me from all my unknown sins." In this way the people can learn to find comfort in God's grace and not in their own contrition, confession, and satisfaction, as the Antichrist and his disciples teach.

As far as the statement is concerned which says that in ancient times only public sins were confessed, I leave the proof to the history books and to the epistles of St. Paul. I have spoken only of mortal sins known to the person himself, though they may be unknown to everybody else. Beside these sins, I say, there are still others which only God knows. We ought, therefore, leave people in peace and not force them to search out all their sins, since this is impossible anyway. We should let them confess those sins that occur to them at the time and of which they are aware. Then they can concentrate more on their faith in God's grace than on the thoroughness of their confession.[41]

THE NINTH ARTICLE

When we undertake to make a full and complete confession of all our sins, we do nothing but show that we are not willing to leave forgiveness to the mercy of God.[42]

This article is already proved by the one above and by the second article, for if it is true, as David says in Ps. 19 [:12] that since no one knows all his sins, we must needs leave the unknown sins to the mercy of God. And we must not rely on our own confession or contrition, but on his grace, and ask in humble and fearful prayer that he will cleanse us from sin, as Scripture tells us here.

Moreover, if we have shown in the discussion of the first and second articles that all the saints lament the sin in their flesh, from which they cannot free themselves, then we must admit that the sins which remain must be commended to God's grace. If he were to judge them strictly—as he will do in the case of those who despise his grace—they would all be found to be mortal sins. The pope's condemnation of this article is no surprise, for they [the papists] teach us always to rely upon our own works and the pope's power, and never upon God's mercy. Thus fear of God and hope are obliterated in the hearts of Christians. But St. Augustine says in the *Confessions* IX, "Woe to the life of man, however good it be, if it is judged without mercy." [43] If St. Augustine desires that even a good life be commended to God's mercy and knows that it cannot endure God's judgment, should we not be willing to leave some hidden sins to his grace? O, it is disgusting that such evident truths should be condemned by the pope! Pope and papists are an antichristian lot!

THE TENTH ARTICLE

No one's sins are forgiven unless he believes that they are

---

[41] Cf. *Confitendi ratio* (1520). WA 6, 157-169; *PE* 1, 81-101.
[42] From Luther's *Sermon on Repentance* (1518). WA 1, 323.
[43] Luther quotes freely from Augustine's *Confessions*, IX, chap. 13. Migne 32, 778.

forgiven when the priest absolves him. Indeed, the sin remains unless he believes that it is forgiven. For the forgiveness of sin, or infusion of grace, is not enough, but one must believe that sin is forgiven.[44]

From the condemnation of this article, a number of conclusions can be drawn. First of all, it means that that article of the Creed is false and heretical in which all Christians confess, "I believe in the Holy Spirit, one holy Christian church, the forgiveness of sins"; for my article teaches nothing but that we must believe in the forgiveness of sins, as this article of the Christian Creed says. We thank you, O most holy father pope, for teaching what the world never knew before, namely, that the article of the Creed concerning the forgiveness of sins is heretical. But if this one part of the Creed is heretical, then, surely, all its parts are heretical. Here, then, the most holy father pope bluntly condemns the whole Creed, so that I am afraid nobody will believe that such a statement is actually contained in the bull. But it is indeed there, and for this reason they are ashamed that the bull is being translated into German,[45] and that their antichristian and heretical raving is coming to light.

Secondly, it means that a sinner ought to say to the priest who absolves him, "You lie; my sins are not forgiven, as you say, for the holy father, the pope, has lately issued a bull in which he condemns all those who believe that their sins are forgiven and that the absolution is true." He who goes to confession should rather think, "I shall confess, but I shall consider every absolution mere lies, heresy, and error, and call all priests liars, heretics, and seducers, if they absolve anybody; the pope in his bull has ordered me to do this."

Thirdly, it means that Christ himself is a liar and a heretic when he says to Peter in Matt. 16 [:19], "Whatever you loose on earth shall be loosed in heaven." For this tender bull forbids anyone, on pain of ban and stake, to believe that what the priest looses is loosed; that is, no one is to believe that his sins are forgiven him, as my article says. If anyone should doubt that such

---

[44] From the Seventh of Luther's *Explanations* (1518). WA 1, 543; LW 31, 104-105.
[45] Cf. p. 15 n. 8.

abominable statements are written in this bull, let him read it and notice what it condemns. I should myself have believed that the heavens would fall before such things would be proclaimed by the pope. I think the pope has reached the end of his rope.[46] This article, however, is so evidently true that the ears of all Christians are terrified and appalled at the pope's condemnation of it. For it is common practice everywhere in Christendom for Christians to encourage each other to believe and trust in the mercy of God, which forgives their sins. To be sure, the Evil Spirit usually suggests to men, in the hour and anxiety of death, the very thing the pope teaches in this bull, namely, that they ought not to believe that their sins are forgiven. But he does that not in order to help, but rather because he is the enemy of grace and faith and truth. The pope, however, is worse than all the devils, since he teaches it as orthodox and good doctrine. He sits in God's place [II Thess. 2:4] and condemns the Creed. This no devil has ever done. Your end is near, you son of perdition and Antichrist! Stop now, pope, you are going too far!

But let us demonstrate the truth of our article. In Matt. 9 [:2], when Christ heals the paralytic, he says first, "My son, trust and believe, and your sins are forgiven." [47] Here you see plainly that his sins are not forgiven unless he believes that they are forgiven. He also absolves Mary Magdalene because of her faith, for his words are, "Go in peace; your faith has saved you" (Luke 7 [:50]). You see, the faith which helped her and blotted out her sin was there first. Christ himself does not ascribe the forgiveness of her sins to his absolution, nor to his keys, nor to his power, but to her faith. Yet the pope pretends that sins are forgiven because of his power, not because of man's faith. It is obvious what kind of spirit tells him to say that.

Everybody knows that the priest's absolution is a verdict—not his own, but God's—which demands faith, by virtue of Christ's words, "Whatever you loose on earth shall be loosed in heaven." The priest says, "I absolve you," that is to say, "I loose you," or, "Your sins are forgiven." What sense does it make that the sinner

---

[46] In his manuscript Luther said, "I think that all the devils have at once entered into the pope." WA 7, 372. He chose the milder form for the printed edition.
[47] Luther's translation is based on the Vulgate.

is not supposed to believe this divine verdict? Go ahead, pope, burn and condemn books! God shall overthrow you and give you up to madness, and you will receive the reward which you have deserved for always resisting divine truth. Let him who feels like it doubt that the pope, who spreads all these errors throughout the world and receives in return the wealth of the nations, is the true, chief, and final Antichrist. Thank God, I know him.

THE ELEVENTH ARTICLE

You must not trust that you are absolved because of your contrition, but because of the word of Christ when he says to Peter, "Whatever you loose, shall be loosed." I say that when you receive absolution from the priest you must firmly believe that you are absolved, whatever the status of your contrition.[48]

The truth of this article has been sufficiently demonstrated through those we have discussed above. Who would confess or repent if he did not believe that his sins would be forgiven? What would a priest say if I were to come to him and say, "Sir, I have committed such and such sins and am sorry, but I do not believe that you can absolve me." He would certainly consider me insane. But this is what this bull teaches us to do and it condemns the very faith which my article teaches.

Suppose it were true that our sins are forgiven because of our contrition, as the bull teaches, and not because of God's word alone, as my article says. If this were so, a man could boast before God that he had attained grace and forgiveness by his own contrition and merit and not solely by the mercy of God. This is abominable and terrible and an utter denial of grace. For God's mercy and grace are bestowed freely upon the undeserving, as St. Paul says in Rom. 5 [3:24], "We have been acquitted and justified freely and out of pure mercy," and Ps. 25 [:11], "For thy name's sake, O Lord, pardon my guilt." [The Psalmist] does not say, "for my sake," or, "for my name's sake," or, "for my merit's sake."

Moreover, if it has been shown above that the dear saints still

---

[48] From Luther's *Sermon on Repentance* (1518). WA 1, 323.

have sin and that sin strives against grace and grace against sin, then it is clear that grace is given not only to those who have not merited it, but even to those who have merited evil and who are enemies of grace. How then shall our contrition be so meritorious that God forgives sins for its sake? Would he not rather forgive it for his own sake? He says through the prophet Isaiah, "I will turn my displeasure away from you, for my name's sake, for my own sake I do it, that I may not be profaned. My glory I will not give to another," etc. (Isa. 48 [:9, 11]). But if our sins were forgiven because of our contrition the honor would be ours and not God's. He would also be profaned, as though sins were forgiven for some other reason and not only for his Name's sake.

And King Manasseh prayed[49] that God would forgive his sins for the sake of God's loving kindness and promise, without regard to his own merit or contrition. Why make a long story of it? If anyone's sins are forgiven because of his contrition, as this accursed bull declares in lying and blasphemous fashion, then let him do away with the prayer that we all say, "Lord, be gracious to me, a poor, unworthy sinner." Let him say instead, "Lord, forgive me, a worthy and well-deserving and quite sufficiently holy man, my sins, and rebuke the centurion in the gospel who said, 'Lord, I am not worthy to have you come under my roof'" [Matt. 8:8]. If the pope and his saints are so worthy that God must forgive their sins because of their contrition, I would advise the pope to put on his triple crown, saddle his steed with gold and pearls, ride with all his pomp into God's presence, and defy Him with his own great worthiness. And if God should not forgive the pope's sins, let the pope place God under the ban and chase Him out of heaven. How far will you go, O devilish pride? It is easy to see why you want to be called "most holy" in all the world. Keep it up and your blasphemy and raging against God will come to an end.

For this reason I still insist and warn everyone to give God the honor, and not trust that his sins are forgiven because of his own contrition. No contrition is sufficient in God's sight. Forgiveness is the result of the sheer mercy of God. He wants us to honor,

---

[49] This is a reference to the apocryphal Prayer of Manasseh, verse 14. Though Luther listed it at the end of the Apocrypha of the Old Testament, even Roman Catholics do not consider it "canonical." Cf. also II Chron. 33:18-19.

praise, and love him as one who is gracious to us unworthy and undeserving men. Beware of this bull and of those who teach such doctrine.

THE TWELFTH ARTICLE

If it were possible that anyone could confess without contrition, or if a priest were to absolve anyone thoughtlessly or in jest, nevertheless, if such a person should believe that he has received absolution he is most certainly absolved.[50]

In the entire gospel Christ made everything depend on faith when he said, "All things are possible to him who believes" [Mark 9:23], and again, "Be it done for you as you have believed" [Matt. 8:13]. Therefore it is true that although the priest may be jesting, nevertheless, if I receive his absolution in earnest and have faith, the result does not depend on what he does, but on faith. I said this in order to show how important and necessary a part of repentance faith is. Everything depends on it. And although faith is not possible without contrition, as I said above when I showed that the infusion of faith and grace is accompanied by a great turmoil, yet, if it were possible to have faith without contrition, faith alone would be sufficient. For God did not make the offer of his grace dependent on contrition or any other work but only on faith, when he said, "He who believes will be saved" [Mark 16:16].

And why should not a thoughtless absolution be valid, since St. Paul says in Ephesians [Phil. 1:15-18] that the Word of God is valid and helps those who believe, even when it is preached by his enemies and persecutors? Furthermore, don't they all admit that the sacraments are efficacious though administered by wicked and unbelieving priests, indeed, even if the priest hates the penitent? Surely sin and unbelief are worse than jesting and thoughtlessness. And, they must also admit that he who sincerely desires the sacrament receives its benefit, even though the priest should arbitrarily withhold it, so completely does everything depend on the faith of the penitent.[51] As he believes, so he receives,

---

[50] From Luther's *Sermon on Repentance* (1518). WA 1, 323.
[51] This is a reference to the so-called *votum sacramenti* or "desire for the sacrament."

whether the priest gives or withholds the sacrament, whether he be in jest or in earnest. In whatever way the sacrament comes to us, it is God's sacrament and can be received in faith. But God's friend in Rome,[52] the pope, would like to obliterate this faith and seduce us into trusting his power rather than God's sacrament, pretending that he has the power to forgive sins, without our faith. May God protect all Christian hearts against this Antichrist and apostle of Satan!

THE THIRTEENTH ARTICLE

In the sacrament of penance and in the remission of guilt, pope and bishop do no more than the humblest priest. Indeed, if a priest is not available, any Christian could do just as much, even a woman or a child.[53]

Look here, this article really hits the sore spot. This had to be suppressed and condemned! For if this article were allowed to stand it would knock the very keys out of the Roman idol's coat of arms. But condemnation won't do. He cannot legitimately refute it and I shall prove it right now.

It has been clearly shown in the preceding pages that it is not the work of the priest but the faith of the penitent which effects the forgiveness of sins. For if the pope and all the priests together were to give absolution to a sinner it would not be valid, nor would it help him at all unless the sinner believed it. The word stands firm, "He who does not believe will be condemned" [Mark 16:16]. Against it there is no help. Indeed, how could the absolution of the pope and all the priests be of any avail without faith? If even Christ and God himself were to pronounce the absolution, without faith it would be of no avail. Is it not true that God every day preaches and works wonders among men, yet they help nobody except those who believe in him? If, then, forgiveness depends entirely upon faith and not on the office or power of the priest; and if the pope can do as little toward the bestowal of faith as the humblest priest, and the priest as little as a woman or a child, I should like the pope to explain to me what he does in this matter

---

[52] In his manuscript Luther wrote, "blasphemer in Rome." WA 7, 378.
[53] From Luther's *Sermon on the Sacrament of Penance* (1519). WA 2, 716.

that is more than an ordinary priest does? Let me have your pearls of wisdom, my dear pope! But I shall be glad to tell you what you do that is more than an ordinary priest does. You display great banners with keys on them, you sell bulls, you have the bells ring,[54] you cheat entire countries and nations out of their money, their goods, their bodies, and their souls, and you lead them with you into the abyss of hell. This is what you do that is more than other priests and Christians do.

It has been said above that the heretical Donatists,[55] who were overcome by St. Augustine, and who tried to make all the sacraments dependent upon the sanctity of the priests and not the faith of the penitents, were nevertheless more tolerable and better than the pope and his bishops who want to bind the sacraments to rank and power. For if a holy priest does no more in the sacrament than a sinful priest, how can a great high priest do any more than a lowly and insignificant priest, since holiness is far more important than power? It is, therefore, obvious that the pope has exactly the same right to the sole possession of the keys that Lucifer, when he was in heaven, had to the throne of God. For the keys are given only for the sake of the sacrament of penance, which is the common property of all Christians. No one has a greater or smaller part in it, save in proportion to his faith.

I would like to ask another question, most holy father pope: Do you also have a sacrament of baptism that is different from what all priests and Christians have? By virtue of your exalted rank, do you do more when you baptize than does a priest, a layman, a woman, or a child? Speak up! Have you lost your voice? If you have another baptism, then St. Paul condemns you in Eph. 4 [:5], when he says, "One Lord, one faith, one baptism," etc. But if the sacrament of baptism is the same among all Christians, so that in an emergency a layman, a woman, or a child may administer it—which happens every day—why should not the sacrament of the keys, i.e., penance or absolution, also be common property? Is it not also a sacrament just like baptism? And is your mass any different from that of all other priests? Can you give more of the

---

[54] This is a reference to the procedure at the sale of indulgences.
[55] Cf. p. 41 n. 37, above.

body of Christ than our chaplain? Why, then, do you make an exception of the sacrament of the keys with your claim to do more in this sacrament than all the rest of Christendom? You are seeking to establish your own sacrilegious power over the churches, and out of the sacrament of the keys, which is the equal and universal property of all, you build your own unequal and special power and tyranny. If all the sacraments have the same effect in the hands of every man who administers them, then you cannot reserve to yourself this one sacrament of the keys and make it into a sacrament of your own, different from that which all of Christendom has in common.

Therefore all Christians should be on guard against this antichristian poison of the pope. If all baptisms and all masses are equally valid, wherever and by whomever they are administered, then the absolution also is equally valid wherever and by whomever it is pronounced. Everything depends on the faith of him who receives it, not on the holiness, learning, rank or power of him who administers it. We cannot divide baptism and give the pope and the bishops a part of it which is different from that which all Christians have. Neither can we divide the mass and the keys in order that the pope may have a mass and a sacrament of the keys different from those which all of Christendom has. But if he has a different sacrament, or a better sacrament, then St. Paul excludes him from Christendom, for he says in Eph. 4 [:5], "One Lord, one faith, one baptism."

To be sure, the pope and the bishops reserve to themselves the disposition of certain cases and certain sins. But that is a matter of custom and human law and has gained ground by force. Even so, however, they do no more than others in these cases as far as the remission of guilt is concerned. Only in regard to the remission of the penalty or punishment is there a difference. But it is the remission of guilt which belongs properly to the keys and the sacrament of penance and it requires faith. The remission of the penalty does not require faith, but is a matter of experience which can take place without faith and does not properly belong to the sacrament of the keys. My article, however, speaks of the remission of guilt, and this, like baptism and the mass, is the common possession of all and cannot be seized by persons of high rank or power, as the pope and his followers pretend in lying fashion.

THE FOURTEENTH ARTICLE

No one ought to say to the priest that he is contrite, nor ought the priest demand that he do so.[56]

This, too, is an error in your eyes, holy father pope, but now you will have to admit it to be true, for I can prove it as follows. Whether our contrition is genuine or not is a question which cannot be left to our own discretion, but must be left to the judgment of God. Therefore, no one can say without presumption that he is truly contrite. St. Paul says in I Cor. 10 [II Cor. 10:18], "Not the man who commends himself is accepted, but the man whom the Lord commends," and in I Cor. 4 [:4], "I am not aware of anything against myself, but I am not thereby acquitted. It is the Lord who judges me." And David says in Ps. 19 [:12], "Lord, who knows all his sins?"

If a man were required to say that he was truly contrite, he would be driven to presumption and to the impossible task of knowing all sin and evil in his heart. And since all the saints still have sin and evil within them, it is impossible for anyone to have such contrition as will be adequate in God's judgment, but they all say with David, "Lord, enter not into judgment with thy servant, for in thy sight will no man living be found justified" [Ps. 143:2]. If no one will be found justified, how will anyone be found contrite, since contrition is the beginning of justification? Why, then, O pope, do you teach pride and presumption to Christians so that they run head-on into God's judgment?

Christians ought to be so instructed that every penitent would know that before God no contrition is worthy and sufficient. He ought therefore to say, "Behold, dear Lord, I know that I will not be found truly contrite before thy judgment, and that there is still much evil lust in me which hinders true contrition, yet, because thou hast promised grace, I flee from thy judgment, and because my contrition is nothing in thy sight, I put my trust and my hope upon thy promise in this sacrament." And if the priest begins to

---

[56] From Luther's *Sermon on Repentance* (1518). WA 1, 322.

inquire about his contrition, he ought to say, "Sir, in my own eyes I am contrite, but in the presence of God it is but a poor contrition, with which I am not able to stand before Him; yet I trust in His grace, which you are now, at His command, to promise me." Thus the people should always be urged to have faith, for at death contrition will be far too great and faith far too small. God's promise in the sacrament is sure; our contrition is never sure. For this reason God would have us build not on our uncertain contrition, but on his certain promise, so that we may be able to persevere in every time of trouble.

THE FIFTEENTH ARTICLE

They are greatly in error who, when communing, rely on the fact that they have confessed, or that they are not aware of any mortal sin, and have said their prayers. Such people eat and drink judgment to themselves. But if they believe and trust that in the sacrament they receive grace, this faith alone makes them pure and worthy.[57]

This I have taught for the sake of those people of timid conscience, who prepare themselves for the sacrament with much worry and woe and yet have no peace and do not know how they stand with God. For it is not possible for a heart to be at peace unless it trusts in God and not in its own works, efforts, and prayers. St. Paul says in Rom. 5 [:1], "By faith we have peace with God." But if peace comes only through faith, it cannot be achieved through works, prayers, or anything else. Experience also teaches that even though a man may work himself to death, his heart has no peace until he begins to yield himself to God's grace, and takes the risk of trust in it.

Similarly, St. Peter teaches in Acts 15 [:9] that God cleanses the heart only by faith. Surely, then, the sacrament must always be preceded by faith, without which no prayers cleanse, as this article teaches. Besides, it has been sufficiently shown above that all works done without faith are dead and sin, as St. Paul teaches

---

[57] Cf. Luther's *Sermon on the Worthy Preparation of the Heart to Receive the Sacrament of the Eucharist* (1518). WA 1, 329-334.

in Rom. 14 [:23]: "Whatever does not proceed from faith is sin." How, then, can confession, prayer, and other preparation [for the sacrament] be without sin, when they are made without faith? Faith alone must always be the proper cleansing and worthy preparation.

Of course, I do not condemn these prayers and preparations! But nobody should trust in them. Rather he should have something more important than these preparations, namely, faith. Since in the sacrament God promises and offers his grace (as was said in the first article) prayers and works are not enough; rather, this divine promise must be believed, otherwise our unbelief will make God a liar. If you go to the sacrament with many preparations but without this trust, what else are you doing but saying to God, "In the promises of this sacrament thou liest, and thou wilt not give me grace." O, O, O you wicked bull! Mind what you teach! Mind what you condemn!

They have driven us away from this faith and from this way of using the sacrament by means of the word of St. Paul (I Cor. 11 [:28]), "Let a man examine himself, and so eat of the bread and drink of the cup." They have interpreted this saying to mean that we should examine our consciences for sin, although it means rather that we should examine ourselves for faith and trust, since no man can discover all his mortal sins, as has been shown above from Ps. 19 [:12], "Lord, who knows his sin?" Moreover, not to be conscious of mortal sin is not enough, for St. Paul says in I Cor. [4:4], "I am not aware of anything against myself, but I am not thereby acquitted." Why then do they drive us into such impossible, futile, and worthless works and why do they conceal the very faith for which a man ought to scrutinize or examine himself most of all? As was said under the previous article, they are always trying to drive us away from faith and into works; I wish we would be driven away from works and into faith, for the works will surely follow faith, but faith never follows works.

THE SIXTEENTH ARTICLE

It would be advisable that the church, in a general council, should decree that both kinds[58] *be given in the sacrament*

---

[58] The elements of the Lord's Supper are known as the two "kinds."

to the laity; and the Bohemians,[59] who receive both kinds,
are neither heretics nor schismatics.[60]

[In the debate] on this article, St. Paul easily wins over the pope, but he will not be put under the ban by his holiness and he does not care about the bull. Indeed, he puts the pope and all his bulls and followers under the ban, for he says in Gal. 1 [:8], "He who preaches otherwise than you have been taught in the gospel, though he were an angel from heaven, let him be banned and accursed." Listen, pope, that means you! According to the Gospels of Matthew, Mark, and Luke, Christ instituted both kinds at the last supper and gave both kinds to all and said to all, "This do, as often as you do it, in remembrance of me."[61] But the pope teaches differently and gives only one kind, a half-sacrament. For this reason he is assuredly under the curse and ban of St. Paul. Pope, if you, with the help of all your friends can crack this little nut and show that you are not banned and condemned before God, I am ready to recant everything that I have ever written in all my life and say that you are pope indeed. Otherwise, don't hold it against me if I call you the Antichrist, whom St. Paul bans and curses as one who changes his Lord's ordinance and resists and perverts His gospel. You cannot say anything or produce anything on your behalf, and you know it. Why, then, do you set your capricious will against so obvious and clear a text of the gospel? Why don't you tell us to deny also the Lord's Prayer?

They claim Christ gave both kinds to the apostles and priests only, and commanded them to give either one or both kinds to the laity.[62] My question is, "Where is this command written?" I think they received it in their pipe dreams.[63] It is a wanton lie and a fictitious addition. When Christ gave the cup, he added the word, "all," and said, "Drink of it, all of you" [Matt. 26:27]. He did not

---

[59] The adherents of John Huss (1369-1415).
[60] From Luther's *Treatise on the Blessed Sacrament* (1519). WA 2, 742.
[61] Luther is thinking of Matt. 26:26f.; Mark 14:22f.; Luke 22:17f.; however, the quotation is from I Cor. 11:23f.
[62] Cf. *Babylonian Captivity of the Church*. PE 2, 178-187; WA 6, 502-507.
[63] *Im finster rauchloch.*

say this when he gave the bread, doubtless because he wished to forestall this Roman sacrilege and heresy, foreseeing that they would some day rob his Christians of the cup. It would be more in accordance with the gospel if they withheld the bread, for he does not say, "Eat of it, all of you," but, "Drink of it, all of you." O how they would shout and rave if the word, "all," had been spoken with the bread and not with the cup. No one would be able to contain them. Yet when they are so plainly caught by a clear text, they deny that they are caught or bound by it.

Again in the hymn, "Celestial Word," [64] the church sings how he gave his disciples flesh and blood under the two kinds in order to feed the whole man, who is twofold in nature. If the church is right in singing this then they certainly ought to give both kinds to all Christians. Not only the priests, but the laity also are men and twofold in nature and the hymn sings of this food as whole food for the whole man.

But we will present still stronger reasons. St. Paul says in I Cor. 10 [:17], "We are one bread and one body, even as we all partake of one bread and one cup." [65] I ask whether the laity are not also Christians and members of the Christian body of whom St. Paul here says, "We are all one body"? I hope everybody will admit that. Why, then, does the pope want to segregate them and allow only the priests to be Christians? For he will not allow all to partake of the one bread and the one cup, though St. Paul says here that all those who belong to the body are to partake of the one bread and the one cup (if they are able to do so and are not hindered, but more of that later).

Afterwards, in I Cor. 11 [:23-26], he says, not to the priests but to all Christians in the city, "I received from the Lord what I also taught you." (He does not say, "What I have taught only to your priests.") "The Lord Jesus on the night when he was betrayed,

---

[64] A reference to the hymn, *Verbum Supernum Prodiens,* by Thomas Aquinas. The third stanza reads:

> Quibus sub bina specie
> Carnem dedit et sanguinem
> Ut duplicis substantiae
> Totum cibaret hominem.

H. A. Daniel, *op. cit.,* I, 254, CCXLI.

[65] Luther seems to refer to I Cor. 10:17, but he quotes freely.

took bread, and when he had given thanks, he broke it, and said, 'Take and eat, this is my body which is given for you. Do this in remembrance of me.' In the same way also the cup, after supper, saying, 'This cup is a new testament in my blood. Do this as often as you drink it, in remembrance of me.'" Here you can see what the Apostle received of the Lord and gave to the Corinthians, namely, both kinds, as he says in such clear and explicit words that I am amazed that these schismatic Roman Christians and "half-sacramenters" do not blush or blanch when they see them.

He says further, "As often as you eat this bread and drink the cup, you proclaim the Lord's death until he comes" [I Cor. 11:26]. He does not say, "As often as you priests alone eat and drink," but speaks to all of them. Nor does he say they are to do all this till the pope come and ordain it otherwise, but until the Lord himself shall come at the last day.

Again, "Whoever, therefore, eats the bread and drinks this cup in an unworthy manner is guilty of the body and blood of the Lord" [I Cor. 11:27]. He does not say, "Whatever priest," but in general, "Whoever among you all." Also, he does not say that such a person is guilty of the body only but also of the blood of Christ. He always mentions both together, eating and drinking, bread and cup.

Again, "Let a man examine himself, and so eat of the bread and drink of the cup" [I Cor. 11:28]. He does not say, "Let the priest alone examine himself," but every person in Corinth who is a Christian should examine himself, for, of course, he does not write this epistle to the heathen. Nor does he say, "Let a man eat only of the bread and drink not the cup," as the pope teaches, robbing us of our own sacrament.

And again later, "Anyone who eats and drinks unworthily, eats and drinks judgment upon himself, as one who does not respect the Lord's body" [I Cor. 11:29]. That, too, is said to all and the drinking is bound to the eating, though the pope separates it from the eating and does not think much of it.

Finally the Apostle says, "That is why many of you are weak and ill, and some have died" [I Cor. 11:30], since you eat and drink unworthily. I hardly think that this punishment and chastening came upon the priests alone, for he says, "Many of you are ill." Otherwise he could have said, "Many of your priests are ill." What can the Roman seducer bring forward against these mighty sayings of St. Paul?

Moreover, the long-established practice of all of Christendom in the whole world stands against him. This practice still continues among the Greeks,[66] whom even Rome itself dare not call heretics or apostates because of it. Why, then, should I let the Bohemians or anyone else be reviled as heretics, because they receive both kinds according to the teaching of Christ and St. Paul, and according to the custom of all the world except the pope? Besides, at the Council of Basel it was decided that the Bohemians do right. Does this bull condemn its own council? [67]

These are the reasons why I have recanted this article,[68] and still recant it, as one that I have expressed far too mildly and gently. I assert now that on this point the Greeks and Bohemians are neither heretics nor schismatics, but the most Christian people and the best followers of the gospel on earth. I beseech them, through Christ our Lord and by means of these writings, to remain constant in their views without allowing themselves to be led astray by the perverted and sacrilegious laws of the Roman tyrant and Antichrist. In sheer wantonness he takes one element and half of the sacrament away from the Christians when Christ himself and all the apostles gave it to them, and the church all over the world has used it for such a long time.

The pope commands the priests to receive both kinds and gives as his reason that it is not proper to receive one kind only, since both kinds constitute one whole and complete sacrament, which is not to be divided. On the other hand, he keeps the laity from taking one of the two kinds and again gives as his reason that one kind is a whole sacrament. Thus he tosses God's words and sacraments about like a juggler. The sacrament is whole and not whole when and where he pleases. He is free to contradict himself and to lie and deceive as the situation may demand. Thus the priests have a sacrament different from that of the laity, just as he

---

[66] Luther refers to the Holy Orthodox Catholic Apostolic Eastern church.
[67] The Council of Basel (1431-1437) allowed the use of both elements to the Bohemians. Cf. Karl Joseph von Hefele, *Conziliengeschichte* (2d ed.; Freiburg, 1873-1890), VII, 572f.
[68] In his *Babylonian Captivity of the Church* (1520). WA 6, 498; PE 2, 172.

claims to have different keys and a sacrament of penance different from that which all of Christendom has.

In the second place, I say that the pope and all who knowingly abet him in this matter are heretics, apostates, under the ban, and accursed, for they teach contrary to the gospel and follow their own ideas against the common usage and practice of the whole of Christendom. Heretics and apostates are people who transgress the teaching of their fathers, separate themselves from the common usage and practice of all of Christendom and, without reason, out of sheer wantonness, invent new usages and practices contrary to the holy gospel. This is exactly what the Antichrist in Rome does in the matter of the sacrament and in many other questions. Yet he lifts his shameless, blasphemous mouth to heaven and slanders the Greek church, claiming that it is schismatic and apostate. It is he himself who is the chief cause and sole author of all schisms and divisions. This is plain as day and all historical records show it.

However, I want to exclude the poor masses of the people from this condemnation and apologize for them. It is not their fault that they receive only the one element in the sacrament. The pope and his followers must bear all the guilt and my condemnation affects them only. This situation is just like that of baptism. If anyone should desire baptism and the pope would sacrilegiously withhold it from him and deprive him of the sacrament, his faith and desire for baptism would be accepted by God as though he were actually baptized, since he did not cause the obstruction. But the pope, who withheld baptism from him, would be a heretic and not a Christian. We must even endure it that the pope and his followers do not preach, though that is a still higher obligation. Nevertheless, we must not join them in wrongdoing on this account, but only suffer the wrong they do us.

Although it is the pope's duty to give us the sacrament under both kinds, if he does not do it and thus robs us, we can endure his encroachment and injustice and yet remain good Christians in the sight of God, receiving the fruit of the whole sacrament through our faith and desire. What could we do if the pope or the Turk took both kinds from us? What do prisoners and sick people and young children do now? None of them can receive either kind, yet all of them can receive the fruit of the sacrament. So it was in ancient days when some holy fathers lived for many years in the wilderness and never went to the sacrament.

But I speak only of those who desire both kinds; they should receive both kinds and not be refused. The pope is not the lord of the sacrament but its servant and in duty bound to give it to anyone who may desire it, as is also the case with baptism, penance, and the other sacraments. Christ has compelled no one to take the sacraments. He does not say, "You shall do this," but, "When you do this, remember me!" He has not commanded us to do it, but to remember him when we do it. When we want to do it, he left up to us. The pope seizes this freedom and takes possession of it; he compels us to go to the sacrament once a year,[69] which Christ does not do. Thus he is in all his deeds, his commands, and his prohibitions, the very opposite of Christ as befits a true Antichrist.

I do not say this to incite anyone to lawless revolt against the pope's tyranny (for we ought to suffer tyranny and wrong and it does us no harm), but only that everyone may understand this matter and be properly instructed and observe how Christ and the pope compare, how things ought and how they ought not to be done in Christendom. It should help people avoid becoming involved in the pope's sin, error, and destruction by defending his acts and calling his wrong right and praising it, as do the lackeys who surround him. When anyone does us bodily harm we ought to suffer it patiently and confess our guilt to God, but we are not bound to say that the offender is right or praise him as though he had done well. In the same way, even though the pope withholds the gospel and the sacraments and takes them away from us, we ought to endure it and confess our sins to God who permits the rule of the pope as a punishment for our sins. We have deserved that Antichrist rule over us, but we ought not to praise him and defend him as though he were doing well, and call him "most holy" into the bargain. On the contrary, we ought to bear witness in public against his demonic and heretical tyranny, and rebuke it as Christ rebuked the evil deeds of the Jews, even though he was willing to suffer evil at their hands.

---

[69] Pope Innocent III (1215). Cf. Carl Mirbt, *Quellen zur Geschichte des Papsttums und des römischen Katholizismus* (4th ed., Tübingen, 1924), No. 331, p. 181.

To bring this matter to a close, I am prepared to change this article and will now say: It would be good if not only a general council, but every bishop in his own diocese were to decree again that both kinds, the whole sacrament, be given to the laity, thus following the gospel and never mind the pope. For it is the bishop's duty to fight against the wolf in defense of the sheep of Christ, whom Christ has committed to his care. It is the bishop's task to protect the gospel with life and limb since he represents Christ.

But if that cannot be achieved I advise every Christian layman to remember that his Lord, Christ, has instituted both kinds in the one sacrament. For this reason let him heartily desire both kinds and believe. Then he will receive the holy sacrament half with the body and half with the spirit, since the dangerous times of the Antichrist permit no more. Let him also cry to God that because of our sin we are robbed of the sacrament as Christ has given it to us and the Antichrist has taken it from us. For if anyone despises the two kinds and does not even desire them he is not a Christian. Don't pay any attention to their twaddle that the whole sacrament is received in the bread. Christ knew very well that we receive everything in one kind, indeed by faith alone, without the sacrament, yet it was not without reason that he instituted both kinds.

THE SEVENTEENTH ARTICLE

The treasures of the church, out of which the pope grants indulgences, are not the merits of Christ and of the saints.[70]

The pope and his hypocrites, in order to praise the indulgences and to make them appear valuable in the eyes of the poor people and to usurp the treasures of the world, have invented this doctrine, and teach, to the great dishonor of Christ, that Christ's merits are the treasure from which the indulgences come. But if asked what evidence for this view they have in Scripture they puff themselves up and boast of their power, and reply, "Is it not enough that we say so?" Against this attitude I propose this article and can base it on Scripture.

---

[70] The bull has combined parts of Thesis 56 and Thesis 58 from Luther's *Ninety-Five Theses* (1517). WA 1, 236; LW 31, 30.

In John 6 [:51] Christ himself says that he is the living bread from heaven, and that he who eats of this bread will live for ever. Isaiah 53 [:4] says that Christ has borne our sins. No Christian is so naive as not to know that Christ's merits and suffering take away our sins and save us. All believe that he died for our sins. From this it is clear that Christ's suffering and merit are a living treasure and give everlasting life to all who share in it. But even my opponents must admit that the indulgences do not give life, but are dead, through them no one is made better, let alone given life. They do not take away sin, but the penalty for sin. Now, no one but the pope and his sycophants is so foolish as to hold that discarding or remitting a penalty makes anyone better, though imposing a penalty may indeed make a man better, as we learn from reason, experience, Scripture, and truth.

This is the reason why the indulgences and the merits of Christ dovetail like life and death, day and night, Christ and Belial [II Cor. 6:15], the pope and a Christian. And they do have the right name for it, for indulgence[71] means "to relax" or "to remit," and now everything good ceases and every kind of disaster is admitted.[72] The pope leaves sin unpunished, indeed he takes away the penalty of sin which God has imposed and demands. So far as possible he lets sin go free and does not check it. Indeed, he protects and fosters sin, for he remits the penalty and asks and accepts money in its place. This is why St. Paul, writing to the Thessalonians [II Thess. 2:3], calls the pope a "man of sin" and "the son of perdition," for he permits and encourages sin, and thereby leads all the world with him to the devil, using his lying and deceitful indulgences.

Struck by this truth and left without an answer they invent the fiction that the merits of Christ can be applied in two ways. In one way, as we just said, they give life, in another way they render satisfaction for our sin. I answer, Yes; but the merits of Christ are used in many ways. They are used to get money, to obtain high rank and honor, to secure luxury and ease, to lead the world into war and bloodshed and all kinds of misery. Is there anything that is used more shamefully at Rome and in the whole Roman

---

[71] In German: *Ablass.*
[72] In German: *zulassen.*

church than Christ's name and his merit? The pope with all his lackeys would have been a beggar long ago if he had not had Christ to sell and to exploit as a screen for all his malice. The name of Christ must now cover up all the ruin that the rule of Antichrist has brought about all over the world. Christ himself foretold this in Matt. 24 [:5]: "Many will come in my name and they will lead many astray." Thus the indulgences and their hucksters, coming in the name of Christ and of his merits, lead the whole world astray, so that even the elect are scarcely safe from them.

THE EIGHTEENTH ARTICLE

Indulgences are a pious fraud practiced upon Christians; they are remissions of good works and belong to the things that are permitted but not necessary.[73]

Some of the people who recognized the worthlessness of the indulgences, but did not venture to oppose the teacher of sins in Rome, have had a saying which asserted that the indulgences are a "pious fraud," that is to say, although they were really worthless and deceived the people, nevertheless they were a reason for the contribution of money, which was considered a good work. In this way, though fraudulent, they served a worthwhile and godly purpose. When I made this statement I agreed with these men and said the same thing, for then I did not know better.

But now that the holy father pope orders me to recant, and condemns this article, I will be obedient and say, "I confess my error; this article is not true." And this is the reason: The indulgences are not a pious fraud, but an infernal, diabolical, antichristian fraud, larceny, and robbery, whereby the Roman Nimrod [Gen. 10:9] and teacher of sin peddles sin and hell to the whole world and sucks and entices away everybody's money as the price of this unspeakable harm. If this recantation is not enough, I will improve on it some other time.

But this is how I prove it: God says in Ps. 89 [:32], "I will punish their transgression with the rod and their iniquity with scourges." And St. Paul says in I Cor. 11 [:31], "If we punish

---

[73] From the *Disputation of Johann Eck and Martin Luther* (1519). WA 2, 356-357.

ourselves, God will not punish us; but when he punishes us, he chastens us, that we may not be condemned along with the world."

Here you can see that sin must be punished, either by God, by man, or by our own selves, if we are not to be condemned with this world. Yet the pope would blind our eyes to these clear words and through his indulgences let all sin go unpunished, so that we be condemned with this world, as St. Paul here says. He wants to hide this abomination behind Christ's merits and then sell it, and Christ's merits must serve him while he flies in the face of this clear word of God. O pope, O pope, enough is enough!

THE NINETEENTH ARTICLE

Indulgences do not effect the remission of the punishment or penalty which divine justice demands for actual sin.[74]

THE TWENTIETH ARTICLE

They are deceived who believe that indulgences save, and are profitable to the soul.[75]

THE TWENTY-FIRST ARTICLE

Indulgences are necessary only for those who are guilty of public mortal sins, and are really granted only to the lazy and to weaklings.[76]

THE TWENTY-SECOND ARTICLE

There are six kinds of men for whom indulgences are neither necessary nor useful: The dead, the sick, those who have good reason for being unable to obtain them, those who are without mortal sins, those whose mortal sins are not public, and those who do better works.[77]

In honor of the holy and most learned bull I recant everything that I have ever taught about indulgences and I am most heartily

---

[74] *Ibid.* WA 2, 357.
[75] From Luther's *Explanations of the Ninety-Five Theses.* WA 1, 587.
[76] *Ibid.* WA 1, 612 and 609.
[77] *Ibid.* From the Thirteenth. WA 1, 552; LW 31, 119-123.

sorry for every good word that I have ever said about them. Do not be troubled, good people, when the pope here pretends that indulgences are profitable to men's souls and save them. That is a doctrine that has been unknown until now; even the pope himself had really never heard of it. It is the old dragon from the abyss of hell who speaks in this bull [Rev. 17:8]. Hold on to the truth that indulgences are not what the pope pretends they are, for no sin can go unpunished, as has been said. If an angel from heaven says otherwise, we are not to believe him [Gal. 1:8]. And if my books deserve to be burned, it is most certainly because on the question of indulgences I have played into their hands. I have yielded too much to the pope and his followers.[78] I myself condemn such doctrine to the flames.

THE TWENTY-THIRD ARTICLE

Excommunication is only an external penalty, and does not deprive men of the common prayers of the church.[79]

Observe how the pope tries to be God. In the preceding articles he has usurped the power to save souls by means of indulgences; in this article he usurps the power to damn souls by means of the ban. Neither of these functions are, however, in the power of any creature, but are the exclusive function of the exalted divine Majesty. St. Paul prophesied concerning the pope, "He will sit and rule in the church of God, claim that he himself is God and oppose and exalt himself against everything that is God" [II Thess. 2:4].

I have defended this article sufficiently in the *Treatise Concerning the Ban*.[80] I will only add briefly that the Christian life, based on faith, neither pope nor devil can give or take away. While faith remains, nothing can harm us—neither death, nor hell, nor even the sin we have committed—as St. Paul says in Rom. 8 [:28], "All things work out for the best for believers," or Christians. For this reason the ban can be nothing more than an external penalty, that is, exclusion from the fellowship of church and sacraments. The pope

---

[78] In his manuscript Luther wrote, "to the devil and Antichrist." WA 7, 404.
[79] From Luther's *Sermon on Excommunication* (1518). WA 1, 639.
[80] *Treatise Concerning the Ban* (1520). WA 6, 63-75; PE 2, 37-54.

says in his own law[81] (though he seems to have overlooked that he, for once, taught something good) that the ban is medicine, not destruction, therefore it can do no inner harm, but only help and improve.

THE TWENTY-FOURTH ARTICLE

Christians should be taught to love the ban rather than fear it.[82]

This article has been condemned because the pope wants to remain God and have everyone fear him more than the exalted and true Majesty. Nevertheless what has been said before has proven this article true. Since the ban is a penalty for sin and a medicine for the soul, he who has deserved it ought to bear up under it patiently and gladly, though, to be sure, he ought to fear the sin by which he might deserve the ban. Just as a child ought to be afraid to do wrong, but, if it does wrong, it should suffer the penalty gladly and kiss the rod. Since it is God's will that we willingly suffer death and love all suffering, how much more ought we to love and willingly suffer this fox's tail and motherly rod? The pope and his church are an exception. Because of their own blindness they are quite properly afraid, as it is written, "Un-Christian sinners are afraid when no one pursues them" [Prov. 28:1].

THE TWENTY-FIFTH ARTICLE

The Roman bishop, the successor of St. Peter, is not by Christ's appointment vicar of Christ over all the churches of the world.[83]

This is another of the key teachings which abolish the holy gospel and replace Christ with an idol in Christendom. Against it I have proposed this article. I stand by it and can prove it as follows:

First, since everything that is done in the church is proclaimed in clear and plain passages of Scripture, it is surely amazing that

---

[81] Canon law, e.g., Sexti Decret. lib. v. tit. XI cap. I, *Aegidii Perrini Opera* (Lyons, 1556), p. 643.
[82] From Luther's *Treatise Concerning the Ban* (1520). WA 6, 70; PE 2, 47.
[83] From Luther's *Defense Against the Malignant Judgment of Johann Eck* (1519). WA 2, 628.

nothing is openly said in the whole Bible about the papacy. This is especially strange since my opponents consider the papacy the most important, most necessary, and most unique feature in the church. It is a suspicious situation and makes a bad impression that so many matters of lesser importance are based upon a multitude of reliable and clear passages of Scripture, while for this one doctrine no one has been able to produce a single clear reason. It is clearly stated in the gospel that St. Peter is a fisherman and an apostle, which they consider a matter of small importance compared with the papacy; yet there is not one single letter which states that St. Peter is above all the churches in the world.

At this point I would like to have it understood that I do not propose this article because I wish to repudiate the pope. Let him have as much power as he will, it makes no difference to me, and he is welcome to it. But there are two things I can neither tolerate nor keep silent about. First, he and his supporters torture, violate, and blaspheme the holy Word of God in order to establish their power. Second, they revile, slander, and anathematize the Greeks, and all others who do not submit to the pope, as though these were not Christians. They act as if being a Christian meant being bound to the pope and to Rome, while St. Paul and Christ have bound it only to faith and to God's Word, of which no one knows less or has less than the pope and his followers. And yet, though without faith and God's Word, he wants to be not only a Christian, but the god of all Christians and condemn all those who do not worship him, no matter how sound their faith and their gospel.

Moreover, if the pope were sensible, he would welcome less trouble, and he would not load all the affairs of the world on his own shoulders. It is surely impossible to tie the whole world to one place and transact all its business there.

But watch how they torture and insult the holy words of God in order to establish their prevaricated power. Christ says to St. Peter in Matt. 16 [:18], "You are Peter"—that is a rock—"and on this rock I will build my church, . . . I will give you the keys of the kingdom of heaven . . . and whatever you loose on earth shall be loosed in heaven." Here they interpret the rock to mean St. Peter, and pretend that it is the papal power on which Christ builds his church, and that, therefore, all churches ought to be subject to the pope's power. According to the teaching of these experts the church built on the rock means the church subject to the pope: an interpretation of his words Christ has had to suffer all these years.

Now, in order to bring their lies and guile clearly into the open, and to make them blush for shame, let us examine Christ's words. If to build the church upon a rock means nothing but to be subject to the pope, as they say, it follows that the church can be built and exists without faith, without the gospel, and without any sacraments (for what is built is built and needs no further building). The power and authority of the pope are one thing; faith, sacraments and gospel are quite another thing. If, therefore, the church is built on the pope's power, it is evident that for the building of it the pope's power and authority are sufficient, and faith is not necessary, or anything else. Especially since the pope and his followers live, as a rule, without faith or the gospel and the sacraments, indeed, they despise them like heathen, and yet his power remains rock, building, and church, as they say. Isn't this a fine explanation of Christ's word! If the papists have the power to interpret Christ's word any way they please, who will stop someone else from saying that the rock and the building of the church are an ass and a cow, or whatever else his nightmares tell him?

Again, in this same passage, Christ speaks of this rock and of his church and says, "the gates of hell shall not prevail against it" [Matt. 16:18]. Here Christ says clearly that against his rock and building and church the very devils shall not prevail. If, then, the rock is papal power and the building represents submission to this authority, how does it happen that this building and authority have in fact collapsed and the gates of hell have prevailed against it? For all Christendom has fallen away from the pope; for example, the Greeks, the Bohemians, Africa, and the whole Orient! Or to be more accurate, they never were built upon this rock. Now, if Christ, who cannot lie, promises that the gates of hell shall not prevail against his building, and no one can deny that the Orient has fallen away, it follows that Christ speaks the truth and the pope lies, and the building is not obedience to his power but something else, which the gates of hell have not been able to break down.

And it cannot be said that these people are no longer Christians because they do not obey the pope and are not built on him, since the pope himself and all his followers wish to be considered Christians, though they do not obey God in a single letter, and live, for the most part, without faith. So far they have been successful with their lies in maintaining that those who do not agree with them on this point are heretics and they themselves good Christians, though they do not take their stand with God and Christ on any point. Thus they make monkeys and fools of all the world, and define the terms "Christian" and "heretic" to suit themselves.

But let us leave their false interpretation and take up the true meaning of these words. To say that the gates of hell cannot prevail against this building must mean that the devil has no power over it; and this happens when the building is based on firm faith and stands without sin. Where faith is lacking or sin is present, there the devil rules and prevails against the building. Thus St. Peter teaches us [I Pet. 5:9] that we are to fight the devil with a strong faith, for the devil centers his attack on faith. From this it follows that this rock is Christ himself, for this is what St. Paul calls him in I Cor. 10 [:4]. The building is the believing church, in which there is no sin, and to build is nothing but to become a believer and free from sin, as St. Peter also teaches in I Pet. 2 [:5] that we are to be built into a spiritual house on Christ the rock.

Now, since the pope and his authority and those who obey him walk in sin and horrible perversions and are the devil's henchmen, as everyone can see, it must be a lying invention that the rock and the building, which Christ puts beyond the reach of the gates of hell, mean the papal power and rule. This power the devil has brought into subjection to himself. If the power of the pope were the "rock" in Christ's words it could not do any evil, for Christ does not lie. But before our very eyes papal power has become the devil's power, a power for evil now as in the past.

Come on, you papists, crack this nut! This Scripture passage won't do any more, the citadel has been conquered, the pope has fallen, and he has nothing to stand on. For this saying of Christ has been the only basis on which the papacy has relied and built its claims all these many years. Now its lies and falsehoods have been revealed. If we have gained nothing else from the pope in this controversy we have at least liberated this passage of Scripture. In fact, this wins the war and decapitates the papacy, for this passage speaks stronger against the pope than for him. He who tells a single lie is assuredly not of God and everything else he says is suspect. But since the pope has lied about this fundamental doctrine and this key passage of Scripture on which it is based, and since he has perverted God's word and deceived the world with his false rule, what St. Paul says of him is certainly true, that the coming of the Antichrist shall be through the activity of the evil spirit, who enters only through lies and false interpretations of Scripture [II Thess. 2:9].

Now you lie prostrate, dear pope! If you can honestly talk your way out of this predicament and turn your lies into truth I will admit that you have been made pope by God. But all this is not Luther's work. The credit belongs to John Huss.[84] As it is written, "The righteous man who is dead shall condemn the ungodly who are living" [Wisd. of Sol. 4:16].

It won't do to quote some of the holy fathers who called St. Peter the rock and foundation of the church. First of all, because Christ's words take precedence over the words of all the saints. They have erred often; Christ never erred. Secondly, because no saint has ever said that the pope is this rock. They have called St. Peter the rock, not because of his power, but because of his faith, and if the pope will follow him in faith, we are ready to call him a rock too, provided only that the "rock" continues to be "faith" and does not turn into "power." But if he has no faith he shall not be called a rock.

But they produce another proof-text. It is in the last chapter of John [John 21:15-19], where Christ says three times to Peter, "Peter, do you love me?" and Peter answers three times, "Yes, Lord, I love you"; then Christ said three times, "Tend my sheep!" They try to use this passage to place the pope over all Christians; but no clear passage with which to prove so great a claim has been found and this passage here is quite obscure. Nobody can suppose that God would have established such a great institution, as they claim the papacy to be, without a single clear passage of Scripture. Moreover, this passage, too, undermines the papacy as can be easily seen. Three times Christ demands love from St. Peter before

---

[84] The Bohemian reformer, burned at the stake at Constance, July 6, 1415, challenged papal supremacy.

he commends the sheep to his care. This shows clearly that the tending of the sheep does not belong to him who is without love. And since the pope and the papacy are without love, "tending the sheep" cannot refer to the papacy. It is, therefore, a lie and a false explanation to apply the word "tending" to the loveless rule and power of the papacy. If we are willing to allow Christ's words to be thus torn to pieces and distorted, I might as well say that the rule of the Turk means tending the sheep. But if the words are to keep their true meaning, then there must be love or we cannot speak of a shepherd. Who can get around this?

And the evil spirit has taught them that "to tend" means to preside. How will they prove this interpretation? Must we simply take their word for it and be satisfied when they boast and crow and say, "This is the way we read it, hush up and don't contradict us"? But I will go a step further and say that these words, "to tend," have such a profoundly spiritual meaning that even if the pope were as holy as St. Peter, and even if he kept his canon law most diligently, he would still not be a shepherd. "To tend" means to supply the teaching which gives life to the soul, namely, faith and the gospel. If the pope were to attend to this task he would have to live in constant expectation of death and offer his soul for the sheep. In this way, St. Augustine has correctly interpreted this passage,[85] that to tend means here to give one's life for the sheep and for the gospel. And this is how Christ himself interprets these words immediately afterwards when he shows Peter the martyrdom that he must suffer in order to "tend" the sheep. It is impossible to do this without love.

It is indeed disgusting that this noble, spiritual, mighty, and precious word of Christ is so shamefully tortured and applied to the idle, pompous, and luxurious power of the papacy. The most accurate interpretation which they offer applies these words to the pope's laws, but even these laws poison rather than tend the sheep. We accept as Christ's meaning, therefore, what St. Augustine also holds, namely, that in Peter all preachers are taught that they are not to preach unless they love Christ and are ready to give their lives for the sheep.

---

[85] Augustine, *On the Gospel of John.* Migne 35, 1967.

If "to tend" means to be pope, then the church must be without a pope as often as the pope does not love and does not preach. And this is most certainly true, for where the gospel is not preached there is no church, and this papacy is as useful to the church as the fifth wheel to a wagon; in fact, it is altogether harmful. But of this I will say more some other time. Again, if "to love" and "to tend" meant papacy, there would be as many popes as there are men who love and tend the sheep. It could not be otherwise. And this cannot be denied, for whoever loves and tends is a pope. Thus the words of God, which the pope applies to himself, always go against him. It does not help his case to say that the pope does not himself tend the sheep, but does the tending through others. Why, then, is he not also pope through others? If "to tend" means to be pope, then he can just as well be pope through others as he can tend through others. If the one is impossible, so is the other. He must do his own tending or he cannot himself be pope. The word "tend" cannot be milked and forced any old way.

And now I will show that St. Peter was subject to the other apostles rather than their master. In Acts 8 [:14] we read that the apostles and elders sent St. Peter and St. John to Samaria to strengthen the Christians there. If, then, St. Peter was a messenger, subject to the others, why does his successor or rather his oppressor, the pope, claim to be subject to no one? If St. Peter had been the superior by divine right, he should have sat in his chair, as the pope does now, and given the orders and done the sending, and not let himself be sent. He should have rather suffered ten deaths than allowed himself to be humiliated, contrary to God's ordinance. This is the way the popes act now; they would rather drown the whole world in blood than give up their supremacy.

They have not solved their problem; it hits them so hard that they reel dizzily and know not what to answer, but they are not silent. They prattle about the Arians[86] and how the Holy Spirit is not less than the Father, even though the Father has sent him. But they do not see that this argument fits into this discussion like the papacy fits into the church. The Holy Spirit is not sent in his own person, like St. Peter, but, with the Father and the Son he sends

---

[86] Followers of Arius who denied that Christ is of the same substance with the Father.

himself. That means he reveals himself in the dove, in the clouds, and in believing hearts, as the Book of Wisdom says [Wisd. of Sol. 19:7] and Augustine explains. For this reason the pope's partisans must now stop and confess that the pope is not sovereign, but rather equal with or beneath the others, if his rule is to be of God and not of the devil. It is contrary to God and his holy Word that the pope exalts his sacrilegious power over everything, when he ought to do no more than to tolerate it, should we exalt him.

Scripture shows clearly that St. Peter never made or sent apostles, or gave orders to them. Even with the aid of all the other apostles he could not make St. Matthias into an apostle [Acts 1:15-26]. They obtained him from heaven. Here Christ shows incontestably that all the apostles were created by him alone and are equal. This ought also to make all bishops equal and unite them, not under one authority and sovereign power as the pope's partisans deceitfully suggest to us, but in the unity of faith, baptism, love, and the Spirit, so that they would be one people, as St. Paul teaches in Eph. 4 [:4-16]. What a tempest they would raise if they could find that St. Peter sent out a single apostle, as we find that he was himself sent out! Nevertheless, they say our argument is not valid and their fable is the true version. But I think that I have produced sufficient evidence to show not only that the papacy hangs in the air, without any foundation in Scripture, but also that it raves against Scripture.

THE TWENTY-SIXTH ARTICLE

The words of Christ to Peter, "Whatever you loose on earth shall be loosed in heaven," are to be understood only of those things that were bound by Peter himself.[87]

How much the pope would like to be a god and be able to turn Christ's words around and decree, "Whatever I bind and loose in heaven, you shall loose and bind on earth." Thus he would be able to bind what God looses and loose what God binds. Then our God would be banished and could do nothing but the will of the pope. This is what happened in the days of John Huss.[88] In those days the

---

[87] From the Fifth of Luther's *Explanations* (1518). WA 1, 536; LW 31, 93.
[88] Cf. p. 71 n. 84, above.

pope commanded the angels in heaven to lead to heaven the souls of those pilgrims who died on the way to Rome.[89] John Huss objected to this horrible blasphemy and more than diabolic presumption. This protest cost him his life, but he at least caused the pope to change his tune and, embarrassed by this sacrilege, to refrain from such proclamation. But the rogue's face still shows. Since the pope could not keep his hold on heaven and hell, having over-extended himself, he nevertheless wants to take purgatory captive. Though he must admit that he cannot cast anyone into purgatory or bind him there, he wishes to free those that are bound there and bring them out. If you ask on what grounds he can do this, he says, "I am pope."

But enough of this! The words of Christ expressly state that his authority is on earth, not above it or beneath it. Binding and loosing apply in the same situation. The words are, "Whatever you bind on earth," and, "Whatever you loose on earth." The binding is as effective as the loosing, and the latter goes no farther than the former. We, therefore, abide by Christ's words and disdain papal sacrilege.

Moreover, all priests use the words of Christ when they absolve, and no absolution is granted except by virtue of this same word and promise of Christ. If, then, these are the very same words, why does the pope try to do more with them than the humblest priest? If the words have the same meaning, they have the same power, and if that power allows the pope to reach into purgatory, it gives every priest the same right. See how the pope fools and deceives the whole world. He selects from the divine Word whatever he wants, even though it belongs equally to everybody, and pretends to drink the best wine out of the very cask from which others can scarcely get water. God's plain and simple Word with its uniform power is gold for him, but he will not let others pass it as copper. Stop it, pope, the game has gone far enough!

To interpret this passage to mean that the keys are used for

---

[89] When in the year 1500 thousands of pilgrims died on the way to Rome as the result of the plague, it was rumored that Pope Clement VI had once given orders to the angels to carry the souls of those who died on a pilgrimage to Rome immediately to paradise. This rumor, however, was based on a bull which was most probably spurious. Cf. WA 30[II], 282 n. 2; PE 2, 244 n. 1.

the remission of penalties is likewise dangerous. Christ did not give these words so that St. Peter might have power to do anything, but they are given to our faith, which is to hold fast to them in order that our sins may be forgiven. St. Peter is only a servant in this matter. He can hold these words up to us, but what he can do with them depends on our faith. He may remit penalty and guilt a thousand times over, and yet accomplish nothing, unless I believe in it. Faith makes the keys effective and powerful, unbelief makes them ineffective and powerless. Without faith there is in these words none of the power which the pope arrogates to himself, deceiving both himself and us. If God himself cannot give heaven to him who does not believe, how should the pope by means of the keys give heaven to a person who does not believe? But the remission of the penalty does not properly belong to the power of the keys, for that is a public transaction, and there is no room in it for faith, which believes only invisible things, namely, the forgiveness of sins in the eyes of God.

There have been some who use this passage to make the Roman bishop into a pope, because Christ says, "Whatever you bind shall be bound." But since all priests absolve by virtue of these same words, these words cannot be the property of St. Peter and the pope, but must belong to all in common. If these words refer to the papacy, either all priests who absolve by virtue of these words are popes, or else no one can absolve except the pope. The pope can no more make absolution common property than he can make the papacy common property, for they depend on one and the same word and "binding" and "papacy" are one and the same thing, as they themselves say. Here you can see how they distort the holy words of God. What is common property is said to belong to the pope and what is given to our faith is used to confirm his power and tyranny.

THE TWENTY-SEVENTH ARTICLE

It is certain that it is not within the power of the pope or of the church to establish articles of faith or commandments regarding morals and good works.[90]

[90] From Luther's *Explanation of the Articles Debated at Leipzig* (1519). WA 2, 427.

There is nothing I should be happier to hear than exactly what are these articles of faith and commandments concerning morals and good works which the pope or the church can establish. Then we can send the Holy Spirit and Christ to school and have them properly disciplined since they have been so forgetful and negligent and have not correctly and adequately taught us the Christian faith and good works. Most learned disciples of the pope, open the mouth of your wisdom and tell us what these articles and commandments are. Go ahead! If not, well, then, let me tell you.

Christ foretold them in Matt. 24 [:15, 24], "When you see the desolating sacrilege spoken of by the prophet Daniel, standing in the holy place (let the reader understand) . . . false Christs and false prophets will arise and show great signs and wonders, so as to lead astray, if possible, even the elect." And St. Paul spoke of them in I Tim. 4 [:1], "Now the Spirit expressly says that in later times many will depart from the faith by giving heed to deceitful spirits and doctrines of demons, through the pretensions of liars whose consciences are seared, who forbid marriage and enjoin abstinence from foods which God created to be received with thanksgiving by those who believe and know the truth."

See here! Shouldn't the pope have power to establish doctrines and articles of faith, when this prophecy of him is so clear that even the spirits who inspire him are expressly mentioned?

Moreover, in Col. 2 [:8], St. Paul teaches us how we should deal with such doctrines when he says, "See to it, that no one makes a prey of you by philosophy and empty deceit, according to human tradition, and temporal commandments which do not teach of Christ." Here we see that we should listen to Christ alone and flee from the commandments of man. Such commandments may appear to make us godly, but are only deceit and the destruction of faith. Christ himself says in Matt. 23 [:10], "Call no man master upon earth. You have one master, even Christ." And St. James [James 3:1] commands, "Let not many of you be masters, dear brethren." Even St. Peter is not silent and says in II Pet. 2 [:1], "There will be false teachers among you who will teach according to their whim." And there are countless other passages of the same sort.

Hence the experts in Rome have recently pronounced a holy

decree[91] which establishes that the soul of man is immortal, acting as if we did not all say in our common Creed, "I believe in the life everlasting." And, with the assistance of the mastermind Aristotle, they decreed further that the soul is "essentially the form of the human body," and many other splendid articles of a similar nature. These decrees are, indeed, most appropriate to the papal church, for they make it possible for them to hold fast to human dreams and the doctrines of devils while they trample upon and destroy faith and the teaching of Christ.[92]

But let us look at the source from which they derive their authority to make articles of faith and laws. "Not everything that is necessary," they say, "is written in the Bible; therefore Christ has committed this authority to the church, as St. John says in the last chapter of his Gospel [John 21:25], 'But Christ did many other signs which are not written in this book; were every one of them to be written, I suppose that the world itself could not contain the books that would be written.'" Note the superior wisdom of the papal partisans. John does not speak of all the signs of Christ, but of the many which he has not recorded. Moreover, he says these "are not written in this book," meaning his own book. He does not deny, indeed he acknowledges, that they may have been recorded in the other books. But our teachers apply his words to the whole Bible, and now the Gospel of John must mean the whole Bible.

That, however, is not the worst. When John says that Christ's signs are not all recorded, these gentlemen interpret that to mean that what we ought to do and their law are not fully recorded. What do you think of that? Doesn't that show how the pope's partisans can interpret Scripture? Listen to these Roman masters of Christendom! Many of Christ's signs are not recorded in John's book, which means that the Bible does not tell us adequately what we ought to know and do. The Holy Spirit must speak to the pope so that he can give and teach us more laws and doctrines. See, now you know why the Holy Spirit was given to the pope and to the Christians.

---

[91] At the Fifth Lateran Council, 1512-1517. Cf. John F. Clarkson (ed. and trans.), *The Church Teaches* (St. Louis, Mo., 1955), p. 149.

[92] Luther objects to the substitution of philosophical ideas concerning the immortality of the soul for the biblical teaching of the resurrection and the life everlasting. Cf. Carl Stange, *Studien zur Theologie Luthers* (Gütersloh, 1928-   ), pp. 287-344.

St. Paul and all Scripture teaches that the Holy Spirit is given in order to fulfil the law, to reduce its burdens, to release us and make us free. As he says in II Cor. 4 [3:6], "The letter of the law kills, but the Spirit gives life," and in Rom. 8 [:2], "The Spirit of life has set me free from the law of sin and death." But the master of all Christians in Rome and his partisans have another Holy Spirit who multiplies laws and forces them upon people, enslaving them with these man-made laws. Forgive me, my God, that I here mention the name of thy Holy Spirit! I know not what to think or what to say against this unspeakable abomination of the Antichrist at Rome, who treats thy Word not only foolishly, but ridicules it as though it were a carnival joke.[93] O God, where are those who earnestly pray to thee, and turn away thine inconceivable wrath?

THE TWENTY-EIGHTH ARTICLE

If the pope, together with a large portion of the church, professed a certain opinion, and even though he were not in error, it would nevertheless be neither sin nor heresy to hold a different opinion, especially in matters not necessary to salvation, until such time as a general council approves one opinion and condemns the other.[94]

Why will they not allow me to hold this article, since it speaks only of things not necessary to salvation? In regard to the conception of our Lady they have admitted that, since this article is not necessary to salvation, it is neither heresy nor error when some hold that she was conceived in sin, although in this case council, pope, and the majority hold a different view.[95] Why should we poor Christians be forced to believe whatever the pope and his

---

[93] The German phrase reads, *fasznacht Schimpff.*

[94] From the Twenty-sixth of Luther's *Explanations* (1518). WA 1, 584; LW 31, 174.

[95] The immaculate conception of the Virgin Mary was a matter of serious dispute between the Dominican and Franciscan orders. The Dominicans, relying on the authority of Thomas Aquinas, denied it. The Franciscans, following Duns Scotus, affirmed it. In 1483, Pope Sixtus IV forbade either party to accuse the other of heresy on pain of excommunication, "since it has not yet been decided by the Roman Church or the apostolic see." Cf. Carl Mirbt, *op. cit.*, p. 243. The Roman Dogma of the Immaculate Conception was proclaimed by Pope Pius IX in 1854.

papists think, even when it is not necessary to salvation? Has papal authority the power to make unnecessary matters necessary articles of faith, and can it make heretics of people in matters which are not necessary for salvation?

For this reason I must now retract this article myself and condemn it to the flames. I have said in this article, very foolishly, that we need not believe the pope in regard to unnecessary matters. I should have said, if the pope and his papists assembled in a council[96] are so frivolous and irresponsible as to waste time and money on unnecessary questions, when it is the business of a council to deal only with the important and necessary affairs of the church, we should not only refuse to obey them, but consider them insane or criminals. When men turn from the serious and necessary affairs of the suffering church to childish and useless trifles, they mock a miserable and poor Christendom. Unfortunately, it is just such foolishness and frivolity that they have committed by dealing in all these recent councils with indulgences and papacy, with episcopal sees and jurisdictions, but with none of those questions which are truly urgent.

But the bull is right when it turns over to the papists and their councils the decision of useless questions. For these mockers of the church ought to be given over by the wrath of God to such a perverse mind that they do not take the necessary things to heart and deal only with unnecessary matters. They deserve no better fate.

THE TWENTY-NINTH ARTICLE

We have now the right to weaken the power of the councils and to contradict their acts, also to pass judgment on their decrees and to confess boldly whatever we think is true, regardless of whether it is condemned or approved by any council.[97]

My papists attack this article with such hate and venom, as though I intended to teach that anybody might arbitrarily and without

---

[96] Cf. p. 78 n. 91, above; also WA 5, 345 n. 1.
[97] From Luther's *Explanation of the Articles Debated at Leipzig* (1519). WA 2, 406; 404.

reason oppose the councils—a thought which was never either in my mind or on my pen. I have said that when anything contrary to Scripture is decreed in a council, we ought to believe Scripture rather than the council. Scripture is our court of appeal and bulwark; with it we can resist even an angel from heaven—as St. Paul commands in Gal. 1 [:8]—let alone a pope and a council!

And why do they condemn me for this article? Why do they not condemn those who first advanced it and whom I have cited as my authorities, such as St. Paul, in Gal. 1 [:8], where he says, "If anyone teach you otherwise than you have heard, even though it were an angel from heaven, let him be banned and accursed"? Listen, you papists! Paul curses an angel from heaven if he teaches contrarily to Scripture, and am I not to have the power to scorn a man if he so teaches? Why don't you also condemn that chapter of Panormitanus,[98] *Significasti, de electione,* which I have cited,[99] in which he says that we should rather believe a layman, if he has plain Scripture and clear reason on his side, than a pope or a council. This opinion is shared by almost all the legal experts, especially the ablest and most learned among them.

What other conclusion can be drawn from this article of the bull except that man's teaching is more important than God's word, and the pope is higher than God, and whatever other horrors follow from such views. Indeed, Lucifer was not guilty of so great a sacrilege in heaven, for he only presumed to be God's equal. God help us! Has it come to this in Christendom that we must hear that

---

[98] Nicholas of Tudesco, O. S. B. (1386-1445), known as *Siculus* or *Panormitanus,* was professor of canon law in various Italian universities and later was archbishop of Palermo. He participated in the Council of Basel, where he sided with Pope Felix V, who appointed him cardinal. Luther thought highly of his *Lectures on the Decretals* and his *Report on the Council of Basel.*

[99] In Luther's *Proceedings at Augsburg,* 1518 (*WA* 2, 10; *LW* 31, 265 n. 13), he had quoted the *Decretum Magistri Gratiani,* Prima Pars, dist. XIX, 1, 2 (*Corpus Iuris Canonici,* ed. Aemilius Friedberg (Graz, 1955), I, 60). Here he is thinking of what Panormitanus says by way of interpretation of the decretal, *Significasti, de electione et potestate,* cap. 4. *Corpus Iuris Canonici* II, cols. 45-50 in his *Lectures on the Decretals* I (Basel, 1518): "Therefore in all questions concerning faith the council stands above the pope so that the pope cannot decide anything contrary to the decisions of the council. For this reason the council can condemn the pope in case of heresy. In questions of faith the opinions of a private citizen must be preferred to those of the pope if the private citizen has better proofs from the Old and New Testament on his side than the pope." Cf. *MA*³ 1, 450.

God and his Word must yield to the pope and his law? The time has come to suffer a hundred deaths instead!

THE THIRTIETH ARTICLE

Certain articles of John Huss,[100] condemned at Constance, are most Christian, most true, and altogether evangelical, and these all Christendom together could not condemn.[101]

As a matter of fact, on this point I have greatly erred, and I have already retracted and condemned this article[102] because I said, "Certain articles of John Huss, etc." Now I say, not only certain articles, but all the articles of John Huss, condemned at Constance, are altogether Christian; and I admit that the pope and his followers acted in this matter like the true Antichrist. He condemned the holy gospel along with John Huss, and replaced it with the teaching of the dragon from hell [cf. Rev. 13:1-18]. I am prepared to defend this thesis, if need be, and by the help of God I will vindicate and uphold it.

In fact, St. John[103] did not go far enough and only began to present the gospel. I have done five times as much, yet I fear that I am doing too little. John Huss did not deny that the pope is sovereign in all the world. He claimed merely that an evil pope is not a member of the body of Christendom, though he is to be endured as a tyrant. For all the members of the body of Christendom must either be holy or be on the road to holiness. But I claim that if St. Peter himself were sitting in Rome today I would still deny that he is pope and supposed to rule over all other bishops by divine right. The papacy is a human invention of which God knows nothing. All churches are equal, and their unity does not depend on the sovereignty of this one man; but as St. Paul says in Eph. 4 [:5], their unity depends on one faith, one baptism, one Lord Jesus Christ, and these are all the common and equal possession of all the parishes in the world.

---

[100] Cf. p. 71 n. 84, above.
[101] From the *Disputation of Johann Eck and Martin Luther* (1519). WA 2, 279.
[102] E.g., in *An Open Letter to the Christian Nobility* (1520). WA 6, 454-457; PE 2, 140-146.
[103] John Huss.

As far as the decretals are concerned, I do not say that they are apocryphal, that is, things it is not necessary to believe, as John Wycliffe said,[104] but rather that they are un-Christian, antichristian, and written by the inspiration of the evil spirit. It is for this reason that I burned them with a joyful heart.[105]

THE THIRTY-FIRST ARTICLE

A righteous man sins in all his good works.[106]

This article annoys the great saints of work-righteousness, who place their trust not in God's mercy, but in their own righteousness, that is, on sand. What happened to the house built on sand in Matt. 7 [:26] will also happen to them. But a godly Christian ought to learn and know that all his good works are inadequate and insufficient in the sight of God. In the company of all the dear saints he ought to despair of his own works and rely solely on the mercy of God, putting all confidence and trust in him. Therefore we want to establish this article very firmly and see what the dear saints have to say about it.

Isaiah 64 [:6] says, "We are all of us unclean, and all our righteousness is as a filthy stinking rag." You notice that the prophet makes no exceptions. He says, "We are all of us unclean," yet he himself was a holy prophet. Again, if our righteousness is unclean and stinking before God, what will our unrighteousness be? Moreover, he says "all righteousness," making no exception. Now, if there is such a thing as a good work without sin, this prophet lies, which God forbid! Is not this passage from Isaiah sufficiently clear? Why then do they condemn my article, which says nothing but what Isaiah says? But we are glad to be condemned along with this holy prophet.

Again, Solomon says in Eccles. 7 [:20], "There is no man on

---

[104] The English reformer who died in 1380 and exerted great influence on John Huss. The statement which Luther quotes was one of Wycliffe's articles condemned in 1418 at the Council of Constance. Cf. Carl Mirbt, *op. cit.,* pp. 229f.

[105] On December 10, 1520, Luther, his colleagues, and his students burned the papal decretals and also the bull, *Exsurge Domine.* WA 7, 161-182; LW 31, 383-395. Cf. E. G. Schwiebert, *Luther and His Times* (St. Louis, 1950), p. 490.

[106] From Luther's *Explanation of the Articles Debated at Leipzig* (1519). WA 2, 416.

earth so righteous that he does good and sins not." I trust this passage is clear enough, and it corresponds with my article almost word for word. And now, since Solomon is here condemned, look, his father David must also be condemned. He says in Ps. 143 [:2], "Lord, enter not into judgment with me, thy servant, for no man living is righteous before thee." Now, who is God's servant but the man who does good works? How, then, does it happen that this very man cannot face God's judgment? Surely God's judgment is not unjust. If a work were actually altogether good and without sin, it would not flee God's just judgment. The defect, then, must of necessity be in the work, which is not pure. It is for this reason that no man living is justified in God's sight and all men need his mercy, even in their good works. Here you papists have an opportunity to show your learning—not merely by inventing bulls, but by answering such passages of Scripture.

Back in the first two articles[107] I have shown that all the saints struggle against their sinful flesh, and continue to be sinners as long as they live in the flesh which is at war with the spirit. At one and the same time, they serve God according to the spirit, and sin according to the flesh. If, then, a godly man is at the same time justified by reason of the spirit, and sinful by reason of the flesh, his work must certainly be like the person, the fruit like the tree. In so far as the spirit participates in the work, it is good; in so far as the flesh participates in it, it is evil, for Christ says, "A good tree bears good fruit, an evil tree bears evil fruit" [Matt. 7:17]. God always judges the work according to the person, as it is written in Gen. 4 [:4], "And the Lord had regard for Abel and his offering, but for Cain and his offering he had no regard." First he looks at Abel and Cain, only afterwards at their offerings. And here too, since the person is not altogether pure, the work can never be altogether pure. If the author is not altogether competent, the work will not be entirely competent either. Every work must be like its author; this is the common consent of reason and experience.

But if they say here, as they always do, "Yes, but this impurity is not sin but rather an imperfection, or weakness, or defect," my reply is that it is indeed a defect and a weakness, but if that is not

---

[107] Cf. pp. 19-29, above.

sin I am prepared to say that murder and adultery are not sins either but only defects and weaknesses. Who has given you papists the power to twist God's Word and to call the impurity of a good work weakness and not sin? Where is there a single letter of Scripture supporting your side? Must we believe your nightmares, unsubstantiated by Scripture, when you refuse to believe our clear texts? Is it not common knowledge that nothing separates us from God except sin? As Isaiah says (Isa. 59 [:2]), "But your iniquities have made a separation between you and your God." If, then, David says that even God's servants cannot face his judgment and no man living is justified in his sight, then this weakness must certainly be sin, and he who will not allow that any living man is justified in his sight includes most certainly also those who walk in good works. Unless, of course, they are neither "men" nor "living."

Augustine says in his *Confessions* IX,[108] "Woe unto every human life, even the most praiseworthy, were it to be judged without mercy." Look how this great heretic, St. Augustine, speaks brazenly and sacrilegiously against this holy bull. Not only does he attribute sin to a good life, but he condemns even the very best life, which doubtlessly abounds in good works, as though it were nothing but mortal sin, if judged without mercy. O, St. Augustine, are you not afraid of the most holy father pope?

St. Gregory, too, speaks of that holy man Job and says, quoting Job 9 [:3], "Job, that holy man, saw that all our good works are nothing but sin, if God should judge them. Therefore he said, 'If one wished to contend with God, one could not answer him once in a thousand times.'" [109] Gregory, how can you say this? How dare you say that all our good works are nothing but sin? Now you are under the pope's ban, and a heretic far worse than Luther. For he only says that there is sin in all good works; you make them out to be nothing but sin. I can see plainly that you do not want to be canonized by the most holy father pope, for you contradict him and make him into a heretic and Antichrist with this holy bull.

The same St. Gregory says later, referring to the same chapter, "We have now said many times that all human righteousness will be

---

[108] *Loc. cit.*
[109] Gregory the Great, *Moralia*, IX, chap. 2, 3. Migne 75, 859.

found unrighteousness, if strictly judged. For this reason Job [Job 9:15] says, 'Though I had done something righteous, I will not answer God and contend with him, but make supplication to my judge.' " [110] God's judgment is not false or unjust, but true and just. If it finds unrighteousness in our righteousness, that unrighteousness cannot be fictitious, but must really be present. It cannot be merely a "defect" or a "weakness," but must be a damnable sin, which prevents salvation, unless mercy intervenes, and accepts and rewards our works out of sheer grace.

If these passages do not help to substantiate my article, then may God help it! I would much rather be condemned with Isaiah, David, Solomon, Paul, Augustine, and Gregory, than praised with the pope and all the bishops and papists, even though all the world were made up of pope, bishops, and papists. Blessed is he who should die for this cause! Amen.

THE THIRTY-SECOND ARTICLE

A good work, even though well performed, is still a venial sin.[111]

This article follows clearly from what has been said before. David does not say, "No man living is worthily rewarded before thee," but, "No man living is justified before thee." Now, "to be not justified" is nothing else than "to be damned." And Augustine does not say, "Woe to some who live good lives," but, "Woe unto the most praiseworthy life, were it to be judged without grace." Here the word, "woe," means nothing but damnation. St. Gregory does not say, "All human righteousness is found to be imperfect," but rather, "All human righteousness will be found unrighteousness, if strictly judged." And again, he does not say, "All good works are affected by sin," but, "All our good works are nothing but sin." Therefore I must retract this article too, and this is what I now say:

A good work, even though well performed, is a venial sin according to God's merciful judgment, and a mortal sin according

---

[110] *Ibid.*, chap. 18. Migne 75, 875.
[111] From the Fifty-eighth of Luther's *Explanations* (1518). WA 1, 608; LW 31, 216.

to his strict judgment. Look, how the most holy father forces me to make such strange recantations as a result of this bull. Here he tends the sheep of Christ by teaching them not to recognize their sin, their own nature, or God's judgment, and not to yearn for God's mercy, but to run against God with the horns of their pride up in the air and thus plunge into the abyss of hell. Woe unto you, Antichrist!

THE THIRTY-THIRD ARTICLE

The burning of heretics is contrary to the will of the Holy Spirit.[112]

This I can demonstrate, first of all, by reference to history. From the beginning until now the church has never yet burned a heretic, and never will, though in ancient times there were many heretics of various types. Secondly, I can show the soundness of this article from their own words. For if a pope or bishop is a heretic they only depose him and do not burn him. In fact their own law,[113] which they claim has come from the Holy Spirit, teaches that. In the third place, they have no word of Scripture which would prove that the burning of heretics is the will of the Holy Spirit. But if they say that John Huss[114] and Jerome of Prague[115] were burned at Constance, I reply that I was speaking of heretics. John Huss and Jerome of Prague were good Christians who were burned by heretics and apostates and antichristians, namely, the papists, for the sake of the holy gospel, as I said above.[116] Following this example the pope and his heresy-hunters have burned other good Christians in other places, fulfilling the

---

[112] From the Eightieth of Luther's *Explanations* (1518). WA 1, 624; LW 31, 245.
[113] Luther refers to some laws of the ancient church which stipulate that a bishop or presbyter who is discovered in mortal sin is to be deposed and not excommunicated. Cf. *Canones Apostolorum* XXV, C. H. Turner (ed.) *Ecclesiae Occidentalis Monumenta Juris Antiquissima* (Oxford, 1899), I, 18. Cf. also Paul Hinschius, *Das Kirchenrecht der Katholiken und Protestanten in Deutschland* (Berlin, 1888), IV, 739 n. 1.
[114] Cf. 71 n. 84, above.
[115] Jerome of Prague (b. *ca.* 1379), follower and friend of John Huss, was burned at the stake at Constance on May 30, 1416.
[116] Cf. pp. 82-83, above.

prophecy concerning the Antichrist that he will cast Christians into the oven. It was for this reason that Pope Alexander VI [1492-1503] ordered the burning of that godly man of Florence, the Dominican Girolamo Savonarola and his brethren.[117] That is the way in which the holy church of the papists serves God. To do better they would consider a disgrace.

Isaiah 2 [:4] and 11 [:6] portray the Christian church as free from bloodshed, saying, "They shall beat their swords into plowshares and their spears into sickles and scythes and shall not kill or hurt anyone on my holy mountain," that is, in Christendom. And in Luke 9 [:54-56], when the disciples wanted to call down fire from heaven upon the city which did not want to give Christ shelter, he rebuked them and said, "You do not know of what spirit you are the children, for the Son of man came not to destroy men's lives, but to save them." The papists should defend themselves against these passages of Scripture; instead they brag of their sacrilege and would force us to grant that their intentions and actions are lawful, and leave it at that, even when they are contrary to Scripture.

Furthermore, according to the canon law, the clergy are strictly forbidden to bear arms.[118] Yet no one spills more Christian blood than the most holy father, the pope. Nowadays he tends the sheep of Christ with sword, gun, and fire, and is worse than the Turk. He embroils kings and princes, and lands and cities in war, yet this does not make him a heretic or Turk, a murderer or a tyrant, but he is the vicar of Christ and grants indulgences, sends out legates and cardinals in order to promote the war against the Turk. His papists make excuses for their false god and say that it isn't the pope who goes to war or burns anybody. He sits in his holy chair at Rome and prays—probably his bed-time prayers—and only commands the temporal power to fight and burn. That is exactly what the Jews did. They turned Christ over to Pilate and the Gentiles to have him crucified, but they themselves, like great

---

[117] Girolamo Savonarola (1452-1498), the Florentine revival preacher, was burned at the stake with the approval of the papacy.
[118] *Decretalium D. Gregorii Papae IX*, lib. iii. tit. I, cap. 2. *Corpus Iuris Canonici*, ed. Aemilius Friedberg (Graz, 1955), II, col. 449. Cf. *LW* 31, 244 n. 126.

saints, would not even enter Pilate's house; yet St. Stephen, in Acts 8 [7:52] called them the murderers of Christ, and died for it. And now, because I have called the pope, who murders both body and soul, the greatest murderer the world has ever seen since its beginning, I am in the pope's eyes a heretic. God be praised, that I am a heretic in the eyes of his holiness and his papists!

This, our present Babylon, is like the first, and what the mother lacked the daughter has supplied. Genesis 11 [:1-9] shows that the first Babel defended its faith with fire only and burned Christ's ancestors. This Babylon in Rome burns Christ's children. The evil spirit knows full well that if the pope were to defend himself in books, he could not last for an instant and he would be exposed as the very dregs of all heresy and the Antichrist. To protect himself against what others write he has resorted to fire and outrageous tyranny, and now the one Babylon is as godly as the other.

They taunt me, asking why I am so timid and do not come to Rome. Did Christ run of his own accord to Annas, Caiaphas, Pilate, and Herod and ask them to kill him? I thought it was enough to stand my ground and not to flee and to wait for them where I am till they came for me, as they came for Christ. Then they could lead me wherever they want. But they say that I ought to run after them and urge them to kill me. They put everything so cleverly. Why don't they have the courage to refute my writings or to come to me and conquer me with their superior wisdom? Ah well, let the blind lead the blind!

THE THIRTY-FOURTH ARTICLE

To fight against the Turks is nothing but to strive against God who is punishing our sins by means of the Turks.[119]

It is a scandal how the pope has all this time led us by the nose with this war against the Turks.[120] He has used it to make off with our money, destroy many Christians, and cause much misery. When will we learn that the pope is the devil's most dangerous tool?

---

[119] From the Fourth of Luther's *Explanations* (1518). WA 1, 535; LW 31, 88.
[120] PE 2, 85.

Was it not the pope who incited the good King Ladislas[121] of Hungary and Poland, and many thousand Christians, to make war upon the Turks, and was he not miserably defeated at Varna, because he obeyed the pope, and at his command broke the treaty which he had earlier made with the Turk? Is it not heresy to teach in regard to perjury that the pope has the power to break an oath? How can a man become a heretic who can do anything he pleases? Yet what misery has recently come to Hungary as a result of this same war against the Turks, which was begun with a Roman indulgence. But we remain blind as far as the pope is concerned.

But this article does not mean that we are not to fight against the Turk, as that holy manufacturer of heresies, the pope, charges. It means, rather, that we should first mend our ways and cause God to be gracious to us. We should not plunge into war, relying on the pope's indulgence, with which he has deceived Christians in the past and is deceiving them still. The historical books of the Old Testament, especially Josh. 7 [:1-26] and Judg. 18 [20:12-48], and many other passages, show clearly what it means to fight against an angry God and against an enemy whom we have deserved. All the pope accomplishes with his crusading indulgences and his promises of heaven is to lead Christians with their lives into death and with their souls into hell. This is, of course, the proper work of the Antichrist. God does not demand crusades, indulgences, and wars. He wants us to live good lives. But the pope and his followers run from goodness faster than from anything else, yet he wants to devour the Turk. This is the reason why our war against the Turk is so successful—so that where he formerly held one mile of land he now holds a hundred. But we still do not see it, so completely have we been taken in by this Roman leader of the blind.

---

[121] In 1443 the Hungarian king forced the Turks to sue for peace on condition of restoring Serbia and quitting the Hungarian frontier. The following year, at the instigation of the papal legate, Cardinal Cesarini, who claimed that since the treaty of 1443 had not been approved by the pope, the king did not have to abide by it, Ladislas took up arms again. The result was a severe defeat at the battle of Varna on November 10, 1444, in which the king and the cardinal were both killed. Cf. M. Creighton, *A History of the Papacy* (Boston, 1882), II, 248-249.

THE THIRTY-FIFTH ARTICLE

No one is certain that he is not continually committing mortal sin, because of the most secret vice of pride.[122]

This article follows logically from the thirty-first and the thirty-second. For David says, "Lord, enter not into judgment with me, thy servant, for no man living is righteous before thee" [Ps. 143:2]. And St. Gregory writes at the end of his *Moralia*,[123] "How can we ever be saved, when our evil works are absolutely evil and our good works never absolutely good?" Again, Job 9 [:21] says, "Though I were godly, even this my soul does not know," and again, "I am afraid in all my works, for I know thou dost not spare the sinner" [Job 9:28]. Commenting on this, St. Gregory says,[124] "What I have done openly, I see; but what I have suffered secretly, I do not know." This means that no one can fully know his secret pride, as this same teacher says many times, and through it all works are made unclean and cannot stand in the light of God's just judgment. This is what David says in Ps. 19 [:12], "Lord, who can discern his errors? Clear thou me from hidden sins."

Therefore I must retract this article, too, and I say now that no one should doubt that all our good works are mortal sins, if they are judged according to God's judgment and severity and not accepted as good by grace alone. The saying of St. Paul in Rom. 3 [:19-20; 11:32] holds true, "The Scripture consigns all men to sin, so that all the world may be guilty before God and know that no one can be justified by good works, but that God has mercy upon all and justifies them solely through grace." This is the true Christian doctrine, which teaches a man to fear and trust God, and then he can love and praise Him, for he now despairs of himself and relies for everything that is good upon the grace of God. The pope and his papists intend to destroy throughout the world this love, praise, and fear of God, and this faith. In fact he has begun this and is continuing this work as it is written in Mic. 2 [:9], "You have taken away my praise from them for ever."

---

[122] From the Thirteenth of Luther's *Explanations* (1518). WA 1, 553; *LW* 31, 121.
[123] XXXV, chap. 20. Migne 76, 780.
[124] *Ibid.*, IX, chap. 34. Migne 75, 889.

THE THIRTY-SIXTH ARTICLE

Since the fall of Adam, or after actual sin, free will exists only in name, and when it does what it can it commits sin.[125]

This article should be sufficiently clear from what has been said above. St. Paul says in Rom. 14 [:23], "Whatever does not proceed from faith is sin." Where, then, is this freedom, if of its own power it cannot do anything but sin? Again, St. Augustine says in his work, *On the Spirit and the Letter*, chapter IV,[126] "The free will, without God's grace, can do nothing but sin." What do you say now, pope? Is it freedom to be without power to do anything but evil? You might as well say that a lame man walks straight, though he can only limp and never walk straight. It is just as if I were to call the pope "most holy," though St. Paul calls him a "man of sin and son of perdition" [II Thess. 2:3], and Christ calls him "the desolating sacrilege" [Matt. 24:15], the head of all sin and destruction. The papists have so distorted the meaning of words that they have created a new language and confused everything, just like the builders of the tower of Babel. Now "white" is called "black," and "black," "white," to the unspeakable damage of Christendom.

Paul says in II Tim. 2 [:24-26], "Teach those who oppose the truth: God may perhaps grant that they will repent and come to know the truth, and they may escape from the snare of the devil, after being captured by him to do his will." Where is the free will here? It is the prisoner of the devil, not, indeed, unable to act, but able to act only in conformity with the devil's will. Is that freedom, to be a prisoner at the mercy of the devil? There is no help unless God grants repentance and improvement. This is what Christ said in John 8 [:33-36] when the Jews claimed that they were free. He said, "Truly, I say to you, everyone who commits sin is a slave of— or owned by—sin . . . if the Son makes you free you will be free indeed." And St. Augustine changes the term, "free will," in his work *Against Julian*, II,[127] and calls it "a will in bondage."

---

[125] From Thesis 13 of the *Heidelberg Disputation* (1518). *WA* 1, 354; *LW* 31, 40. *Wenn er thut das seine (dum facit, quod in se est)* is a scholastic phrase which implies that a Christian can do meritorious works agreeable to God.
[126] Augustine, *De spiritu et littera*, I, chap. 3, par. 5. Migne 44, 203. Cf. *LW* 31, 49 n. 8.

Furthermore, in Gen. 6 [:5] and 8 [:21] Moses says, "Everything that the heart of man craves and desires is evil at all times." Listen here, my dear papists, Moses bears witness against you, what have you to say in your defense? If there is a good thought or will in man, at any time, we must call Moses a liar, for he calls all thoughts and all desires of the human heart evil at all times. What kind of freedom is it that is always inclined to evil?

To bring the matter to an end, in the preceding pages[128] it has been said repeatedly that godly and holy men who live out of the resources of God's powerful grace, struggle against their own flesh with great pains and peril, and the flesh fights against grace with all its strength. It is a profound and blind error to teach that the will is by nature free and can, without grace, turn to the spirit, seek grace, and desire it. Actually, the will tries to escape from grace and rages against it when it is present. Whose reason is not shocked to think that although spirit and flesh are the two greatest enemies, yet the flesh is supposed to desire and seek its enemy, the spirit? Surely, every man knows from his own experience how all his powers fight against grace in order to expel and destroy it. My opponents' position suggests that when nobody can control a wild and ravenous beast with chains you let it go free and it will chain itself and go into captivity of its own accord.

These teachings have been invented in order to insult and detract from the grace of God. They strengthen sin and increase the kingdom of the devil. Scripture says of man, in Gen. 6 [:3], that he is altogether flesh, and the flesh is most directly opposed to the spirit according to Gal. 5 [:17]. And yet they confuse everything and say that the free will, which is utter flesh, seeks after the spirit. In other matters the frivolity and blindness of the pope could be tolerated, but when it comes to this chief article of the faith it is a pity that they are so senseless. Here they completely ruin everything that God has given us through Christ. St. Peter prophesied accurately when he said in II Pet. 2 [:1], "There will be false teachers among you who shall deny the Master who bought them." Who is this Master but Christ, who has bought us with his own precious blood? Who denies him more than those who ascribe too

---

[127] Augustine, *Against Julian*, II, 8. Migne 44, 689.
[128] Cf. pp. 19-29, above.

little to his grace and too much to free will? For while they will not allow that to be sin and evil which is indeed sin and evil, neither will they allow that to be grace which is indeed grace and which should drive out sin. Just as a man who refuses to admit that he is sick will not allow medicine to be medicine for him.

But even if they were right, it would still be safer if they would ascribe all good to grace alone and grant that all our actions are sin. There is no danger if I confess before God that even a good work is sin, and then seek his grace which I can never pursue too much. But cruel danger threatens those who confess a thought to be good which in fact is not good. And since my opponents seek, follow, and defend the dangerous path so stubbornly and abandon the safe path, and, indeed, persecute those that walk in it, it is well to note that their doctrine is not of God, but altogether suspect.

For this reason I would wish that the words, "free will," had never been invented. They are not found in Scripture and would better be called "self will" which is of no use. But if anyone wishes to retain these words, he ought to apply them to the newly created man, so as to understand by them the man who is without sin. He is truly free, as was Adam in Paradise, and it is of him that Scripture speaks when it deals with our freedom. But those who are involved in sins are not free, but prisoners of the devil. Since they may become free through grace you can call them men of free will, just as you might call a man rich, although he is a beggar because he can become rich. But it is neither right nor good to play tricks with words in matters of such great importance. A simple man is easily deceived by such tricks and teachers of this kind are called sophists. Ecclesiasticus 34 [:11-13] says, "I have learned many things from many words, and have found the way in which these words are used strange and bewildering. Sometimes I have been in deadly peril of soul because of these things, but I have been delivered by the grace of God." We ought, therefore, avoid the sophists, and speak clearly and plainly as does Scripture, especially when we speak of God's most profound design. This error about "free will" is a special doctrine of Antichrist. Small wonder that it has spread all over the world, for it is written of this Antichrist that he will seduce the whole world. Only few Christians will be saved [II Thess. 2:10]. Woe unto him!

THE THIRTY-SEVENTH ARTICLE

That there is a purgatory cannot be proved by those Scriptures[129] which are authentic and trustworthy.[130]

The existence of a purgatory I have never denied. I still hold that it exists, as I have written and admitted[131] many times, though I have found no way of proving it incontrovertibly from Scripture or reason. I find in Scripture that Christ, Abraham, Jacob, Moses, Job, David, Hezekiah, and some others tasted hell in this life. This I think was purgatory, and it seems not beyond belief that some of the dead suffer in like manner. Tauler[132] has much to say about it, and, in short, I myself have come to the conclusion that there is a purgatory, but I cannot force anybody else to come to the same result.

There is only one thing that I have criticized, namely, the way in which my opponents refer to purgatory passages in Scripture which are so inapplicable that it is shameful. For example, they apply Ps. 66 [:12], "We went through fire and through water," though the whole psalm sings of the sufferings of the saints, whom no one places in purgatory. And they quote St. Paul in I Cor. 3 [:13-15] when he says of the fire of the last day that it will test the good works, and by it some will be saved because they keep the faith, though their work may suffer loss. They turn this fire also into a purgatory, according to their custom of twisting Scripture and making it mean whatever they want.

And similarly they have arbitrarily dragged in the passage in Matt. 12 [:32] in which Christ says, "Whoever speaks blasphemy against the Holy Spirit will not be forgiven, either in this world or in the world to come." Christ means here that he shall never be forgiven, as Mark 3 [:29] explains, saying, "Whoever blasphemes against the Holy Spirit never has forgiveness, but is guilty of an eternal sin." To be sure, even St. Gregory[133] interprets the passage

---

[129] The Latin text of this assertion reads, *sacra scriptura, quae sit in Canone.* WA 7, 149.
[130] From the *Disputation of Johann Eck and Martin Luther* (1519). WA 2, 324.
[131] Cf. *Unterricht auf etlich Artikel.* WA 2, 70.
[132] Johann Tauler (*ca.* 1300-1361), a Dominican monk who, under the influence of his teacher Meister Eckhart, taught at Strassburg a deeply mystical piety.
[133] Gregory the Great, *Dialogorum Libri,* IV, chap. 39. Migne 77, 396.

in Matthew 12 to mean that some sins will be forgiven in the world to come, but St. Mark does not permit such an interpretation, and he counts for more than all the doctors.

I have discussed all this in order to show that no one is bound to believe more than what is based on Scripture, and those who do not believe in purgatory are not to be called heretics, if otherwise they accept Scripture in its entirety, as the Greek church does. The gospel compels me to believe that St. Peter and St. James are saints, but at the same time it is not necessary to believe that St. Peter is buried in Rome and St. James at Compostella[134] and that their bodies are still there, for Scripture does not report it. Again, there is no sin in holding that none of the saints whom the pope canonizes are saints, and no saint will be offended, for, as a matter of fact, there are many saints in heaven of whom we know nothing, and certainly not that they are saints, yet they are not offended, and do not consider us heretics because we do not know of them. The pope and his partisans play this game only in order to fabricate many wild articles of faith and thus make it possible to silence and suppress the true articles of the Scripture.

But their use of the passage in II Macc. 12 [:43], which tells how Judas Maccabeus sent money to Jerusalem for prayers to be offered for those who fell in battle, proves nothing, for that book is not among the books of Holy Scripture, and, as St. Jerome says, it is not found in a Hebrew version, the language in which all the books of the Old Testament are written.[135] In other respects, too, this book deserves little authority, for it contradicts the first Book of Maccabees in its description of King Antiochus, and contains many other fables which destroy its credibility. But even were the book authoritative, it would still be necessary in the case of so important an article that at least one passage out of the chief books [of the Bible] should support it, in order that every word might be established through the mouth of two or three witnesses. It must give rise to suspicion that in order to substantiate this doctrine no more than one passage could be discovered in the entire Bible; moreover this passage is in the least important and

---

[134] Santiago de Compostella, a famous place of pilgrimage in Spain.
[135] Jerome, *Preface to the Books of Samuel and Malachi.* Migne 28, 600ff.

most despised book. Especially since so much depends on this doctrine which is so important that, indeed, the papacy and the whole hierarchy are all but built upon it, and derive all their wealth and honor from it. Surely, the majority of the priests would starve to death if there were no purgatory. Well, they should not offer such vague and feeble grounds for our faith!

THE THIRTY-EIGHTH ARTICLE

The souls in purgatory are not certain of their own salvation, at least not all of them, nor has it been proved from Scripture or by reason that they are not in a position to acquire merit and to grow in love toward God.[136]

THE THIRTY-NINTH ARTICLE

The souls in purgatory sin continually as long as they seek rest and dread punishment.[137]

THE FORTIETH ARTICLE

The souls released from purgatory through the intercession of the living obtain less reward than if they themselves had satisfied the requirements of divine justice.[138]

These three articles I have discussed merely as scholarly problems. I have frequently admitted that they were merely my opinions and that I cannot offer definite proof to substantiate them. What I think about them can be read in my *Explanations.*[139] The papists and their shyster-lawyers condemn me for them, but advance no other argument except their own arbitrary opinions, based neither on Scripture nor on reason. They do not reply to my references to Scripture or my reasons. But I won't let that worry me, and disdain their mere condemnation as much as they disdain my

---

[136] From the *Disputation of Johann Eck and Martin Luther* (1519). WA 2, 342.
[137] From the Eighteenth of Luther's *Explanations* (1518). WA 1, 562; *LW* 31, 136.
[138] From the *Disputation of Johann Eck and Martin Luther* (1519). WA 2, 340f.
[139] *Explanations of the Ninety-Five Theses* (1518). WA 1, 530-628; *LW* 31, 83-252.

arguments and reasons. In fact the pope and his shyster-lawyers understand less of these questions than a log on the ground.

My advice is that no one allow the pope to invent new articles of faith, but be willing to remain in ignorance, with St. Augustine,[140] about what the souls in purgatory are doing and what their condition is. For us it is enough to know that they suffer great and unbearable pain and crave your help. But if you wish to discuss this question then you must leave room for surmise and differences of opinion, as I do. Do not make your own ideas into articles of faith as that abomination at Rome does. For then your faith may become a nightmare. Hold to Scripture and the Word of God. There you will find truth and security—assurance and a faith that is complete, pure, sufficient, and abiding.

THE LAST ARTICLE

The prelates of the church and the secular princes would do no wrong if they wiped out all the mendicant orders.[141]

In this article, indeed in this whole bull, Johann Eck was the pope's Holy Spirit, and this man is as reluctant when it comes to lying as he is reluctant when it comes to talking. This Holy Spirit is, in fact, just like the pope whom he inspires. They are two villains of the same sort. I have not spoken of prelates and princes, except that I said I wished there were no mendicant orders. This I still say, and many godly people say it with me. Amen.[142]

Who will send the pope and his shyster-lawyers to school and teach them to speak Latin before they start writing bulls? Are these mendicants "letters" or "paintings" that they can be "wiped" away[143] as the pope here lisps and stammers? Even if his rule lasts, I think the pope will never learn to speak his own language, so far has he gone in the neglect of all knowledge and honor. I never

---

[140] *Enchiridion ad Laurentium* 109. Migne 40, 283.
[141] From Luther's *Larger Treatise on Usury* (1520). WA 6, 42.
[142] The printed text of this treatise ends here. The section which follows is crossed out in Luther's manuscript and does not belong to the official version.
[143] Luther objects to the use of the word, *delere*, in the Latin bull as a translation of the German word, *abtun*. In Luther's German this word means "to give up," "to remove," as in I Cor. 13:11 and II Kings 18:22 in his translation of the Bible.

said that the ecclesiastical and secular princes should "wipe out" or destroy the mendicants. But I have said that I wished there were no mendicant orders, and actually I know that the pope, the bishops, and the priests deep down in their hearts agree with me. But they condemn my words, even though they believe in them more than I do. But I see that Johann Eck has here been the pope's Holy Spirit, and he is a man as reluctant when it comes to lying as he is reluctant when it comes to talking. In fact, the whole bull is his, as he, quite needlessly, admits. It is obvious that father and child are so much alike neither can deny the other. It seems I must have liars and villains for opponents. I am not worthy in the sight of God that a godly and honorable man should discuss these matters with me in a Christian way. This is my greatest lament.

But I still say that it is sin and shame to have begging going on in Christendom, and it is still more abominable that priests whose business it is to preach and to administer the sacraments should be begging and that the mendicant orders are established by the pope as a Christian estate. Begging was not allowed among the Jews in the Old Testament, and yet we Christians, who ought to be filled with love for our neighbor, consider begging a great honor. We ought to be ashamed in the sight of God and man that a Christian man goes publicly begging among us. We ought to anticipate men's wants and help the poor so that there would be no need for begging. But this too is one of the Antichrist's tricks. He has established the mendicant orders, for otherwise he would be short of apostles, be too weak against the bishops and pastors, and would not be able to raise his throne above heaven and earth.

LUTHER AT THE
DIET OF WORMS

1521

Translated by Roger A. Hornsby

INTRODUCTION

Luther's appearance at the Diet of Worms was in many ways the most dramatic public event of his career. Its religious and political significance was immediately apparent to all his contemporaries and resulted in a great many reports from both friends and foes of the Reformation.*

In order to present as comprehensive a picture as possible we have translated the most complete document prepared by the friends of the Reformation (pp. 105 to 123) and the report of the papal nuncio Aleander (pp. 123 to 130) who was the master mind behind the opposition to Luther at Worms and who had played an important part in the futile attempts to prevent the reformer's appearance at the diet.†

The authorship of the first report has not been established. It has been attributed to Luther himself, to Spalatin, to Bucer, and some others. For many reasons Paul Kalkoff's suggestion deserves attention. He believes that Luther's friend and companion, Justus Jonas, wrote the report with the help of Luther, Schurf, and Amsdorf.

Aleander's report is based largely upon the minutes of Johann Eck, the secretary of the archbishop of Trier. Eck (not to be confused with the Dr. Johann Eck who had opposed Luther at Leipzig) had been selected to act as Luther's interrogator because his record showed unwavering support of the sale of indulgences. While at first Glapion, the father confessor of Emperor Charles V, had been designated to question Luther in public, the fact that he was a French Franciscan made his selection too obviously prejudicial to the cause of the Reformation. Eck was equally reliable as far as the supporters of the papacy were concerned and he was a lawyer and a German.

This means that our reports are prepared by partisans on opposing sides of the issue. Yet a comparison shows such wide and surprising agreement that it appears possible to establish fairly accurately what actually transpired.

Our translation, prepared by Dr. Roger Hornsby of the State University of Iowa, is based upon the critical text in *WA* 7, 814-857.

---

* This material has been collected in *Deutsche Reichstagsakten,* Vol. II: *Deutsche Reichstagsakten unter Kaiser Karl V* (Gotha, 1896). *WA* 7, 814ff.
† For a comprehensive analysis of the diet and the personalities who dominated it, see Paul Kalkoff, *Der Wormser Reichstag 1521* (München and Berlin, 1922).

LUTHER AT THE
DIET OF WORMS

In the Name of Jesus, 1521

*The Account and Actions of
Doctor Martin Luther the Augustinian
at the Diet of Worms*

On the third day after Misericordias Domini Sunday [April 16], Doctor Martin Luther, an Augustinian monk by profession, traveled to Worms in the year of our Lord 1521, summoned by Emperor Charles V, king of Spain, archduke of Austria, etc., who in the first year of his reign held his first royal assembly in this city. Dr. Martin had proposed for debate at Wittenberg, a city of Saxony, certain propositions against the tyranny of the bishop of Rome, which were attacked in the interim and burned by many, although they were confuted by no one either by the Scriptures or by reason. Because of this, the affair began to tend toward unrest, for the people were supporting the cause of the gospel against the clergy. Therefore, it seemed advisable, at the instigation of the Roman legates, for him to be summoned by an imperial herald, letters of safe conduct having been granted for this purpose by the emperor and the princes. He was summoned. He came and stayed at the house of the Knights of Rhodes, where he was hospitably received, greeted, and visited through the entire night by many counts, barons, gilded knights, and nobles, both ecclesiastical and lay.

On the day after his arrival, the fourth day [after Misericordias Domini Sunday; April 17], Ulrich von Pappenheim, a nobleman and master of the imperial cavalry, sent by the emperor, came before luncheon and showed Dr. Martin the order of Charles, appointed four o'clock in the afternoon as the hour of the audience, for which he had come, before his imperial majesty, the electoral princes, electors, the dukes, and the rest of the imperial estates. As was proper, Dr. Martin readily accepted this order.

Immediately after four o'clock on that day, Ulrich von Pappenheim came and with him Caspar Sturm, imperial herald for Germany, who had summoned Dr. Martin at Wittenberg and brought him to Worms. These two invited him and accompanied him through the garden of the house of the Knights of Rhodes into the quarters of the Count Palatine. To avoid any possible annoyance at the hands of the throng, gathered in great numbers along the customary route to the imperial palace, he came into the audience hall through some side streets, as if by stealth. However, he did not escape the notice of many who were barely held back by force from entering. Many climbed to the roof tops in their eagerness to see.

Now when he stood in the presence of his imperial majesty, the electoral princes, electors, and the dukes, in short, all the imperial estates who were then in attendance upon the emperor, Dr. Martin was warned by Ulrich von Pappenheim not to say anything without being asked.

Then Johann Eck, general secretary of the bishop of Trier, the speaker for his imperial majesty, made the same statement, first in Latin, then in German, as follows: "His imperial majesty has summoned you here, Martin Luther, for these two reasons: first, that you may here publicly acknowledge if the books published so far under your name are yours; then, whether you wish all these to be regarded as your work, or whether you wish to retract anything in them."

Thereupon Dr. Jerome Schurff,[1] a Swiss from St. Gallen, who stood with Martin, cried in a loud voice: "Let the titles of the books be read." Here the secretary of Trier recited by name those books of Doctor Martin which had once been printed at Basel, among which were listed the *Commentaries on the Psalms,* the little book *On Good Works,* the *Commentary on the Lord's Prayer,* and other Christian books which were not controversial.

After this Dr. Martin made the same statement in German and Latin in reply to the questions:

---

[1] Professor of canon law at the University of Wittenberg who acted as Luther's lawyer during the trial.

"Two questions have been put to me by his imperial majesty: First, whether I wish all the books bearing my name to be regarded as my own work; second, whether I intend to stand by them or, in fact, retract anything from those which have been published by me till now. To these two questions I shall respond, briefly and to the point [and to the best of my ability].[2] First, I must indeed include the books just now named as among those written by me and I shall never deny any of them.

"As for the next question, whether I would likewise affirm everything or retract what is supposed to have been uttered beyond the testimony of Scripture: Because this is a question of faith and the salvation of souls, and because it concerns the divine Word, which we are all bound to reverence, for there is nothing greater in heaven or on earth, it would be rash and at the same time dangerous for me to put forth anything without proper consideration. Since without previous deliberation I could assert less than the cause demands or more than accords with the truth, I might in either case come under Christ's judgment when he said, 'Whoever denies me before men, I also will deny before my Father who is in heaven' [Matt. 10:33]. For this reason I beseech your imperial majesty for time to think, in order to satisfactorily answer the question without violence to the divine Word and danger to my own soul."

After this the princes began a consultation which the secretary of Trier reported as follows:

"Although you, Martin, have been able to learn well enough from the imperial order why you have been summoned, and, therefore, do not deserve to be granted a longer time for consideration, yet, out of innate clemency, his imperial majesty grants one day for your deliberation so that you may furnish an answer openly tomorrow at this hour—on this condition: that you do not present your opinion in writing, but declare it by word of mouth."

After this Dr. Martin was led back to his inn by the herald. In this affair, what happened between his departure to obey the order of the emperor and his appearance in the assembly of the princes

---

[2] A rendering of *ut potero* in the Wittenberg, Jena, and Erlangen editions of Luther's writings.

ought not to be omitted. Luther was admonished by various voices to be brave, to act manfully, and not to fear those who can kill the body but cannot kill the soul, but rather revere Him who is able to cast both soul and body into hell [Matt. 10:28]. Again, "When you shall stand before kings, do not think about what you are saying, for it will be given you in that hour" [Luke 12:11-12]. One of the bystanders shouted, "Blessed is the womb that bore you" [Luke 11:27].

Thus was that day spent.

After four o'clock in the afternoon on the following day, the fifth [after Misericordias Domini Sunday; April 18], the herald came and conducted Dr. Martin to the court of the emperor where, because of the pre-occupation of the princes, he remained until six o'clock, waiting in a great throng of people, becoming exhausted because of the crowd. When the assembly was seated and Martin stood up, the secretary spoke up in these words:

"His imperial majesty has appointed this hour for you, Martin Luther, because you admitted that the books which we named yesterday are yours. Moreover, upon the question of whether you wished any of them to be withdrawn, or whether you approved all which you have published, you requested a period for deliberation, which now has come to an end, although by right you ought not to have sought a longer period for consideration. You knew at that time why you were summoned. Moreover, it is generally agreed that the obligation of faith is so certain for all that anybody, whenever he is asked, should be able to give his certain and constant reasons, not least of all you, so great and so learned a professor of theology. Come then; answer the question of his majesty, whose kindness you have experienced in seeking a time for thought. Do you wish to defend all your acknowledged books, or to retract some?" This the secretary said in Latin and in German, more forcefully, however, in Latin than in German.

Dr. Martin himself replied in Latin and German, humbly, quietly, and modestly; however, not without Christian boldness and firmness, and in such a way that his adversaries would have desired a more abject speech and spirit. For they looked most eagerly for a recantation, some hope of which they had conceived from the request for time to deliberate.

108

The Speech of Dr. Martin Luther
before the Emperor Charles and Princes
at Worms on the Fifth Day
after Misericordias Domini [April 18]
In the Name of Jesus

"Most serene emperor, most illustrious princes, most clement lords, obedient to the time set for me yesterday evening, I appear before you, beseeching you, by the mercy of God, that your most serene majesty and your most illustrious lordships may deign to listen graciously to this my cause—which is, as I hope, a cause of justice and of truth. If through my inexperience I have either not given the proper titles to some, or have offended in some manner against court customs and etiquette, I beseech you to kindly pardon me, as a man accustomed not to courts but to the cells of monks. I can bear no other witness about myself but that I have taught and written up to this time with simplicity of heart, as I had in view only the glory of God and the sound instruction of Christ's faithful.

"Most serene emperor, most illustrious princes, concerning those questions proposed to me yesterday on behalf of your serene majesty, whether I acknowledged as mine the books enumerated and published in my name and whether I wished to persevere in their defense or to retract them, I have given to the first question my full and complete answer, in which I still persist and shall persist forever. These books are mine and they have been published in my name by me, unless in the meantime, either through the craft or the mistaken wisdom of my emulators, something in them has been changed or wrongly cut out. For plainly I cannot acknowledge anything except what is mine alone and what has been written by me alone, to the exclusion of all interpretations of anyone at all.

"In replying to the second question, I ask that your most serene majesty and your lordships may deign to note that my books are not all of the same kind.

"For there are some in which I have discussed religious faith and morals simply and evangelically, so that even my enemies themselves are compelled to admit that these are useful, harmless, and clearly worthy to be read by Christians. Even the bull,[3]

---

[3] Luther refers to the bull, *Exsurge Domine,* issued in Rome June 15, 1520.

109

although harsh and cruel, admits that some of my books are inoffensive, and yet allows these also to be condemned with a judgment which is utterly monstrous. Thus, if I should begin to disavow them, I ask you, what would I be doing? Would not I, alone of all men, be condemning the very truth upon which friends and enemies equally agree, striving alone against the harmonious confession of all?

"Another group of my books attacks the papacy and the affairs of the papists as those who both by their doctrines and very wicked examples have laid waste the Christian world with evil that affects the spirit and the body. For no one can deny or conceal this fact, when the experience of all and the complaints of everyone witness that through the decrees of the pope and the doctrines of men the consciences of the faithful have been most miserably entangled, tortured, and torn to pieces. Also, property and possessions, especially in this illustrious nation of Germany, have been devoured by an unbelievable tyranny and are being devoured to this time without letup and by unworthy means. [Yet the papists] by their own decrees (as in dist. 9 and 25; ques. 1 and 2)[4] warn that the papal laws and doctrines which are contrary to the gospel or the opinions of the fathers are to be regarded as erroneous and reprehensible. If, therefore, I should have retracted these writings, I should have done nothing other than to have added strength to this [papal] tyranny and I should have opened not only windows but doors to such great godlessness. It would rage farther and more freely than ever it has dared up to this time. Yes, from the proof of such a revocation on my part, their wholly lawless and unrestrained kingdom of wickedness would become still more intolerable for the already wretched people; and their rule would be further strengthened and established, especially if it should be reported that this evil deed had been done by me by virtue of the authority of your most serene majesty and of the whole Roman Empire. Good God! What a cover for wickedness and tyranny I should have then become.

"I have written a third sort of book against some private and

---

[4] This seems to be a reference to *Decretum Magistri Gratiani,* dist. IX, c. 8. Migne 187, 50.

(as they say) distinguished individuals—those, namely, who strive to preserve the Roman tyranny and to destroy the godliness taught by me. Against these I confess I have been more violent than my religion or profession demands. But then, I do not set myself up as a saint; neither am I disputing about my life, but about the teaching of Christ. It is not proper for me to retract these works, because by this retraction it would again happen that tyranny and godlessness would, with my patronage, rule and rage among the people of God more violently than ever before.

"However, because I am a man and not God, I am not able to shield my books with any other protection than that which my Lord Jesus Christ himself offered for his teaching. When questioned before Annas about his teaching and struck by a servant, he said: 'If I have spoken wrongly, bear witness to the wrong' [John 18: 19-23]. If the Lord himself, who knew that he could not err, did not refuse to hear testimony against his teaching, even from the lowliest servant, how much more ought I, who am the lowest scum and able to do nothing except err, desire and expect that somebody should want to offer testimony against my teaching! Therefore, I ask by the mercy of God, may your most serene majesty, most illustrious lordships, or anyone at all who is able, either high or low, bear witness, expose my errors, overthrowing them by the writings of the prophets and the evangelists. Once I have been taught I shall be quite ready to renounce every error, and I shall be the first to cast my books into the fire.

"From these remarks I think it is clear that I have sufficiently considered and weighed the hazards and dangers, as well as the excitement and dissensions aroused in the world as a result of my teachings, things about which I was gravely and forcefully warned yesterday. To see excitement and dissension arise because of the Word of God is to me clearly the most joyful aspect of all in these matters. For this is the way, the opportunity, and the result of the Word of God, just as He [Christ] said, 'I have not come to bring peace, but a sword. For I have come to set a man against his father, etc.' [Matt. 10:34-35]. Therefore, we ought to think how marvelous and terrible is our God in his counsels, lest by chance what is attempted for settling strife grows rather into an intolerable deluge of evils, if we begin by condemning the Word of God. And

111

concern must be shown lest the reign of this most noble youth, Prince Charles (in whom after God is our great hope), become unhappy and inauspicious. I could illustrate this with abundant examples from Scripture—like Pharaoh, the king of Babylon, and the kings of Israel who, when they endeavored to pacify and strengthen their kingdoms by the wisest counsels, most surely destroyed themselves. For it is He who takes the wise in their own craftiness [Job 5:13] and overturns mountains before they know it [Job 9:5]. Therefore we must fear God. I do not say these things because there is a need of either my teachings or my warnings for such leaders as you, but because I must not withhold the allegiance which I owe my Germany. With these words I commend myself to your most serene majesty and to your lordships, humbly asking that I not be allowed through the agitation of my enemies, without cause, to be made hateful to you.[5] I have finished."

When I[6] had finished, the speaker for the emperor said, as if in reproach, that I had not answered the question, that I ought not call into question those things which had been condemned and defined in councils; therefore what was sought from me was not a horned[7] response, but a simple one, whether or not I wished to retract.

Here I answered:

"Since then your serene majesty and your lordships seek a simple answer, I will give it in this manner, neither horned nor toothed: Unless I am convinced by the testimony of the Scriptures or by clear reason (for I do not trust either in the pope or in councils alone, since it is well known that they have often erred and contradicted themselves), I am bound by the Scriptures I have quoted and my conscience is captive to the Word of God. I cannot and I will not retract anything, since it is neither safe nor right to go against conscience.

---

[5] Reading *patiantur,* with *EA Var. Arg.* 6, 13.
[6] At this point the narration proceeds in the first person, not in the third person as it had done prior to the speech of Luther. Also, the Eck-Aleander report goes into more detail in its account of the proceedings. Cf. p. 126 l. 32; p. 131.
[7] *Cornutum,* "horned" syllogism—a sophistical, ambiguous reply.

"I cannot do otherwise, here I stand, may God help me, Amen." [8]

The princes deliberated about this speech of Dr. Martin. When they had examined it the secretary of Trier began to tear it apart in this fashion: "Martin, you have answered more impudently than befits your person, and not to the point either. You have made various distinctions among your books, but in such a way that none of them contributes anything to this investigation. If you had recanted those which contain a large portion of your errors, no doubt his imperial majesty, in his innate clemency, would not have tolerated a persecution of the rest which are good. But now you revive those [errors] which the general Council of Constance, composed of the whole German nation, has condemned, and you wish to be refuted by means of Scripture. In this you are completely mad. For what purpose does it serve to raise a new dispute about matters condemned through so many centuries by church and council? Unless perhaps a reason must be given to just anyone about anything whatsoever. But if it were granted that whoever contradicts the councils and the common understanding of the church must be overcome by Scripture passages, we will have nothing in Christianity that is certain or decided. And for this reason his imperial majesty seeks from you an answer, simple and straightforward, either a no or a yes: Do you wish to regard all your works as catholic? Or do you wish to retract anything from them?"

But Dr. Martin nevertheless asked that his imperial majesty not allow him to be compelled to retract contrary to his conscience, captive to and bound by holy Scripture, without the clear arguments of those who spoke against him. If they sought an answer which was unambiguous, simple, and true, he had none other than what he had uttered before: Unless his adversaries by sufficient arguments would extricate his conscience, which was captured by those errors (as they called them), he would not be able to get out of the nets in which he was entangled. Whatever the councils agreed upon was

---

[8] These words are given in German in the Latin text upon which this translation is based. There is good evidence, however, that Luther actually said only: "May God help me!" Cf. *Deutsche Reichstagsakten*, Vol. II: *Deutsche Reichstagsakten unter Kaiser Karl V* (Gotha, 1896), p. 587.

not immediately true; further, the councils have erred and have often contradicted themselves. Moreover, the arguments of his contradictors were not convincing. He was able to show that the councils had erred: he was not able to retract that which the Scripture zealously proclaimed. He added at this place an exclamation, "God help me!"

To these words there was no reply from the secretary except a very few words to the effect that it could not be shown that the councils had erred. Martin said that he was truly able and willing to do that.

However, since darkness had by then come over the whole audience hall, each one departed to his home. As he departed from his imperial majesty and the tribunal, a large group of Spaniards followed Luther, the man of God, with jeers, derisive gestures, and much loud noise.

On the sixth day after Misericordias Domini [April 19], when the princes, electors, dukes, and the nobles of every rank who were ordinarily present at the assemblies, had met, the emperor sent this message, which he had written with his own hand to this council:[9]

---

[9] The emperor's declaration of April 19, 1521, was originally in French. It was printed numerous times in Latin translation. The following is a translation of the original French document in its entirety, as published for the first time in *Reichstagsakten, op. cit.*, 595ff. [WA 7, 841 n. 2]: "You know that I am descended from the most Christian emperors of the noble German nation, from the Catholic kings of Spain, the archdukes of Austria and the dukes of Burgundy. To the honor of God, the strengthening of the faith, and the salvation of souls, they all have remained up to death faithful sons of the church and have always been defenders of the Catholic faith, the sacred rituals, decrees, ordinances and holy customs. After death they have left to us by natural right and heritage these holy Catholic observances, to live according to them and to die according to their example, in which [observances], as true followers of these our predecessors, we have up to now lived. For this reason I am determined to support everything that these predecessors and I myself have kept, up to the present, and especially what has been laid down by these my predecessors at the Council of Constance as well as others. For it is certain that a single friar errs in his opinion which is against all of Christendom and according to which all of Christianity will be and will always have been in error both in the past thousand years and even more in the present. For that reason I am absolutely determined to stake on this cause my kingdoms and seigniories, my friends, my body and blood, my life and soul. For it would be a great shame to me and to you, who are the noble and renowned German nation, who are by privilege and pre-eminent standing singularly called to be defenders and protectors of the Catholic faith, if in our time not only heresy but suspicion of heresy or decrease of the Christian religion should through our negligence dwell after us in the hearts of men and our successors to our perpetual dishonor. And after having

"Our ancestors who were also Christian princes, were nevertheless obedient to the Roman church which Dr. Martin now attacks. And because he is determined to move not even a hair's breadth from his errors, we are not able with propriety to depart from the example of our ancestors in defending the ancient faith, and giving aid to the Roman see. Therefore, we shall pursue Martin himself and his adherents with excommunication, and use other methods available for their liquidation."

However, because he did not wish to violate the agreement which had been granted and signed, he would therefore do his best that Luther might return safely from where he was summoned.

The electoral princes, dukes, and the imperial orders debated this judgment of Charles on the sixth day throughout the whole afternoon, and even on the whole of the Saturday which followed, and during this time Dr. Martin received no word from his imperial majesty.

Meanwhile, he was seen and visited by many princes, counts, barons, knights, nobles, and priests, both religious and secular, not to mention a number of the common people. These constantly besieged the residence, and their desire to see was never satisfied.

Two notices were also posted: one against the Doctor, the other (so it seemed) for the Doctor, although that one is thought by many who were well informed to have been done maliciously by his enemies, so that an opportunity might be found for breaking the safe-conduct, a thing which the Roman envoys most actively sought.[10]

---

heard the obstinate answer which Luther gave yesterday, April 18, in the presence of us all, I declare to you that I regret having so long delayed to proceed against this Luther and his false doctrine and I am no longer willing to hear him speak more, but I am making it clear that immediately, according to the mandate, he be taken back keeping the tenor of his safe-conduct without preaching or admonishing the people with his bad doctrine and making sure that no disorder results. And as I have said before, I am determined to proceed against him as a notorious heretic, requesting of you that you conduct yourselves in this matter as good Christians as you have promised it to me and are held to do it. Given by my hand this nineteenth day of April, 1521.

SIGNED
Carolus"

[10] The report is referring to the so-called "Pledge of the Nobles" signed with the *Bundschuh,* the symbol of the peasants' revolt. Cf. E. G. Schwiebert, *Luther and His Times* (St. Louis, 1950), p. 506; Roland Bainton, *Here I Stand* (New York and Nashville, 1950), p. 187.

On the second day after Jubilate [April 22], before breakfast, the archbishop of Trier announced to Dr. Martin that on the fourth day after Jubilate he should appear at the sixth hour (before luncheon), in his presence, at a place to be designated in the interim.

On the Feast of St. George [April 23], after dinner, [a messenger] returned at the command of his prince, the archbishop of Trier, saying that on the next day at the hour recently designated, Luther should be present at the lodging of his lordship.

On Wednesday, the day after the Feast of St. George [April 24], obedient to the command, Dr. Martin entered the lodging of the archbishop of Trier, accompanied by the latter's chaplain and the imperial herald and followed by those who had accompanied him here from Saxony and Thuringia, and some other very good friends. When he was before the archbishop of Trier, Margrave Joachim of Brandenburg, Duke George of Saxony, the bishops of Augsburg [Christopher von Stadion] and of Brandenburg [Jerome Scultetus], the master of the Teutonic Order [Dietrich von Cleen], Count George of Wertheim, Dr. Bock of Strassburg, and Dr. Peutinger,[11] Dr. Vehus, chancellor of Baden, began to speak and declared: He [Luther] had not been called to this meeting to enter upon an argument or debate, but only out of Christian charity and clemency had the princes sought permission from his imperial majesty to exhort him kindly and fraternally. Next, although the councils had set forth varying views, they did not contradict one another. But even if the councils had erred greatly, they had certainly not thereby destroyed their authority to such a degree that anyone should wish to rely on his own interpretation in opposition to them. Adding many things concerning the centurion [Matt. 8:5-13] and Zacchaeus [Luke 19:2-10] about human institutions, ceremonies, and decrees, and affirming that all these things were sanctioned for the repression of vice according to the temper and vicissitudes of the times, he said that the church was not able to exist without human institutions. The tree is known by its fruit [Matt. 12:33]. Moreover, it is said that many good things are the result of laws. And St. Martin, St. Nicholas, and many other saints had taken part in

---

[11] Konrad Peutinger (1465-1547), humanist, secretary of the city of Augsburg, occupied a mediating position in the religious struggles arising out of the Reformation.

councils. Further he said that his [Luther's] books would excite great disturbances and unbelievable confusion. The common people were using his book, *The Freedom of a Christian*,[12] to throw off the yoke, and to strengthen disobedience. Now we are far from the time when those who believed were of one heart and soul [Acts 4:32]. Therefore, laws are necessary. Moreover, it must be considered that although he [Luther] had written many good things, and without doubt with a fine spirit, such as *Of Threefold Justice* and others, the devil was using this fact and working through secret snares, so that all his works might be condemned in perpetuity. He would be judged from these he had written last, just as a tree is known not by its flower but by its fruit. There he [Vehus] added the quotation about the destruction that wastes at noonday and the pestilence that stalks in darkness and the arrow that flies [Ps. 91:5-6]. The whole oration was an exhortation, full of rhetorical commonplaces about the usefulness and wholesomeness of laws, and, on the other hand, the dangers to conscience and safety, both public and private. As in the beginning, so in the middle and the end, he asserted the same thing, that this admonition was the result of the most kind attitude and singular mercy of the princes. In closing he added threats in a final speech, saying that if [Luther] persevered in his position, the emperor would proceed against him, exiling him from the empire and condemning his works, and he reminded him again that he should think about these things and weigh them.

Dr. Martin answered:

"Most clement and illustrious princes and lords, for that most clement and kind will of yours from which this admonition proceeded, I thank you as humbly as I am able. For I know that I am by far too lowly a man to be warned by such great princes. I have not censured all councils, but only that of Constance because of the most powerful reason that it condemned the Word of God, which is shown in its condemnation of this proposition of John Huss: 'The church of Christ is the community of the elect.' This statement the council at Constance condemned and thus the article of faith: 'I believe in the holy catholic church.' "

---

[12] *LW* 31, 327-377.

117

He [Luther] did not refuse to pay with his life and blood, provided he were not reduced to the point where he might be compelled to retract the clear Word of God. For in its defense it is necessary to obey God rather than man [Acts 5:29]. Moreover, there are two kinds of offenses, one involving charity and the other faith. Offenses against charity depend upon morals and life; those involving faith or doctrine depend on the Word of God and cannot be avoided. For it is not in his [Luther's] power, that Christ should not become a "stumbling-stone" [Isa. 8:14-15; Rom. 9:32-33; I Pet. 2:8]. If the faith were truly preached and magistrates were good, one law, informed by the spirit of the gospel,[13] would be sufficient and human laws useless. He knew that magistrates and men in power must be obeyed, even those who live evil and unjust lives. He knew also that private opinions should give way, for that is also taught in his writings. If only he would not be forced to deny the Word of God he would show himself in all other things most obedient.

When Dr. Martin had withdrawn, the princes talked together about what they should order to be done with the man. Therefore, when he was recalled into the chamber, Doctor [Vehus] of Baden pressed upon him again his former arguments, urging that he should place his writings under the judgment of the emperor and the empire.

Dr. Martin replied humbly and modestly: He did not allow nor would he ever allow it to be said that he avoided the judgment of the emperor, the princes, and nobility of the empire. For so far was he from scorning their judgment that he would permit his works to be examined minutely and severely, on the condition that it be done by the authority of holy Scripture and the divine Word. For the Word of God was so clear to him that he was unable to yield unless taught better by the Word of God. For St. Augustine writes that he had learned that only those books which are called canonical should be given the honor of belief in their absolute truth, and that he believed the rest of the learned fathers, no matter how holy and sanctified, only if they wrote the truth.[14]

---

[13] ". . . *legem Evangelicam unam.* . . ." WA 7, 847.
[14] Luther refers here to a letter of Augustine to Jerome (Letter 82, parts 1, 3). Migne 33, 276 and 286.

St. Paul had written on this same point to the Thessalonians: "Test everything; hold fast what is good" [I Thess. 5:21]; and to the Galatians: "Even if an angel comes from heaven and preaches something different, let him be accursed" [Gal. 1:8], and do not believe him. He [Luther], therefore, besought them all the more not to violate his conscience, bound as it was by the chains of Scripture and the holy Word, by forcing him to deny that clear Word of God. And in order to prove agreeable to them personally and before his imperial majesty, he said that in other respects he would do everything most obediently.

The margrave, elector of Brandenburg, asked him when he had finished whether he had said he would not yield unless convinced by holy Scripture. Dr. Martin answered, "Yes, most clement lord, or by the most clear and evident reasons."

So when the conference broke up, and while the rest of the princes were going into the diet, the archbishop of Trier, accompanied by his secretary, Johann Eck, and Cochlaeus,[15] summoned Dr. Martin into the dining room. With Martin were Jerome Schurff and Amsdorf.[16] The secretary began to argue, in the manner of a casuist, that heresies are almost always born from holy Scripture, like that of Arius which arose from the statement, "The Father is greater than I" [John 14:28], and again, from this passage of the gospel, "Joseph did not know his wife until she had borne her first-born son" [Matt. 1:25]. Then he went so far as to try to overthrow the proposition that the catholic church is the communion of saints. He even dared to make wheat from tares and limbs from the excrement of the body. After he proclaimed these and similar ridiculous and futile arguments, Dr. Martin and Dr. Jerome Schurff reproved him soberly, saying that the arguments did not contribute to the matter at hand. Sometimes Johann Cochlaeus interrupted noisily and tried to persuade Dr. Luther to give up what he had begun, and from now on refrain completely from all writing and teaching. At last they departed. The archbishop of Trier wished

---

[15] Johann Cochlaeus (1479-1552) remained an opponent of Luther and the reformers, continuously attacking them in his many pamphlets and books. Cf. *Catholic Encyclopedia*, IV, 79.

[16] Nicholas von Amsdorf (1483-1565), who had accompanied Luther to the debate with Eck at Leipzig (1519) and to the Diet of Worms.

that they would return after dinner. But the secretary and Cochlaeus did not agree.

After dinner Cochlaeus accosted Dr. Martin in his lodging with the most offensive arguments, in which he was properly restrained by Jerome [Schurff], Jonas,[17] and Tilemann [Conradi]. He did not hesitate to demand that Luther renounce his safe-conduct and debate publicly with him and he exhorted him to recant. Dr. Martin, because of his extraordinary kindness and modesty, dealt gently with the man and warned him, as he was about to go, that he should not yield too much to passion and that since he was going to write against him [Luther] he should offer the authority of divine Scripture; for otherwise he would accomplish nothing.

In the evening the archbishop of Trier announced to Dr. Martin through an emissary, Amsdorf, that his safe-conduct had been extended two days by the emperor so that he [the archbishop] could in the meantime confer with him. Therefore, on the next day Dr. Peutinger and Dr. [Vehus of] Baden would come to Luther and indeed he himself would confer with him.

In the forenoon on Thursday, the Feast of St. Mark [April 25], Peutinger and [Vehus of] Baden attempted to persuade Dr. Martin that he should leave the judgment of his books simply and absolutely to the emperor and the empire. He answered that he would do and endure everything if only they supported themselves by the authority of holy Scripture, for he would trust in nothing less. For God had once spoken through the prophet, "Put not your trust in princes, in the sons of men, in whom there is no help" [Ps. 146:3]. And again, "Cursed is the man who trusts in man" [Jer. 17:5]. And when they pressed him harder he answered that nothing ought less to be entrusted to the judgment of men than the Word of God. Thus they left him, asking him to think over a better answer, and saying that they would come back after luncheon.

After luncheon they returned and attempted in vain the same thing as in the morning. They pleaded with him to at least submit his case to the judgment of some future council. And he granted this, but on the condition that they show him the parts excerpted

---

[17] Justus Jonas (1493-1555) who at the time was professor of jurisprudence at the University of Wittenberg. From 1523 on he devoted his energies to theology, writing, and serving as pastor in various places in Germany.

from his books for submission to the council, and that they judge them by the testimony of Scripture and the divine Word. Upon leaving Dr. Martin they told the archbishop of Trier that he had promised to submit some parts of his works to a council and that meanwhile he would be silent about them. But Dr. Martin had never even considered this, as he had always up to this time refused to either deny or to cast aside whatever concerned the Word of God.

Therefore it came about, through the work of God, that [the archbishop of] Trier summoned Dr. Martin to hear him personally. And when he saw that the situation was different from that which the doctors had reported, he declared that this could not have been corrected unless he himself had heard him say it. Otherwise he would have gone immediately to the emperor and told him what the doctors had reported.

After all witnesses had first been dismissed [the archbishop of] Trier discussed most kindly with Dr. Martin about submitting to the judgment first of the emperor and the empire and then of a council. In this conversation Dr. Martin hid nothing from [the archbishop of] Trier, showing that he could not safely entrust such an important matter to those who, approving the judgment and bull of the pope, attacked and condemned with new commands him who was summoned under a safe-conduct.

Then after Luther's friend was admitted,[18] [the archbishop of] Trier asked Dr. Martin for means with which he might meet the situation. Luther answered that there were none better than those of which Gamaliel had spoken in Acts 5, according to the witness of St. Luke, "If this is the counsel of men, this work will be overthrown, if it is of God, you will not be able to overthrow it" [Acts 5:38-39]. This the emperor and the imperial estates could write to the Roman pontiff. For he [Luther] knew that if his work were not from God, within three years, or even two, it would perish of its own accord.

To [the archbishop of] Trier, who asked what he would do if some articles were selected for the purpose of submitting them to a council, Luther answered that he would accept, provided that they

---

[18] This was Spalatin. WA 7, 854 n. 1.

were not those which the Council of Constance had condemned. [The archbishop of] Trier said that he feared that those would be the very ones. Then Luther said, "About these, I am unable and unwilling to keep silent, for I am certain that by those decrees the Word of God was condemned and I would rather lose my life and head than desert the clear Word of God."

When [the archbishop of] Trier saw that Dr. Martin would never submit the Word of God to the judgment of men, he dismissed him in a kindly manner, and when asked [by Luther] if he would obtain permission from his imperial majesty to leave, he answered that he would properly care for the matter and would report back.

Not long afterward, the secretary of [the archbishop of] Trier, in the presence of the chancellor of Austria[19] and Maximilian,[20] the imperial secretary, read to Dr. Martin in his lodging the emperor's decree:

"Because, although he has so often been warned in vain by the emperor, the electors, the princes, and the estates, he is unwilling to return to the heart and unity of the catholic faith, it remains for the emperor as defender of the catholic faith[21] to act. Therefore, it is the command of the emperor that within twenty-one days from this time, he return to his home under a safe-conduct passage and with his liberty secured, and that on the journey he not stir up the people either by preaching or writing."

The most Christian father, answering very modestly, began thus:

"As it has pleased the Lord so it has happened. Blessed be the name of the Lord [Job 1:21]. First of all to his most serene majesty, to the prince electors, the princes, and the rest of the imperial estates, I give most humble thanks for a favorable and kind audience and for the safe-conduct which has been kept and is to be kept. For I have desired nothing in all this except a reformation according to holy Scripture, and this I have urgently demanded. Otherwise I will endure all things for his imperial majesty and the

---

[19] Johann Schnaidpeck.
[20] Maximilian von Zevenberghen.
[21] Though the title, Defender of the Faith, was officially bestowed, for the first time, on Henry VIII of England by Leo X in October, 1521, its use in this instance has official overtones.

empire: life and death, fame and infamy, reserving nothing at all for myself except only the right to confess and testify to the Word of the Lord. I most humbly commend myself and subject myself to his imperial majesty and the whole empire."

Therefore, on the next day, that is, the sixth day after Jubilate [April 26], after he had paid his respects to his supporters and friends who had visited him frequently, he left after breakfast, at about ten in the morning, accompanied both by those with whom he had traveled there and by Dr. Jerome Schurff, the lawyer of Wittenberg. Caspar Sturm, the herald, after a few hours followed him and found him at Oppenheim and accompanied him according to the verbal order of Emperor Charles.

And so may God for a very long time preserve for his church and his Word this most godly man born to defend and teach the gospel. Amen.

The Minutes of the Trial
of Luther before the Diet of Worms[22]
Dr. Johann Eck, Doctor of Arts and Laws,
Secretary of [the
Archbishop of] Trier
(Let the Notary attest the forms)

The designated notary, in a clear and understandable voice, spoke first in Latin then in German, by order of his holy imperial majesty, and stated what follows in substantially these words:

Martin Luther: His holy and invincible imperial majesty, on the advice of all the estates of the Holy Roman Empire, has ordered that you be called here to the throne of his majesty so you might retract the books edited and published by you in both Latin and German, as well as the contents of these same books; also so you might in like manner recant their violence, form, and tenor according to the earlier order decreed by his majesty and properly brought against you. Wherefore, I ask you in the name of his imperial majesty and of the princes of the empire: First, do you acknowledge that these books here (a bundle of his books and

---

[22] The following is the report of Aleander (1480-1542), the papal nuncio to the court of Emperor Charles V.

writings in Latin and German was shown him) now named publicly to you one by one, which are published with your name as author, are yours; do you recognize them as your works or not? Next, do you wish to retract and recall them and their contents or to cling to them henceforth and to insist on them?

Since this question was separated and divided into two parts for Luther, he answered the first part of the question, that the books, writings in Latin and German, shown to him and just read by title, were his, published at his residence, and that he acknowledged his offspring and would always acknowledge them (and he said in a somewhat lower voice, though still understandable, that some others, furthermore, which were not named were his). To the second part of the question, whether he wished to retract them and their contents and proclaim their recantation,[23] he began to contrive excuses and to seek an escape. He said that he was prepared to yield and to accede to anyone seeking to instruct him from holy Scripture, and since this had not happened to him up to this time, although he had published so often, and since it was a question about a difficult and hard, not to mention a most important, matter (since it was about faith), he was not able to answer extempore and without forethought. Moreover, he asked most humbly that time be given and allowed him to think things over.

While these things were done and thus acted upon, his holy imperial majesty, with the counsel and agreement of all the electors and the other princes, both ecclesiastical and lay, and of the estates of the empire who were present in great number, wished through the celebrated Johann Eck to warn him kindly and gently in the beginning that he should keep in mind the unity of the holy, catholic, and apostolic church, and the general peace and quiet of the Christian commonwealth, and that he should not contrive to rend apart what he ought to respect, venerate, and adore. He should be unwilling to trust in his own opinion and in sacred texts twisted to suit his own understanding, and moving among questionable doctrines and discoveries both foreign and his own, to overturn the whole Christian religion, to arouse the world, to confuse the lowest with the highest, and to seduce so many godly minds and

---

[23] Translated literally, *palinodiam canere*, would mean "to sing a palinode."

souls. He should consider how deeply he is now involved in his own inextricable errors, how difficult, indeed even impossible, it is to rectify them, and how many with his self-assured spirit he, unhappily, has seduced to danger and loss and sent to hell. He should desire, therefore, to come to his senses again and to return to the heart of the faith, and acknowledge and recant his errors. And if he should do this, his majesty on his part promised the hope of pardon and grace, and also that he would obtain those favors easily for him from the most holy [Father]. If, on the other hand, persevering wantonly in his errors, he should not listen to this sound exhortation, his majesty on his part wished to have it made clear publicly, on behalf of the faith by which he had been bound and held to the holy mother church and to the Christian religion, that he would defend the majesty of his and the holy apostolic throne through law. And he should consider what evil and what end would await him afterwards.

Now he had sought an opportunity for deliberation about the second part of the question. Of course he should not have asked this at all, and he certainly does not deserve to obtain it, for the nature and condition of the matter about which he is disturbed has been brought to his attention, for, even in the earlier order issued against him, a revocation which had to be made by him of his works, specifically and by name, and their contents, was introduced and declared to him. Therefore, because he has known for a long time why he was called and what had to be done, he should not drag out with further delay a matter so dangerous and so much at variance with custom. He ought, moreover, to have come here having finished his deliberation on this serious matter. Nevertheless, so that he may not seize the opportunity of complaining, in any way, that action had been taken too hastily, his majesty in clemency wishes to grant the requested deliberation and wishes further to have set and appointed, for making evident and known his deliberation, the following day at the fifth hour after noon, just as his majesty set and appointed that same day and hour for him to accomplish the things demanded.

There was a recess for the day. And after they turned from this to some other business, they adjourned.

When he arrived on the appointed day (let the notary continue) the distinguished secretary, by order of his sacred and invincible majesty, began to speak to him again in the following fashion in Latin and in German:

"Yesterday evening, Martin, you felt that it was burdensome because of the importance of the matter (as you then stated), to answer immediately and extempore that part of the interrogation concerning whether you wished to retract and revoke, together with their contents, the books named to you yesterday from the list, books in Latin and German, edited and published by you and acknowledged to be your works, although in matters of faith and of things in which there lies a danger to souls no delay ought to be given, and especially to men trained and learned in holy letters (the interpretation of which you claim for yourself alone). You ought to be prepared to satisfy anyone demanding a reason about what constitutes your faith and hope. Nevertheless, his sacred and invincible majesty, through his innate mildness and kindness, granted you the opportunity for deliberation and appointed and set this day and hour for that declaration. Thus his imperial majesty and all the estates of the empire look forward and will listen attentively to that."

To these words, Martin answered, requesting them, first of all, to listen kindly to him for the sake of justice and the cause of truth, and then asked to be forgiven if he addressed anyone with less than his appropriate title. If he erred in any way against the customs of courts, they should overlook it, for he was a monk not acquainted with royal courts but with the cells and chambers of a monastery. Later he answered with a rather long digression the questions put to him in the name of his imperial majesty. (This answer, since he took some time to deliver it, and committed it to writing, and since a copy of it was made by me, I have caused to be inserted in this document.) [Here follows text given in this translation, pp. 109-112.]

However, when Luther had finished speaking, the distinguished secretary, at a signal from his holy imperial majesty, began:

"By rights, Luther, you have every reason to think yourself favored, because you have spoken before so kind an emperor, who listened to you for some time with more moderation than you showed in your speech. Do you believe that this most godly ruler heard with equanimity and favor all that which you, with more violence and with greater bitterness than becomes your religion or profession, have used to attack the supreme pontiff? Look how little moderation there is in you, how temperance or modesty is lacking in you! Moreover, what about your deliberation concerning what you were to say: whether or not you wished to retract and to revoke those books which you have acknowledged as your own, together with their contents? You complain that you are treated unjustly if you are compelled to revoke all at once and without discrimination, since not all are of the same sort and kind. You have divided them into three kinds, for there are some in which you have treated simply, sincerely, and evangelically, matters of morals and faith, so that they are regarded as harmless even by your enemies; indeed, even the apostolic bull, otherwise harsh and cruel, considers some of them inoffensive.[24] If you retracted those, you would be doing nothing other than damning those which friends and enemies alike approve. There are others of the kind in which you attack the pope and papal affairs, as you say, and tear apart their morals, vices, abuses, tyranny, and other things of that nature. You say that it is not proper for you to recall these lest you seem to have strengthened the tyranny. The third group are the books which you have written against those who are striving to defend the Roman tyranny and to destroy your own godly doctrines. These are the basis for the dispute. If you should revoke these, the result would be that the Roman tyranny might, with your patronage, rule more violently than it had ever ruled before.

"In these divisions, Martin, you have not distinguished between your dogmas and books sufficiently, since those which you have published after the decree of the supreme pontiff are far more abominable and execrable than those written earlier, and deserve to be condemned, since in them you proclaim as catholic truths the long since rejected heresies of John Huss, and at the same time undercut and weaken the whole authority and majesty of councils. Furthermore, you have not sufficiently answered my questions. Granted that some of your books do not contain harmful doctrine (something which we, however, do not concede): remove the diseased and poisoned dogmas, remove the godlessness, remove

---

[24] Cf. p. 109 n. 3.

the heresies and the approval of heresies, remove those things which damage the catholic faith; no harm will come from that which is sound. His holy imperial majesty will deal most graciously with them if you change your mind, and he will intervene with the supreme pontiff that that which is sound is not destroyed and suppressed with that which is not sound. If, however, you continue to persist in your notorious errors and heresies, as you have begun to do, there is no doubt that all memory of you will be wiped out; all that is sound and unsound will be condemned together with its author. And this is neither new nor unheard of, since in ancient times the books of the Arians[25] and the Montanists,[26] of the Photinians,[27] and likewise of the Nestorians[28] and Eutychians, and other heretics were burned although they contained much godly and catholic religious thought. For no doctrine is more effective in deceiving than that which mixes a few false teachings with many that are true.

"However, Martin, you finally retreat and flee to the place to which all heretics have been accustomed to retreat and take refuge. Of course you say that you are prepared, since you are a human being who is able to slip and fall, to accept instruction out of the holy Scriptures, from anyone at all, high or low. However, up to this time there has been no one (justly, I should think) who has attempted to do what you say, except all the heretics who have

---

[25] Arians were those who shared the view of Arius (presbyter of Alexandria, d. 336) that the Son is not of the same substance with the Father. Their belief was condemned as heretical by the Council of Nicaea, 325.

[26] Montanus, from whom the Montanists derived their name, made prophetic utterance central to his Christian message, claiming on the basis of John 14:26 that the Counselor (Paraklete) was imparting a fuller revelation to him and his followers. Although embraced by Tertullian (d. ca. 220), Montanism as a movement was gradually wiped out through the firm opposition of church and state.

[27] Photinus, bishop of Smyrna (d. 376), regarded the person of Christ as essentially human. Those who share his view and manner of thinking are referred to as Photinians.

[28] Nestorius, patriarch of Constantinople (d. in exile after 451), and representative of the theology of Antioch, got into difficulty initially through his opposition to applying the name, "Mother of God," to Mary. His views and those of his followers, Nestorians, were condemned by the Council of Ephesus, 431. While the followers of Nestorius emphasized the two natures (the human and divine) in the person of Christ, Eutyches, representing an exaggeration of the theology of Alexandria, stressed the one nature (the divine) in Christ. Though not formally condemned, Eutyches was banished after 452.

always done the same thing; and you, just like them, wish holy Scripture to be understood according to your judgment and the workings of your mind. You have come as a spokesman of great, new heresies as well as those long since condemned; for many of the things which you adduce are heresies of the Beghards,[29] the Waldenses,[30] the Poor Men of Lyons,[31] of Wycliffe and Huss,[32] and of others long since rejected by the synods. Is it proper to question again, to drag into dispute, those matters which the Catholic church has judicially settled, matters which have turned upon the usages, rites, and observances which our fathers held with absolute faith, on behalf of which they would have endured all sorts of punishment, all torments, and for which at last they would rather have endured a thousand deaths than to have fallen away from in any way at all? Do you want us to stray from the path which our fathers faithfully trod?

"What will the Jews say upon hearing these things, what the Turks, what the Saracens, and the other sects who are opposed to our faith? How they will break into laughter, how they will mock, that now we Christians argue whether up to this time we have believed what is right. Do not, I entreat you, Martin, do not claim for yourself that you, I say, that you are the one and only man who has knowledge of the Bible, who has the true understanding of holy Scripture, to which understanding the most holy doctors toiling night and day in the exposition of Scripture, have attained through great labor and effort. Do not place your judgment ahead of that of so many distinguished men. Do not regard yourself as wiser than all others. Do not cast doubt upon the most holy, orthodox faith which Christ, the perfect lawgiver, instituted; which the apostles spread through the whole world; which the miracles made

---

[29] Beghards is the name given to a religious society deriving its chief inspiration from Lambert of Beghe (d. *ca.* 1177). Although condemned as heretical, apparently on account of ecstatic practices, by the Council of Vienne (1311), the society continued to exist until the fifteenth century.
[30] Named after their leader, Peter Waldo, the Waldenses stressed apostolic poverty and preaching. On account of their ignorance of Christ's teachings they were not granted the right to preach (1179); when they persisted they were placed under the papal ban (1184).
[31] The Poor Men of Lyons were informed by a spirit closely allied to that of the Waldenses.
[32] John Wycliffe (d. 1384) and John Huss (d. 1415) were declared heretics by the Council of Constance (1414-1418).

clear; which the martyrs confirmed with their red blood. And later, holy doctors, discussing the obscure passages of the prophets, and unveiling the greatest mysteries of both the New and Old Testaments, and with good arguments disputing against heretics, have more amply ascertained it. The result of the holy councils has strengthened it. What the doctors have discussed as doctrine the church has defined as its judgment, the faith in which our fathers and ancestors confidently died and as a legacy have transmitted to us. We are forbidden to argue about this faith by the law of both pontiff and emperor, and since, among many, reasoning and disputing never ends, both are going to judge those who with headlong rashness refuse to submit to the decision of the church. Punishments have been provided and published.

"In order to save time, I purposely pass over the rest of what you said, Martin, as not being pertinent to the matter at hand.

"Therefore it is futile, Martin, to expect a debate of those things which according to the faith you are bound to believe as certain and clear. Wherefore, I think this same question must again be pressed and renewed, that you answer sincerely and candidly, not ambiguously, not dialectically,[33] whether or not you wish to recall and retract your books and the errors contained in them, which have been disseminated by you." [34]

When Luther had given his answer, and since all were worn out by the crowd and the heat and were preparing to depart, the distinguished secretary shouted a few last words because of the shortness of time:

"Lay aside your conscience, Martin; you must lay it aside because it is in error; and it will be safe and proper for you to recant. Although you say the councils have erred you will never be able to prove it, in matters of faith at least, and even in matters of morals I fancy it will be with much difficulty."

Here Martin shouted back that he was able to prove these things.

Then there was a recess.

---

[33] *Non cornute.* Cf. p. 112 n. 7.
[34] At this point Aleander has included in his report Luther's reply which is identical with the one on which our translation is based. Cf. p. 112 l. 22 to p. 113 l. 5. However, Aleander's version does not include the words, *Ich kann nicht anderst, hie stehe ich.*

Books of Martin Luther

In German:

On Good Works
The Freedom of a Christian
To the German Nobility
On the New Testament and Mass
Defense and Explanation of All the Articles
To the Secretary at Stolpen
Appeal to a Council
A pamphlet signed J. G. [John Grünenberg]
What Those Who Are Accused of Reading Martin's Books Should Answer
A certain sermon on the Man Pictured with a Shepherd's Staff
A second quarto volume entitled, *To the Goat*
A certain book of eight quartos against the pope.

In Latin:

A large volume printed at Basel, in folio
Babylonian Captivity of the Church
Defense and Explanation of All the Articles
On Good Works
Commentary on the Lord's Prayer
Appeal to a Council
Why the Books of the Pope Were Burned
Sermon on Preparation for Death
A Commentary on the First Thirteen Psalms
Against the Execrable Bull of the Antichrist

AGAINST LATOMUS

1521

Translated by George Lindbeck

INTRODUCTION

The low countries, Belgium and Holland, became involved very early in the controversy over Luther and his theology. At first Luther was considered just another disciple of Erasmus of Rotterdam and the men who had opposed Erasmus in earlier controversies went immediately into action against Luther. The theologians of the University of Louvain in Belgium openly condemned Luther's writings as early as 1519.*

In March, 1520, Luther replied, publishing both the condemnation and his disdainful answer.† In May, 1521, one of the teachers at Louvain published a comprehensive defense of the original condemnation.‡ This teacher was Jacobus Masson, born in Cambron about 1475. He had studied at Paris and joined the faculty at Louvain in 1510, remaining there until his death in 1544. Like so many of his contemporaries in academic life Masson had changed his name and was known as Latomus.

His book against Luther was not his first literary effort. In a previous work§ he had taken issue with the humanistic enthusiasm for the ancient languages. Indirectly he had attacked Erasmus, the great leader of the humanists. The latter replied on March 28, 1519‖ and the result was that Latomus acquired the reputation of an enemy of the new learning among all the friends of humanism. Luther, too, was familiar with this earlier controversy and therefore called Latomus a "detractor of linguistic competence."

Latomus' book against Luther reached the reformer during his stay at the Wartburg on May 26, 1521. Luther felt that a reply

---

* *Facultatis theologiae Lovaniensis doctrinalis condemnatio Martini Lutheri,* WA 6, 175.

† *Responsio Lutheriana ad condemnationem doctrinalem per magistros nostros Lovaniensis et Coloniensis,* WA 6, 181-195.

‡ *Articulorum doctrinae fratris M. Lutheri per theologos Lovaniensis damnatorum ratio ex sacris literis et veteribus tractoribus* (1521).

§ *De trium linguarum et studii theologici ratione dialogus* (1519).

‖ *Apologia refellens suspiciones quorundam dictiantium dialogum D. Jacobi Latomi.*

was necessary but resented taking time from his translation of the Bible to answer a man whose theological competence did not impress him.

However, Latomus' book did deal with the heart of the theological controversy. In seven sections he discussed the effect of sin on good works, free will, the sacrament of penance, the universality of idolatry and of offenses against the first commandment, virtue and knowledge as they are found in the sinner, purgatory, and indulgences. In his reply Luther had to work without a library. He was handicapped because he could neither check Latomus' quotations nor quote passages from the fathers except the ones he knew by heart. Yet, in spite of these difficulties the refutation of Latomus became a forcefully presented explanation of the relationship of sin and grace, law and gospel, and justification and sanctification. Some of the central ideas of Luther's theology are here presented as clearly as anywhere in his writings.

Our translation is based upon the text in *WA* 8, 43-128. It was prepared by Dr. George Lindbeck of Yale Divinity School.

AGAINST LATOMUS

*Luther's Refutation of Latomus' Argument
on Behalf of the Incendiary[1] Sophists of
the University of Louvain*

1521

To the Honorable Justus Jonas,[2] (Dean of the Clergy) of Wittenberg, my superior in the Lord, I, Martin Luther, send greetings in the Lord.

I also, my good Jonas, would like to congratulate you on the office you have recently assumed. Unable to be present in person,[3] I have decided to send you this "Latomus" of mine. He is no longer a detractor of linguistic competence.[4] You need not fear him, for that Ishbibenob has been vanquished by the strength of our Abishai[5] [II Sam. 21:16-17]. Neither is he the tardy advocate justifying the crime of the Louvainian arsonists with a malicious pretense of modesty and an unfortunate verbal subtlety. Nor is he the one whom you have seen glorying in the lord pope and his bull. But, I send you a "Latomus" who—purified by Luther's holy water—seems to be freed from the ghosts and hobgoblins with which until now he has been disturbed, and with which he was wont to trouble devout hearts.

---

[1] The bull, *Exsurge Domine,* threatening Luther with excommunication, also included a demand to burn his books. In compliance with this demand some of Luther's books were burned in Louvain (cf. *Why the Books of the Pope and His Disciples Were Burned* (1520). *LW* 31, 381-384). For this reason Luther speaks of the members of the faculty of the University of Louvain as "incendiary."

[2] Following the Leipzig Debate (1519), Justus Jonas (1493-1555) became a supporter of the evangelical cause. He accompanied Luther on his journey to Worms in 1521, and had recently become professor of canon law at Wittenberg.

[3] Luther was at the Wartburg.

[4] This refers to Latomus' earlier *Dialogue on Three Languages,* in which he argued that knowledge of Greek and Hebrew is not necessary for the theologian. Cf. Introduction, p. 135.

[5] Erasmus. Cf. Introduction, p. 135.

If the Louvainians had published their opinion[6] at the proper time and, as is proper for learned men, had consulted together before acting, they would neither have condemned nor destroyed my writings, nor would they like fools seek to justify themselves only after the deed. This much I hope to show. Latomus' book certainly shows me how easy it is to sit in one's corner and babble against an absent Luther: "This is heretical, this is erroneous." But in public they would not have had confidence in their strength and daring to deal with the matter. This persuades me that if the bull had not inflated Latomus' confidence he would never have published his illustrious "Argument." Therefore he boasts as of a deed well done and, dreaming of the bull's antique and antiquated terrors, believes that his booklet will alarm the world. For this reason he now fearlessly dares to play against Luther with God's mighty Scriptures. I'd just as soon have such an act approved by such a bull. I would not want it otherwise than to be condemned by such a bull. The bull, indictment, judge, and advocate all agree beautifully. May the Lord Jesus protect me and all devout souls from their contagion and their company! Amen.

Truly it won't be easy for you to believe how unwillingly I have torn myself away from the peace-giving words of Christ, with which I have been occupied on this my Patmos,[7] in order to waste my time reading the nonsense of this prickly and thorny sophist. Indeed, the man is sophistic from the sole of his foot to the crown of his head. Swollen with the flatulent bull, he writes with such confidence that he considers both industry and discernment unnecessary. He is content to babble whatever he has read or swallowed. It is a great bother to reply to him, for in doing so you can neither exercise skill nor increase your learning, and yet you are forced to waste precious hours. I suspect the man of believing that Luther has been spirited away or has been condemned to eternal silence so that they may once again freely dominate the public with sophistic tyranny. They consider me not a little guilty for its decline and fall. O that its downfall were complete; I would gladly

---

[6] Cf. Introduction, p. 135.

[7] Luther's reference is to the Wartburg where he was occupied with translating the New Testament into German.

be guilty, even unto death, of this seven times unforgivable sin (if we are to believe the most holy priests of the bull).

However, I am concerned that while we bravely battle over grace and good works, we do not in the meantime deprive ourselves of grace or of works. When I consider these fearful times of wrath, I ask only that my eyes become fountains of tears so that I may bewail this latest desolation of souls [Jer. 9:1] which this reign of sin and of perdition is producing. Seated in Rome in the midst of the church [II Thess. 2:4], this monster vaunts itself as God, is flattered by the bishops, compliantly aided by the sophists, and there is nothing that the hypocrites are not willing to do for it. "Therefore hell has enlarged its appetite and opened its mouth without any bounds" [Isa. 5:14], and Satan plays at the damnation of souls. There is no one among us who, seriously and with tears, stands in this day of fury and builds up a wall for the house of Israel [cf. Jer. 9:1; 15:20]. So, full of anger against blasphemers like Latomus, who deal sophistically with serious matters and compel us to interrupt better tasks in order to concern ourselves with their senseless insanities, I invoke these words against their flinty foreheads: "All my enemies shall be ashamed and sorely troubled; they shall turn back, and be put to shame in a moment" [Ps. 6:10].

In order not to detain you with too long a letter, I shall answer the main points of Latomus' preface in a separate introduction. Meanwhile accept this testimony of my esteem for you and ask the Lord for me that I may be delivered (for so I now dare to pray with the Apostle) from the evil and unbelieving men [II Thess. 3:2; cf. Rom. 15:31] who inhabit this Babylon, and that a door be opened to me [Col. 4:3] for the praise of the glorious grace of the gospel of His Son [Eph. 1:6]. I, for my part, pray the Lord to give you His Spirit so that you may lecture on those most pestilent decrees[8] of the Antichrist, which you are commissioned to teach, with the purpose of which I have told you; may you be an Aaron clothed in holy garments—that is, armed with the sacred Scriptures—so that, grasping the censer of prayer [Rev. 8:3] you may go forth to encounter this devastator in the midst of the Romish fire which now consumes the world. It is soon to be extinguished by another fire

---

[8] Cf. p. 137 n. 1.

coming from heaven at the advent of our Savior, for whom we wait. See to it, my brother, that you teach so that what you are teaching must be forgotten, and that [your students] know that they must flee as something deadly whatever the pope and papists hold and assert. Since we do not have the power to abolish this public and world-wide evil, and are compelled to administer the sacrilegious provinces of Babylon, it remains for us so to administer them as to recognize that they are completely different from Jerusalem our home, and that they are its adversaries, ravagers, and enemies of insatiable cruelty. Thus we shall not smile and caress our bondage as do those who perish, in whom the gospel of the glory of God is hidden [II Cor. 4:3]. Do not lightly regard your ministry for, alongside the poisonous refuse and insane foolishness of the pope, you present the saving and life-giving gospel of Christ. Thus young men may have an antidote against this venom—the mere smell of which kills a man—until such time as they learn to reject evil and choose the good for themselves. This Immanuel is commended to you [cf. Isa. 7:14]. Therefore be hardy and strong. Do not fear this Baal-peor [Num. 25:3] for if we only believe, it is scarcely a Baal-zebub [II Kings 1:2]—that is, a man of flies. For we believe that Jesus Christ is the Lord, blessed in eternity—Amen!—who will perfect and confirm you and his little church which is with you. Be strong in Him.

In the place of my exile, June 8, 1521.

ON THE PREFACE OF LATOMUS[9]

First of all, Latomus charges that from the beginning I expressly submitted my writings to the pope. It is in accordance with his sophistic self-assurance to imagine this. To be sure, I regret that I did quite seriously submit them, for my sincere opinion of the pope, councils, and universities was no different from the common one. Although much of what they said seemed absurd to me and completely alien to Christ, yet for more than a decade I curbed my thoughts with the advice of Solomon: "Do not rely on your

---

[9] Luther is thinking of the letter by Latomus dedicated to Rudolf de Monckedamis in the preface to Latomus' work, *Articulorum doctrinae fratris M. Lutheri per theologos Lovaniensis* . . . (1521). WA 8, 37; cf. also p. 139, ll. 22-23.

own insight" [Prov. 3:5]. I always believed there were theologians hidden in the schools who would not have been silent if these teachings were impious. I then still believed that scarcely anywhere were there fewer stupid blockheads and asses—but now I would say scoundrels—than at Louvain. However, in view of what has happened, knowledge of the true situation—as well as courage—has grown. For they made their ignorance and vileness glaringly apparent, offending the sign which is spoken against [Luke 2:34]. If they had not so completely unmasked themselves, if they could have further dissembled, they would in the end have certainly made me into a crazy fool. However, I give thanks to my Lord Jesus Christ who, on account of this assault, has repaid me a hundred times [Matt. 19:29] with the knowledge—of which I am now convinced—that the pope is the Antichrist, the sign of the end prophesied throughout the Scriptures, and that the universities are indeed the ultimate in the synagogues of Satan, in which the rule belongs to those Epicurean swine,[10] the sophistic theologians.

He [Latomus] says that I lack the evangelical modesty which I enjoin, and that this is especially true of the book in which I replied to the sophists of Louvain when they condemned my teachings.[11] Now I have never insisted that anyone consider me modest or holy, but only that everyone recognize what the gospel is. If they do this, I give anyone freedom to attack my life to his heart's content. My boast is that I have injured no one's life or reputation, but only sharply reproached, as godless and sacrilegious, those assertions, inventions, and doctrines which are against the Word of God. I do not apologize for this, for I have good precedents. John the Baptist [Luke 3:7] and Christ after him [Matt. 23:33] called the Pharisees the "offspring of vipers." So excessive and outrageous was this abuse of such learned, holy, powerful, and honored men that they said in reply that He had a demon [John 7:20]. If in this instance Latomus had been judge, I wonder what the verdict would have been! Elsewhere Christ calls

that would have been rather silly

---

[10] Horace, _Epist._ I. 5, 16: _Epicuri de grege porcum_ (a hog of Epicure's herd). Relying on memory Luther quotes freely: _Epicurei illi porci._

[11] Cf. _Condemnatio doctrinalis librorum Martini Lutheri per quosdam magistros nostros Lovaniensis et Coloniensis facta. Responsio Lutheriana ad eandem damnationem._ WA 6, 174-195.

them "blind" [Matt. 23:16], "crooked," "liars," "sons of the devil"
[John 8:44, 55]. Good God, even Paul lacked evangelical modesty
when he anathematized the teachers of the Galatians [Gal. 1:8]
who were, I suppose, great men. Others he calls "dogs" [Phil. 3:2],
"empty talkers" [Tit. 1:10], "deceivers" [Col. 2:4, 8]. Further, he
accused to his face the magician Elymas with being a "son of the
devil, full of all deceit and villainy" [Acts 13:10].

I hold that the sophists have no right to judge me, for they
themselves see that my work does not disagree with the apostles,
Christ, and the prophets. But according to such teachers as
Latomus, in our day we show evangelical modesty when we kneel
before godless and blasphemous bishops and sophists, and say:
"Gracious Lord, your Grace does well; distinguished Master, your
Excellency speaks well." If you tell them what they are—ignorant,
stupid, godless blasphemers against God's Word, doing incalculable
damage to the service of God and souls—then you are called one
who offends against the whole gospel.

On the other hand, if you flatter them you are not immoderate,
even if you murder every mortal and turn the world upside down.
When has Latomus accused the pope of excess, who is almost insane
in engaging in so many wars and wicked plots? Evidently
evangelical moderation or excess depends exclusively on whether
one venerates papal idols and sophistic idiots! Therefore Latomus—
that moderate enforcer and eulogizer of moderation—not only does
not attack this bloodthirsty bull (whose cruelty would be abhorred
by every godly man even if it did rightly condemn me), but praises,
boasts, relies upon, and glories in it. He is one of those bloody and
deceitful men who affect modesty in words and appearance, but
who meanwhile—unless one yields—breathe out threats and blood.
No one whom this bull can please will persuade me that he is a
moderate and upright man. I prefer to be frank and not have
anyone misled by flattery. I can testify that although my shell may
be hard, still my kernel is soft and sweet. I wish no one harm, but
desire everyone to carefully consider these things with me. Just as
my harshness has hurt no one, so it has deceived no one. Whoever
avoids me suffers nothing from me; whoever bears with me is
profited. In Prov. 28 [:23], Solomon says, "He who rebukes a man
will afterward find more favor than he who flatters with his tongue."

Next, in order to emphasize my offense, he cites an ancient author, whom he [Latomus] considers wise, on the question of how to reprove the Roman bishop. His opinion is that one ought neither speak out fully nor remain completely silent, but the way to do this escapes him. No wonder, for in order to appreciate such exalted bulls one must be ignorant of what even children know and, on the other hand, know what even the angels do not know. In bearing the title of "Master of Theology," Latomus professes to know about divine things, and indeed asserts in this book that he is among the wisest. Yet this miserable man is ignorant of the present circumstances of daily human life, nor does he know how one ought to counsel souls in danger. He is certain of what is done by the souls in purgatory who are so far removed from our senses and of whose state Scripture says nothing (although they [the sophists] claim that everything taught by them and the pope is abundantly found in Scripture). However, I ask that we leave the sophists to their own devices, for nothing properly suits them except hypocrisy, flattery, and lies. Let us look again at the ancient author whom Latomus thinks so wise. He advises three things: First, that the cities and princes stop demanding what is unjust, and that they refuse it even when it is offered. In this way we begin by freeing ourselves of what we object to in the pope, for it is insolent not to bear with those faults in the superior which one suffers from oneself. Second, he advises prayer; third, patience. So speaks this wise man.

His first recommendation is a pious wish, that is, a mere conjecture rather like one we ourselves can think of: "If an ass flew, it would have wings." In the same way we may think, "If no one demanded what is wrong, the pope would become better." But why not the other way around, "If the pope reformed himself, then no one would dare to demand what is wrong"? What happens when—as is usually the case—nothing is demanded of the pope, yet he, of his own accord, rages furiously? Above all, what happens when he cares nothing for the gospel and performs none of the episcopal duties described in I Timothy 3? [I Tim. 3:2ff.]. Is it then enough to think, "If no one demanded what is wrong"? Doesn't everyone in the whole world already think, not only what that wise man suggested, but also what I have added? Who does not want this? And what more can one do? After all, who controls

143

princes and cities (making exception now of that power of God which he tells us, in the second place, to seek through prayer)? Yet he does not advise us, as someone might try to do, that, "It is the fault of the rulers and people that the pope is wicked." Let us rather think, "If only the devil would stop riding the pope he would become good," and so blame the devil that the pope is evil. You also can use this advice and think, "O that I were blessed, here and in the future." This is the best way of getting to heaven. Actually the world has already gone beyond the recommendation of this wise man. For whom is prayer everywhere offered more than for the pope? Similarly, whose tyranny is more calmly borne than that of the pope? Is there anything left, then, of the advice of this sage? What a beautiful picture of the pope this wise man paints, in which first the sheep begin to find their own pasture, and the people lead themselves along the way, preparing pasture for the shepherd and a path for the guide! Notice how well this wise man agrees with his eulogist, Latomus. It seems to Latomus that one ought not be completely silent; to this wise man of his, that one ought to be completely so. Now I'd like to know which of the two lies, the eulogist or the eulogy. Either Latomus lies in considering him wise, or else he lies in holding that one ought not be completely silent. Nor is the sage consistent, for he recommends silence and yet makes the pope a man who prostitutes himself, telling us that he lavishes ill-gotten gains, which ought to be refused even if they were offered.

As Hilary well says,[12] it would be hard to defend the cause of truth against the godless if wisdom had to examine all that godlessness dares. Let us look further into the secrets of this sanctified guile. Our author says that you must bear with your ruler's fault since you also suffer from it. So everyone keeps quiet—for, according to Latomus' sage, the command to silence is general—and so all suffer, even against their will, from this same fault. But are not those who are free from it allowed to speak up? Why does he order them to be quiet? I am all in favor of proper and well-informed appreciation of this admirable bull; but since this clever bit of dramatics is doubtless staged precisely against Luther, I

---

[12] *On the Trinity,* VI, 15. Migne 10, 577.

would like to learn what fault he shares with the lord pope. Or am I guilty of the entire Hydra's[13] nest of Roman crimes? But since he who is called to preach the gospel is bound to proclaim it to every creature [Mark 16:15], I ask whether the pope is not a creature? Why isn't it permissible to speak the truth freely and openly to him? But enough of this. The reward of such flattery is what such crass stupidity deserves. Therefore, we shall turn from this sevenfold stupid and blasphemous wise man and learn what is right for free witnesses of the free gospel, and think and act accordingly.

Indeed, the greater the prince, especially in the church, the less his faults should be tolerated and the more sharply should they be rebuked. It is not right to bind the Word of God for the sake of a man [II Tim. 2:9]. God knows no respect of persons [Acts 10:34]. As is said in Psalm 119 [:46], "I will also speak of thy testimonies before kings, and shall not be put to shame." Kings are rebuked in Psalm 2 [:10]: "Now therefore, O kings, be wise; be warned, O rulers of the earth." Further examples are provided by all the prophets who, though taken from the common people, reproved kings, priests and, most especially, prophets. Whom did Christ upbraid? The people? Was it not rather only the great? Latomus tries to conceal these examples, and in lying fashion ignores what even children know. Isn't such flattery sickening?

It will be said, however, that Christ was God. True, but he emptied himself, took the form of a servant [Phil. 2:7]. It was not as God that he rebuked, but he was an example to all preachers that they should deal gently with the common people but not with the princes, for it is these latter who are responsible for the misfortunes of the multitude. Or must one be silent because God's wrath has made the evil into rulers, as Latomus flatteringly says? Indeed he is a man of profound insight who, in contrast to Christ, spares the princes, but not the common folk! Truly he is the best of appraisers, who rates crimes not according to deserts, but according to the rank of those who do them, and he blames the sins of the rulers on the people. For he teaches that crime should not be treated as crime, but only proclaimed when committed by

---

[13] Cf. LW 31, 237 n. 119.

the little man, and kept quiet when committed by the great. What do these enemies of the cross want except to remove the stumbling block of the cross? He knows there is no danger in rebuking the people, but this can't be done to the rulers without suffering for it. Men of this sort are hirelings, dumb dogs unable to bark [Isa. 56:10], who see the wolf coming and flee [John 10:12] or, rather, join up with the wolf. Christ isn't like this. His horns are caught in the thornbushes [Gen. 22:13]; descending, he touches the mountains and they smoke [Ps. 144:5]. He catches Leviathan's head in a fish trap,[14] penetrates into the terrible circle of his teeth,[15] pierces his jaw with a ring [Job 41:2] and, like Samson, slays lions [Judg. 14:6]. In short, the whole of Scripture testifies that the voice of the Lord breaks cedars [Ps. 29:5] and assaults only that which is exalted: the mountains of Israel, the oaks of Bashan, and lofty castles. This is clear to any child and yet exceeds the comprehension of a teacher in Israel [John 3:10].

I grant that one ought to respect superiors, but not to the extent of offending against the Word of God—which is God himself. We ought to obey him, rather than men [Acts 5:29]. If the faults of any magistrate must be tolerated, it is those of the secular, rather than the ecclesiastical authority; among other reasons, because the ecclesiastical [authority], unlike the secular, does not come from God. God does not recognize this priestly crowd which rules today. He has placed within the church only evangelists and ministers of the Word. Nor did men appoint these priests, for they rather exalted themselves against the will of men and of God, even as the giants did before the flood [Gen. 6:4]. However, the real reason they cannot be tolerated is because a bishop who neglects the Word, even if saintly, is a wolf and apostle of Satan while, in contrast, the failings of a civil magistrate do not endanger souls. He who does not guard the sheep against wolves differs not at all from a wolf. Although we know the devil does not sleep, we flatter the sleeping bishops; nay, rather, we defend the helpers of the devil and kill and condemn those who stir them up and remind them of their duties. I ask, what madness surpasses this? Thrice cursed be

---

[14] Cf. Vulgate version of Job 40:26 (corresponding to RSV 41:1).
[15] Cf. Vulgate version of Job 41:5 (corresponding to RSV 41:14).

146

the man who does the Lord's work fraudulently, who flatters the pope, who winks at and plays along with hell's wolf, and who has no pity on the many souls of his brethren, purchased by Christ's blood, but now perishing miserably. If Latomus had written nothing else, this single hellish recommendation would be enough to show that he is full of the spirit of Satan. What hope is there for these sophists to read, understand, and teach the Scriptures with godly zeal? How can they proclaim Christian doctrine? Lastly, how can one expect salvation from those who consider that advice wise which consists exclusively of the very words of Satan, and who take the affairs of the church, the faults of the shepherd, and salvation of souls as lightly as if they were only the crimes of a civil tyranny destructive of body and wealth? Wretched man that I am, I am afraid that I have been far too sparing and moderate toward the pope and the bishops, companions and playmates of the devil, and that I have not sufficiently considered the thousands of souls destroyed forever by these ultimate scourges of the world, this Antichrist together with his sophists and bishops.

"But," Latomus says, "sedition is dangerous and wouldn't improve matters." That sounds like the Jews. They feared that Christ would lead an insurrection so that the situation would not have become a hair's breadth better, but, on the contrary, worse. Should Christ have therefore kept silence? And who told you things won't become better? Is this a theological affirmation: "Because they don't listen, you shall be silent"? So the sedition which ravages bodies is feared, but that which ravages souls is excused. Thus, the prudent man fears what ought not to be feared and prefers outward peace to the eternal salvation of souls. Is there anyone able to detest as he deserves this cowardly slave, this corrupt sycophant, with his sickening advice? Such persons the pope rightly approves, and these are the people by whose judgment books are condemned and burnt.

Never is there less reason to fear sedition than when God's Word is taught, for God—who is the God of peace—is then present. Yet if these idolatrous priests refuse to hear, and proceed to increase their oppression by prohibiting, condemning, and burning, and if some rebellion or calamity should overtake them, then one would laugh and mock as does Wisdom in Prov. 1 [:26]. Responsibility lies not with the Word which has been proclaimed, but—as is said in the same chapter—with the godlessness which does not listen to the reproaches and reproofs of Wisdom. Nor can Latomus evade the issue by saying that he speaks, not of the gospel, but of reprimands, for we know that the gospel of Christ cannot be taught without reprimanding. As Wisdom says, its reproofs are despised [Prov. 1:30]. This [the Word of God] is the salt of the earth which stings in order to purify, pierces in order to heal, rebukes in order to save, kills in order to make alive. Whoever teaches otherwise babbles flattery, not the gospel.

We come now to another point. Out of respect for Louvanian foolishness, Latomus does not want to absolve me of the suspicion of hiding heresy under the pretext of academic discussion. As is asserted by the words of the Roman bishop, Leo[16] [Leo the Great, pope 440-461], which he frequently cites, one ought not to dispute about what is decided through the prophetic and gospel writings. Furthermore, my manner of disputing is not scholastic, not truly scholarly, but heretical, for I have engaged in it simply in order to attack, not in order to search for the truth. Here you see that Latomus freely invents these stories, for again I say in the beginning I disputed with complete sincerity, until I realized that our professors are idiots and swine. Since then, as he himself admits, I have not claimed that I was engaging in scholarly discussion, but rather was ready to expose myself to the fire [for the truth]. Our honorable friend lies. Never was I so hypocritical as to pretend merely to discuss what I was resolved to confess. However, let us suppose that it seems I wanted in the wickedness of my heart simply to argue. What authority forbids this? Leo's? Who gave Leo the authority to prohibit it? Or did this come from the faith of Latomus and the apathy of the sophists? Well then, did Jesus never refuse to answer the Jews when they maliciously tried to trick him? Is the word of Leo worth more than the example of Christ? This is the unconquerable and perpetual folly of the sophists: to exalt the words of men and conceal the words of God.

Here is something even more fantastic: Leo has acted only to prevent [his] opponents from engaging in disputation; he did not for-

---

[16] *Epistles* 42, 43, 47, and 78. Migne 54, 816-818; 821-826; 839-840; 907-909.

bid answering them. From this Latomus infers that there is no need to answer the opponent, and that it is on the basis of this highly prudent advice that the University of Louvain proceeded against Luther. So, if the Turks start a war against us—which, of course, they are not permitted to do—and will not be restrained, let us send the Louvainian theologians to them as ambassadors, for they will say, "You are not allowed to fight, for if you do we shall condemn you." Then we shall let them ravage, and vaunt ourselves as victors. Accordingly there is now no need of Paul's counsel and command that bishops hold firm to the sound doctrine of godliness so that they may be able to confute and stop the mouths of those who contradict it [Tit. 1:9]. Rather, it is enough that they ought not dispute, and that idiots and idols be secure. Why not lay aside prayer and all the arms of the Spirit? Let us stop resisting the devil and announce to him, "You are not allowed to disturb the church." That is what we do in reality. This is the faith of Latomus; this is how he deals with the sayings of the fathers.

Is it not indeed arrogant and presumptuous of so moderate a man impudently to assert that his views are prophetic and evangelical for [after all] the words of Leo refer to the prophets and gospels? [17] Were then the prophets and evangelists from Louvain? Truly Luther didn't know this, and by some great miracle, no man other than Latomus, I believe, knows of it. He is equally arrogant in asserting that my disputation is against the truth. This infallible judge and evangelist means by "truth" the opinions of the Louvainians, while the foolish Luther believes that it is the task of the judge, and not of the disputants, to determine the truth. It is also the conceit of sophists and the pride of firebrands to say that one should not have winked at my errors. They were not, and are not, proved to be such. But it is enough for him that the opinion of the evangelists and prophets of Louvain is the truth, and that these [my views] are contrary to it.

It is clearly evident that the main point of the council described by Latomus in his Preface was this: "We are the teachers, the judges; we cannot err, the world obeys us, and whatever we say is an article of faith, evangelical, prophetic." In my booklet[18]

---

[17] Cf. p. 148 n. 16.
[18] Cf. p. 135 n. †.

against them, didn't I plainly announce what Latomus here admits? If I were an enemy of this [theological] faculty, I would not have been able to censure more strongly the pride, conceit, rashness, ignorance, dullness, and malice of this council than does Latomus in his magnificent preface. Every letter breathes Moabitish pride [Num. 22:1ff.] and an arrogance which is even more than sophistic. So much can a single bull inflate a single bubble that Latomus speaks of this controversy as if everything were non-controversial, thereby practically making these distinguished asses into gods.

I approve and agree that erroneous books must be burnt, but not—as is foolishly maintained by these arrogant new prophets— those which have not yet been proved to be in error. I have myself burnt papist books[19] so that these professors of ours may see that the burning of paper requires neither skill nor ingenuity. Our scullions and serving boys can do as much. As is said, fire settles no arguments. The people in Acts 17 [19:19] did not burn books until they saw the truth and knew that they were harmful. Our professors have followed an easier course, but that which needs hard work and was part of their office they have left to the hearts of the faithful because the judgment stands: the Louvainians do not err.

I am sorry that at the time when those Jewish books annoyed the sophists[20] Maximilian did not turn their devices against them, remove these sophistic worms, grasshoppers, locusts, frogs and lice, and urge on them the pure and only Scriptures. This would have been much more beneficial advice, and far more necessary, than to debate the books of the Jews by exhausting the subject with such absurd and such stupid articles. I was heartily ashamed of the name of Christian because our prophets and elders made among us so great an ado about nothing. Yet we deserve no better thanks than what we now hope will shortly be given us. Meanwhile, it pleases me greatly that the pope has approved the judgment of the

---

[19] Cf. *LW* 31, 381.
[20] Luther refers to the controversy concerning the destruction of Jewish books involving the baptized Jew, Johann Pfefferkorn, and the humanist, Johann Reuchlin. Maximilian I (Emperor, 1508-1519) ordered the confiscation of Jewish books in 1509. The order was set aside in favor of securing the opinions of theological faculties at Köln, Mainz, Erfurt, Louvain, and Paris. The faculty at Louvain sided with Pfefferkorn.

five universities in this matter. What could be more appropriate to that renowned and glorious throne, that ultimate adversary of Christ?

Furthermore Latomus says that in the thesis which they have condemned, "The saints did not live without sin," he did not condemn the proposition itself but the false conclusions which we have drawn from it. And he marvels that we do not fear the world's judgment when we attack them because of this condemnation. I simply don't understand. Perhaps he requires his readers to understand intuitively this mysterious logic of his. As we shall see, he uses it in his book—perhaps he will there explain it. In the meantime, I laugh at the success and triumph on which he prides himself: namely, that he has shown that the fathers oppose me frequently, not occasionally; basically, not in passing, etc. "Unless," he says, "my opponents want to claim that the fathers were inconsistent." Latomus does not suppose that we would assert this, for he is sure we are not prophets. So he shouts, "Hurrah, hurrah, woe to the vanquished!" But we have not been idle while our antagonists have been reading these fathers whom they before despised. We have found that the fathers were often human, erring, inconsistent, and asleep. Thus even this triumph of Latomus rests on sand, and his book will collapse as soon as I attack it.

Finally this most gentlemanly host offers a foretaste of his booklet. He says that some of my statements are opposed to the principal articles of the faith. Let us drink up, and after finishing this elegant appetizer, we shall see what articles of faith are basic at Louvain.

THE FIRST of the condemned propositions is this: God commands the impossible.[21] The way this honest and upright man treats this proposition leaves me breathless. Even the addition of the words, "us," and, "without the grace of God," which he cannot deny are in my pamphlet, makes no difference to him. Now we ask, what is this hard and unmerciful principle of faith which denies that the

---

[21] Cf. *Disputation Against Scholastic Theology* (1517), Thesis 68: "Therefore it is impossible to fulfil the law in any way without the grace of God." *LW* 31, 14; cf. also *Explanations of the Ninety-Five Theses* (1518), Thesis 58, *LW* 31, 212-218.

precepts of God are impossible for us, that is, beyond our strength in the absence of grace? Was its author Paul, or Christ, or Moses? No, it is merely a human decretal, based on Jerome, according to which, "Whoever says God commands the impossible is anathema." [22] This obscure and ambiguous statement of a man is so emphasized by the sophists that they completely close their minds and do nothing but shout, "Anathema, anathema, anathema!" so that by their own voices you may judge them mad. One must be silent and yield to this human word no matter how many scriptural texts most obviously, clearly, and abundantly deny it. This tender decretal allows not a syllable of clarifying commentary, but it must be hurled and thrust with its full rigidity into all ears, and imprinted on all hearts, to the great peril of the faith and of the knowledge of the grace of God. All this must be done for no other reason than because it is a human statute, and because our professors are accustomed to using it as an infallible rule in their decisions. Thus this decretal has not a little strengthened free will.

This principle of faith is just as ambitious and insolent as Romulus, who would not let Remus, his brother and partner, rule in their joint kingdom. For there is another decree, alongside this scandalous one, which is genuinely godly, holding that, "Whoever says we can fulfil God's commands without divine grace is anathema." [23] No one emphasizes, extols, inculcates, and insists on this poor decree for, as I said, it has been forced to yield the kingdom to its brother. This is not a principal article of faith, and our teachers judge and condemn nothing by means of it. Why so? Because it is too godly. Almost all the professorial writings oppose it.

Besides, observe the extraordinary fairness of our professors. It is not enough for them to conceal this poor decree. They quench

---

[22] The statement which approximates Luther's quotation occurs in Jerome's *Dialogue Against the Pelagians*. Migne 23, 537.

[23] This may be a reference to the decrees of the Synod of Orange (529) which were confirmed by Pope Boniface II. Here we read: "7. Without grace, and merely from natural powers, we can do nothing which belongs to eternal salvation; neither think nor will in a proper manner (*ut expedit*), nor consent to the preaching of the gospel. . . . 20. God works much good in man which man does not work; but man works no good the performance of which God does not enable him to do. . . . 22. That which man has of his own is only falsehood and sin. What he possesses in truth and righteousness he has from God." Karl Joseph von Hefele, *Conziliengeschichte* (2d ed., Freiburg, 1873-1890), IV, 152ff.

and disembowel it by adding this insipid gloss: "God's commandments may be fulfilled in two ways: one way according to the
actuality of the deeds [commanded]; another, according to the
intention of him who commands." [24] By finding this way of escape,
how neatly they have cheated the truth! From this they deduce
that grace is not needed in order to fulfil God's commands, but only
for the fulfilment of a divine intention which is exacted above and
beyond the commandments. Thus God is an unjust overseer who
is not satisfied with the carrying out of his orders, but demands that
they be carried out by grace. So grace is not grace, but a sort of
exaction. Free will certainly satisfies God's law, but God is not
content with this. This is the most godless and blasphemous opinion
of all, but, as I said, this is what is done with this poor decree.

Now if with devout diligence, you wish to qualify the first
decretal [that God does not command the impossible] so that
"impossible" may also be taken in two senses—either in grace, or
outside of grace—they resist you with hand, and fire, and sword.
They won't let you touch it. So unless you profess exactly what it
says they shout: "He's a heretic, heretic, heretic, for he denies the
decrees of the fathers, disbelieves the Holy Church, and does not
hold to the principal articles of faith!" I implore you, what else
can you do, except let this generation of vipers prepare itself for
unquenchable fire? Can you doubt that the sophistic monster is
indeed the synagogue of Satan? Observe how confidently this
bombastic Latomus advances a decretal of one sort against me,
and how professorially and provincially he keeps silent about the
other. No doubt he wants to deceive the ears of the whole world,
so that no one will discover how godlessly the Louvainians behaved.

Even more, observe the importance attributed to this unholy
and blasphemous interpretation [of the second decretal]. They
teach that so much can be effected by works actually performed,

---

[24] The "modern" theologians (Duns Scotus, William Occam, Gabriel Biel)
whom Luther here opposes, reason that man can, as a result of his *free will*,
"actually do" the will of God, but only as a result of *grace* is he able to do it,
"in accordance with the intention of him who commands." Cf. Gabriel Biel,
Commentary on the Sentences, 1, II, dist. 28K, as quoted in Karl Holl,
Gesammelte Aufsätze zur Kirchengeschichte, I, 173. Cf. also, *Die Bekenntnis-
schriften der evangelisch-lutherischen Kirche* (Göttingen, 1952), p. 74 n. 2.

providing they are done with all of one's natural powers, that God necessarily and infallibly grants grace to them. This is, "to do what is in one," [25] even though Paul, and after him Augustine, loudly thundered that man through the law, without grace, only becomes worse, "because the law brings wrath" [Rom. 4:15] and, "came in to increase the trespass" [Rom. 5:20]. Thus they have cancelled the whole New Testament by this blasphemous opinion, and have led us unfortunates, now only nominally Christian, to the place where Christ is of absolutely no use except to teach us.

What need is there to report their frivolous talk about mere [informis], acquired, general, and special faith, as well as about the principal articles of the faith? It comes to this, that even if it is impossible without grace to fulfil the commands of God with respect to the intention of him who commands, still it is in your hands, and very easy, to acquire the grace which results from works actually performed. Thus free will reigns not merely in acting rightly, but even in fulfilling the intention of him who commands— that is, to put it plainly, in the very grace of God; for it is certainly in its [free will's] hand whether grace comes or does not come. From this they derive [teachings] concerning values that are morally good, [morally] neutral and—what shall I say?—as many principal articles of faith as there are sayings of the fathers, decrees of the councils, ordinances of the pope, and opinions of the professors. You see from this that the world is almost drowning in a flood of such principal articles of faith. What then of the consequences and conclusions drawn from these principles? And although this is the seven-times blasphemous "modern theology," [26] as no one can deny, that impure and impudent mouthpiece of Louvain dares in addition, with jaws wide open, to babble to the world that the teachings of the ancients are the same as those of these recent authors. He still persists in harmonizing their statements and opinions, so that he joins Christ to Belial, and mingles light with darkness.

However, if we look at the whole scene, we see how many

---

[25] Cf. *Disputation Against Scholastic Theology* (1517), Thesis 26. LW 31, 10.
[26] Cf. p. 153 n. 24.

important pronouncements of Scripture have been forced to yield to this scandalous doctrine. For instance, the whole of what Paul says in Rom. 8 [:3-4]: "For what the law, weakened by the flesh, could not do, God, sending his own Son in the likeness of sinful flesh and for sin, condemned sin in the flesh, in order that the righteousness of the law might be fulfilled in us." Unless you force "the righteousness of the law" to mean "the intention of Him who commands," you will see that Paul here explicitly affirms that it was impossible that the righteousness of the law be fulfilled in us by the law. If it was impossible by the law, which was given as a help, how much more impossible was it without the law! Indeed, it was so utterly impossible that the help of the law was a hindrance. For he says that the law was weakened in these impossible things, that is, it was not fulfilled because of the sins of the flesh. They, however, say that it was not fulfilled as He who commanded *this is close* intended. So then, contrary to what Paul says, it was not through *to Augustine,* the fault of the flesh that the law was unfulfilled, but through the *+ to Luther!* fault of what God intended, for, not being content with the fulfilment of the commandments, He required grace. Thus the law was strengthened through the flesh, but weakened through the intention of Him who commanded.

These are mad and blasphemous voices. But, as I said, Paul's divine voice must be silenced among moths and corruption so that this principal article of faith, the decretal, may reign. Yet he says in Acts 15 [13:38-39] that, "Through this man forgiveness of sins is proclaimed to you, and by him everyone that believes is justified from everything from which you could not be justified by the law of Moses." Apparently the Apostle didn't know enough Greek to be able to say that it is difficult to be justified—he had to say that it was impossible. Again in Acts 15 [:10] Peter says that this is a burden, "which neither our fathers nor we have been able to bear." Peter, what are you saying? that they cannot bear it? Have they not borne it as far as the "actual performance" of works is concerned? Have they not sacrificed, been circumcised, and observed everything? I see that you [Peter] do not know the principal articles of faith and rave in many ways against the theology of Louvain. At this point Latomus says, "Peter speaks [only] of circumcision, as is shown by the beginning of the chapter." Could they then not bear circumcision? No, he speaks rather of the law of Moses. Just a little earlier it is written: "Some believers who belonged to the party of the Pharisees rose up, and said, 'It is necessary to circumcise them and to charge them to keep the law of Moses'" [Acts 15:5]. This is the burden which Peter says is impossible. What does he finally decide? He says, "But we believe we shall be saved through the grace of the Lord Jesus, just as they will" [Acts 15:11]. Peter, don't you know about "the actual performance" of works which carries the burden and compels grace to come?

I shall omit what is told the Hebrews [Heb. 7]—and not just in one place—regarding this impossibility. Christ also said in Matt. 19 [:24], "It is easier for a camel to go through the eye of a needle than for a rich man to enter the kingdom of God." When his disciples—shocked that it is impossible to be saved—said, "Who then can be saved?" [Matt. 19:25], he knew nothing of this principal article of faith. He did not deny, but rather affirmed, the impossibility of this salvation. Nor did he change it into something merely difficult, but spoke thus: "With men this is impossible, but with God all things are possible" [Matt. 19:26]. He said this not only of the rich, but in response to the question, "Who then can be saved?" Therefore, since the ministry of the Spirit—that is, as the Apostle says, the preaching of grace—ought to prevail especially in the New Testament, one must wish either that Jerome had never made this statement [condemning the assertion that God commands the impossible], or that it had remained buried in darkness. For Christians should preach nothing but the glory of God, that is, to confess our impossibility and God's possibility even as Christ does here. All the shameful obstructions—of which this decretal is one of the greatest—able to establish and inflate free will must be removed so that the knowledge of the pure grace of God and of our misery may be preserved.

However, it greatly disturbed this man [Latomus] that I said that even in grace not all the commandments of God are perfectly fulfilled in this life. This is not my opinion, but Augustine's in chapter 19 of the *Retractions* I[27]—at this we shall look later. Now

---

[27] Augustine, *Retractions,* I, 19, 3. Migne 32, 615.

when I said this does not happen, I did not deny that it could happen. This splendid sophist has not learned his logic well enough to know that, "does not happen" differs from "cannot happen." He infers, "Therefore you say it cannot happen." Yet who doubts that God could give to someone so much grace that he would fulfil [the Law] completely (as we believe he did in the case of the Blessed Virgin), granted that he does not do it in every case? If the decretal opposes this, let it go hang and be damned.

This writer is afflicted with another fault from which sophists always suffer. Latomus' entire book equivocates by begging the question, which is the very worst way of arguing. The perpetual foolishness of the sophists is to seize upon that which must first of all be proved and demonstrated, and assume that it is an infallible rule of faith. This is what he does here. Latomus ought first to have demonstrated that, "The perfect fulfilment of God's commands," signifies that, "The commandments are completely satisfied so that forgiveness is not needed." It is this which Augustine, and I, and the Scriptures deny. He, however, rushes on unhesitatingly, secure in the possession of a principal article of faith which needs no demonstration. While believing that he devastates everything with the sword of the Spirit, he plays the fool before us with the stubble and straw of his [personal] opinion. Not even this decretal of his supports this view, for we say that all the commandments of God are fulfilled, not by our perfect deeds, but in the abundantly forgiving grace of God. Here there is nothing impossible, but rather total perfection. Thus we say something much better than if we were to assert that everything could be fulfilled by works alone without the pardoning mercy of God. As I said, he must prove that his "impossible" means what he thinks it does. However, our opponents themselves admit that grace is never fully given in this life. Since grace is not granted except for the fulfilment of the commands of God, it follows that, in so far as these are not fulfilled, to that extent grace is not complete. Because the professors say this, it is not to be condemned; if Luther had said it, it would have been an error.

THE SECOND THESIS: Sin remains after baptism. Latomus condemns this proposition—which I have proved on the authority of Paul [Rom. 7][28]—by the authority of Gregory.[29] Viciously begging the question, he explains that in Paul "sin" is not "sin," but "weakness." He acts as if he had successfully established that one must expound the passage as if Paul did not know which words he ought to use, or as if I am not permitted to use his words. Let us look at the proof from Gregory: "Christ said, 'He who has bathed is clean all over'" [John 13:10]. I shall disregard the carelessness of Latomus who promised to weigh, not merely count, the witnesses—that is (he speaks with sophistic artifice) he wants to count, not weigh them. Instead I shall dispute with Gregory. "Tell me, Gregory, where does Christ say what you say? Shouldn't you cite Christ's words textually? You quote, 'He who has bathed is clean all over,' but Christ really said, 'He who has bathed does not need to wash, except for his feet, but he is clean all over' [John 13:10]. From whence comes this soiling of the feet after bathing? Doesn't he assert complete cleansing in such a way that the feet, nevertheless, have need of washing? What can be made of this except that sin is completely forgiven in baptism and yet remains, even as Paul says in Rom. 7 [:18ff.]. The feet are to be washed all through life, even in the case of those who are cleansed. Therefore Christ says, 'You also ought to wash one another's feet'" [John 13:14].

Doesn't this text speak for me, and against Latomus? All sins are washed away, yet something remains to be bathed. The meaning is clear. How could all be washed away unless they were pardoned and remitted through grace? How could cleansing still be necessary unless [sin] still remained? We shall come back to this later. At the moment, Latomus' confidence must be destroyed so that he may see that sometimes the fathers were but men, and so come to recognize the fallacious way—I have called it begging the question—in which he argues. He ought first to have shown that, "to be clean all over," means that no sin remains after baptism. Gregory's words

---

[28] Cf. *The Leipzig Debate* (1519), Thesis 2. *LW* 31, 317.
[29] *Epistles*, IX, 45. Migne 77, 1162. "In the gospel the Lord says, 'He who is bathed does not need to wash, but is clean all over.' If, therefore, sins are not entirely removed in baptism, how is it that he who is bathed is clean all over? For he cannot be said to be clean all over if any sin remains. . . . Nothing, therefore, remains of the contagion of sin to him whom the very One who redeemed declares clean all over."

do not demand this interpretation, or if they do, they must be denied. Our opponents, having injected their own views into the words of the fathers, rush forward as [would] an ass under the pelt of a lion. These deceitful workers manufacture principal articles of faith for us, not from the opinions of the fathers, but from their own, which they impose on what the fathers say.

THE THIRD THESIS: It is not necessary to confess all mortal sins to the priests. Latomus says that this was condemned by a general council, and that therefore it is indeed condemned—this, according to his logic, is a necessary inference. Yet what Scripture supports that council? If a council is valid without Scripture—if it is enough for the capped and shaven to congregate—why don't we assemble the wooden and stone statues from the churches, place mitres and caps upon them, and say that there is a general council? Isn't it most villainous for a council to act and decide apart from God's Word? In a book of mine[30] published in German—which I shall put into Latin when time permits—I completely deny (and at greater length) that confession should be required. The traditions of men must be abolished from the church. Latomus agrees in his *Dialogue*[31] that men can repeal them; and this rule of confession is nothing other than a tyrannical exaction of the pope unsupported on any scriptural grounds.

THE LAST THESIS: Every good work of the saints while pilgrims in this world is sin.[32] He makes this out to be absurd. To this great man it seems directly opposed to the [Athanasian] Creed: "They who have done good go into life everlasting."[33] Here he triumphs in earnest and insists that it is shameful to ask for reasons in such a matter. Thus this ferocious man speaks threateningly so that no one will make common cause with me. This is what the Jews did before Pilate: "If this man were not an evildoer, we would not have handed him over to you" [John 18:30]. Truly they are shameless and stupid mortals who do not believe at the mere nod of our Louvainian professors. As if they were like other men who can err

---

[30] Luther refers to *Concerning Confession and the Pope's Power to Order It* (1521). *WA* 8, 129ff. Actually it was not published until *Against Latomus* had appeared, and Luther never found time for a Latin version.
[31] Cf. Introduction, p. 135 n. §.
[32] Cf. *Heidelberg Disputation* (1518), Theses 6 and 7. *LW* 31, 45-46.
[33] P. Schaff, *Creeds of Christendom* (New York, 1931), II, 70.

and will evil! This is out of the question, for their act has been approved by the bishop of their bulls, that is, bubbles by a bubble.

Consider the villainy of these men who never fail to interpret the sin which I mentioned as present in good works as being of the sort which they call "damnable," for it is only this kind which opposes [the statement], "They who have done good shall enter into life everlasting." They themselves admit that good deeds in which venial sin is present are not against this Creed. They even maintain what Gerson says: "No venial sin is venial by nature, and God's grace takes away more than it positively bestows, so that it is only by the mercy of God that sin is venial." [34] You will be surprised that Latomus does not at first deny the possibility of venial sin—for instance, negligence—in every good work. According to him, it is not absurd that in this way there could be sin in a good work. This is not against the Creed. And the only reason for this is that I did not say it while they did.

Later on I shall force them to agree—perhaps they will willingly concede—that it is uncertain that any work of any man, no matter how good, is without sin, for [even] they compel no man to assert this of his good works. Now notice that what is uncertain can nevertheless be—perhaps even they think so. Yet if someone else says this, it is so absurd and contrary to the Creed that they would like to think nothing more absurd could possibly be said. Yet this uncertainty prevents them from asserting the opposite, and therefore from denying or condemning my thesis. Latomus deals with all the statements he cites from the fathers by begging the question, for he does not prove that his quotations apply; that is, that [they say] there is no sin in [good] works. No matter how many of the fathers say there are good works, this does not condemn [my thesis]—nor do I deny anything that they say.

In short, dear reader, you have in this preface of Latomus the portrait (*eikonos*) of a sophist. Here you see the sophist's picture superbly sketched. In appearance and words it simulates modesty, but it is so swollen with haughtiness, arrogance, pride, malice, villainy, rashness, superciliousness, ignorance, and stupidity that there is nothing to surpass it.

---

[34] John Gerson (d. 1429), *Opera Omnia*, ed. Du Pin (Antwerp, 1706), III, 10.

The first article attacked by Latomus is this: Every good work
is sin.[35]

First, he deduces unacceptable consequences from this thesis;
second, he opposes it with contrary [views]; third, he impugns my
premises. In driving this Sennacherib [II Kings 19:28; cf. Isa. 37:29]
back to his own land, I shall begin with the last point and thus
start by defending my own position.

In order to deprive me of that wonderful verse in Isa. 64 [:6]
which reads, "We have all become like one who is unclean, and
all our righteous deeds are like filthy rags," he interprets it so that
neither he nor I can use it. He makes the application of the verse
uncertain, citing some who think it refers to the Assyrian captivity
of the Jews, others to the Babylonian, and others to the Roman.
Together with Jerome and Lyra,[36] he agrees with the last view.
Fourthly, and finally, if it applied to believers, he takes refuge in
synecdoche, a frequent figure of speech in Scripture. According
to this, "all righteous deeds" would stand for "some righteous
deeds." However, he advances nothing definite. Jerome's authority
is not enough, for, as that author himself wrote to Augustine,[37] he
was accustomed to do little more than recount the views of others
in his commentaries [and so Latomus'] opinion wavers.

This, then, is the first reply to everything which he infers,
establishes, and builds upon this opinion. In fighting one must use
certainties. To Latomus this authority is uncertain, and useless
against me. I, then, must seek one which is powerful and sure
against him. First, I agree and prove that this verse applies to the
captivity of the Jews and is spoken in the name [*persona*] of the
captives. It does not refer to the Assyrian captivity, for the city of
Jerusalem was not then destroyed nor the tribe of Judah taken
captive, and yet this is what the prophet here laments. Now if I
can show that it must not be understood of the Roman captivity,

---

[35] *Op. cit.,* p. 159 n. 32.
[36] Nicholas of Lyra (d. 1340) was the French exegete who stressed the literal
as opposed to the allegorical sense of Scripture. Luther frequently cites him in
his commentaries on books of the Bible.
[37] *Jerome to Augustine,* Migne 22, 919: "I confess frankly that I read the
writings of the fathers, and complying with universal usage put down in my
commentaries a variety of explanations that each may adopt from the number
given the one which pleases him."

I shall have demonstrated that it necessarily refers to the Babylonian.

First, let us look at the text [Isa. 64:5-12]: "Thou meetest him that is joyful and works righteousness, those that remember thee in thy ways. Behold, thou wast angry, and we sinned; in our sins we have been a long time, and we shall be saved. We have all become like one who is unclean, and all our righteous deeds are like filthy rags. We all fade like a leaf, and our iniquities, like the wind, take us away. There is no one that calls upon thy name, that bestirs himself to take hold of thee; for thou hast hid thy face from us, and hast delivered us into the hand of our iniquities. Yet, O Lord, thou art our Father; we are the clay, and thou art our potter; we are all the work of thy hand. Be not exceeding angry, O Lord, and remember not our iniquity forever. Behold, consider, we are all thy people. Thy holy cities have become a wilderness, Zion has become a wilderness, Jerusalem a desolation. Our holy and beautiful house, where our fathers praised thee, has been burned by fire, and all our pleasant places have become ruins. Wilt thou restrain thyself at these things, O Lord? Wilt thou keep silent, and afflict us sorely?"

Latomus, like a champion jumper, leaps boldly over the barrier opposed to his interpretation by the words "and we shall be saved." [38] These cannot be understood of reprobate Jews, but are without doubt spoken in the name [*persona*] of elect believers. Afterwards, coming to, "Thou meetest him that is joyful," he says, "Who is this who works righteousness, whom the Lord meets as one that is joyful? If these words, as M. [artin] would like, are to be understood of any believers of any time" — then, perhaps fearing to be a poor interpreter, he suddenly falls silent as if he had bitten a pebble, so that one doesn't know what he asks.

Latomus agrees with his authorities who hold that these things are said in the name of those who look toward Jerusalem and the temple, and who wish to rebuild them so that they may sacrifice and praise God as had their fathers. This truth I also affirm, not because they say it—for I believe nothing because of them—but because the text which convinces them also convinces me. Other-

[38] RSV reads, "and shall we be saved?" (RSV also has a footnote, "Hebrew obscure"; argument based on Vulgate text.)

wise, why would the prophet so copiously multiply complaints, and so diligently lay before God the destruction of the city, if he were not asking God to be merciful and rebuild it? Surely it is because he asks to be healed that he exposes the wound to the physician. Finally, when he says, "And all our pleasant places have become ruins," he adds, "Wilt thou restrain thyself at these things, O Lord?" What does, "Do not restrain thyself," mean except, "Do not remain idle"? For if He never rebuilds, He indeed cuts Himself off from what has been once destroyed. Is it not therefore most clear and certain that these words are groans and prayers for the rebuilding of Jerusalem? Otherwise I do not see why our author presses, insists, amplifies, and enlarges so much. So with these obstinate sophists one must doubt even the self-evident until it becomes certain.

It follows that what the prophet pleads for with these words and groans is of such a nature that it can be rebuilt. The Holy Spirit is not so foolish as to incite unto prayer for the manifestly impossible. Now it is definitely the case that, after [the appearance of] Christ, God is to be worshiped neither in a mountain, nor in Jerusalem, but in spirit and truth, as Christ says in John 4 [:21, 23]. The Spirit made known this future mystery to Isaiah so that he knew and foretold it more clearly than any one since David. At the same time Haggai [2:9] predicts this "final temple." Daniel [9:27; 12:11] also foresaw that at the end, after Christ, there would come a destruction so conclusive that it would be impossible to repair it [the temple] as the Jews hoped. Therefore these complaints and entreaties cannot refer to the times after Christ, but to the Babylonian captivity alone, in which it was right for the soul to hope, desire, and pray for the restoration of the city.

We must beware of attributing blasphemy to the Holy Spirit as if he sometimes spoke in the name of the godless and blasphemous. Psalm 109 [:7] plainly says that the prayer of the Jews during the Roman captivity was sinful and abominable. In Ps. 16 [:4] Christ says that he will not take their names upon his lips. How then could the spirit of Isaiah in the name of blasphemers recite their blasphemies before God with so much humility, such godly professions, so sincere a heart and zeal? His prayer then must also have been sinful and blasphemous. It is indeed scriptural that the

Spirit prays about and for the godless, but never in their name. It is the Spirit of the Body of Christ, and helps the saints in their weaknesses, groaning and interceding for them [Rom. 8:26]. Who does not feel that Isaiah's prayer is even of this sort? So Christ wept over Jerusalem, but not in the name of Jerusalem; Paul also [prays] for the Jews, but not in the name of the Jews. But here Isaiah identifies himself with those for whom, and with whom, he prays.

Therefore, since it would be dangerous to assert that of which there is no example in Scripture, we must limit ourselves to what is. Let us confess that the Spirit of the Body of Christ never speaks, works, lives, and abides in the name of an alien, that is, diabolical, body, but always in the name of its own Body. Whoever praises God cannot bear the name of him who blasphemes God, for he who bears the name, and He whose name he bears, ought at least to agree in word, meaning, and desire, even if not in power and action.

There is an irreconcilable opposition between these Jews and the Spirit of God. Yet if He spoke through Isaiah in their name, would He not much more speak in the same manner even today? His words remain, and the present occasion strongly urges it. We cannot deny that these are the words of the Spirit, for they are in the sacred canon. If they are of the Spirit, then they are godly, faithful, and holy, and this, as you see, befits the character of the Jews least of all. If He were merely to quote the words of the ungodly, then the opinion of our opponents could be accepted, but it cannot be admitted that He prays and acts in their name. In Isaiah [14:13; 10:8f.; 36:4f.] the Spirit does recite the proud words of Babylon, Ashur, and Sennacherib. In Ezekiel [29:3] He recounts the words of the great dragon of the river, and of many others, but He speaks only in the name of the godly and of those who belong to Him.

This is clearly stated in the text: "Behold, consider, we are all thy people" [Isa. 64:9]. Now don't we know who God's people are? The Jews are no longer this people, as is said in Hosea [1:9]: "Call his name Not my people, for you are not my people and I am not your God." But our text says, "Yet, O Lord, thou art our Father; we are the clay, and thou art our potter; we are all the work of thy hand" [Isa. 64:8]. Are the Jews now sons and not rather

164

enemies? Are they not potter's clay which would not be molded because they do not know the potter? Are they not now rather the work of Satan than of the potter? It is captious to object that they call [Him] "Father," "potter," "maker," only in a general sense. The prophet speaks in the Spirit, and his words proceed from the disposition of the Spirit in which God is Father only of the children who are faithful, just as in the Lord's Prayer we worship the Father in the Spirit. [Latomus] will not hear the name of the "Father" mentioned, especially in the New Testament, if the Spirit does not inspire it. However, this definitely ought to be expected if these things were said in the name of the Jews, since, as I said, the occasion is urgent, and the words still remain.

It is now, I think, sufficiently plain that these words cannot be said in the name of the unfaithful people. This will be even plainer when we see their full meaning.

Now Latomus contends that universal statements in Scripture usually have a particular meaning. This is the case in, "All seek their own" [Phil. 2:21], for this does not apply to Titus [Timothy?] and many others. Also here, where all righteousness is called unclean, he wants to understand this as some of the righteousness of some people. Latomus is here either blinded by malice and envy, or he is notably stupid, for he not merely plays with inept examples, but he rashly misinterprets this figure of speech. If it is permissible to play so arbitrarily and groundlessly with figures of speech, what prevents giving new meanings to everything? I might say that Ps. 1 [:3], "In all that he does, he prospers," can be understood as, "In some things he prospers"; Ps. 2 [:11], "Blessed are all who take refuge in him," as, "Some who take refuge in him"; Ps. 5 [:6], "Thou destroyest all those who speak lies," as, "Some who speak lies." I ask you, what jesting with Scripture does this lead to? It is not the business of so great a theologian as Latomus to assert what can be said, but what ought to be said. It is not a question of what whimsical trifling can do, but of what conscientious interpretation must show, especially as this braggart proclaims himself as one who weighs, not merely enumerates, the testimonies of Scripture, and as one who convicts Luther of wrongly citing them. Does saying, "I can understand it thus and thus," constitute a weighing of the testimony of Scripture and a demonstration of the incorrectness of my use of it? Haven't I already shown that the error of which these sophists are guilty is that they are able to understand everything in "one way or the other," but never wish to understand it as they should? They don't confute the adversary, but rather confound the divine Scriptures.

Next, if Latomus so vividly remembers this figure of speech in this place, why does he snore so loudly in what follows where it is said, "There is no one that calls upon thy name, that bestirs himself to take hold of thee"? [Isa. 64:7]. Couldn't he also make this particular—that is, "some," or "many," call not upon thy name? In this way he would have guarded against the compulsion to make so awkward and insipid a digression in order to prove that there have never lacked those who call upon the name of the Lord. Doesn't this figure of speech occur in the negative? What about Isa. 57 [:1]: "The righteous man perishes, and no one lays it to heart; devout men are taken away, while no one understands"? Didn't Isaiah understand what he himself said? Or is only Latomus allowed to find a figure of speech wherever he wishes and where it doesn't suit [him], find none. This prudent man perceives that, unless figuratively interpreted, "All righteousness is unclean," argues against him. Therefore it must be invalidated. In contrast, "There is no one who calls," does not oppose Luther when it is figuratively understood, and so one must not understand it that way. Meanwhile this great man did not consider that by such rash arbitrariness he would supply his opponent with plenty of openings. I have the same right to alter the meaning of these two expressions so that now both, now one or the other, are figurative or not figurative. But is this the way to deal with Scripture?

Again, this distinguished theologian, who figuratively assigns, "All our righteousness is unclean" to believers, afterwards applies this verse literally to the final destruction of [Jerusalem]. Our opponents interpret the passage in this way so that they may have somebody of whom it can be non-figuratively asserted that all their righteousness is unclean. So Latomus claims the freedom to be arbitrary in explaining the Scriptures even when he adduces it in earnest and fights for the faith against the worst sort of heretics. If—Christ forbid—I were a heretic and were confronted with this kind of smoke screen [larvae], I would be confirmed in my view and would hold all their opinions suspect because of their uncertainty and trifling. I would not believe that they were genuine and true. So much the more, therefore, do I now condemn and detest them.

Well then, farewell to these Louvainians and their new way of theologizing—and with one word I shall conquer and overthrow the whole of Latomus. He so often cites authorities, sophistically reasoning that a good work is not sinful, that I shall resort to this subterfuge, synecdoche, and say that a good work is to be understood as partly good and, similarly, a sin as partly sinful. He himself thus uses synecdoche to explain that some of the righteousness of some [people] is not well done. What is easier than to conquer with weapons taken from the enemy himself? Observe that this is the Louvainian and Latomian way of separating the meaning of Scripture from its context, consequences, and circumstances. Yet to call them blockheads and stumps is [considered] treason.

So much for this "Louvanity" and veritable vanity. Let us replace it with Augustine's opinion, which is that of ordinary common sense and of truth itself. "Figurative language proves nothing." [39] Although he says this of sacred types [of the relationship of image and reality in the realm of the holy], it can be properly applied at least as well to rhetorical figures of speech. In no writings, least of all the divine, is it right in mere whimsy to grasp at figurative meanings. These ought to be shunned, and the pure, simple, original sense should be sought, unless the context or an evident absurdity forces one to recognize a figurative expression. Wouldn't there otherwise be a Babel of words and languages in the world? Silence would then be better than speech. Let us present a crude example of this, for our professors at Louvain are excessively crude. When the poet says, "From Troy's fair stock shall Caesar come," [40] you can, following your whim, decide to take this figuratively to mean that "Caesar" stands instead of "Caesars," but will you convince the grammarians? Again, you can suppose that the verse, "Take care, O Roman, to rule the nations with

---

[39] Not a quotation, but the idea is expressed, for example, in Letter 93 (to Vincentius) cap. VIII. Migne 33, 333-335.
[40] Virgil, *Aeneid*, I, 286.

imperial sway," [41] refers literally to a single Roman citizen, but what would the grammarians say? Similarly in Ps. 16 [:11], "Thou dost show me the path of life": your fancy might lead you to say that the path is an earthly one, trodden by bodily feet, yet you would then follow error instead of the [true] path. What need is there of further examples? We acknowledge that everything is full of figures, but they must be considered with [sound] judgment for which no certain and adequate rule can be formulated. However, I have yet to find an example of the sort of figurative use of universal expressions which Latomus here imagines. We are guided by two [rules]: [we assume figurative speech if the result would otherwise lead to] absurdity of meaning, and the circumstances in which the words are spoken. Thus in the case of the, "sword upon the thigh," in Ps. 45 [:3], and the two swords of the disciples in Luke 20 [22:38], the context more forcefully shows that they are not made of iron than does the absurdity [of such an interpretation]—though that also holds. On the other hand, when it is said that he who has left a wife shall receive a hundredfold in this life [Matt. 19:29], it is the absurdity of the [literal meaning] which compels us to understand that this does not refer to physical leaving and receiving.

Thus in the present case, it is not enough for my Latomus to say that "all" can be figuratively understood as "some." I will tolerate no figure as long as it is not required by an absurdity or by the necessity of the circumstances. I shall urge upon him that he ought to understand the simple, proper, and primary meaning of, "All our righteousness is unclean." He ought to do this, I say, because there is here no absurdity nor opposition to what is found in Scripture. So this text still stands unconquered and laughs at Latomus' efforts and his premature boasting. It proves that all our righteousness is unclean, and that every good work is sin. Yet I marvel that he has here forgotten the evasion that he uses everywhere else. He could say that uncleanness is nothing else than imperfection. This is what he does with the words "fault" and "sin" on the ground that he and his fellows are used to devising meanings for words, and natures for things [substantias res] in accordance

---

[41] Ibid., VI, 851.

with conjecture. But this high-spirited hero hoped that an outstanding victory would for once make him more notable than had this other subterfuge.

One may add another reason why a figurative interpretation is here out of place. In Scripture, as a rule, where the universal—exclusive, as one might say, of all synecdoche and particularity—without any doubt is absolutely and perfectly asserted, the universal affirmative is not simply stated, but the universal negative is added. It is thus in Rom. 3 [:11-12], quoting from Ps. 14 [:3], "All have turned aside, together they have gone wrong. No one understands; no one seeks for God; no one does good." Here Paul uses and confirms this rule, concluding that absolutely all Jews and Greeks—that is, all the sons of men—are under sin. The Apostle's argument in this passage would collapse if synecdoche were not excluded, for then—contrary to his intention—he would demonstrate nothing regarding the necessity of grace. Such also is the case when he quotes [in Rom. 4:7] from Ps. 32 [:1-2]: "Blessed are those whose iniquities are forgiven, and whose sins are covered. Blessed is the man against whom the Lord will not reckon sin, and in whose spirit there is no deceit." Notice that in order fully and comprehensively to express forgiveness, it was not enough to state affirmatively that sins are forgiven and covered, but he added that they are not imputed, and that deceit is not in the spirit. In the same way Lam. 2 [:2] says, "The Lord has destroyed without mercy all the beauteous things of Jacob," in order to show that nothing beautiful remained. In Ps. 28 [:5] it is said, "He will break them down and not build them up," so that one might not suppose that He will only partly destroy them. In accordance with this same rule, Isa. [64:6ff.] combines many affirmations and negations, saying, "We have all become like one who is unclean, and all our righteous deeds are like filthy rags. We all fade like a leaf, and our iniquities, like the wind, take us away." What follows is stated negatively: "There is no one that calls upon thy name, that bestirs himself to take hold of thee." This means that all righteous deeds are polluted to such a degree that absolutely no one has anything which in Thy sight is good enough to cause Thee to restrain Thy anger. Thus the very foundation of this frivolous invention of Latomus is overturned. Synecdoche, to be sure, is a most sweet and necessary figure of speech and a symbol of God's love and mercy, for sometimes when He is said to strike and destroy, one is not to understand that He strikes all or completely annihilates, for He touches the whole when He touches a part.[42]

However, I argue in this way not because I concede to Latomus that this figurative mode of expression, synecdoche, is present in the places he adduces, but because I admit that this figure is frequently found in Scripture. It may be that this sophist, as he attacks so great a rock with fragile straws, will see that it is easy enough to dispose of his little ditties, and in more than one way. Now I do not remember seeing any scriptural texts which use that form of synecdoche in which a universal expression stands for the particular. Latomus forces synecdoche upon the ones he cites, for they have not the least trace of it. He even refutes himself when he says that an expression of this sort ought to be limited to its subject matter, so that Isaiah's, "to destroy the whole earth" [Isa. 13:5], obviously refers not to the world, but to the land of Babylon. Similarly in the Gospel of Luke (2 [:1]), the "world" which is mentioned is not the totality of all lands, but the Roman Empire. "There was darkness over all the land" [Matt. 27:45], is thought to refer only to the land of the Jews, for the Roman authors do not mention this darkness (except for the account of Dionysius of Heliopolis, whose extant epistle is in my judgment certainly spurious).[43] In addition to all this, our author does not use synecdoche when he applies "all righteousness is unclean" to the people in the Roman captivity.

Now in the case of the verse, "The whole head is sick, etc." [Isa. 1:5], there are two reasons why synecdoche is not present: First, because the expression is universal; next, because the negation is added, "there is no soundness in it" [Isa. 1:6]. Also, as Paul explains in Rom. 9 [:29], this pertains to the Jews forsaken [by God] after Christ in whom the whole head is truly sick, with no health in it. However, they were already sick in the time of Christ, for he speaks against those who were then, and remain, outside of

---

[42] Following the conjecture of Robert Frick in *MA*³, suppl. vol. 6, p. 170, the sentence beginning with "Synecdoche, to be sure . . . part," has been transposed.
[43] The Pseudo-Dionysius (or Dionysius the Areopagite) was reputed to be an immediate disciple of the Apostle Paul, but actually lived much later, presumably in the fifth century.

Christ. Thus also the verse in Jeremiah [6:13], "For from the least to the greatest of them, every one is greedy for unjust gain," certainly applies to the mass of those who are avaricious, excluding the godly. So Paul's statement, "They all look after their own interests" [Phil. 2:21], also refers to its [particular] object and subject matter. Otherwise, when Paul concludes that all men are under sin [Rom. 3:9], and says that all fall short of the glory of God [Rom. 3:23], he would have included himself, Abraham, and all the godly, but he spoke against those that acted without true faith. So, as I said, Latomus—disturbed by the troublesome consciousness of error, and desiring to escape, but not being able to—plays with inept examples. The evident proof that he is convicted by the unconquered truth is that this miserable man so anxiously seeks so many hiding places. Consciousness of truth does not thus waver and quake. This wretched sophist seeks these remedies too late.

Yet we do find this figure, synecdoche, in the gospel: for instance, "So will the Son of man be three days and three nights in the heart of the earth" [Matt. 12:40]; similarly, "The robbers who were crucified with him, reviled him" [Matt. 27:44]; and most clearly in Ps. 78 [:18], "They tested God in their heart by demanding food." This [last] is said in reproach, as if of the whole people of Israel. In contrast, Ps. 105 [:40]—"They asked and he brought quails"—is said in praise; but in both cases we find synecdoche, the whole standing for a part. It is especially in the prophets that this figure of speech often dominates. Yet in the present case, Isaiah's words cannot be thus applied to "some," for he includes himself and does not simply speak to others, as in the places mentioned above. He personifies, that is, presents a person who speaks of himself when saying, "we all," "all our righteous deeds." He does not say "they," or "you," etc.

There still remains the problem of how these things can refer to the faithful. It is not, I believe, necessary to prove that they were indeed faithful and godly, for, in obedience to God at the word of Jeremiah, they had delivered themselves into captivity, some voluntarily, others because they were finally coerced. Christ and the apostles were still in their flesh.[44] We could call them godly and faithful simply because of this, since it is rightly believed that the

---

[44] That is, were to be born from them.

line of Christ's descent through the entire human race even to the Virgin Mother was an elect and holy seed. I shall therefore first summarize, and then take up the text.

I have taught[45] that our good works are of such sort that they cannot bear the judgment of God, as is said in Ps. 101 [Ps. 143:2], "Enter not into judgment with thy servant; for no man living is righteous before thee." Since, however, His judgment is true and just, He does not condemn works which are wholly blameless. He wrongs no one, but as it is written, "He will render to every man according to his works" [Rom. 2:6]. It follows, therefore, that our good works are not good unless His forgiving mercy reigns over us. Our good works are evil, if the judgment of Him who renders to every man threatens us. This is the way to teach the fear of God and hope in him. Yet in accordance with Latomus' rantings, my calumniators condemn this godly wisdom, extol their works, deprive men of fear and hope in God, make them proud with their pestilent doctrines, and invent a good work which is worthy of praise, glory, and reward.

This teaching I have confirmed with this text of Isaiah's—and rightly so, as far as I can now see; indeed, it is now more firmly established for me than before the wanton mockery of Latomus. Isaiah means to say that God, being angry and having thrust the people into captivity and destruction, does not deal with them in mercy, but in judgment—no, rather in wrath. Even if under this judgment there are just and godly men whose righteousness—apart from judgment and under mercy's rule—could be pure, still nothing of this is now of any use to them, so that they are like the most polluted of those who are even now sinners. God in this wrath does not recognize them, but abandons the godly and ungodly alike. He does not restrain himself. What else, then, does he do but so deal with those that are just that he makes it appear they are not just? Nevertheless, because he judges truly and righteously, it must be that those who are under this judgment are at the same time righteous, and yet unclean. In this way he shows that no one ought to rely on his own righteousness, but solely on His mercy. This is also the meaning of Job 9 [:22]: "It is all one; therefore I say,

---

[45] Cf. *The Leipzig Debate* (1519), Thesis 2. *LW* 31, 317.

he destroys both the blameless and the wicked." This is not said of him whose innocence is counterfeit, and yet he destroys him not unjustly. So also here, Isaiah means the genuinely just and pure, for the Spirit does not speak in the spirit of the godly about the pseudorighteous, nor in the person of the pseudorighteous. Their righteousness is completely genuine and yet it is as if it were unclean, for they suffer everything which the wicked suffer, yet not innocently before a righteous God even if they are guiltless before men and our own conscience.

This is also the meaning of Ps. 44 [:17-18], which is spoken by those who have endured many evils: "All this has come upon us, though we have not been false to thy covenant. Our heart has not turned back, nor have our steps departed from thy way." This is what He says through Jeremiah 48 [49:12], "If those who did not deserve to drink the cup must drink it, will you go unpunished? You shall not go unpunished, but must drink." In what way were they not under judgment and yet drank? They were so before men and their own conscience. Thus it was in the case of Job, whom the Lord proclaims blameless and yet he [Job] speaks very differently in chapter 9—for otherwise the just God would not have afflicted either him or the righteous Jews. Again, He says in Jer. 31 [30:11], "I will chasten you in just measure, and will by no means leave you unpunished." Therefore, if he judges, we all sin before him, and perish if he is angry; and yet if mercy covers us, we are innocent and godly before him and all creatures. This is what Isaiah says here.

It must be understood that the "worker of righteousness" in this place [Isa. 64:5] does not refer to him who acts justly, as does "he who does what is right" in Ps. 13 [15:2]. Righteousness of the latter sort is here called wholly polluted, while the first text refers to a maker—that is, author—of righteousness, who makes righteousness prevail in his day. Thus it is in Jer. 23 [:5]: "He shall reign as a king and deal wisely, and shall execute justice and righteousness in the land." Also in Ps. 119 [:121]: "I have done what is just and right." Fortunate and happy are the times in which there are makers of righteousness who yet at the same time must be doers of it. This whole passage bewails these times of wrath in which, although there are just and good men, still righteousness cannot rise up because it is checked and restrained by the wrath of God. The godly are destroyed with the ungodly, for their righteousness is accounted nothing, and God's wrath does not let them accomplish anything whatsoever. Thus one may at length apply this passage in this way.

"Thou meetest him that joyfully, etc." [Isa. 64:5]. When the times are happy, and the justice which is the kingdom of Thy grace prospers, then Thou art kind, Thou meetest men and dost receive them with open arms, they call on Thy name and Thou hearest, they arise and find Thee, they hold to Thee, and Thou carest for all as in the time of Moses in the desert. There is then a walking in Thy paths, and remembrance, praise and thanksgiving to Thee for the benefits Thou hast poured forth. But now when Thine anger rages and the times are sad, we are nothing but sinners; Thou dost not meet, nor art Thou found or adhered to. Although there are those who are good and righteous, yet there is not one of them who rises up and adheres to Thee, or calls upon Thy name for us. He does not dare. There is now no praise to Thee for benefits, but only lamentation over our misfortunes. Just as in the time when justice flourished, the sins of these others were made white as snow, and Thou didst not punish them—indeed, didst not account them sins—so in these times of wrath when justice is destroyed, Thou dost reckon even all our righteousness unclean, and dost punish it [the righteousness] together with the sin of the others, dost overwhelm it together with evil, thrusting us into the power of our iniquity, and letting that happen to us which our sins deserve, so that it is as if all of us were filthy. Thus when mercy is removed, our iniquity carries us away like wind, and all our righteousness is helpless against it.

This is the way people speak of an angry prince. No one, not even his children or his wife or his friends, dares speak or plead with him regarding what angers him. It is thus that the prophet complains of the wrath of God which is so great that it treats the righteousness of all the godly as if it were sinful and unclean. They neither dare, nor can, appease him and call upon him. When compared to this burning and vehement prayer, it is indeed a cold opinion [to suppose] that this verse refers to the unholy righteousness of the godless. If ever this prayer could be prayed, it can be prayed today. There are many who are godly, but the Antichrist pope is so powerful that the elect are dragged, not simply into penitential suffering, but even into error, and there is no one who arises, holds, and calls upon God's name for us miserable men.

It seems clear enough to me that this interpretation fits beautifully with what follows, although to people like Latomus, it has the defect that they do not believe the Holy Spirit speaks in earnest, but [think] he merely speaks of a spurious righteousness. If this were so, the prophet would not complain that they have become unclean, since they would already be unclean. He testifies that the righteousness is genuine; and so the question is how it became filthy and polluted, for what happens to it is the contrary of what usually happens to genuine righteousness, for it [righteousness] cannot rise up and cling to the angry God in the day of wrath, whereas there is nothing it cannot do in the time of grace. Therefore the harshness and fury of judgment simultaneously ravage the just and the unjust, and mercy alone saves all those who are saved. Dear reader, you see, I believe, why this passage, with all its consequences, together with the proper sense of the words and the unity and simplicity of the meaning, and without using the wayward redundancy of the sophists of Louvain, favors me, stands unshaken, and scoffs at the barking of this Scylla. It holds, I say, that when the covering cloud of grace is removed, a good work is by its nature unclean, and it is pure and worthy of praise and glory only through forgiving mercy.

Consequently this passage not only supports my opinion, but also, at the same time, presents an illustration of its own teaching. For apart from forgiving mercy, God treats good works in the manner of which we hear Isaiah complaining. Yet the Just Judge would not thus deal with them unless they were truly evil and unclean. From this we learn how bounteous is the grace of God toward us, how he favors the unworthy so that we may be grateful from our innermost heart, and may love and praise these riches of glory and of the grace of God. Such worship of God and knowledge of the truth is quickly destroyed by these sophistic drawers-of-conclusions and makers-of-qualifications, who exalt themselves as the sole interpreters of Scripture, and yet do nothing except tear it to pieces and render it ambiguous and obscure.

At the same time, this answers the splendid quibbling with which Latomus so vigorously maligned Luther as absurd, just because I said that this passage applies not only to the Jews—in whose name I admit it is spoken—but to the saints of all the ages. This same Spirit who was in Isaiah in the midst of his time and tribulation was also in Job, in Abraham, in Adam, and is still in all the members of the whole Body of Christ from the beginning to the end of the world, and is with each and every one in his particular time and tribulation. Unless, perhaps, Paul ought not to have said in II Cor. 4 [:13], "We too believe, and so we speak," because he did not experience the same rapture and [live] at the same time as David. Times change, as do things, bodies, and tribulations, but the same Spirit, the same meaning, the same food and drink abide in all and through all. If this does not please them, then let the Louvainian arsonists decide to burn the Psalter of David and create a new one which will celebrate "our triumphs" over Reuchlin and Luther. The old Psalter commemorates the deeds of the Jews and so does not suit us moderns. Blind moles! Judging not according to the Spirit, but according to works, you look at the surface of the divine writings just as the Jews in the desert stood at their tent doors and saw nothing except the back of Moses entering into the tent of the tabernacle of the Lord [Exod. 33:8].

WE NOW PROCEED TO WHAT REMAINS.

Since I had maintained[46] that this passage does not refer to legal righteousness which puffs up, rather than humbly groans as does this text, Latomus says that I assume what is false, since the whole passage is supposed to refer to those proud Jews asking for temporal liberation. He demonstrates this falsity [of mine] by referring to a distinguished authority—namely, the opinion of Latomus, who believes that this text is to be understood of the Jews. So these men dare to build everything on their own [opinion] and condemn everything else. From this it follows that the Holy Spirit may sometimes act proudly in the person of the proud, and speak haughtily before God. Finally, with the same rashness, Latomus dares to add that the preceding chapter is to be understood

---

[46] *Resolutiones Lutherianae super propositionibus suis Lipsiae disputatis* (1519). WA 2, 411.

of the same proud men speaking proudly: "Why dost thou make us err from thy ways? We have become like those over whom thou hast never ruled" [Isa. 63:17, 19]. As the context is the same, Isaiah is here supposed to be speaking in the same spirit.

Further, when I denied that the righteousness of the law is evil, and condemned [only] the use which makes it censurable, Latomus showed again how learned he is in Holy Writ. He adduced II Cor. 3 [:10]: "What once had splendor has come to have no splendor at all, because of the splendor that surpasses it." He believes that I have not read Ezek. 19 [20:25]: "I gave them statutes that were not good." If he were to say this to me in person, I would think, if he were friendly, that he jests, or, if he were malicious, that he mocks. Nevertheless, we shall say a little about this for the sake of others. Many are persuaded that Paul deals in the above text with the ceremonial righteousness which is now repealed; yet he is speaking of the whole law, and comparing law with grace, not law with law. This error comes from the fact that they suppose the gospel is the teaching of laws. In brief then, let us point out that there are two ministries of preaching; one of the letter, the other of the spirit. The letter is the law, the spirit is grace. The first belongs to the Old Covenant, the second to the New. The glory of the law is the knowledge of sin; the glory of the Spirit is that revelation, or knowledge, of grace which is faith. Therefore the law did not justify: indeed, since human frailty found it unbearable, grace is veiled by it on Mount Tabor even to the present time.

Unless protected by grace, no one can withstand the power of the law. This is the reason Moses veiled his face [II Cor. 3:13]. It is because of this that the Jews do not understand the law even to this day. They seek to establish their own righteousness, and do not want that it become sin so that they may be subjected to the righteousness of God. The glory of the law makes all become sin, as Rom. 3 [:9; cf. Gal. 3:22] says, "All men are under the power of sin." Thus the law is the strength of sin, working wrath and death; but the spirit makes alive. Therefore that verse of Ezekiel [20:25], "I gave them statutes that were not good and ordinances by which they could not have life," has to do with the whole law, not only with ceremonies. Also, Paul's statement, "What once had splendor has come to have no splendor at all," refers to the entire law. The whole law was holy, just, and good, as Paul says in Rom. 7 [:12]; but because of our fault, that which is good cannot be good to us, nor does it make us alive, but kills. God himself, the highest good, is not good to the ungodly but their greatest dread and distress, as Hos. 5 [:12, 14] says, "I am like a moth to Ephraim, and like dry rot to the house of Judah. For I will be like a lion to Ephraim, and like a young lion to the house of Judah."

So the error of our teachers is that they know absolutely nothing of the Scriptures, nor understand either what is law, or what is grace, or what is ceremonial, or what is legal. Being thus confused, they follow one instead of the other. I say, therefore, that just as the law of the Decalogue is good if it is observed—that is, if you have faith, which is the fulness of the law and of righteousness— so also it is death, and wrath, and no good to you if you do not observe it—that is, if you do not have faith. This is so, no matter how many good works you do—for the righteousness of the law, that is, of the Ten Commandments, is unclean and abolished by Christ even more than is [the righteousness] of ceremonies. It is precisely the righteousness of the law which is the veil over the face of Moses, and which the glory of faith removes. Also, whatever is in the ceremonial law is good if you observe it by faith, not with works; that is, if you do it so as to know that righteousness is not in [works], but in faith. On the other hand, it is death, wrath, and no good, if you observe it without faith; this is the same as not observing it. It is clear, then, that the whole law is the letter which kills, but the life-giving Spirit is the grace in faith on Christ.

Now, since through Moses God gave the written law, not the law of faith, He rightly says [Ezek. 20:25] that the statutes He gave them are neither good nor life-giving, for they could not make persons alive nor good. Grace, however, is the law of life which makes persons good, and righteous, and alive. Therefore Paul wants the ministers of the New Covenant to be ministers of grace, not ministers of the law. Their office is not that of Moses, which has passed away, but that of Christ, that is, the preaching of the splendor of grace [II Cor. 3:6]. I would like to learn from our professors how they know that Ezekiel, and Paul in II Cor. 3, are speaking of the ceremonial law. Do they not allege it simply out of their heads, or from the testimony of men? In this way these

filthy swine rush in and seize upon the words of Scripture, understanding them in whatever way they please, and daring to fight for
the faith before they consider whether their weapons are imaginary
or real.

Indeed, in reference to that text from Isaiah, "all our righteous
deeds," and "we all are unclean," which I treated[47] so as to urge
that the meaning is universal, for it says, "we" and "all," "all" and
"our"—this most ingenious dialectician turns the argument around,
saying that the way to reason is rather this: the prophet does not
say "all," but "we all"; not "all righteous deeds," but "our righteous
deeds." He wants the text to apply to the ungodly Jews, not to all,
nor to the faithful. This has already been sufficiently refuted as
resting on the wavering opinion of Latomus. I have proved that
the text applies most accurately to the faithful and especially to the
very best of them.

However, this resourceful theologian has another way of
escape. "Be it so," he says. "Then the prophet would simply have
said, 'all righteous deeds,' and 'all are unclean.'" Invoking his
protectress, hyperbole or synecdoche, he maintains that the application must still be limited to a part or to some. If you ask him how
he proves the presence of this figure, and the necessity for limitation,
he replies that it is found in other places in Scripture, as was shown
above: for instance, "The whole head is sick," etc. [Isa. 1:5]. Here
you see again that when Latomus is the teacher everyone is free to
allegorize and play with Scripture as he pleases. This is what at
Louvain is called the scholarly weighing of the testimony of
Scripture, solid teaching, and an auspicious triumph over heretics.
By the same sort of scholarship I shall now easily prove that this
citation from Isaiah signifies one single, impious Jew. I shall also
check Latomus so that he cannot make out from this text that their
[the Jews'] righteousness is unclean, nor apply this passage to them.
This is the way to do it: If he says, "All your righteous deeds are
filthy," I shall reply that because of the figurative language, this
must be limited to a few, just as in, "The whole head is sick." Taking
these few—say, two—we say to them, "All your righteous deeds are
filthy." But they say, "No, this is a figure of speech in which the

---

[47]Cf. p. 176 n. 46, above.

whole stands for a part." Won't we seem to you, dear reader, to have theologized splendidly? Since Latomus is satisfied to fight on the basis of similarities in Scripture, I believe that because he once read that a virgin gave birth, he will make virgins into mothers as often as he wishes, content because he can show a text in which this happened.

You see that the efforts and habits of the sophists are such that, whatever they do, everything becomes changeable and uncertain. They insist with so much rigor and stubbornness upon the very sound of the words of that decretal of theirs, "Let him be anathema who says that the commandments of God are impossible," that they absolutely will not admit a syllable of pious interpretation, and declare the whole world heretical if it so much as murmurs against it. Why do they do this? Because it is theirs, a merely human word derived from men. Yet when one uses God's Scripture against them, they abound in numberless subterfuges, so whatever they are capable of thinking becomes immediately an article of faith—and what they think is never simple, constant, and the same. I suppose that if Christ today were to cry from heaven, "Luther's opinion is true," they would find some distinction in the meaning of "true" so that they would not be compelled to return to the [true] way. However, you dear reader, as you take those wandering eyes as evidence that here is an adulterous woman, so also among our professors there is no zeal for simple truth, but rather wavering and inconstant mockery. If I had to labor thus over suppositions, similitudes and variations, I wouldn't want to be a Christian, for how could I hope to find the solid truth among these billows and tempests? What, then, is left? Most certainly, since Latomus cannot prove that this passage is figurative, he will be compelled to admit the authority of the literal, simple and proper meaning that—apart from God's mercy—all righteous deeds are filthy, and all men unclean.

ANOTHER TEXT, ECCLES. VII [20]

"Surely there is not a righteous man on earth who does good and sins not."

Latomus attacks—finally even threatens me—so that I will stop blackening the glory of the saints, for according to him their glory is their work which is without sin. In this way Psalm 3 [:3]: "Thou, O Lord, art my glory," means, "You are my good work without sin"; and Psalm 89 [:17], "For thou art the glory of our strength," means, "You are our good work without sin." Thus, clearly enough, we make gods for ourselves just as is said in Exod. 32 [:23], "Make us gods." Properly speaking, this refers to good works, and it is in these that the saints of Latomus glory. Isaiah 3 [2:8] agrees with this: "They bow down to the work of their hands, to what their own fingers have made." Now the saints of God are ashamed of their works before him and glory in him alone. Jeremiah 9 [:23] shows this: "Let not the mighty man glory in his might." Paul says in I Cor. 10 [1:31], "Let him who boasts, boast of the Lord." But, as I said, our professors speak with such excessive intelligence that they reveal that in their hearts they think their notion of godliness is superior to what the apostles and prophets could understand. What Latomus really thinks of faith and works is evident enough from his own mouth, speaking out of the abundance of his heart. Nature prevails over art, and he cannot conceal it.

In reference to the text we are now considering, this most prudent weigher of evidence has omitted the consequences, circumstances and—as he calls it—the thread of the discourse, for he senses danger, and therefore flees, first to the expositions of others and then, in his peculiar way, to another passage of Scripture. Although I would not persist in my opinion if I had only this one verse; still I base my opinion on it because there is absolutely nothing with which I can satisfactorily refute it. Nor can Latomus; nor, I believe, can anyone else. Because it seems to grant my contention in the clearest terms, and because this is the only meaning we can find in it until the Spirit gives us a better one, I have joined this verse to those which are evident and infallible. I have often toyed with the interpretations of it on which Latomus depends, but it obstinately persists in conspiring to agree with my other texts. Although what Latomus brings up isn't new, he still believes that Luther hasn't seen any of it: and this credulity was enough to impel him to write.

It is easy to say that the statement "There is not a righteous man on earth who does good and sins not," is the same as I Kings 8 [:46], "There is no man who does not sin." Because he does this, Latomus slips out of his difficulty, for in our text, "righteous" and "man," as well as "doing good" and "not sinning," are connected, while Kings simply mentions "man" and "not sinning." He ignores the consequences of the text and the circumstances in which it was written, although he has promised to investigate these above all. However, I who do observe and adhere to them, understand that it is not for me to assert that a man, and a righteous man, are the same, or that sinning and doing good are identical with not sinning. I fully admit I would have been embarrassed if Latomus, acting as the advocate of my opinion, had advanced this verse against me, contending that Scripture almost always uses "man" in a bad sense for "sinner." This is done in Gen. 6 [:3] and 8 [:21]: "My spirit shall not abide in man, for he is flesh;" and in Paul, "Are you not merely men?" [I Cor. 3:4]. He often says, "I speak as a man" [Rom. 3:5] or "the day of man" [I Cor. 4:3]. Finally, Ps. 82 [:7] reads, "You shall die like men."

One must either reject this text by making evident from Scripture that this is not its meaning, or one must yield to it as long as its teaching is that of many other passages. It is a single witness, but when a second and third agree with it, the word is established in its mouth. Just because I don't know how to explain it away, I am freed from the task [of interpreting it] as long as I yield to it (for it is supplemented by other and more certain witnesses) until the Spirit shall have revealed that a man and a righteous man are the same, and that to "do good and not to sin" is identical with sinning. Meanwhile I shall follow what the words say; and, as I said, shall not follow them, but leave them doubtful, if they are the only ones which speak thus. Yet even if this is the only scriptural text which expresses this meaning, still it is safer to affirm than deny it. No one sins if he denounces his good works before God as useless, as sinful, as nothing at all, and with Job fears everything.[48] It is dangerous—indeed, godless—to exalt and praise even a single work before God. This consideration compels the acceptance of our interpretation even if, as Latomus would have it, the text gives it only apparent support. Now, since he turns away from what it clearly says, as he fears only lest it have a hidden meaning, and

---

[48] Thus in the Vulgate version of Job 9:28.

as the sense is neither completely obscure nor completely evident, certainly a godly meaning, or no meaning, is preferable to an impious one. It happens that here, according to the Hebrew, "doer of good," signifies a producer of good works whose goodness is not simply personal, but effective and fruitful for others. Yet it is said that such a one sins; and so, even more, the one who simply acts well, is a sinner. Nevertheless, if my bit of Hebrew may be relied upon, I would assert that this is the meaning of the original, for it reads, "Surely there is not a righteous man on earth who does good and sins not." The first part, "There is not a righteous man on earth," certainly affirms what Latomus advances from the book of Kings, "There is no man who does not sin." Indeed, it is apparent that it says more. Now, what follows explains that even a righteous man sins in doing good, for the Hebrews know that in expressions of this sort the conjunction is generally superfluous; as, for instance, in Gen. 17 [:14]: "Any male whose flesh is not circumcised, and he shall be cut off from his people"; or in Exod. 13 [12:15]: "Whoever eats what is leavened, and that person shall be cut off from Israel." In the same way, "Who does good and sins not," here stands for, "Who sins not when he does good."

Latomus has not weakened the conclusion implied by my earlier argument[49] to the effect that it seems superfluous for Solomon to add, "who does good and sins not" to "a righteous man," as if there were someone righteous who does not do the good. He plays around with "falling" and "sinning," but this does not disturb me, for I do not ask what Bede[50] or any other man says, but what they ought to say. One ought to pay attention to God's Scripture only, and not simply to what is said, but also who says it. Nor does that other verse from I Kings 8 [:46] help him, for he must first prove that it agrees with his view and opposes me. He cannot simply list quotations, but he must refute. Otherwise why doesn't he also cite, "In the beginning God created the heavens and the earth"? I ask how often must he be told not merely to list passages,

---

[49] Cf. p. 176 n. 46. WA 2, 412.
[50] Latomus had quoted Prov. 24:16, and had appealed to Bede (673-735) who had explained this passage as having to do with trivial, everyday sins which even the righteous cannot avoid in this life.

but to refute mine, just as I have brought forward contrary passages, not parallel or similar ones? I won't listen to, "Such and such is said in another place," but I would listen [if he were to say], "The contrary is clearly stated in another place." Let him stop saying, "So and so can be said," and give us, "Such and such must always be said." He ought to do this, because those who are approved by the bull have judged, condemned, and burned, and so it would be dishonorable of them to rely on what merely "can" be said, and not show that it "must" be said. What will the world think if they themselves make it appear that they have inflicted, executed, and approved so sure a sentence upon so doubtful [a foundation]? Who will not then affirm that Latomus, that champion of the truth, has been publicly confounded in his arguments and in what he asserts is true, and that he has written with no other purpose than to quibble and mock, rather than to teach and defend? This is the worst sort of sophistry, and an attack on the intelligence and good sense of the world. I for my part do not want to insist on even one of my statements which merely "could" mean what I claim. Unless they "must" have this meaning I am ready to let them go and consider them merely open questions. Even if Latomus had been able to show that my propositions are not conclusive, this still does not justify the people who have to give account for my condemnation and who have burned my propositions as if they were not merely inconclusive, but ought never to have been uttered. With what levity or stupidity do you who have made Christ the subject of your discussion soon take up another tune and sing of Hector of Troy!

Among other things, he uses fallacious arguments against Luther, just as if I knew no logic and were ignorant of dialectics. He says, "There is no more validity in this reasoning: 'there is no righteous man who does good and sins not, therefore by one and the same act the righteous does good and sins,' than there is in this: 'there is no man who lives and does not see death, therefore he who lives is at the same time dead.' It is as if one were to say that there is no man who is awake and does not sleep, and from this to want to infer that someone is therefore simultaneously awake and asleep; or, similarly, say that there is no man who lives and does not eat, and therefore whenever he lives he eats." [51] So far, Latomus. I would like to be given one of his pupils who had even for a day heard lectures on dialectic, so that I might examine him on the skill of his teacher. Tell me, boy, is it true, as the first principles of Aristotle would have it, that all those inferences are valid which presuppose that anything follows from the impossible? For instance, does this properly follow from the rule that anything may be inferred from the impossible: three and two equal eight, therefore the devil is God? Now as soon as the antecedent is true, the consequence also is true. So, in this way, is it not proper to infer: there is no man who lives and does not see death, therefore he who lives is at the same time dead? Here the antecedent is impossible, since no living man sees death, and so from the same antecedent there also follows the opposite conclusion: therefore no one is dead and alive at the same time. In the same way, is not this a legitimate inference: there is no man awake who does not sleep, therefore he is simultaneously awake and asleep? For the contradictory also follows: therefore he is not simultaneously awake and asleep. This is so because the antecedent is impossible, since a man who is awake cannot sleep, nor conversely. So also, does this not follow: there is no man who lives and does not eat, and therefore whenever he lives he eats, and does not eat, and exists, and does not exist, and whatever else you want to deduce? Why therefore does your teacher deny and condemn this mode of inference? Why does he trifle about so serious a matter? Or is it that the bull approves even this remarkable achievement? You see, dear reader, that sophistic envy is so blind that it cannot even grasp ordinary common sense nor the rudiments of a schoolboy's learning.

But perhaps some disciple of Latomus says, "Our distinguished professors really mean this: there is no man who lives and will not see death some time in the future; and, there is no man awake who does not at some time sleep—namely, at a time other than when he is awake; and, there is no man who lives and does not at some time eat—not, however, during all the time he lives. From these premises it does not follow that he is simultaneously living and dead, awake and asleep, living and eating." I am grateful for this sound

---

[51] Cf. Latomus, *Works*, fol. 8ᵇ. In this reference, the last example cited by Luther is lacking in the *Works* of Latomus. Cf. WA 8, 75 n. 4.

information. Yet it frees our distinguished professors from one absurdity while plunging them into two [others]. The first is that they are ignorant of grammar and don't know the difference between the present and future tense, for they express something future by means of the present tense, and omit many adverbs. Perhaps this is a punishment for that earlier slander against linguistic skill;[52] so that now they are speechless and unable to express those [accidental] attributes of the soul which, according to Aristotle, as Latomus says in his *Dialogue,* are the same in all. I grant that it is completely invalid to infer: there is no man who lives and (as Ps. 89 [:48] has it) will not see death, or will not at some time see death, therefore he is simultaneously alive and dead. So also, it is completely wrong to infer: there is no man who is awake and does not at some time sleep, therefore he is awake and asleep at the same time. Nor is this correct: there is no man who lives and does not at some time eat, therefore whenever he lives he eats. But against whom do they fight with these absurd inferences? Has Luther said: there is not a righteous man on earth who does good and at some [other] time sins not, therefore he does good and sins simultaneously? Who forces this adverb, "some time," on me? Who will dare to say that Solomon adds it?

The other absurdity of these professors of ours is one into which they almost always fall. It is what is called "begging the question." Because Latomus does this so often, I shall not find it burdensome to admonish him frequently, for perhaps he is capable of learning a few rules of logic from this dispute. So I say that Latomus must prove that Solomon inserted the adverb, "some time," thus limiting sin to evil works exclusive of good works. Instead, he takes this as proved, and fallaciously demonstrates what is denied by means of what is denied.

Even if this were not a fallacy, he still fails in regard to essential and accidental predication. For I meant and now [expressly] say (what makes every hair of our professors stand on end) that sin, as long as we live, inheres essentially in good works, just as the ability to laugh inheres in man. (I speak after the fashion of Aristotle, not of the sophists, for they still don't know what is an essential or

---

[52] This is another reference to the Reuchlin controversy. Cf. p. 150 n. 20.

proper attribute according to Aristotle.) [In contrast], food, sleep, and death are attributed to man by accidental predication. Consequently, just as it does not follow that because a man is always capable of laughing, therefore he always laughs, so it does not follow that because a man lives, therefore he is always awake, eating, or dying. However, this does follow: a man lives, therefore he is capable of laughter, of eating, of sleeping, of dying, etc. In the same way, this follows: a man does good and therefore sins, because a man doing good is a subject which has sin as its attribute, just as was postulated on the basis of what Solomon says. So I shall emulate Latomus in drawing essential consequences and do it better than he does, and shall support my necessary conclusions with true and necessary examples. In this way, the following may be correctly inferred: there is no sophist of Louvain who treats of Scripture and does not distort the meaning and condemn the truth; therefore, it is in the same work that he treats of Scripture and distorts it. This follows, because it pertains to sophists sometimes to treat of Scripture, but it is a property of theirs to distort and condemn it. Thus this also is a correct inference: there is no theologizer of Louvain who preaches and does not tell his dreams and fables, therefore, as often as he preaches, he tells fables. This is so, because a theologizer pretends to speak the Word of God, but his property is to teach fables instead of it. Again, there is no hypocrite of Louvain who celebrates mass and does not adore an idol, therefore as often as he celebrates mass, he adores an idol. It is so, because all these antecedents are necessary and essential, for they could not be otherwise. Good reader, forgive my frivolity and blame it on Latomus, for he is not afraid to slander by trifling with these grave matters of truth. I didn't want to deal with this quibble but, remembering the ostentation and the bull, I was afraid that simple people might believe that this doggerel amounted to something, which, if true, would have reduced my opinion to an incredible absurdity. Therefore he had to be paid back what he deserved. He is one of those whom the pope approves[52a] and calls faithful cultivators of the Lord's field, not, however, in order to favor them, but simply to spite me—and yet they pride themselves on this alone.

[52a] Leo X in the introduction to the bull, *Exsurge Domine,* June 15, 1520. Cf. *WA* 8, 77 n. 1.

Latomus cites a passage from Jerome[53] to the effect that, "No man sins not," means that there is no one who is perpetually free from sin; that is, it ought to be understood that the righteous doer of good is not sinless, but sometimes sins, just as we read of David, who did all the will of God and yet sometimes sinned [I Kings 15:5]. Here again, however, Latomus presents his, "It can be said," and does not show that this is what ought to be said. Who, I ask, doubts that the saints sometimes sin? What Latomus must prove is that this is Solomon's meaning in the present verse. [So] another fallacy in this place is that he argues on the basis of similarities. A third fault is that of begging the question, for he does not prove that the similarity exists. I concede that he is right about the meaning of what he cites from Jerome, but I deny that Solomon's meaning is similar or the same. What is to be done? Once again I shall shout at you, Latomus. Do you hear? The argument which supports you is this: a good work is not a sin. Therefore you ought to refute the view that a good work is sin, instead of proving that the saints sometimes sin, or instead of refuting the view that the saints never sin. No one disputes with you regarding these. Now Jerome, in the passage cited, is not thinking of this text from Solomon, so stop saying that he proves it has the meaning which Latomus proposes. This is a remarkably silly deduction: Jerome says that the saints sometimes sin, and are not perpetually free from sin; therefore Solomon intends to assert the same when he says that, "There is not a righteous man on earth who does good and never sins." Why don't you say also that Paul's statement, "If a girl marries she does not sin" [I Cor. 7:28], is the same as what Peter says, "Brethren, be sober, be watchful"? [I Pet. 5:8]. You draw conclusions but do not prove them. Next, you want by your own authority to force the meaning of one passage into another, as if the world ought to yield and believe you without any evidence. Collect as many texts as you wish, but remember to prove that their meaning is the one you want them to seem to have. This, Latomus, is the task you have undertaken, and unless you do it you have done nothing. However, my opinion and my Solomon stand firm, and convict you and your associates of being arsonists and blasphemers.

---

[53] *Dialogue Against the Pelagians*, III, 4. Migne 23, 599-600.

It is questionable whether Jerome rightly deals with the statement that, "David did all the will of God and yet sometimes sinned," for according to Jerome, God said "all the will," but did not add "perpetually." [54] This, however, will not be considered further, for it is alien to our purpose. We say that God's entire will is done in the sense that he pardons all our good works, just as Augustine says, "The commandments of God are fulfilled when those which are not done are forgiven." [55] Here we are not discussing those grave sins into which the saints sometimes fall, but the daily sins remaining in us which our opponents call venial. Jerome's interpretation seems to me quite stiff, for "doing all" is made to refer to some of the time, or the greater part of the time. However, because of that figure of speech, synecdoche, I don't criticize him. Yet he clearly errs when he falsely charges that Paul either sinned or did not do a good work when he wrote Timothy about the parchments [II Tim. 4:13], and, indeed, as often as he thought of the necessities of this life.[56] Where is the braggart who said he would weigh, rather than merely enumerate, his witnesses? I say that it is an error to assert that Paul did not here do well. Paul himself speaks better: "Whether you eat or drink, or whatever you do [I Cor. 10:31] do everything in the name of the Lord Jesus" [Col. 3:17]. The ordinary life of the righteous is nothing except pure good works, for Christ does not leave a single hoof of his sheep in Egypt. I say this so that the sophists may know that just as the holy fathers have sometimes sinned—and as Latomus proves by the example of David cited from Jerome—so they have sometimes erred, as I have here proved in regard to Jerome. Accordingly their authority is worth most when it has clear scriptural support; if not, don't let them [the sophists] prattle and boast to me of victory just because the authority of some of the saints is on their side. We are in a struggle in which one must be supported by divine, certain, and evident testimonies. It is only in private discussions and popular presentations that human witnesses are effective.

Yet, because he cites Paul as an example of one who did a good work without sin, let us represent the situation in dramatic terms.

---

[54] *Ibid.*, p. 600.
[55] *Retractions*, I, 19. Migne 32, 614.
[56] Jerome, *op. cit.*, p. 474.

Let us take St. Paul or Peter as they pray, preach, or do some other good work. If it is a good work without sin and entirely faultless, they could stand with appropriate humility before God and speak in this fashion: "Lord God, behold this good work which I have done through the help of Thy grace. There is in it neither fault nor any sin, nor does it need Thy forgiving mercy. I do not ask for this, as I want Thee to judge it with Thy strictest and truest judgments. In it [my work] I can glory before Thee, because Thou canst not condemn it, for Thou art just and true. Indeed, I am certain that Thou canst not condemn it without denying Thyself. The need of mercy which, as Thy petition [in the Lord's Prayer] teaches, forgives the trespass in this deed is canceled, for there is here only the justice which crowns it." Latomus, doesn't this make you shudder and sweat? And yet it is certain that all this could, indeed should, be said by so just a man, for it is especially before God that truth ought to be spoken, nor ought one to lie because of God. The truth is that a work without sin deserves praise, needs no mercy, and fears not the judgment of God. Indeed, it is proper to trust and hope in it and in the gift of grace which has been [once] received, for we have something with which to encounter God himself, and his judgment and truth, so that we ought no longer fear him, nor rely on his mercy. Isn't it true, Latomus, that all this must happen as a consequence? For even if God destroys good creatures, he does not condemn or disapprove of them. Thus although God can destroy such a saint and his work, yet he cannot condemn or disapprove, for the truth stands firm: "You love righteousness and hate wickedness" [Ps. 45:7]. So, through God's grace, we may in this life, and before his judgment day, stand over against God and fearlessly neglect both his mercy and his judgment.

However, what happens then to Psalm 101 [143:2]: "Enter not into judgment with thy servant; for no man living is righteous before thee"? Do we here have synecdoche, so that "no man living" stands for many or some of the living? But Paul says in I Cor. 4 [:4], "I am not aware of anything against myself" (look at all the good works!) "but I am not thereby acquitted." How is it that you are not acquitted, since there is righteousness and no sin in a good work? You have certainly preached the gospel with all your strength, and you have gathered a collection [for Jerusalem], as

Latomus says, with all the accompaniments of virtue even as Aristotle would enumerate them. Surely you cannot deny that this is good work; how, then, are you still a sinner in all this? Or, is it that you are not a sinner and so not justified in what you say? Or do you lie in calling yourself not justified when you are justified? If you heard Latomus, you would not say, "I do not even judge myself, it is the Lord who judges me" [I Cor. 4:3, 4]. Rather you would say, "I judge myself, for a good work does not fear His judgment, for He is himself just." Either people like Latomus blaspheme God's mercy and judgment with their good works, or else you, Paul, lie. Indeed, you blaspheme the truth taught by them. You cannot hold at one and the same time that, "I have a work without sin" and, "I am not justified in this." Do not make God unjust so that he would not acquit a good work without sin. What would he condemn in it? Imperfection? This is not sin, but punishment which even increases goodness, so that it is perhaps better to have many imperfections[57] of this sort, rather than a few.

However, you cite Jer. 17 [:16]: "Thou knowest that that which came out of my lips was right in thy sight. And I have not desired the day of man; Thou knowest I have followed thee, my Shepherd."[58] And Hezekiah says in II Kings 20 [:3], "Remember now, O Lord, I beseech thee, how I have walked before thee in faithfulness and with a whole heart, and have done what is good in thy sight." My reply is that he does not say he has not sinned in any of these things, but he means just about what the Apostle does: "I am not aware of anything against myself, I have done what is pleasing to you and whatever is commanded, but I am not thereby acquitted." He speaks only of what he is conscious. Lastly, in the Psalms and frequently in other places, the saints invoke God's judgment in favor of their cause and against their enemies. However, it is not in this that those who are guiltless before men and their consciences are justified before God, but because of someone else, namely Christ. If therefore the Apostle dares to say that he is not aware of anything against himself and yet is not justified in this, how much more are Hezekiah and Jeremiah not justified in what they

---

[57] This is a reference to the Roman Catholic teaching that the "imperfections" in the baptized are not truly sins.
[58] Luther quotes Jer. 17:16 freely from the Vulgate text.

recount, for it is far greater and more perfect to be aware of nothing than to walk in truth and do what pleases God. As Jerome and Latomus prove, they [Hezekiah and Jeremiah] could say this while being aware of something against themselves.

On the other hand, when the Word is at stake another question arises. Here Paul dared to say that because God cannot lie or deny himself (for the Word is his, not ours), we can stand before him with confidence and declare: "I know that Thou canst not condemn this Word for it is justified in itself; it is not at all a matter of being aware of nothing, it does not fear Thy judgment or seek mercy, for we can hold it up to Thee since it is in all things like unto Thee, etc." But about the use, office, and exposition of the Word we cannot talk this way, for here that which belongs to us is added. Therefore Jeremiah well says that, "What came out of my lips was right in thy sight." In short, so certain are we of the pure truth of the Word, that we ought to die for it; but who would dare to die for his own good works even if they are wholly without fault? When Paul writes to Timothy [II Tim. 4:7ff.], "I have fought the good fight, I have finished the race, I have kept the faith. Henceforth there is laid up for me the crown of righteousness, which the Lord, the righteous judge, will award to me on that day," he does not say that he is justified in all this, but, like Hezekiah, he speaks in the assurance of mercy. It is through its benefit that he awaits the crown of glory, although he is aware of nothing against himself. All believers do this, for hope does not await wrath, but glory, as is said in Tit. 2 [:13]; and not through works, but rather through God's mercy.

However, what if Latomus and his crowd evade these consequences by saying, "We don't want this to happen, for no one is certain that he has done such works"? What do I hear? Are we stoics, or academics so that we have no certainty? I really don't believe that they are that foolish. What is more absurd than to teach good works and at the same time not know what good works are, nor be able to exhibit a single example of them? Paul has no doubts at all, nor does David. He does not say, "I am doubtful," but "I am not aware of anything against me." And Hezekiah does not say, "I am doubtful whether I have done what is pleasing before you." Nor does David say in Ps. 7 [:8], "Judge me according to my doubts," but "according to the integrity that is in me." Again, Paul does not doubt that he sinned in working, for he does not say, "But I doubt whether I am thereby acquitted," but rather, "I am not thereby acquitted." David does not say, "Who knows if any man living is righteous before thee," but "No man living is righteous before thee" [Ps. 143:2]. If one must doubt what good works are, who would be persuaded to do them? Who would want, knowingly and with foresight, to run doubtfully and aimlessly (as the Apostle says) and box as one beating the air? [I Cor. 9:26]. Surely there will never be any peace, if it is necessary to have good works, and no one in his whole life knows when he has them. Wherefore God cares admirably for us by making us certain of two things. First, he teaches in Gal. 5 [:22] what good works are manifest. "The fruit of the spirit is love, joy, peace," etc.; and, in Matt. 7 [:20], "You will know them by their fruits." [On the other hand,] He has made us certain that they [the good works] are not sinless and faultless (so that our trust is not in them), with the result that we can acknowledge in a confession without doubt or falsity that we are sinners in all our works and are men whom mercy has found. Further, in order that we may have unfailing peace, he has given us his Word in Christ, on which we rely with confidence, secure from all evil. The gates of hell, together with all sins, do not prevail against that Word. This is our rock of refuge where we, with Jacob, can wrestle against God [Gen. 32:28] and, so to speak, dare to press hard upon him with his promises, his truth, and his own Word. Who will judge God and his Word? Who will accuse or condemn faith in his Word? Let people like Latomus stop blackening the glory of God, muzzle their blaspheming mouths, and no longer raise up idols for us out of our dubious and unbelieving works, so that we may not change our glory into the likeness of a calf which eats hay.

Finally, he is indignant at being accused of not understanding what sin is according to the usage of Scripture. "Let us see," he says, "what sin is in Scripture." Next, he takes sin in four ways: First, as standing for the cause of sin; second, for its effect or punishment; third, for a sacrifice for sin; and fourth, for the guilt itself by which the soul stands accused. I marvel that these fertile drawers of distinction have not taken sin in a fifth way as standing for the reward of sin; and then, so that we might have the whole of Aristotle, they could make a distinction between essential and accidental sin. Now if I ask where in Scripture this team of four sins appears, I am told that Origen and Ambrose call the devil sin, and that according to Augustine,[59] lust [*concupiscentia*] and the motions of sin remain after baptism. From this I conclude that Ambrose, Origen, and Augustine are holy Scripture. Thus not only are gods multiplied through good works, but also the writings of the gods through sins. After all, what sort of gods would these be if they did not give us divine writings? In the next place, Latomus denies that the one who has the second sort of sin, that is, lust or the motions of sin remaining after baptism, is to be called a sinner. Let us pass over this astonishing assertion and get to the point. Here I entreat you, dear reader, be free and a Christian. Do not swear allegiance to any word of man, but be a steadfast adherent of the holy Scripture. If it calls anything sin, beware of being influenced by the words of any of those who—as if they could speak better—deny sin itself, wishing to name it sometimes an imperfection, sometimes a penalty, sometimes a fault, and thus weaken and mock the Word of God, for none of these terms are found in Scripture. Believe me, the Holy Spirit is quite capable of expressing his meanings in suitable words, so that there is no need for human inventions. It is unbelievable how Paul torments the sophists in Romans 6, 7 and 8, for he there named the lust which survives baptism sin, and not penalty. They would pay a great deal, if they could, to get rid of this word.

If St. Hilary has given us the right advice, nothing should be asserted beyond the heavenly precepts;[60] but whoever has tried to do this has either not understood, or failed to make others understand. This is exactly what happens to our opponents in regard to the word "sin" in this text of Paul. The sophists don't notice how absurd and unworthy of belief it is to call "sin" in this place the "penalty of sin," and that this can be supported by no other scriptural testimonies (which, as Paul advises Titus [Tit. 1:9], must be done when disputing, so that the mouth of the adversary may be stopped). Yet it is not only impossible to teach that sin in this place means penalty, but, in addition, not even the Louvainian

---

[59] *Against Two Letters of the Pelagians,* I, 13. Migne 44, 562.
[60] *On the Trinity,* II, 1-5, *passim.* Migne 10, 51-54.

notion of theologizing can do anything to produce one single text of Scripture in which sin in this way signifies penalty—and this would be true, even if the text did not compel one to understand it, of sin itself. However, since this is the point on which almost the whole question turns, and since the entire confused and shapeless mass of Latomus revels in sporting and equivocating about sin, we must act to assert the truth so that the adversary will not have occasion to mock. To be sure, he will still take the opportunity to mock if we cannot prove through Scripture that one must make distinctions and equivocate about sin just as he does—and just, in fact, as neither he nor we can do. Therefore we must abide in the simple and steadfast meaning [of sin], nor go beyond it until manifest authority compels us to. So we must go back to what was said a little earlier.

First of all, do not doubt that "sin" is used in Scripture in a single very simple way, not in many different ones. Do not let those verbose sophists wrest this away from you. Indeed, sin is simply that which is not in accord with God's law. The meaning of Rom. 7 [:7] stands firm, "Through the law comes the knowledge of sin" [Rom. 3:20], just as, conversely, through sin comes ignorance of the law. For sin is the darkness which is illuminated and revealed by the law in order that it may be recognized. Now we freely admit and rejoice that Scripture very often uses figures of speech such as synecdoche, ellipsis, metaphor, and hyperbole. Indeed, in no other writing is figurative language more common. Thus "heaven" is throughout Scripture a simple and univocal word which designates the vault of the sky, and yet it is used as a metaphor for the apostles in Ps. 19 [:1]. Everyone knows what the simple word "earth" signifies, but metaphorically it means the godless who are trampled under by vice and evil. To anyone who contends that this word none the less has many meanings, I reply that I do not object if he wants to say this. But what kind of dictionary will it be that will teach us [the meaning of] these words since such figures of speech are left to the choice of those who use them or to their whim, as they say. Horace tells us: "You will speak superbly, when skilful combinations make an old word new." [61] For instance, everyone considers "banner" a simple term. Yet when I say "banner of the

---

[61] *The Art of Poetry*, I, 46-48.

cross" or "banner of the word," everyone sees that a familiar word has been admirably transformed into a new one. However, if you made proper meanings out of these excellent innovations, how would you ever stop? Would you write in the dictionary that "banner" sometimes signifies the cross when it is publicly exhibited, and the gospel when it is preached? Persius says that an onion has a tunic[62]; must you therefore write: "Note that 'tunic' signifies the skin of an onion"?

For this reason I am not pleased with those Hebrew scholars who, following the precedent furnished by the Chaldean targumists, Onkelos and Jonathan,[63] distinguish so many different meanings of a single word. For the benefit of the uneducated, they seem to make it their business [to take] away what Scripture expresses in the most splendid and beautiful figures, strip it for the benefit of the uneducated, and present the crude and simple sense. Hence, for no good reason, equivocations arise in this language and a veritable Babylonian confusion of words. The mind and understanding are wondrously distracted by this variety. If, wherever possible, you were to set down one simple meaning and place all the imagery and figures of speech alongside, then you would quietly and easily remove all the confusion, marvelously help the memory and understanding, and even give sweet pleasure to the mind. I don't know what sort of power images have that they can so forcefully enter and affect one, and make every man by nature long to hear and speak in imagery. Isn't it true that, "The heavens declare the glory of God," [Ps. 19:1] sounds much sweeter than, "The apostles preach God's Word"? When Moses warns against worshiping the stars in Deut. 4 [:19]—"Beware lest you worship them, things which the Lord your God has allotted to all the people under heaven"—you will hear nothing sweeter, fuller, and more powerful than if you substitute the Hebrew word[64] in its simplicity, for it includes a metaphor. The Hebrew speaks of the "things with which the Lord your God has caressed all the people under heaven."

---

[62] *Satires*, IV, 30.
[63] The reference is to Aramaic translations of and commentaries on the Old Testament from the second century A.D.
[64] *Chalaq*. Luther combines here the two meanings of the Hebrew word, *Chalaq*, "to allot" and "to flatter, to caress."

How much godly learning, how much emotion, how much delight there is in these words! Just think, even as a mother fondles her child upon her knees, so the Lord God has given the stars of the heaven to all peoples as if to flatter and caress them, and in order to draw them to himself by his most sweet and tender goodness and to invite them to his love by these gentle benefits. Now if you come to me with an equivocation and contend that that word properly signifies in this place "allotted," or as our Jerome translates it, "created," I am compelled to yield. Yet of how much loveliness you have deprived me by speaking too properly and too literally! You have thrown me from paradise to earth, although in the figurative expression, I grasped your meaning with delight. Who does not see that God caresses a person by [supplying] his needs, and gives us his blandishments for our portion, so that it is for this reason that "portion," "part," "lot," and "inheritance" are spoken of? Thus you can say, "These are God's caresses and my portion." It seems that the elliptical significance of the word, "divide," is brought out in this way, for instance, in Gen. 49 [:7]: "I will divide them in Jacob." In contrast, Ps. 5 [:9] has, "They flatter with their tongue," instead of retaining the more favorable expression, "They caress with their tongue." Thus, if you make three words out of the one word which means divide, caress, create, since the authors use it sometimes figuratively, sometimes literally, you can express it in a single designation, and, as a result, more gracefully and clearly.

So also, when it is said in Deut. 6 [:7], "And you shall tell[65] them [these words] to your children," it sounds more forceful to say, "And you shall engrave them on your children." That this was not simply a matter of telling is shown by what follows: "You shall talk of them when you sit in your house, and when you walk by the way, and when you lie down, and when you rise." If you object that engraving is done with iron, not with words, so that you are compelled to express the proper meaning of the word by "repeat, tell, inculcate," I shall allow you to do this, but shall continue to believe that the first meaning is the more agreeable, and perhaps the only one. For Paul seems to want to imitate the power of this word

---

[65] Vulgate. The Hebrew word is *shanan*.

in II Tim. 3 [4:2]: "Be urgent in season and out of season, convince, rebuke, and exhort." What does this mean except that the Word of God must be assiduously expounded and inculcated, engraved and polished? This must be done so that the traditions of man do not enter in and make dull the Word of God, and so Eccles. 10 [:10] puts it this way: "If the iron is blunt, and one does not whet the edge, he must put forth more strength." When it says in Exod. 32 [:25], "Seeing the people were naked [Hebrew: *para*] for Aaron had stripped them on account of the shame of the filth, and had set them naked among their enemies," I do not hesitate to improve the translation: "And when Moses saw that the people had broken loose (for Aaron had let them break loose when he raised them up to their shame)." This word is imitated by Paul in speaking to the Galatians [5:4, 11]: "You are severed from Christ, and the stumbling block of the cross has been removed"; that is, the stumbling block has disappeared, is no longer effective, for Christ does not work within you. Thus also Aaron, with his calf, moved the people so that they were neither led by God nor did God deal with them, and they, having broken loose from divine works, were aroused to glorying in their own righteousness. By putting it this way, don't I beautifully encompass not only nakedness itself, but also what it points toward? Namely, that afterwards the priests acted as did Aaron and, having drawn the nation away from God's law and nullified the divine activity, they made much of the people on account of their own works. Thus Paul says, "They desire to have you circumcised that they may glory in your flesh" [Gal. 6:13]. Moses mentions this glory when he says that the people were let loose by Aaron, and yet were raised up to their shame (so that Aaron also was dishonored, for it was through his action that this had happened to the people). Jerome's translation ("on account of the shame of the filth, had set them naked among their enemies") makes no sense either of the text or of the subject matter unless one makes everything equivocal (which I don't prohibit). It is from this word [*para*] that the king of the Egyptians gets the name "Pharaoh," for he is king of the sort of people who have broken loose from God's works and turned to their own works.

Still another example is provided by Ps. 119 [:23, 15], which often repeats the word "meditate," as in, "Thy servant will meditate[66] on thy statutes," and "I will meditate[67] on thy precepts." The word is used in various ways, yet all its meanings may easily be combined into one which is, in the vernacular, "give friendly attention" or "recommend oneself." [68] In Gen. 4 [:4-5] it is said, "The Lord had regard[69] for Abel and his offering, but for Cain and his offering he had no regard." The word is translated differently in Prov. 8 [:30-31]: "I was delighted every day," and again, "My delights were with the children of men." Isaiah 17 [:7-8] reads, "In that day men will be inclined to their maker, and will not be inclined to their idols," and Isa. 66 [:12], "Upon the knees shall they caress you"; while in contrast Isa. 6 [:10] has, "Shut their eyes." I ask if these are all proper meanings, so that the same word signifies "meditate," "be inclined," "be delighted," "have delights," "caress," "shut," and perhaps other things? Is it right to make so many terms out of one when you can combine all, or most, into a single meaning and simply vary the figurative uses? "The Lord had regard for Abel," means that while Abel was doing this, God turned his thoughts to him. Wisdom is "delighted every day" says that when the sons of men act in a certain way, God directs his thoughts toward them and generously recommends himself to them. Thus a man turns sweetly toward God, and thus a mother fondles her child on her lap, fixes her gaze upon his, and holds him caressingly. So also God shuts men's eyes by making them voluntarily concentrate on their own strivings, and thus be blinded. Similarly, my "meditation is on thy statutes" when, despising everything else, I turn myself to them. In short, I include all this variety of meaning in the notion of turning, and preparing and attending to a thing freely and sincerely.

These things have been considered in order to show that Scripture is crammed with figurative language, so we ought not to make as many separate words and meanings as there are figurative expressions—for then what need would there be for such expressions?

---

[66] The Hebrew word is *shaashuim*.

[67] The Hebrew word here is *shaa*.

[68] The reading in the original is: *Amicabiliter applicare, sese insinuare, teutonice freuntlich zu yhm thun, feyn zu yhm stellen.*

[69] Here Luther confuses *shaah*, to glance, look, with *shaa*, to delight in, Ps. 119 [:23, 15].

So, coming to the point of this discussion, we see that when Christ is offered up, he is made sin for us metaphorically, for he was in every respect like a sinner. He was condemned, abandoned, put to shame, and in nothing different from a true sinner, except that he had not done the sin and guilt which he bore. He says in Ps. 69 [:4], "What I did not steal must I now restore?" In order that it may not be doubted that he acknowledges these sins as his own, he says in the same place [v. 9], "The insults of those who insult thee have fallen on me"; and again, "Thou knowest my folly; the wrongs I have done are not hidden from thee" [v. 5]. However, in metaphors it is necessary that something be different from the real thing, because, as they say, similarity is not identity. At the same time, there must be a likeness between the thing and that which represents it, for otherwise there wouldn't even be a representation. Paul saw this in Rom. 8 [:3], "God sent his Son in the likeness of sinful flesh"; and in Heb. 4 [:15], "One who in every respect has been tempted like as we are, yet without sinning." In this trope there is a metaphor not only in the words, but also in the actuality, for our sins have truly been taken from us and placed upon him, so that everyone who believes on him really has no sins, because they have been transferred to Christ and swallowed up by him, for they no longer condemn [the believer]. Just as figurative language is sweeter and more effective than is crude and simple speech, so also real sin is burdensome and intolerable to us, while transferred and metaphorical sin is wholesome and most delightful.

Therefore, in I Cor. 10 [:4] Christ is rightly called "the Rock" by the Apostle; just as "the Rock was Christ," so Christ truly is sin. Similarly, Christ is the bronze serpent, the paschal lamb, and all the other things which are said of him. Yet this is no reason for us to say that "bronze serpent," or "rock," has two separate meanings. No one ever says that "paschal lamb" sometimes means a sheep, and at other times Christ; nor does anyone say that "Aaron" is sometimes a name for Christ, and at other times for Amram's son [Exod. 6:20]; or that "David" is in one sense the son of Jesse, and in another sense Christ; or that "Solomon" is in one sense the son of David, and in another sense Christ. Yet we truly say that Christ is David, Solomon, Aaron, and all the other Old Testament types. On account of this Christ, who was made sin, is called sin because of his likeness to the offerings of the Old Testament, so that it is the likeness, not the differences, of sin present in all those things which makes room for these figurative uses in place of the usual meaning. My opponents, however, discuss sin as if its four species were as different as heaven and earth. Because of this dissimilarity in meaning, the understanding is dulled, the mind confused, and all grace—both the word and the content—is destroyed. Paul, discussing sin in the way which asserts similarity, says in Rom. 8 [:3] that, "For sin, he condemned sin"; that is, for the sin through which Christ was made sin (for our sin was transferred to him), our sin was condemned in him, as we now shall see.

We therefore say that the sophists really do not know what sin is according to the usage of Scripture, for when they talk of "penalty" they dream in an unscriptural way of something very different from sin. As I said, Christ was in every respect similar to sin except that he did not sin, for all the evil which follows sinful acts in us, such as the fear of death and hell, was felt and borne by Christ. The sophists themselves do not understand what they have invented about guilt and the attribution of punishment. Contrary to what they say, Christ felt that attribution, and was similar to one to whom sin is attributed, although without guilt. What is an attribution which one does not feel? Absolutely nothing. So, as I said, Christ differs not at all from a sinner of our own day who has just received the sentence that he must be condemned to death and hell. It was an effective attribution, wholly genuine, except that he did not deserve it, and was delivered up for us without having done anything to merit it. However, this is a thing rather to be experienced than to be discussed and grasped in words. We say further that the sophists partially grasp what the substance of sin is (namely, an offense against God and a transgression of God's law), but they know absolutely nothing of what it is in the categories of quantity, quality, relation, action, and passion. I shall here deal with this matter in such a way as to respond once and for all to everything that Latomus has brought forward. This is out of consideration for the reader, for this book would grow beyond measure if I were to proceed point by point.

We shall treat of sin in terms of these categories, thus speaking in a most barbarous way for the benefit of the sophists so that they may perhaps be able to follow us. Nonmetaphorical sin, wherever it exists, is in its nature truly sin. Looked at from the point of view of the character of substance (which is not susceptible of degrees) one sin is no more a sin than is another. However, one may be greater or stronger than another, just as one substance may be larger than another; and yet a fly is just as much a substance as is a man, and a weak man as a strong man. Furthermore, so that they won't trip me up in what I say, I here specify that I am using "substance" in the manner of Quintilian, not Aristotle, according to which one can state in regard to everything in the world, first, what it is, then its quantity, then its quality, and so on for the rest. Aristotle agrees whenever he discusses the matter, but the sophists attribute what they call "whatness" [70] [not only to things], but also to every category. For example, when discussing righteousness in accordance with the categories, one arranges the parts of the discourse so that first comes what it substantially is, then its quantity, quality, what it is related to, what it does, what affects it, where it is, and at what time, what it has, and what its situation is. In my judgment, an acquaintance with the categories, if rightly employed, would here be most useful for the exposition, memory, knowledge, and understanding of things, but this is completely unknown in the schools of the sophists.

To be sure, as I said, the sophists do understand something of the substance of sin; but after baptism and the infusion of the power of God, the condition of sin is such that it is not yet entirely reduced to nothing, but it is so subjected and broken down that it cannot now do what it once could. But what could it do? It made us guilty before God, tyrannically plagued the conscience, dragged us day by day into greater and greater evil, was mighty in quantity, quality, and action, governed in time and place, for it prevailed always and everywhere in all our powers and at every hour. The category of passion did not apply to it, for it did not suffer the law's accusation, nor would it even be touched. It was situated in the heart, turned its face downwards, and hastened to hell. Further, it was the relation of all the worst things which were opposed to

---

[70] *Quidditatem.* Thus Luther is using "substance" to refer to the "nature" or "essence" of a thing. Cf. *MA*⁸, *op. cit.*, pp. 174-175.

grace and subject to the anger and wrath of God. Thus it ruled, and we served it.

Now when the kingdom of God arrived [the other] kingdom was divided, the prince of the world was cast out, and the head of the serpent was trampled down even to the refuse and remains which by our care are at last to be eliminated. Similarly, after the children of Israel had entered into the land of Canaan, killed absolutely all the kings and destroyed their power, there still remained a natural and genuine part of the annihilated peoples of the Canaanites, Jebusites, and Amorites (as is written in Judges 1). They did not rule, nor were they equal to, the children of Israel, but were tributaries and servants, until at last David, having established the kingdom, wiped them out. So also we, having been called into the kingdom of faith by the grace of baptism, gain the rule over sin, for all its powers are smitten. Now only grumbling remnants, possessing the nature and character of what was destroyed, remain in the members. These we ought to extirpate by our own exertion, but this will happen only when Our David, having established the kingdom, will be enthroned in his majesty. Now the issue between myself and the sophists is whether or not this sin which remains must be truly considered sin. As was said, it cannot be denied, as they would like to do, that it is called sin by the Apostle; and so they take refuge in the interpretations and distinctions of the fathers. It therefore has come about that the voice of Paul is silenced throughout the world, so that there is no one left who calls that particular sin by the name with which Paul refers to it, for they suppose it to be an absurd and dangerous doctrine. It is as if the Holy Spirit were insufficiently foresighted, or did not know the words with which to speak safely—and teach us to speak—of His own affairs. Hence, in order to reintroduce the use of the Pauline word, we here reject once and for all everything that all of the fathers have said when they called this remainder lust, weakness, penalty, imperfection, fault, or whatever else they supposed it to be. To them we oppose Paul, our, that is, the Gentile's, apostle, for that edifying author calls it [the remaining sin] "sin," not in one place, but always, and never penalty, never imperfection, never weakness. For not even Augustine, even though he is of all the fathers the best, was free to change the expression Paul used and to invent another.

We therefore say that we would yield and grant that sin in this passage does not signify sin, but rather penalty, only if it were proved not to be genuine sin because of the absurdity of this opinion or of its consequences; otherwise we would not yield even to an angel from heaven who spoke against it. What more do you want, you sophists? I can excuse the fathers who were tempted, or driven by necessity, vigorously to deny that sin remains after baptism, for they fought against those who absolutely denied grace. It was therefore in order to commend grace that they asserted that all sin is taken away. What they say fits the subject matter beautifully and well, for their opponents disputed regarding the reign of sin, denying that it is removed; but this is a godless view, for the whole of sin is truly annulled so that it definitely no longer reigns. Nevertheless, Augustine himself in many places clearly calls it [the remaining sin] both fault and sin. For instance, he says in a letter to Jerome[71] that no man has so much love in this life that it need not be increased. He asserts that, "In so far as it is less than it ought to be, it is a fault," and then continues: "Because of this fault, in God's sight shall no man living be justified. On account of this fault, if we say we have no sin, we deceive ourselves, and the truth is not in us. Because of this fault there is not a righteous man upon earth that does good and sins not." This is what Augustine says. So you see that Augustine also understood this text of Scripture to the effect that a person in doing good [also] sins, for he calls it a fault that he does not yet work with a love which is large enough, explaining that the only thing lacking in his action is complete love. Isn't this clear enough?

Latomus, however, cites some passages as showing that Augustine always asserts the same meaning for fault. (However, as I said, I do not entirely believe Augustine, so that my opponents cannot say that I base myself on him only when he agrees with me— it may be that he is as thoroughly inconsistent as Latomus infers, but that is no concern of mine.) What happened was that when Latomus saw that Augustine had been condemned in condemning

---

[71] Letter 167, 4. Migne 33, 739.

Luther—which, before their rash deed, none of the sophists could see—he was so thunderstruck that for a long time he was not himself. Returning to his senses, he thought, what shall I do? It is shameful to be beaten, so I shall do this: I shall imagine that the Latin language, together with the Greek and Hebrew, has become extinct everywhere through the power of my *Dialogue*,[72] or if something has survived, I shall say it is not a language, just as I say that this sin is not sin. Because the pope has approved our deed, it will be easy for us to compel the rest of the world to come to the faculty of Louvain in order to ask the meaning of words. Therefore, since the word "fault" occurs so often in Augustine that it is even more troublesome than the term "sin" in Paul, we shall establish, ordain, and enact by the power of our faculty that "fault" shall mean what we want it to, namely, an imperfection, and not that which lacks what it ought not to lack, or something contrary to the law of God. If anyone says otherwise, he will know the wrath of the bull and of those who "tail" after it. Signed and sealed, etc.

I ask you, my readers, who are surprised to see me make fun of the sophists in this way, whether my indignation over their unheard-of audacity and shameless fawning is not justified? Shouldn't I mock at those who are not satisfied to mock God's Scriptures, the sayings of the fathers and rational evidence, but in addition go on to gag the mouths of the whole world and plainly transform all men into beasts, as if we didn't know our language? The whole world at all times has called that a fault which is contrary to the moral virtues, and this expression is so generally used in connection with faults and virtues that even their Aristotle calls sins nothing other than faults. Yet they dare to come forward and deny everything (whether ours, theirs, or God's) and in front of everybody, not only say that a fault is not contrary to virtue, but that it is not contrary to the grace of God. So behold, O Louvain, your arsonists, the enemies of languages and of truth, and you, O Roman Antichrist, behold your cultivators [of the Lord's field]![73]

Because of all this, we despise their whorish impudence, and join Augustine with Paul. What the latter calls sin, the former calls

---

[72] *Dialogue on Three Languages.* Cf. Introduction, p. 135.
[73] Cf. above, p. 187.

fault. We know that even in reference to the body a fault is something culpable and reprehensible, and deserving of censure. This is the universal usage of the Latin language. Therefore let us listen to what Paul says of sin in Rom. 8 [:3ff.]: "God sent his own Son in the likeness of sinful flesh and for sin, he condemned sin in the flesh, in order that the righteousness of the law might be fulfilled in us, who walk not according to the flesh but according to the Spirit." What does this mean, "sin is condemned for sin"? We have said that Christ was made sin for us, just as II Cor. 5 [:21] puts it: "For our sake he made him to be sin who knew no sin, so that in him we might become the righteousness of God." Sin is used in the same way both places. Allegorically or metaphorically, Christ is the sin for which God has condemned our true sin, for on what account are our sins removed if not for the sake of Christ who was made sin for us? This is certainly not done for our own strength and merits but for the sin of God, that is, for Him whom God has made sin. I now ask why it is not said that He extinguished sin, but is carefully stated that He condemned sin. We do not believe, as do the sophists of Louvain, that Paul, who was a chosen vessel, lacked the words to speak with foresight in well-chosen and proper terms. What then is condemned? He adds "in the flesh," precisely asserting that there is sin in the flesh, although condemned. That man is indeed condemned whose robberies and wicked crimes are not simply forbidden, who is not simply arrested and imprisoned, but on whom the verdict is pronounced and who, bearing the sentence of death, is led to execution so that, even though he has not yet suffered, nothing can happen to him except to be taken away. Where then is the power of such a robber?

So also through baptism, sin in us is arrested, judged, and wholly incapacitated so that it can do nothing, and is appointed to complete annihilation (although he who indeed conspires with what has been condemned falls under what is said in John 16 [:8, 11]: "The Spirit will convince the world of judgment, because the ruler of this world is judged.") We ought to believe that sin is condemned, and that this judgment is just, and we ought also to carry out that judgment. But what are the chains with which sin is held captive? (Isa. 5 [11:5]): "Righteousness shall be the girdle of his waist, and faithfulness the girdle of his loins." Psalm 68 [:18] says, "Thou didst ascend the high mount, leading captives in thy train, and receiving gifts among men." Who indeed does not know that a robber at large is no less a robber than one who is imprisoned? But the strength of the latter is quenched so that nothing is weaker than one to whom death is near, for he cannot do what as a robber he wants to do. Yet, although miserable, he is still a robber, so that if released, he would do what a robber does. Thus sin in us after baptism is in its nature truly sin; but only according to substance, and not in its quantity, quality, or action, for it is wholly passive. The motion of anger and of evil desire is exactly the same in the godly and the godless, the same before grace and after grace, just as the flesh is the same before grace and after grace; but in grace it can do nothing, while outside of grace it gets the upper hand. Because of this Paul says in Rom. 8 [:2], "For the law of the Spirit of life in Christ Jesus has set me free from the law of sin and death." Why does he not say that, "It has set me free from sin and death"? Has not Christ set us free from sin and death once and for all? Paul, however, is speaking of the proper operation of the law of the Spirit, which does what Christ has merited. Indeed, Christ once and for all absolved and freed everyone from sin and death when He merited for us the law of the Spirit of the Life. But what did that Spirit of Life do? He has not yet freed us from death and sin, for we still must die, we still must labor under sin; but in the end He will free us. Yet He has already liberated us from the law of sin and death, that is, from the kingdom and tyranny of sin and death. Sin is indeed present, but having lost its tyrannic power, it can do nothing; death indeed impends, but having lost its sting, it can neither harm nor terrify. These then are two places in which Paul calls "sin" that evil which remains after baptism.

It is for this reason that in Rom. 8 [:13] and Col. 3 [:5], Paul recommends the putting to death of what is earthly; that is, such things as anger, passion, and covetousness. He uses unmistakable terms, not simply speaking of sin, but calling it by its names: anger, passion, covetousness. Yet these new linguistic authorities would persuade us that these are not the names of either faults or sins, for the Apostle is writing to saints and believers. They therefore pretend that passion in this place is not a fault, but the penalty of sin and a certain imperfection which is not against the law of God.

207

Was it not then already the penalty of sin before baptism? Why then was it sin? Is its attribution [to Christ] enough to change the thing and its nature? If so, they would have to fill almost all of Paul with new words, and erase the original ones. Thus Rom. 6 [:12]: "Let not sin therefore reign in your mortal bodies, to make you obey their passions." What could have been said more clearly? Sin and its passions are in the body, but one must take care that it does not reign. This then is a third text, and here is a fourth: "For sin will have no dominion over you, since you are not under law but under grace" [Rom. 6:14]. Notice that he writes to those who live under grace, and says that they are not to be ruled by sin. This must be understood as referring not to the sins of others, but to our own sins, for who can resist the sins of others, or prevent another from sinning? A fifth text of the same sort: "Our old self was crucified with him [Christ] so that the sinful body might be destroyed" [Rom. 6:6]. He says our old man is crucified, and yet the sinful body must be destroyed even in us. He would never say that Christ destroys the imperfect body, or the body of punishment. Observe that we have five clear passages in which he speaks of sin, in addition to the places which we have not enumerated where Paul speaks of individual faults. Yet these insignificant vendors of smoke would compel all these heavenly thunderings to yield to an invented interpretation, spawned out of their own heads, unconfirmed by a single text of Scripture. We shall deal later with the seventh chapter [of Romans], which is closely related to this.

What then, are we sinners? No, rather we are justified, but by grace. Righteousness is not situated in those qualitative forms, but in the mercy of God. In fact, if you remove mercy from the godly, they are sinners and really have sin, but it is not imputed to them because they believe and live under the reign of mercy, and because sin is condemned and continually put to death in them. This is a most glorious pardon which comes through baptism. Surely, if you look at it carefully, it is almost greater to accept as righteous him who is still infected by sin than him who is entirely pure. [However], it must not therefore be said that baptism does not remove all sins; it indeed removes all, but not their substance. The power of all, and much of the substance, are taken away. Day by day the substance is removed so that it may be utterly destroyed. I am neither the first nor the only man to say this since the [days of the] Apostle. Augustine's words are these: "All sin is forgiven in baptism, not so that it no longer exists, but so that it is no longer imputed." [74] Do you hear? Even after forgiveness there is still sin, but it is not imputed. Are you so little satisfied with this ineffable mercy of God which justifies you from all sin, accepting you as if you were without sin, that you push on further to put to death what He has himself already condemned and brought close to extinction? This is a manifest absurdity and compels Latomus to hold that the Apostle must not be understood to be speaking properly of real sin. Do you say that what is not imputed is now no longer sin? But this is what I want, that nonimputation [of sin] is not ascribed to the work and its nature, but to mercy. Latomus, however, sets aside forgiving mercy and claims that according to nature sin is no longer present. This truly is to rob God.

What has just been said supplies, I believe, the defense for the thesis that all good work is sin unless it is forgiven by mercy. They themselves [my opponents] cannot deny that the fruit exhibits the nature of the tree. Now it has been shown that the tree is not without sin, even though this [sin] has been condemned and forgiven. Even Augustine in *Retractions* I, 19 (where he discusses whether the commands of God are fulfilled in this life) concludes that, "The commandments of God are fulfilled when those which are not done are forgiven." Does he not here clearly say that the commandments are fulfilled by the forgiving mercy of God, not by the works which are done? But what is forgiven if not sin? It is therefore clear that the sophists depend on making a mockery of words when they say that this is not sin, for they admit that it is called sin by Paul; and so according to them you can say, "Good work is not sin, yet it is called sin," just as was said above regarding what is impossible: "The command of God is not impossible, yet it is called impossible." It is as if you were to parody the statement of Demodocus reported by Aristotle,[75] and say, "The Louvainians are indeed not fools, but they do what fools do." That is, they put on

---

[74] *Retractions*, I, 19. Migne 32, 614.
[75] *Nichomachean Ethics*, VII, 8.

such an act in order to prevent these words, "sin" and "impossible," from keeping their generally recognized meaning and for no other reason than that it goes against their opinions, and our professors do not want to be put to shame by the truth.

Because we are speaking of sin, I would like to forewarn the reader so that he may have something with which he can briefly respond to everything Latomus brings forward. Observe, first, that Latomus proceeds in everything as if the sin which I assert were nothing, and as if it had already been long overcome, for it is the practice of the sophists to rejoice before the victory and viciously to beg the question. Consequently he believes that whatever he can piece together out of the Scriptures and fathers which denies the sinfulness of believers argues against me. Therefore against all these, use the words of Paul in Rom. 6 [:12]: "Let not sin therefore reign in your mortal bodies." Thus you will know that it is one thing for sin to rule, and another thing for it to be ruled. Do you understand? In this way you will be able to say in the manner of Latomus that willing a sin is different from performing it, even though it is one and the same sin, whether theft or murder. So tell him when he comes accompanied by clouds of witnesses: Teacher, thou enumerator, but not weigher, of testimonies, you have effectively proved that sin does not rule in the saints or in their works, but you have not proved that there is there no sin which is ruled, or sin of the sort which Paul mentions when he says, "Do not obey the passions thereof." [76] "Thereof"—do you hear that, Lord Latomus? "Thereof," that is, of the sin which does not rule in the body and yet is present with its passions in the body. Luther never talks of sin reigning in the saints. You are not behaving well, for you are not doing what you promised. You wanted to refute Luther, and instead you refute something you have dreamed up.

For example, when Paul says in I Cor. 7 [:28], "If you marry, you do not sin, and if a girl marries she does not sin," your Lordship cites this against Luther, but not conclusively. For this means the same as, "Let not sin therefore reign in your mortal bodies," and so refers to the sin which reigns, as is shown by the context which deals with the saints in whom sin does not rule.

---

[76] Rom. 6:12. The translation follows the Vulgate.

Does not Luther emphasize I John 3 [:9] much more than you: "No one born of God commits sin; and he cannot sin"? "If a girl marries she does not sin" is weaker than, "she cannot sin." Paul too speaks in this way in Rom. 6 [:14]: "For sin will have no dominion over you"—that is, you cannot sin—"since you are not under law but under grace."

Now neither Latomus, who says that a girl who marries does not sin, nor Luther, who says that a girl who marries cannot sin, can deny that a girl who marries sins in discharging her obligations to the flesh. Everyone agrees on this, and it is proved by Ps. 51 [:5], "Behold, I was brought forth in iniquity, and in sin did my mother conceive me." How does the one who marries both sin and not sin? Or does Latomus restrict "marrying" to what is done during the betrothal before the privacies of the marriage bed? I don't believe that he would quibble so obviously, but he might. What then will he do with Paul's previous injunction that, "The husband should give to the wife her conjugal rights, and likewise the wife to her husband"? [I Cor. 7:3]. Does he not here recommend the work of conceiving in sin of which David speaks? The one who marries gives himself heartily to this task. But Latomus also says that the saints often sin, and venial sin can accompany a girl's marrying; so contrary to the Apostle, a maid in marrying will sin.

But look at this daring Apostle who, even without the consent of the faculty of theology of Louvain, speaks further: "Do not refuse one another except perhaps by agreement for a season, that you may devote yourselves to prayer; but then come together again, lest Satan tempt you through lack of self-control" [I Cor. 7:5]. What are you doing, Paul? Do you, who lack the letter and seal of the faculty of theology of Louvain, dare to attribute incontinence to the saints, even to those whom you instruct to take time for prayer? Surely you are a Tatian,[77] a defender of the Cataphrygians,[78] who implicates marriage in sin, and not only marriage but the saints of God. That entire exhibition of absurdity which Latomus produced against Luther now falls on you. In the future your books will be burnt; after that, a terrible bull will endorse the faithful "cultivators of the Lord's field," and then Latomus will arise, proving by a

---

[77] An apologist of the second century, who allegedly left the church again.
[78] Montanists, a sect movement of the second century, originating in Asia Minor.

comprehensive demonstration that incontinence is not incontinence but simply a weakness and penalty. When Satan tempts [the saints], he does not tempt them to incontinence, but to weakness, and if it happens that they consent to incontinence, they do not assent to sin but to a weakness and penalty, and so when they sin they will really not sin. See, [Paul,] you are disgraced as a future heretic.

Because of this it happens that all the divine commands prohibit weakness and the penalty of sin, rather than sin itself. A new theology has come into the world according to which sin consists of consenting to an infirmity and penalty, rather than to sin. God has not commanded us to avoid sin, but weaknesses and the penalties of sin. The meaning of Rom. 6 [:12] becomes this: Let not the penalty of sin reign in your mortal bodies—or, let not weakness reign in your mortal bodies—to make you obey its passions. On the other hand, it will be sin to consent to that which is neither sin nor condemned. Plainly the new notion of sin is this: weakness is neither sin nor condemned, and yet if you consent to a thing which is neither condemned nor culpable, you sin.

marvelous satire!

However, if these sophists had wanted to care for the souls of the godly, they would have omitted misleading words and presented the matter simply as it is, in some such way as this: Look here, good brothers, we confess that good works are pleasing to God and that it is wholly through them that we are saved, but they are good not because they are without sin, but because they are done while fighting against sin. The entire good of the work is that although sin is in us, still we fight with ourselves so that it will not govern, and so that we will not obey its lusts. This is so, although the rigor of the divine law can demand that this conflict not be in us, for as the wise man says, God did not in the beginning create us thus: "God made man upright, but they have sought out many devices" [Eccles. 7:29]. We are hampered by evil so that we are not wholly within His law, and a part of us which fights against us is opposed to His law. Yet He has promised mercy and forgiveness to all who, at the very least, do not consent to this part of themselves but fight against it and are eager to annihilate it. This eagerness pleases Him, not because of its worth, but because he is kind and has promised to accept it. Therefore so that you will not be arrogant or proud, you have in yourself reason to fear judgment and severity and there is nothing to turn to except mercy. It is through mercy, not through your efforts, that your works are good. You will therefore judge yourselves one way in accordance with the severity of God's judgment, and another in accordance with the kindness of His mercy. Do not separate these two perspectives in this life. According to one, all your works are polluted and unclean on account of that part of you which is God's adversary; according to the other, you are genuinely pure and righteous. As testimony that you are thus purified, you have the symbol of baptism, through which all sins are most truly forgiven you—entirely forgiven, I say, but not wholly abolished. We believe that the remission of all sins has been without doubt accomplished, but we daily act in the expectation of the total removal and annihilation of all sin. It is those who labor toward this who do good works. Behold, this is my faith just because it is the catholic faith. The sophists who attack this do so in order to exalt our confidence in works and so diminish the work of both the mercy and justice of God, as is said in Ps. 10 [:5]: "Thy judgments are on high, out of his sight." So therefore they overturn both the fear of God and our confidence. Otherwise they could be borne with, but now they pant to destroy and demolish that which is the chief bulwark of salvation, and our portion, and they either sport or rage about less important things.

However, you will say to me: This distinction between the sin which reigns and that which is reigned over is new; it is yours, and you have arbitrarily posited it. To this I reply: So be it; dislike it if you will—I refuse to dispute about words—go make yourself another. At least this phrase, "sin which reigns," is not my invention, but is cited from Paul. Call the other kind, which does not reign, by whatever name you please, although Gen. 4 [:7] favors me: "Its desire shall be under you, and you shall master it." Here subjugated sin is certainly described. Even the sophists are compelled to concede that venial sin differs from mortal sin. Although they assert that venial sin does not harm, rule, or damn, they yet most truly and properly call it sin; nor do they say that the mortal and the venial are of two different kinds or natures, but they assert that they are both departures from the law of God and contrary to it. I ask nothing more than that they permit me in this way to call sin what remains after baptism so that it, like what they themselves call venial sin, may require mercy and be in its nature faulty and evil. If you consent to this [sin], you have made sin to reign, you serve it and have sinned mortally. From this point of view I have already recalled often enough what Paul says in Rom. 6 [:12], and from this I will not allow myself to be separated. I say that they cannot deny that two evil things survive baptism, sin and its passions. The words of Paul are self-evident: sin, the tinder [*fomes*], is natural evil, while passion and lust are its motion. It is this, he says, which must not be obeyed, which must be destroyed, "so that the sinful body might be destroyed" [Rom. 6:6]. They may name these two things whatever they please, but they shall not get rid of the fact that this was said by Paul. Paul wanted them to be destroyed and put to death and so, because they are condemned to be put to death, it follows that they are evils, faults, and sins. Weaknesses, penalties, and the things involved in our mortality are not subject to legal restraint, nor can they be brought within our range of choice. Who can slay death and the penalties of sin except God alone, [acting] without [dependence on] us? Commandments have to do with sins and the things which make us subject to punishment. Therefore when Paul commands us not to obey certain things, but to put them to death, he certainly means sins, rather than punishments, things pertaining to our mortality or weaknesses. What sort of law would this be: Do not obey ulcers, do not obey fever, do not obey hunger and thirst, do not obey nakedness and bondage; and do not obey the passions of any one of these? Aren't all these weaknesses, penalties, and things pertaining to mortality? No, what must not be obeyed is sin, and sinners and their suggestions, which are also sin.

Nevertheless it is stupid of us to labor with so many words over such obvious things when we have the Apostle asserting sin and evil passion with such clear and distinct words. Who, if he is not satisfied with Paul's words, would be persuaded by ours? I wonder what they would have done if Paul had spoken obscurely and written "evil" and "infirm" instead of "sin"; or if instead of "obey" and "not reign," he had said "be watchful" and "abstain," as Peter does: "Abstain from the passions of the flesh" [I Pet. 2:11]. What a confident and happy triumph they would have here celebrated! Now, since they cannot resist the daylight, they contrive to obscure it with clouds and create darkness in the middle of the day, so that sin is not sin and Paul appears to have lied. Even if the fathers appear to favor them, we must not adhere to them but rather to Paul; and if, [on the other hand,] they spoke the truth, [we still must adhere to Paul,] because they speak more obscurely and less forcefully than he does. Paul's words are too clear to need any gloss; indeed, interpretation rather obscures them. Nevertheless, as I said, even though the fathers sometimes call this [remainder] "sin" and "fault," yet they more often speak of the sin which reigns. Consequently I might say this to our sophists who fight against me with the statements of the fathers: You discuss and demonstrate the clearest of divine matters with what is human and obscure. Therefore, since even your Aristotle forbids the demonstration of the unknown through the unknown, the obscure through the obscure[79]— much less the manifest through the obscure—I conclude that you are clumsy disputants who constantly and in everything beg the question. This is the sum total of Luther's response to, and refutation of Latomus. Luther is ruined if it can be proved that the sin, in the text cited from the Apostle Paul, is not truly and properly sin; but if this cannot be proved, Latomus is ruined. As it cannot be proved except through some self-contradictory statements of the fathers— which, even if not contradictory, are in addition human—our opponents ought to prefer the divine words without whose authority nothing must be asserted. It follows that Latomus, and all that he says, is ruined and that Luther, and all that he says, stands firm.

Yet I compliment the confidence and constancy of Latomus who, once having undertaken the defense of the cause of the stubborn sophists, did nothing unworthy of the sophistic character and obstinacy, but treated, mistreated, twisted, and forced in whatever way he wished everything human and divine which stood against him. We have already seen this happen. So many testimonies of Scripture prove that God's commandment is impossible for us that nothing is more evident, and yet, like deaf adders, the sophists close their ears [Ps. 58:4] and turn away their eyes, holding before the public that single and unique decretal of theirs, which is to be received once and for all: Whoever says that God commands the impossible, let him be anathema. This human word must rule, all

---

[79] *Prior Analytics*, II, 16; *Topics*, V, 2.

must approve it, nor ought any interpretation touch it. But the divine thunders must be silenced and cast down, and one must accept just any arbitrary interpretation of any rascal whatsoever. The word of man is sacred and to be venerated, but God's Word is handed over to whores. It is thus also here where so many bolts of sacred lightning testify that sin and evil passion remain after baptism. These are openly called anger, lust, covetousness, and incontinence—names which, by universal consent and in all languages, are customarily used to designate faults and sins. The sophists, nevertheless, rise proudly up, hold their ears, close their eyes, and turn away their heart just so that they may fill all ears with their human word, and alone may occupy the stage so that no one will bark against their assertion that after baptism only weakness and penalty remain. The divine oracles are silenced, Paul surrenders, and so does our daily experience and that of all the saints. If these fail to yield, then the sophists adopt a disguise, saying that imperfection and weakness are represented under the name of sin, and warning that they cannot accommodate themselves to our interpretations. Latomus acknowledged earlier that the saints often sin (in his sense of the word) by inadvertence, through ignorance or in other ways, and that is what Paul calls the lust of the flesh in the mortal body to which we are not obedient, that is, do not consent. He says that we sin unwillingly, for you cannot consent when you are ignorant, unwilling, or do not deliberate. Because Paul calls this sin, he [Latomus] finds it necessary to understand the word "sin" as referring to penalty—this for no other reason than that the Spirit and not man has spoken. Thus the meaning of sin and of penalty is dependent on the arbitrary choice of the sophists. Who, I ask, would not swear that this is more than Moabitic arrogance? [Isa. 16:6].

Does this mean, you ask, that I do not believe what the fathers say? To this I reply: Should I believe? Who has commanded that I believe them? Where is the precept of God regarding such belief? And why don't they believe these fathers of theirs—especially Augustine who wished to be free and commanded everyone to be free in regard to all human writings? [80] The sophists have imposed

---

[80] Letter 93 (to Vincentius) cap. X. Migne 33, 338-343.

tyranny and bondage upon our freedom to such a point that we must not resist that twice accursed Aristotle, but are compelled to submit. Shall we therefore be perpetually enslaved and never breathe in Christian liberty, nor sigh from out of this Babylon for our Scriptures and our home? Yet you say they were saints and illuminated the Scripture. Who has shown that they made the Scriptures clearer—what if they obscured them? By whose pronouncement do you prove that they threw light on Holy Writ? Will you say in the fashion of Louvain and Cologne that, "it seems so to me," and, "so they say"? To be sure, they may say so and it may seem so, but let them prove the thing to me, or else stop urging me with their empty words. I am commanded to believe the Word of God, not their fancies. There is one teacher, even Christ, and the fathers are to be tested by the judgment of the divine Scriptures so that it may be known who has clarified and who has obscured them. Thus Paul orders us to "test everything; hold fast to what is good" [I Thess. 5:21]. In I Cor. 14 [:29] he says, "Let two or three prophets speak, and let the others weigh what is said." He commands that all be tested and that there be no exceptions—neither Augustine, nor Origen, nor any man, not even the Antichrist, the pope. But doesn't obscure Scripture require explanation? Set aside the obscure and cling to the clear. Further, who has proved that the fathers are not obscure? Are we once again going to have your, "it seems," and their, "they say"? What did the fathers do except seek and present the clear and open testimonies of Scripture? Miserable Christians, whose words and faith still depend on the interpretations of men and who expect clarification from them! This is frivolous and ungodly. The Scriptures are common to all, and are clear enough in respect to what is necessary for salvation, and are also obscure enough for inquiring minds. Let everyone search for his portion in the most abundant and universal Word of God, and let us reject the word of man, or else read it with discrimination. This is enough regarding this matter, and much more than enough.

PART THREE

Latomus next takes up Paul's Romans 7. He here confirms my opinion, and publicly displays that he has written his book, not out of zeal for the truth, but with the intention of perverting and deceiving the world simply in order to mitigate the shame of the book burning and of the blasphemous verdict. However stubborn and obstinate he may be, still he is pale and trembling as he goes silently and cautiously through the words of Paul. He seems to fear every dot, lest a chasm appear and swallow up the wretched sophists. After passing beyond these dangers and arriving in his own territory, he digresses and heaps together the statements of the fathers as if he wanted it thought a miracle that a sedentary and unoccupied reader could patch and press together so much irrelevant stuff. Perhaps he plans and hopes that sheer quantity will terrify me so that I will not write a second time, for it would take an infinitely long volume to reply to a single point of his. Yet this hope deceives him, for my writings are well-founded so that his are overthrown, and there is no need to answer every single point. In summary, Latomus' way of escape is this: What Paul says in this chapter simply shows that a weakness which may be called sin remains after baptism. Nevertheless, the Spirit, in controlling that weakness, works in such a way that it is not to be considered a sin worthy of damnation, nor does a man therefore serve sin, nor sin in doing good works. Here you see, first of all, that Latomus simply delays, misleads the reader, and gains time, while treating a question other than the one proposed. He has undertaken to discuss the question of sin mercifully forgiven, for he has himself testified in more than one place, that it is of this that I speak. Then by means of, and after, all this tumult of testimonies, he concludes in this way: "See, this [the sin in the baptized] is not a sin worthy of damnation." What he ought to have concluded is that this is not a sin, and so not even pardonable, nor in need of mercy. It is as if I were to have said that a laugh is a venial sin, and you—after spewing out all your spittle and exhausting your supply of sweat—were to contradict me by finally panting forth, "Look here, a laugh is not a mortal sin." This is the way Elihu argues with Job [Job 32ff.]. Do you think it takes only a small amount of patience to tolerate, in matters so necessary and sacred, the worthlessness, deceits, and devices of those who exalt themselves as the teachers of the whole world? I do not now complain that they are ignorant of what sin is, but rather that they maliciously disguise and deny their ignorance, and impose their shameless falsehoods on devout hearts.

Nevertheless, this timid runaway sophist gives me confidence. I shall confront him with Paul face to face so that he cannot escape; I shall pursue and overtake him, and shall not turn away until he is consumed [Ps. 18:37]. Either Latomus kills Paul, or Paul, Latomus, and in vain does Latomus trust in human protection. I therefore first ask whether I, as a Christian professing the gospel, am allowed to call sin what the Apostle Paul calls sin. I am here not arguing anything whatsoever about the meaning of sin—I shall see about that later. I simply want to be answered as to whether it is permissible for me to use this Pauline term. If it is not allowed, then Paul is erased. If it is allowed, why do the sophists bellow such terrible words against me just because I have called a good work a sin? Are they not permitted to call a good work an imperfection and a weakness? What then? Are they forcing me to use their words? Why are they unwilling to be compelled to use my words and Paul's? They don't want to call it sin. So be it. I also don't want to call it weakness and imperfection. But they say that the holy fathers have interpreted it as weakness and imperfection. That may be, but who forces me to use the words of the fathers, who forces me to forsake Paul's words? They say that it is absurd and dangerous; but this is no longer to turn against me, against Luther, but against Paul and the Spirit of Christ. "But you do not use the word 'sin' the way Paul does." Who has told you this? "A comparison [of the sayings] of the fathers and yours"? But who made the comparison? "We." Who are you? Who assures us that you cannot err? Is it because the bull has approved you? Now who has made you certain that the fathers have rightly expounded the word of Paul? Don't you hear? What are you muttering? Oh, so you now see that everything the sophists have advanced has come out of their own heads! To you, Latomus, leader of the sophists, I have something special to say. Your shoulders are overburdened with this affair, for it is of such a nature and such a weight that neither Cicero nor Demosthenes dealt with anything like it. Before God and men I accuse all of you as arsonists, blasphemers, murderers, and ravagers of Christian piety. Don't think that you can still argue and play around. It is a serious matter that we are dealing with.

You were apprehended in shame—for from the beginning you hastened after fame—and so now finally confusion arises, that is, you bellow, thunder, and rave so that with dulled ears you refuse to listen to anyone. All you do is hurl out this senseless clamor: There is no sin, there is no sin, there is no sin in a good work. Whatever I bring forward, interpret, and expound amounts to nothing. You rave against this word [sin] for no other reason than that you fear that what was condemned by you will be revived again through Paul to your shame. With unbelievable impudence, Latomus even interprets all my uses of this term as referring to mortal sin worthy of damnation, while he wants it to signify only weakness for Paul. This honest and veracious man always interprets me as harshly and offensively as he can, suppressing my meaning—for even he has admitted that I speak of what is pardonable—for he wishes the world to understand that I call sin what he wants to be considered sin. On the other hand, he gives so mild an interpretation of the word as it is found in Paul that he completely eliminates it. How great a writer is this Latomus who has the right to emphasize and suppress words according to his whim, rather than the intentions of the authors! Truly I promise you and the world that I do not wish to use this word otherwise than does Paul, and I call upon the name of the Lord, asking Him to oppose me, if I shall have used it in any other way. What more would you have? As you know, this is the word I will hold fast, and I don't want your words and those of the fathers. I want, as I say, to call sin what you call a defect or imperfection, and will you force me to do something else? I am not in the least moved by your most violent uproar. I see you have reasons for instigating it, viz., so that you won't succumb and be discovered to have heedlessly rushed into so great a crime. This was to be foreseen beforehand.

And so we come to the meaning of this word. Paul calls that which remains after baptism, sin; the fathers call it a weakness and imperfection, rather than sin. Here we stand at the parting of the ways. I follow Paul, and you the fathers—with the exception of Augustine, who generally calls it by the blunt names of fault and iniquity.

Now we come to the chief point of disagreement. Is it only by forgiving mercy, or is it by its very nature, that this sin—or, as you

prefer, infirmity—is not opposed to God and his law? Doesn't this
summarize our dispute? I have Paul's term on my side. Everyone
knows what it signifies, namely, that which by its nature is opposed
to God unless it is forgiven. You have, as it seems to you, the fathers
in your favor, who assert that it is not by nature against God and
his law. However, in the first place, you have not proved that this
is their intention, for it is easy for me to refute everything you bring
forward if I insist that they speak of sin apart from mercy. They
most truly say that that "sin-grace" [*peccatum-gratiae*]—so I phrase
it in my mind—makes absolutely no one liable to punishment: it
does not damn, or harm, and has absolutely nothing in common
with sin outside of grace. Latomus, don't I say the same thing?
What then is my blasphemy, when we agree to the extent of both
asserting that there is nothing destructive in this, which I call sin
and you call weakness? Why rave against me and so atrociously
wrong me when you cannot prove by the fathers something different
from what I said? Is it because I didn't follow the leadership of
you who condemned and burnt me before judging me? But,
Latomus, audacity and fire will neither influence nor terrify me.
It may be that there is some father of whom I have not yet taken
notice. As for Augustine, Jerome, Ambrose, Gregory, and Bernard—
I know them, and so it is in vain that you raise such clouds [of
witnesses] against me. Yet there may be somebody who asserts
that what remains [after baptism] is by its nature not opposed to
God and his law, and who denies that it is only by the forgiving
mercy of God that it is not against God and his law. When you
find such a one—and I hope you find him when the mule has
offspring—what have you then revealed, what accomplished, what
conquered? Who will convince me that this is Paul's meaning?
Or won't I be allowed to doubt this meaning? Am I not allowed to
murmur to myself that, although this is a holy man, still he is a man
and on this point savors of the human? Who knows if something
different from what he has seen is hidden in the Apostle? This is
especially likely because the Apostle so freely and openly talks of
sin, although he could, if he wished, have spoken as does this other
man. Who has given him the right to legislate for us and for our
understanding? Christ said that "none of you keeps the law"
[John 7:19]. Latomus, would you and your sophists wish to

condemn these thoughts of a devout heart to burning and to hanging? What if such a man cannot do otherwise? His cause may be just, for he is certain that God speaks through Paul, whose words are to be reverenced and not dishonored, while in the other case, he is not sure whether it is God or man that speaks.

What shall we do now? You say that we should go to reason and common sense. I thank you, for I am thereby liberated from any man's authority in this matter. Your reasoning may then [properly] pride itself on flowing from one of the articles of faith, namely, that we believe that the remission of all sins is given in baptism, as Paul himself teaches in many places. This is also the way your church fathers reason, and it pleases me. But why was Paul not at all influenced by this reasoning to refuse the name of sin to what remains after the remission of all sins, while the fathers were influenced so that they, as you say, deny sin? You have discovered two distinct types of sin in order to retain both this reasoning and the term Paul employs, for you were not able to harmonize them in any other way. Yet you cannot prove this distinction by any scriptural text. You cannot deny that it is a human invention which seems to you to be a necessary postulate on account of the reasoning mentioned above. Isn't this so—I understand you, don't I? I have said nothing against this ignorantly or without deliberation, so I plainly had no need for you to act as my teacher. Now what if I, by the illumination of the Spirit, have found a way to retain unharmed the godliness of the articles of faith, and at the same time, keep Paul uninjured because I need not allegorize any of his words in a forced and unheard-of manner? What if I can take them simply, properly, and appropriately in the sense they have in other places, and in this way satisfy the argument you urge to the effect that this equivocal term occurs only in this place, that is, in Paul, and nowhere else in Scripture—if so, will you begrudge me this? If you don't want to accept this, would you want to rob me of my joy when we agree so beautifully about the most important matters? I shall not allow myself to be drawn away from the simple meanings of God's Word providing I can make good sense of them while retaining loyalty to the faith; but as for your human inventions, I will definitely not yield to them.

However, you say: If we essentially agree, what makes you

produce such unholy verbal novelties, and why don't you make common cause with us without creating scandals? My answer is that I prefer to drink from the source, rather than from the rivulets. Will you prevent me from doing this? I am concerned about two things. First, I want to have the Scripture in the purity of its powers, undefiled by any man, even if he is a saint, and not spiced with anything earthly. You are the ones who have not avoided profane novelties of words,[81] as Paul says, but have annulled the holy things of God by wanting to clothe them with human interpretations and spice them with earthly condiments. My soul, like Ezekiel's, is nauseated at eating bread covered with human dung [Ezek. 4:12]. Do you know what this means? My second concern is that you cannot any longer honestly deal in honest words with the mystery of sin and grace. Further, you do not understand nor love it, and have become cold, pallid, sad, and slack in the praise and love of God. Man's word when added to the divine, veils the pure truth; nay rather, as I said, it is the human dung which covers it, as the Lord figuratively says in Ezekiel. This truth is the manna which must be preserved in golden vessels, and not be turned and tossed in the hands of men. Now therefore, you ask about my way of solving this problem. I shall answer, though I suspect that you, who pant after the garlic and melons of Egypt [Num. 11:5] and have already long suffered from perverted tastes, will not be pleased. However, I am satisfied that you will not be able to refute it, but that it can convict you of distorting the Word of God in giving it a sense which it has nowhere else. Everyone feels that it is shameful to hear such things from Christians, not to mention theologians.

The divine Scriptures deal with our sin in two ways: in one way, through the law of God, and in another way, through God's gospel. These are the two Testaments of God, which are ordained for our salvation so that we may be freed from sin. The law deals with sin only in order to reveal it, as Paul says in Rom. 3 [:20], "Through the law comes knowledge of sin." This knowledge teaches two things: the corruption of nature, and the wrath of God. Rom. 7 [:7] speaks of the first: "I should not have known that lust is sin if the law had

---

[81] I Tim. 6:20. Cf. the Vulgate.

not said, 'You shall not covet.'" For nature did not call this wanton itching sin, but rather its evil use on the bodies of others, as in debauchery, adultery, and fornication. Similarly, it does not call anger and avarice sin, but rather their expression in theft, fraud, slander, murder—and so also for other vices. As yet I do not know whether sin ever refers in Scripture to those works which we call sin, for it seems almost always to refer to the radical ferment which bears fruit in evil deeds and words. It is the law which reveals that what was before unknown and dead (as Rom. 5 [:13][82] says) is properly speaking sin, and that it is very much alive, though hidden under the false works of the hypocrites. Paul says that Scripture consigns all men to this sin [Gal. 3:22]. Yet it can never remain hidden so that it does not produce its fruits (which are of different sorts in different people, for you are not able to indicate any single evil work to which you can consign all men, for there are many). Rom. 4 [:15] speaks of the second point: "The law brings wrath," because as is said in Gal. 3 [:10], "Cursed be everyone who does not abide by all things written in the book of the law, and do them." So also [it is said in] Rom. 5 [:12], "death through sin," and Rom. 6 [:23], "the wages of sin is death." Up to this point the light of the law instructs us, teaching us that we are under corruption and wrath, and designating all men as liars and sons of wrath. We would perhaps have disregarded corruption and been pleased with our evil unless this other evil, which is wrath, had refused to indulge our foolishness and had resisted it with terror and the danger of hell and death, so that we have but little peace in our wickedness. Plainly wrath is a greater evil for us than corruption, for we hate punishment more than guilt.

So the law reveals a twofold evil, [one] inward and [the other] outward. The first, which we inflict on ourselves, is sin and the corruption of nature; the second, which God inflicts, is wrath, death, and being accursed. These are, if you wish, guilt and penalty, but in using these terms we have talked far too poorly and coldly of guilt and penalty, inventing I know not what relations and imputations. In accordance with Scripture, we should speak fully and bluntly of sin—or guilt, or inward evil—as a universal corruption

---

[82] Cf. also Rom. 7:7-8.

of nature in all its parts: an evil which inclines us to evil from our youth up, as is written in Gen. 6 [:5] and 8 [:21]. So great is this wrath that there is nothing profitable in those things which seem good as, for instance, arts, talents, prudence, courage, chastity, and whatever natural, moral, and impressive goods there are. The common sense of all men can detect nothing wrong with these things, so that today even our theologians number them among the goods, attributing nothing evil to them, for although they do not merit the kingdom of heaven when they are present apart from grace, still, on the other hand, neither do they merit hell nor punishment. If they had not heard of the necessity of grace, our theologians would be ready to assert plainly that they can even merit heaven, for they suppose that these things lack nothing that the law requires, but only what grace supplies. They teach that the law has been fulfilled [by them], but not the gospel. They next add that so great are these goods that they congruently and infallibly merit grace, so that they will become completely good, not, to be sure, by their own intrinsic merit, but nevertheless through their own merit.[83] It must be added that God himself does not deny that these [virtues] are good—for this cannot in fact be denied—but he rewards and bedecks them with temporal benefits, such as power, wealth, glory, fame, dignity, honor, enjoyment, and the like. Thus a covering—not merely of its own beauty, but of divine recompense— is added to this natural blindness which does not know the true good; thus it confidently and stubbornly maintains that it is good. This is the chief reason for the prophetic task, this is why all the prophets were killed, for they reviled these works and insisted on those which are more genuinely good. For prophecy was nothing else than the burnishing, activating—if I may speak thus—and application of the law; or, as is said in logic, the subsumption which declares whether any particular good work falls in the class of the truly or falsely good. Hence we are surprised at much that is condemned in the ancient books. Hence God warned them not to follow their own understanding but to listen to his voice. He therefore always provided prophets who applied the law practically

---

[83] *Si non proprio merito, tamen per proprium meritum.* Cf. *Apology to the Augsburg Confession*, Art. IV, 19, Concordia Triglotta, p. 125.

and, so to speak, showed by example of these good things what the law is.

Therefore it is only the law which shows that these [virtues] are evil—not, to be sure, in themselves, for they are the gifts of God, but because of that deeply hidden root of sin which is the cause of men being pleased with, relying, and glorying in these things which are not felt to be evil. This is now and always the innermost evil of sin, for trust, pleasure, and glorying must be in God alone, as Jer. 9 [:23] says: "Let not the wise man glory in his wisdom, let not the mighty man glory in his might, let not the rich man glory in his riches." All these are goods, but they are freely distributed among the evil more often than among the good, so that Ps. 73 [:2f.] complains of the danger on account of this—his "steps had well nigh slipped." Yet as I said, all these fall under wrath and the curse, nor do they profit anyone, nor indeed, prepare a "congruence to grace," but rather fatten the heart so that it neither desires nor senses the necessity of grace, as says Ps. 119 [:70]: "Their heart is curdled like milk." The Hebrew puts it better: "Their heart is gross like fat." These people are properly accused in Scripture of being godless, unbelieving, and stiff-necked, for they can neither restrain their unbridled inclination toward these apparently good things nor recognize in them the law and their sin. Through these things, they always suppose themselves to excel in obedience to God all others who are truly righteous. For them all preaching is vain; they are bloodthirsty and deceitful men [Ps. 5:6]. In brief, they have fulfilled the law and do not need grace except in order to meet, as I said, a certain addition in the divine requirement. For them, Moses is veiled, nor can they bear his shining[84] face.

In the midst of so much wisdom, goodness, righteousness, and religiousness, they will not to be evil, nor can they recognize that they are, because they do not listen. You see, therefore, how incomparably the law transcends natural reason, and how bottomless is the sin of which it gives us knowledge. Therefore all are under wrath, since all are under sin.

The gospel, on the contrary, deals with sin so as to remove it, and thus most beautifully follows the law. The law introduces us

---

[84] Luther, following the Vulgate, writes "horned" (*cornutam*).

to sin and overwhelms us with the knowledge of it. It does this so
that we may seek to be freed and to sigh after grace, for the gospel
also teaches and preaches two things, namely, the righteousness and
the grace of God. Through righteousness it heals the corruption of
nature. This is done by the true righteousness which is the gift of
God, namely, faith in Christ, as Rom. 3 [:21] says, "But now the
righteousness of God has been manifested apart from the law";
also in Rom. 5 [:1], "Since we are justified by faith, we have peace,
etc."; and Rom. 3 [:28], "For we hold that a man is justified by
faith." Almost always in Scripture, this righteousness which is
contrary to sin refers to an innermost root whose fruits are good
works. The companion of this faith and righteousness is grace or
mercy, the good will [*favor*] of God, against wrath which is the
partner of sin, so that he who believes in Christ has a merciful God.
For we would not be completely happy in this good of righteousness,
and we would not highly esteem God's gift, if that was all there
was, and it did not gain for us the grace of God. Here, as ought to
be done, I take grace in the proper sense of the favor of God—not a
quality of the soul,[85] as is taught by our more recent writers. This
grace truly produces peace of heart until finally a man is healed
from his corruption and feels he has a gracious God. It is this which
fattens the bones and gives joy, security, and fearlessness to the
conscience so that one dares all, can do all and, in this trust in the
grace of God, laughs even at death. Hence, just as wrath is a greater
evil than the corruption of sin, so grace is a greater good than that
health of righteousness which we have said comes from faith.
Everyone would prefer—if that were possible—to be without the
health of righteousness rather than the grace of God, for peace
and the remission of sins are properly attributed to the grace of
God, while healing from corruption is ascribed to faith. Faith is the
gift and inward good which purges the sin to which it is opposed.
It is that leaven which is described in the gospel as wholly hidden
under three measures of meal [Matt. 13:33]. The grace of God,
on the other hand, is an outward good, God's favor, the opposite of
wrath. These two things are distinguished in Rom. 5 [:15]: "For if
many died through one man's trespass, much more have the grace

---

[85] Cf. Thomas Aquinas, *Summa Theologica* 1 II, ques. 109-112. As cited in
MA[3] 6, 177.

of God and the free gift in the grace of that one man Jesus Christ abounded for many." He calls faith in Christ—which he more often calls a gift—the gift in the grace of one man, for it is given to us through the grace of Christ, because he alone among all men is beloved and accepted and has a kind and gentle God so that he might merit for us this gift and even this grace.

John 1 [:17] reads thus: "The law was given through Moses; grace and truth came through Jesus Christ"; and later, "full of grace and truth" [v. 14]. Now the truth which flows from Christ to us is faith, and grace accompanies faith on account of the grace of Christ, as is indicated earlier in the same place: "From his fulness have we all received, grace upon[86] grace" [v. 16]. What grace, and upon what grace? Our grace, so that God may favor us, upon Christ's grace, with which God favors him; or, as it says, "The law was given through Moses, but grace and truth came through Jesus Christ." We therefore have two goods of the gospel against the two evils of the law: the gift on account of sin, and grace on account of wrath. Now it follows that these two, wrath and grace, are so related—since they are outside us—that they are poured out upon the whole, so that he who is under wrath is wholly under the whole of wrath, while he who is under grace is wholly under the whole of grace, because wrath and grace have to do with persons. He whom God receives in grace, He completely receives, and he whom He favors, He completely favors. On the other hand, He is angry at the whole of him with whom He is angry. He does not divide this grace as gifts are divided, nor does He love the head and hate the foot, nor favor the soul and hate the body. However, He does give the soul what He does not give the body, and He gives the head what He does not give the foot. It is thus in the entirety of the church which stands under the same grace of God, as Rom. 5 [:2] says, "Through him we have obtained access to this grace in which we stand." He is diverse and multiform in his gifts. So also, conversely, he is unfavorable to the whole of the one to whom he is unfavorable, and yet he does not punish the whole. Rather, one man remains wholly under wrath through the sin of one member, while another remains wholly under grace through the one

---

[86] "For" (pro) in original.

gift of one work. As was said, grace must be sharply distinguished from gifts, for only grace is life eternal (Rom. 6 [:23]), and only wrath is eternal death.

Now we finally come to the point. A righteous and faithful man doubtless has both grace and the gift. Grace makes him wholly pleasing so that his person is wholly accepted, and there is no place for wrath in him any more, but the gift heals from sin and from all his corruption of body and soul. It is therefore most godless to say that one who is baptized is still in sin, or that all his sins are not fully forgiven. For what sin is there where God is favorable and wills not to know any sin, and where he wholly accepts and sanctifies the whole man? However, as you see, this must not be attributed to our purity, but solely to the grace of a favorable God. Everything is forgiven through grace, but as yet not everything is healed through the gift. The gift has been infused, the leaven has been added to the mixture. It works so as to purge away the sin for which a person has already been forgiven, and to drive out the evil guest for whose expulsion permission has been given. In the meantime, while this is happening, it is called sin, and is truly such in its nature; but now it is sin without wrath, without the law, dead sin, harmless sin, as long as one perseveres in grace and his gift. As far as its nature is concerned, sin in no way differs from itself before grace and after grace; but it is indeed different in the way it is treated. It is now dealt with otherwise than before. How was it treated previously? In such a way that it was existent, known, and overwhelmed us; but now it is treated as non-existent and as expelled. Despite this, it is truly and by nature sin. Indeed, it is ingratitude and injury to the grace and gift of God to deny that it truly is sin. To be sure, for grace there is no sin, because the whole person pleases; yet for the gift there is sin which it purges away and overcomes. A person neither pleases, nor has grace, except on account of the gift which labors in this way to cleanse from sin. God saves real, not imaginary, sinners, and he teaches us to mortify real rather than imaginary sin.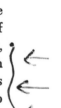

You see that in the treatment of sin and grace, I seek and wish to understand and to speak in this simple and Pauline way. It is sound and pure, grasped absolutely without any difficulty, requires no distinctions, is marvelously attractive and clear, and opens up all

Scripture. Here it is not necessary to say that in Paul sin is a name for weakness, but rather one must say that it means real sin. It is in this way that the grace and gift of God are truly and purely praised, for if anyone denies that this is real sin, he is ungrateful and blasphemes the gift of God. I say and teach thus so that every man may know that he has just as much sin in every one of his own works as the amount of sin which has not yet been expelled from him. As is the tree, so is the fruit. Thus he will not boast before God of the cleanliness which he has in himself, but will rather glory in the grace and gift of God, and in the fact that he has a gracious God on his side who does not impute this sin and, besides this, has given the gift through which it is purged away. He therefore confesses the truth that if he must be judged according to the nature of his works apart from grace, he cannot stand before His face; but now, because he relies upon grace, there is nothing which can accuse him. Are these things as obscure as are the huge volumes of the sophists crammed with sin and grace? Do they not beautifully meet the words of Paul, the piety of faith, and that argument—which seemed compelling—that sin is to be taken as referring to penalty? What is easier than to say that sin is to be dealt with either according to the law, or according to the gospel? If you treat it in terms of law alone, it is wrath and death, but if in terms of the gospel alone, it is grace and life—although truly and naturally remaining sin in both cases. All the citations from the fathers which deny that there is sin in the righteous must be understood in terms of grace, but not in terms of law or of the nature of sin. For Christ has liberated us so that we are no more under the law, but under grace.

However, you [my opponents] will say that the holy fathers deny sin [in the righteous], and I have not proved that sin must be taken in this way. I answer, first, that I understand and teach nothing godless, and alien to the faith. You admit this, don't you? I shall prove more, for I show next that the received meaning of sin everywhere in Scriptures is the one I take it to have. I thus effectively prove that it must be so taken, for nothing should be asserted in [questions of] faith without scriptural precedent. Next, there are two different ways in which your proof utterly fails. First, you have not shown that the fathers deny that sin must be taken, or can be taken, to have the meaning I accept; because, even if they call it weakness and deny sin, still they can be seen to do this, not from the point of view of the nature of sin, but from that of the grace of God—and you have nothing with which to oppose this. Now even if they genuinely deny that this is, in its nature, sin, yet they do not prove what they think and say, nor is it an article of faith. Rather, they speak dangerously, for they speak without scriptural precedent. So you show neither that they mean to say that sin simply signifies debt, nor that they prove it ought to do so. You have discovered this extremely puzzling word, "debt" [*reatus*], and you want to say that this is what sin formally signifies; but Scripture is plainer, and speaks in an easy and obvious manner of corruption and wrath. You do not show that whatever the fathers rightly say of the remission of all sins, the washing away of sins, and finally, of the glory of baptism, amounts to the same thing as the view that, as far as its nature is concerned, no sin is left. Nor do the fathers prove them to be the same. Paul, as well as Peter, opposes all. The latter speaks of the passions of the flesh that wage war against the soul [I Pet. 2:11]; the former of the sin in the mortal body which lusts against the spirit [Gal. 5:17; Rom. 6:12]. They compel us to view the statements of the fathers as referring to the grace with which the baptized are favored and to the gift which is opposed to sin, rather than to the law and the nature of sin. So, Latomus, all your assertions are empty and refuted; they are scattered like dust before the face of the wind. Therefore, since this opinion of mine favors godliness, agrees with the words of Scripture, and is simple and sound both in its expression and content, I will not let "sin"—as a term applicable to all men and to all their works in this life—be taken from me, even though I confess that there is nothing of sin or of evil works in them from the perspective of God's grace. He who does not wish to follow me may disregard this and follow others; but he should know that he relies on human, I on divine, testimonies. I will not allow him to believe in Augustine, who interprets the Apostle, more than in the Apostle himself, who so often speaks of "sin" [in the baptized].

We shall now see how Scripture agrees with this opinion. In the last chapter of Luke [24:47], Christ says that repentance and forgiveness of sins are to be preached in his name. Why was the forgiveness of sins not enough? Is there not agreement in this: repentance is the transformation of corruption and the continual renewal from sin which is effected by faith, the gift of God, and the gift of grace is forgiveness, so that in that case the wrath against sin ceases? He does not teach us to preach the fictitious penance of the sophists, as it is taught to this hour. There must be repentance and renewal so that sin may be expelled as long as there is preaching, as long as there is life. Can you thus harmonize these two [repentance and renewal] with weakness and penalty? Who would do penance for weakness, or who would renew the penalty? The same is implied by the word of John the Baptist which is repeated by Christ: "Repent, for the kingdom of heaven is at hand" [Matt. 3:2; 4:17].

What is this except to change one's life, as is done by faith in purging away sin, and to be under the rule of God, as is accomplished by forgiving grace? John calls this a worthy fruit [Matt. 3:8] if sin is purged and outward works are not feigned. This agrees so beautifully with the parable of the leaven and the three measures of meal in Matt. 13 [:33] that nothing could be more apt. The agreement is lost if you call sin weakness and penalty. Indeed, you have already spread such darkness with these words that you neither see nor understand the parable. The parable of the man half-dead cured by the Samaritan [Luke 10:30ff.] also pertains completely and first of all to this matter. This man was not healed all at once, but was raised up all at once in order to be cured. The Levite and the priest, ministers of the law, saw him, but did not help. So as I said, the law makes sin known, but it is Christ who heals through faith and rescues through God's grace. So also John [13:10], "He who has bathed is clean all over," namely, through grace; and yet it is through active faith that the feet, that is, the remaining sins, are cleansed. Further, we are the branches of Christ, the Vine, because we bear fruit as if in every respect clean, and yet the heavenly Vinedresser prunes us that we may bear more fruit [John 15:2].

You cannot adapt any of these passages to weaknesses and penalties without immediately destroying the meaning of washing, purging, and healing—except what you can make out of vague venialities. However, that results in a superficial meaning which picks off the leaves but does not pluck out the root. To borrow a simile from Latomus, this method of curing is like shaving hair where it will grow anew. The gift of God is not like this, for it works at killing the roots and cleanses [simply], not the act, but the person himself, so that venial faults cease, or at least multiply less luxuriantly. In vain you will resist the venial sins if you do not extinguish the "tinder" of sin from which these other sins develop. Sin always covets, but you resist its lust not only when you resist its agitations but when you kill sin itself. This is done through the gift of faith, which kills and crucifies what Paul calls the old man of sin, and which wears him out with various afflictions. An illustration I used before also applies here: After coming into possession of the Land of Canaan, the children of Israel did not annihilate the remnants of the Amorites, Jebusites, and Canaanites. These remnants were of the same nature as the original peoples— and yet our professors teach that infirmity and penalty are not evil, but they are rather to be tolerated as useful just as if they were not to be wiped out.

Therefore, in conclusion, since Paul speaks in Romans 6 of "sin in your mortal bodies" [v. 12], of "sin having no dominion" [v. 14], of "the sinful body to be destroyed" [v. 6]; in Romans 8, of being "set free from the law of sin and death" [v. 2]; in Romans 7, of "sin working" [v. 13], of sin "at war" and "making captive" [v. 23], of "serving the law of sin" [v. 25]; in I Cor. 7 [:5], of "incontinence"; in I Cor. 5 [:8], of "the old leaven of malice and evil"; in Eph. 4 [:22], of "the old man"; in Col. 3 [:5, 8], of "anger," "evil desire," and "covetousness"; in Heb. 12 [:1], of the "sin which clings so closely"— in short, since he always calls it by the name of sin and vice, I would not yield (even if he had called it sin only once) even to an angel. Now since in so many passages he steadfastly asserts the same thing, who are these men that they should compel me to set their interpretations on the text and erase Paul's words? I reject their opinion, and say that sin and trust [in God][87] are simultaneously present in us and in all our works as long as we are on this earth. So if my Louvainians had listened to me before, and had attended more to the Word of God than to man's, they would certainly have

---

[87] Latin: *fiducia.*

known a purer truth which would have preserved them from so monstrous a blasphemy, sacrilege, crime, and offense; and thus they would now not have rashly burned the word of Paul. However, I still offer them the choice of reflecting, recognizing their error, giving God the glory, confessing their wholly indefensible foolishness—and behold, everything will be forgiven them. I would very much like to have fellowship with them and never remember their trespasses, just as I don't want God to remember mine. Yet if they persist in what I detest, I shall certainly consider them anathema. The Lord will see whether my excommunication is more or less than that silly, bloody, blasphemous—in short, most worthy of the pope and of Rome—bull. Amen. I believe that with this I have sufficiently asserted, defended, and fortified everything I adduced in reference to this article in the original exposition attacked by Latomus; and that I have established that all that he has brought forward is nothing other than ignorance of Scripture, besides mere presumption and begging of questions.

I shall add one consideration so that I may have the help of reason and experience. Since I am disputing with sophists, we shall proceed from the rule to the example in order to avoid being stoics—for they define as "wise" a man the like of whom they have never seen, just as Quintilian trains an orator.[88] I ask whether the sophists dare to grant that there is any man who can say of a single good work of his that it is without sin, even in the sense in which they speak of sin. I do not believe that they themselves, or any man, would dare to suppose this of his work. If they deny there is anyone who can do this, why do they accuse me so fiercely, for they themselves think even as I. Indeed, they say more than I do, for I was not speaking of venial sins. Now what is absurd in positing sin in all good works? They themselves acknowledge that there is sin in most of them, and that in only a few is there no sin (but they say this last without giving an example and simply in accordance with the rule). If it is not absurd in one or in many, why is it absurd or impossible in all? Aren't we professors wonderful, who can teach a rule without instances? But they say: It is uncertain whose work is good and without sin, yet we cannot doubt that it is

---

[88] *Institutio Oratio*, VIII, *Prooemium*.

without sin. What then shall we do? Shall we lead men into uncertainty with our doctrines? Isn't it absurd to teach uncertainties in the church? When will there then be peace in our hearts? What shall we do in the meantime? Shall we pray for the forgiveness of sin in a good work, or shall we boast of it before God? It is dangerous not to ask for forgiveness if there is sin. On the other hand, it is dangerous to ask for forgiveness where there is, or one supposes there is, no guilt; for one would lie in praying for [forgiveness] for that [work] for which one does not feel the necessity of praying, and would not be fair to the good deed in confessing that it has need of pardon. Should a man be suspended in doubt so that he ought to pray—not only work—with uncertainty? We thank you, O our teachers, for you leave us no certainty, and do not even make us certain whether all things are uncertain.

However, let us pass on. Plainly there is in this life not a single instance of this rule that a good work is without sin. As we said, Paul did not dare to assert this of his own works: "I am not aware of anything against me, but I am not thereby acquitted" [I Cor. 4:4]. However, we need to be certain, and so God in his grace has provided us with a Man in whom we may trust, rather than in our works. For although he has justified us through the gift of faith, and although he becomes favorable to us through his grace, yet he wants us to rely on Christ so that we will not waver in ourselves and in these his gifts, nor be satisfied with the righteousness which has begun in us unless it cleaves to and flows from Christ's righteousness, and so that no fool, having once accepted the gift, will think himself already contented and secure. But he does not want us to halt in what has been received, but rather to draw near from day to day so that we may be fully transformed into Christ.

His righteousness is perpetual and sure; there is no change, there is there no lack, for he himself is the Lord of all. Therefore whenever Paul preached faith in Christ, he did so with the utmost care to proclaim that righteousness is not only through him or from him, but even that it is in him. He therefore draws us into himself, and transforms us, and places us as if in hiding "until the wrath passes away" [Isa. 26:20]. It is thus in Rom. 5 [:1], "We are justified by faith, we have peace with God through our Lord Jesus Christ." Observe, faith is not enough, but only the faith which hides under the wings of Christ and glories in his righteousness. Again, "By whom we have access to God through faith in this grace" [v. 2].

Once again he teaches faith in such a way as to thrust it under the wings of Christ. And this: "He was pleased through him to reconcile to himself all things." Notice the "through him" and "to himself." He further speaks of "making peace by the blood of his cross" [Col. 1:19-20]. What does the Apostle mean except that it is not enough to have that wavering faith of the sophists which, once the gift is received, is supposed to work [by itself]? But faith is precisely that which makes you a chick, and Christ a hen, so that you have hope under his wings. Malachi speaks of "healing in its wings" [Mal. 4:2] so that you will not rely on faith received in the past—for that is to fornicate—but that you may know that to have faith is to cleave to him, to presume on him, because he is holy and just for you. Observe that this faith is the gift of God, which the grace of God obtains for us, and which purging away sin, makes us saved and certain—not because of our works, but because of Christ's—so that we can stand and endure in eternity, even as is written: "His righteousness endures forever" [Ps. 112:3].

However, you may say that we seem to be tormented by a verbal disagreement over a matter on which we essentially agree, for neither party asserts that what remains after baptism—whether sin or penalty—deserves damnation. I answer that we agree on the end—namely, that it is harmless—but not at all on why this is so. For they attribute to nature what belongs to the grace of God and this is intolerable. Further, they lull men into security so that they do not cleanse away sin. They even diminish the knowledge of the mysteries of Christ, and so also the praise and love of God, for they do not consider the goodness spread out over sinners by the lavishness of grace, but rather make nature innocent. If there were nothing else against them, still they speak unscripturally, destroying the soundness of Scripture for no reason at all and darkening the understanding of its contents. So it happens that the loss of its simplicity becomes a stumbling block which leads us farther and farther away from it. This occurred when we first accepted human interpretations as godly, and as more lucid than Scripture itself. Finally other interpretations were added to these interpretations, so that now there is no limit to the increase of glosses on glosses and, in the confusion of words, we are led into the utmost confusion. We now know absolutely nothing at all about Christian truths, and suppose that heathen foolishness is as good and useful as what is ours.

These stumbling blocks and obstacles must be removed, and the way of Zion [Lam. 1:4]—in which they have multiplied long enough—must finally once again be made smooth so that we may be pastured on the pure grain of the sound and simple Scriptures. You see how Latomus makes everything uncertain with his human interpretations. Besides doing this with what comes from men and from philosophers, he goes so far as to consider it allowable to give two explanations of this passage [Rom. 7:14ff.] from Paul, one referring to man under the law, the other to man under grace. This is to teach nothing, and to confuse the mind. The affirmation that Paul is here speaking of man under the law must be absolutely rejected and denied, for he says clearly and obviously enough that he delights in the law of God [Rom. 7:22], and serves the law of God with his mind [v. 25]. This can fit none of the ungodly for, as is taught in [Romans] chapters three and five, they fight against God's law with all their strength. My advice to anyone who cannot firmly hold to the sacred writings in accordance with some definite meaning, is to leave them alone. It is safer to be like the laity and not know them, than to be uncertain regarding them. Satan makes an unbelievable amount of trouble for those who are dying by means of Scripture which is thought of as ambiguous, so I suspect that the devil incites the sophists to make passages uncertain with their trifling and equivocations.

Therefore we shall here ask: Where is that weigher of testimonies who wished to present a justification for the holders of the professorships at Louvain? He himself asserts only what is uncertain, does he not? Does he not do this simply in order to oppose his doubtful opinion to Luther's opinion? Yet those who burned and condemned [Luther's books] were of a different sort; that is, they wanted this to be their declared, certain, and infallible opinion so that it not simply could, but must, be asserted. Latomus says nothing for these miserable men, even though he promised to speak for them alone. So confident was he, that he claimed it must be shameful to ask for reasons in so certain a matter. However, as I

237

said, they did not rely on their reasons, but on the bull. This is why they dared to come forward and, by coming forward, sought simply to mangle the Scriptures and stuff the whole world's mouth with their, "One may speak thus." However, if they had realized their madness and said, "This may be condemned and burned, but we do not yet say that it should and must be condemned and burned"—if they had done this, their deeds would have corresponded to their words. But now, who does not see what they have revealed themselves to be? They have condemned with certainty that of which they today confess themselves uncertain. Although the holy fathers sometimes doubted and wavered regarding the senses of Scripture, yet they never added to this the madness of making formal declarations, and of condemning and burning those of others. So therefore, the reasons promised by this judicious man have not been produced; for he mocked at Luther and his opinion, yet has neither proved his own nor disproved mine. He has made them both uncertain, for the expositions he proposed cannot both be true. From this I conclude that our professors were mad when they condemned me, and knew not what they did. Their advocate, Latomus, is witness to this, for he wrote his book so that this [fact] would no longer be hidden from the world.

When I said that to fight against the law is nothing else than to sin, and that not to do good is to be against the law, Latomus replies that Augustine dares to assert that it is not sin unless one consents.[89] He himself then adds that there is nothing condemned in such people, because they do not sin. Look, how this worthless sophist distorts everything! Who does not see that Augustine is here speaking of mortal sin which comes into being through consent to the passions of sin, rather than denying that these motions are venial sins? Still he pretends that this is against Luther, not because he is ignorant that I am speaking of sin which is not mortal or condemned, but because he maliciously chooses to understand me in this way. Now this is Latomus' logic: Because they do not sin, there is no condemnation; therefore, from the opposite of the consequent, the opposite of the antecedent follows—venial sinners sin; therefore, there is nothing but condemnation for them. This is

---

[89] E.g., *City of God*, I, 25. Migne 41, 38.

the Louvainian way of interpreting the Apostle Paul. They assert that a venial sin is without condemnation, yet make the sin of which I speak one which condemns.

They do not consider it worthwhile to remember how often I have adduced what Paul says [Rom. 8:1] to the effect that, although there is sin—for he had previously said much about sin—still there is there no condemnation [for those in Christ Jesus]. The reason why there is no condemnation is not that men do not sin, as Latomus in lying fashion suggests, but because—as Paul says—they are in Jesus Christ; that is, they repose under the shadow of his righteousness as do chicks under a hen. Or as is said more clearly in Rom. 5 [:15], they have grace and the gift through his grace. So they do not walk in accordance with sin and sinful flesh; that is, they do not consent to the sin which they in fact have. God has provided them with two immensely strong and secure foundations so that the sin which is in them should not lead to their condemnation. First of all, Christ is himself the expiation (as in Rom. 3 [:25]). They are safe in his grace, not because they believe or possess faith and the gift, but because it is in Christ's grace that they have these things. No one's faith endures unless he relies upon Christ's own righteousness, and is preserved by his protection. For, as I have said, true faith is not what they have invented, an absolute—nay, rather, obsolete—quality in the soul, but it is something which does not allow itself to be torn away from Christ, and relies only on the One whom it knows is in God's grace. Christ cannot be condemned, nor can anyone who throws himself upon him. This means that so grave a matter is the sin which remains, and so intolerable is God's judgment, that you will not be able to stand unless you shield yourself with him whom you know to be without any sin. This is what true faith does.

The second foundation is the gift they have received, through which they neither walk according to the flesh, nor obey sin. However, the first foundation is the stronger and more important, for although the second amounts to something, it does so only through the power of the first. For God has made a covenant with those who are in Christ, so that there is no condemnation if they fight against themselves and their sin. Therefore, contrary to Latomus' ravings, the reason why there is no condemnation is not because they do not sin, and it is not because there is no sin in a

clear understanding of the grounding of the imperative in the indicative

good work. This sophist invents these things out of his own head independently of, and in opposition to, the clear text of Paul. He is obviously speaking of mortal sin, because he says that they are in Christ Jesus and do not walk after the flesh. The sophists are simply concerned with minimizing this sin which God so greatly emphasizes, for he wills that one should oppose it [his wrath] with his Son. Indeed, through this harshest of judgments he wants to drive and force all men to Christ so that they—trembling, desperate, and sighing—will shelter themselves under his wings. Those who deny this sin make men rest apathetically and carelessly in the gift they have received. In this way they cheapen Christ's grace and minimize God's mercy, from which necessarily follow coldness in love, slackness in praise, and lukewarmness in gratitude. They know absolutely nothing of Christ. Therefore beware of these most pestilent people, and learn that the works of God are great, wonderful, and glorious. Then you shall know that you cannot make this sin great enough, for absolutely no man can ever discover or comprehend his wickedness, since it is infinite and eternal. On the other hand, you will then discover that the work of God accomplished for you in Christ is boundless, in that he has foreordained such powerful grace for you in Christ. Even though you merit such great evil, it will not permit all this evil to destroy you; and not only does the grace of this Man keep it from destroying you, but it will finally liberate you from it. The glory of grace must be magnified even though it cannot be sufficiently praised, so that Paul exclaims, "Thanks be to God for his inexpressible gift" [II Cor. 9:15]. Therefore do not listen to the cold and languid hissing of the sophists concerning good works without sin, infused faith, acquired faith, and freedom of the will. These are dreams and jokes about this serious matter. You must be drawn into Christ, as is said in Isa. 2 [:10]: "Enter into the rock, and hide in the dust from before the terror of the Lord, and from the glory of his majesty"; and in Song of Sol. [2:14]: "O my dove, in the clefts of the rock, in the covert of the cliff." Make no mistake. The greatness of the refuge indicates well enough how great is this sin—as long as you don't suppose that Christ, the Son of God, is some wooden statue. All the saints tremble before this judgment. They perish unless they have Christ for a hiding place—and yet we still make a game of this dispute about whether there is sin in good works. Thus we [pretend] to know [so much] about the fearful and eternal Majesty— we dispute about him as if we were arguing about an ordinary man.

Next, this maker of distinctions goes farther, saying that there are two causes for the failures which seem to be contrary to the law of God and yet are not sin. The first operates when [in the action] the use of reason is lacking, as in infants, or in those who are sleeping, or the insane; the second, when there is no consent [to the action], as in the case [of the rape] of virgins, etc. Once again, who does not see that he has failed to defend the Louvainians who condemned Luther for holding that in the saints there is sin enslaved by the grace of God; [and substitutes] some figments of his dreams who would have condemned Luther for positing mortal sin in good works? Up till now none of the sophists have so completely overwhelmed me with disgust as this Latomus—so utterly worthless and foolish is his trifling. He is not so stupid as to fail to understand that I am not speaking of the sort of sin concerning which he quotes from the fathers, and about which he himself babbles. He has often testified that he knows this. So it is simply villainous of him to boast—against his own testimony—that I speak of a sin meriting damnation, and to impose this on the world.

Similarly, he holds that an inclination to evil is no hindrance to virtue. It is, he says, neither an evil nor a sin, but on the contrary, he suggests that it has assisted the martyrs toward the good. What is this that I hear? It has helped them toward the good and therefore is not sin! You see that these sophists have an extraordinary desire to blaspheme the grace of God, for they shamelessly attribute to sin what belongs to the grace of God. The devil, the tempter, assists the saints toward the good, and so his temptations are neither evils nor sins! The evils of inclination must be conquered, therefore they are not evil! See how excessively these sophists try my patience. Truly, if I sinned in the pamphlet which I published against their condemnation, I have had to do a great deal of penance for it in bearing his [Latomus'] incredible stupidity, ignorance, and malice. This inclination is sin just because it resists and creates difficulties for the martyrs, although the power of grace shines more brightly because of it. Yet if you look at God's judgment this ought not to be [our] work. It is mercy which spares and the divine gift which

241

conquers. You see, dear reader, what a fearful sin I have taken upon myself when I represented these men as more stupid than a block of wood.

My opponent adds to this that only what is voluntary—especially if it is an actual deed—is sinful, and consequently there is no sin in a good work. This is a deduction from Latomus to Latomus, for what Gregory says is this: "God would never have destroyed the vessels of wrath if they had not been found to have voluntary sin." [90]

Why then does he reward infants and the ignorant with destruction? Latomus here understands what Gregory says of the vessels of wrath and of their sins as referring to the sins of the saints and to good works—otherwise why does he quote this against me, and how [else] would it serve his purpose? He attacks the sin of which I have spoken, showing through Gregory that it is not sin, because only what is voluntary ought to be called sinful. This wearies me. Farewell to this most silly sycophant who understands not a particle of what I say, or of what he says, or of the fathers, or of Scripture—or, if he does understand, he doesn't want to. Nothing is correctly handled in this entire book, so it is worthy of being presented as the advocate for the arsonists of Louvain and the antichristian bull.

Let us look at the Apostle himself, and having placed their interpretations next to him, let us consider and learn how many new terms have been recently created. "We know," Paul says, "that the law is spiritual; but I am carnal, sold under sin" [Rom. 7:14]. They say this means, "I am weakened and chastised, sold under the penalty." So, as "spiritual" is used in an antithesis, it means "healthy, unpunished, and redeemed from penalty." Next, "I do not understand my own actions"—that is, I suffer punishment. "For I do not do what I want"—that is, to go unpunished, "but I do the very thing I hate"—that is, penance. "Now if I do what I do not want, I agree with the law"—that is, I am not punished, "that it is good"—that is, it is the absence of punishment. "So then it is no longer I that do it, but sin"—that is, the penalty, "which dwells within me. For I know that nothing good"—that is, unpunished, "dwells within me, that is,

---

[90] This is a paraphrase. Cf. Gregory, *Works* (Paris, 1705) III, 2, col. 563, as cited in WA 8, 116 n. 3.

in my flesh. I can will what is right, but I cannot do it. For I do not do the good I want"—that is, to go unpunished, "but the evil I do not want"—that is, penance, "is what I do." "Now if I do what I do not want, it is no longer I that do it, but sin"—that is, the penalty, "which dwells within me." "So I find it to be a law that when I want to do right"—that is, what is not punished, "evil"—that is, penalty, "lies close at hand. For I delight in the law of God"— that is, I am unpunished, "in my inmost self, but I see in my members another law"—that is, penalty, "at war"—that is, imposing penance, "with the law of my mind"—that is, my unpunished self, "and making me captive"—that is, punishing me, "to the law of sin"— that is, with the penalty, "which dwells in my members. Wretched man that I am! Who will deliver me from the body of this death?"— that is, from this penalty. "Thanks be to God through Jesus Christ our Lord! So then, I of myself serve the law of God with my mind"— that is, I am free from punishment, "but with my flesh I serve the law of sin"—that is, I am under penalty. "There is therefore now no condemnation, etc." [Rom. 7:15-25].

Even if I were to grant that it is good and right to speak thus, is this an explanation of Paul? And if the fathers speak in this way, have they ever commanded, or could they command, that one must speak thus? Must not God, rather than man, be obeyed? Paul commands, and has the right to command, that you "avoid profane novelties of words," [91] and that you speak as he himself spoke, abiding in the old and sacred words. What is profane if it is not that which is not sacred? Human words are not sacred, for they are novelties which were not used by the Apostle. You may object that *homoöusion*[92] has been accepted in opposition to the Arians. But there were many, and these the most notable, who did not accept it, and Jerome wished to have it suppressed. And so little did they escape danger with this invented word that Jerome complains that

---

[91] I Tim. 6:20 (Vulgate).

[92] This is a reference to the Nicene Creed where, in an effort to define the Christian faith against the Arians, the word *homoousios*, "being of one substance with the Father," has been used. Luther's comment is not an attack against this Creed but against theological terms which are not derived from Scripture. His high opinion of the Council of Nicaea is shown in his work, *On the Council and the Churches*, of 1539. Cf. WA 50, 548ff.

he does not know what poison hides under its letters and syllables.[93] Indeed, the Arians railed at it even more than at the Scriptures. Hilary had no reply to them except that this term signifies what is in fact the case and what is contained in the whole of Scripture.[94] This, however, is not true in the present case. There is no passage of Scripture in which "sin" refers to this penalty; on the contrary, it everywhere stands for wickedness which is opposed to the law of God. So even this comparison—which alone makes Latomus a theologian—does not hold.

Even if the comparison did hold, and even if this were really a precedent, still one could not deduce anything. Rather one must be indulgent to the fathers for having once used a word which is not found in Scripture. Otherwise, if you were to adopt this precedent, it would be permissible to translate all of Scripture into other words, just as the sophists do. Even if my soul hated this word, homoousion, and I refused to use it, still I would not be a heretic. For who compels me to use the word, providing I hold to the fact defined by the council on the basis of Scripture? Although the Arians were in error in regard to the faith, yet—whether their motives were good or bad—they rightly demanded that no new, nonscriptural word be allowed in dogmatic formulations. The integrity of Scripture must be guarded, and a man ought not to presume that he speaks more safely and clearly with his mouth than God spoke with his mouth. He who does not understand the Word of God when it speaks of the things of God, ought not believe that he understands the words of a man speaking of things strange to him. No one speaks better than he who best understands; but who understands the things of God better than God himself? Indeed, how much does a man really understand of the things of God?

Man, wretched being that he is, gives more honor to God either by confessing that he does not understand his Word, or by ceasing to profane his words with his own new ones. In this way God's lovable wisdom will remain among us in its pure and genuine form. The fathers may say what they can, but I want Paul's words

---

[93] Apparently the reference is to Jerome's *Letter to Pope Damasus* (Epist. 15, chap. 14) where, however, he complains about the use of the term *hypostasis*. Luther seems to have confused *hypostasis* and *homoousios*. Cf. WA 8, 117 n. 2.
[94] Hilary of Poitiers, *Against Constantius*, chap. 16. Migne 10, 578.

in this place to be taken literally, for I despise sophistic inventions
about debts, obligations [*reatibus ac debitis*], and similar trifles,
which darken the understanding rather than aid it. The words of
the Apostle are easy [understandable], open, and sure. Their most
bright and burning rays need no human illumination. It seems to
you that you have spoken beautifully when you say: Because there
is there neither debt nor obligation, there is no sin. Yet this is most
obscure, so that, as Nehemiah says [13:24], you speak the language
of Ashdod, and of each separate people, for you have long forgotten
the holy language of your fathers. Away with these outlandish
tongues, and let us recover our genuine and native speech! Why
do you not say this in a much more pure and lucid way: Because
there is no wrath there but rather grace, therefore sin—although it
is real sin—does not condemn? John the Evangelist drank real
poison,[95] but it did not kill him, for the power of faith was present.
Yet faith did not make this real poison into something other than
real poison, such as penalty or weakness. Rather it prevented it
from doing harm. If some one else had drunk it, he truly would
have died. Christ says, "If they drink any deadly thing, it will not
hurt them" [Mark 16:18]. He did not say that it will no longer be
deadly, but rather that it will not hurt them because they drink it
in Christ's name. Otherwise, where would be the glory of the
miracle, if it had ceased to be deadly when it was drunk? The
Chaldean fire was, and remained, real fire, yet it did not injure the
three men [Dan. 3:19ff.]. This was not because it was incapable of
scorching and burning, but it could not touch them even though it
wholly consumed those who were outside the furnace. In the same
way, the sin of which we speak is real sin which subjects all others
to wrath; but there are some whom it does not subject, because
they—not the others—have an antidote, namely, the gift of God
in the grace of the one man Jesus Christ. Filled with this, they do
not walk after the flesh. Is not this so clear and easy that even
the dullest can easily comprehend it? Meanwhile, there are these
subtleties about debt, obligation, the form and matter of sin,
habits, acts, expulsion, infusion, remission, qualities, forms, subjects,

---

[95] This legend was offered as an explanation of why John was traditionally
represented with a chalice. Cf. *The Catholic Encyclopedia* VIII, 493.

intrinsic and extrinsic goodness, intrinsic and extrinsic evil, congruence, meritoriousness, the genera of goods, acceptation, deacceptation—indeed, who can hear (much less enumerate) all the words of these frogs and flies? They themselves do not agree as to who among them are the teachers of the others. Much less, then, can the poor common folk get true knowledge of sin and grace from them, for before you understand what debt and obligation are, you must swallow the latest refuse—ten times resifted—of the philosophers. Away with the monstrous absurdities of the sophists!

So Paul truly says, "I am carnal"—he does not say, "I was carnal"—"sold under sin" [Rom. 7:14]. Now prove to me that "carnal" in Scripture signifies subjection to penalties and weaknesses. Paul does not call himself carnal because he is completely carnal, for the mind is spiritual but the flesh carnal, just as the mind is freed from sin, but the flesh is sold under sin, even as he says: "I serve the law of God with my mind, but with my flesh I serve the law of sin" [v. 25]. Here do not let Latomus mislead you by his positing of two wills. There is the one man Paul, who recognizes himself to be in two different relationships: under grace, he is spiritual, but under the law, carnal. It is one and the same Paul who is under both. The gift makes him spiritual and places him under grace—the grace of the one man Jesus Christ. Sin makes him carnal, but does not place him under wrath; for grace and wrath cannot both be present, nor do they fight with each other in such a way that one dominates the other, as do the gift [of God] and sin. So it is as carnal that "I do not understand my own actions" [v. 15]. However, as spiritual, he does understand, for otherwise how could he declare of himself that he does not understand what he does? In what follows, he calls what he does evil. Consequently he understands the evil that he does, but he does not carnally understand what he spiritually understands. Indeed, carnally he supposes that the sin raging in the flesh is the good which he desires, for thus it appears to the man who does not see that it is evil. "For I do not do the good I want, but the evil I hate is what I do" [vv. 15, 19]. See, he understands good and evil, but it is the spiritual Paul who thus understands, and wills, and hates. The carnal man does not understand the good, but loves and does the evil instead of the good.

It is up to Latomus to adduce texts proving that "carnal" here means something different than in other places—and also differs from what is required by grammar and its ordinary meaning. He should prove that "to know" and "to do" mean here something else than in other passages. He should also prove that "good" and "evil" mean something else in this passage than in others; and that "willing," "not willing," "hating," and "doing" here have different meanings than in other places. Since he cannot do this, and since the meanings of these words in this text are not opposed to godliness, why should we be moved by the interpretations of men? As I said, just as a weak or small man is nevertheless a man, so he who is partly carnal is properly called carnal. If the head of a man has been wounded, we rightly say that the man is wounded; and whoever hurts the foot of a dog is rightly said to have hurt the dog. In the same way, it is Paul who does not understand, because according to the flesh he does not understand; he it is who works [evil], because he works according to the flesh; he does evil, because he acts according to the flesh; and it is evil, because it is against the Spirit and the good. And one must not say that [Paul] does not work, does not act, his deeds are not evil, or he knows fully just because he is not all work, or all action, or totally evil, or knows only in part. So the reason why a man is wounded is not because every part of him is wounded and destroyed, and the reason why a dog is hurt is not because every part of him is hurt and destroyed; for according to the proper and original meaning of these words, wounding and hurting take place even if the smallest member is injured. So also there is here genuine sin, even though the whole man is not destroyed, condemned, and subject to wrath, for grace and the gift [of God] preserve a man so that he cannot sin, that is, he does not consent to sin and perish.

You may object that I have not shown that sin in other passages refers in this same way to what does not condemn. I reply that I have not undertaken to do this, nor is it necessary. My sole purpose [is to show] that sin has the same meaning here as in other places. The fact that I say that sin is here dealt with in a different way has nothing to do with the meaning of sin. Scripture everywhere means the same thing by "sin," but it does not everywhere deal with it, or describe how it is dealt with, in the same way. In some places it is shown how sin occurs, in others how it is forgiven, in others how it is punished, in other places how the punishment is postponed, in others how sin is concealed, in others how it is confessed, in others how it is denied. Who can enumerate the actions, passions, and circumstances of sin? This passage describes what sin does and suffers under grace. It does not deny that sin is present, but rather presupposes that sin is done and exists. Sin is here said to be conquered, even though rebellious, while in other places it is described as a reigning conqueror. It is everywhere absolutely the same, even though it does not everywhere have the same strength, or the same mode of acting or of being acted upon. However, I have shown above from Paul that Scripture does use "sin" in other places in the same way, as far as the meaning is concerned. He uses it to refer to incontinence, evil desire, anger, etc. in Romans 6 and 8—in addition to Romans 7—and also in Gal. 5 [:16ff.], I Cor. 5 [:7ff.], Eph. 4 [:22ff.], I Cor. 7 [:5], Col. 3 [:5ff.], Heb. 12 [:1]. Further, I John 1 [:8] reads, "If we say we have no sin, we deceive ourselves." On the other hand, our opponent cannot bring forward an iota in favor of his meaning. Let us therefore follow Paul: "Now if I do what I do not want, I agree with the law that it is good" [Rom. 7:16]. This is a surprising combination. He agrees with the good law, but not totally, for he does not do as a whole man what he does not will as whole man. Here the whole man neither agrees, nor acts, nor does not want to do this or that; and it is this same man who agrees with the good law, and yet does what he does not will, that is, does what is contrary to the good law which he wills. "So then it is no longer I that do it" [Rom. 7:17]. Who is this "I" who now does not do what it has just been said to do? It is the "I" which I spiritually am, because according to this "I," I am now looked at in terms of the grace which does not allow me to be looked at in terms of the sin which makes me carnal. Everything is washed away, and now there is a self different from the one before grace, for that one was evaluated in terms of sin as wholly carnal. "But sin that dwells within me" [Rom. 7:17]—does this mean that you do not do it, but that which is in you does it? Your hand strikes me, but you do not strike me? It is really so, for it does it against my will, and it is in terms of this latter that I am evaluated. Nevertheless, I truly do it, for a part of me does it; but now I am not evaluated in terms of it. When my hand does evil, it is imputed to me unless my soul is innocent; but the reason for this is not that the hand does not do evil, but because it is not imputed—and it is not imputed because of the innocent soul. So sin is truly sin, but because grace and the gift are within me, it is not imputed; not on account of its innocence—as if it were not harmful—but because grace and the gift reign within me.

"For I know that nothing good dwells within me, that is, in my flesh" [Rom. 7:18]. Because it is my flesh, rather than something alien, what dwells within it is said to dwell within me. How delightfully Paul marches up the middle between flesh and spirit, gayly alternating from one to another by means of this most beloved figure of speech, synecdoche! So, sin really dwells in the flesh, and it is genuine sin. For the Jebusites dwell within our borders, and they will be thorns in our eyes and a scourge in our sides [Josh. 23:13; 15:63; Judg. 1:21] if we don't take pains to eliminate them.[96]

Aren't thorns in the eyes simply pieces of wood in front of your face, which you push against if you don't look where you are going? Thus sin daily disturbs us, hindering our way, and even tormenting us, so that unless it is courageously cleared away, we shall thrust ourselves against it and shall stumble. Indeed it is an evil guest, and yet it dwells within us, in our flesh, in our land, within our borders. Therefore there is nothing good in the flesh, indeed, as I said, there is *nothing* good, not simply a penalty, but sin. "I can will what is right, but I cannot do it" [Rom. 7:18]. Paul himself explains more clearly how in sin the spiritual man does not do evil, but rather wills the good, and yet cannot accomplish this volition on account of the sin dwelling in his flesh. Nevertheless, the fact that it is not accomplished does not mean that this volition amounts to nothing; just as on the other hand, the evil which dwells in the flesh is "nothing" even though "I" do not do it, but rather sin itself. I assert both that evil happens, and does not happen. It happens because sin does it. It does not happen because the mind neither does nor wills it—although this will is not accomplished because of the action of sin. I ask, would such a battle be so carefully described if it were between "penalty" and spirit? Once

---

[96] Cf. WA 3, 439; 4, 543.

again, this opposes the sophists. They should say where in Scripture it is taught that it is the penalty (by which term they think to extricate themselves from the necessity of asserting the issue is sin) which must be avoided, resisted, and so fervently condemned. There is no penalty which Scripture does not command us to bear, and it is precisely this which shows that this evasion is worth nothing. Their commentary as well as their text, their words as well as their cause, are alien to the usage of the entire Scripture, and are alien to the understanding of all godly men. Therefore the absurdity which follows from their commentary is no less than the one they tried to avoid in the text. It is indeed absurd to assert what you can never discover nor prove; but [worse than that] you are forced to hear only the contrary in everything.[97]

"For I do not do the good I want, but the evil I do not want is what I do. Now if I do what I do not want, it is no longer I that do it, but sin which dwells within me" [Rom. 7:19-20]. Observe the faithful herald of grace repeating and emphasizing—as if pointing with his finger—the words, "If I do what I do not want." He does this because earlier he seemed to have spoken less clearly—when he similarly said, "If I do what I do not want" [Rom. 7:16]—for, before drawing the conclusion that, "It is no longer I that do it," he there interposed the words, "I agree with the law that it is good." Here, however, "If I do what I do not want," immediately precedes the conclusion, so that my unwillingness definitely proves that, "It is no longer I that do it"—even though it does happen in me. Therefore, it is necessarily the sin which dwells within me which does it; and so it is impossible to understand this passage as referring to anything except a spiritual man, for it does not refer to those who carry out wicked deeds. Paul here says that these two factors interfere with each other, although in such a way that the spirit prevails, so that it is attributed to him [the spirit] that he does not do nor will the evil. He does not invert the sentence so as to say, "For I do not do the evil I want, but the good I do not want is what I do. Now if I do the good I do not want, it is no longer I that do it, but grace which dwells within me." It is thus that the

---

[97] Luther means that his opponents substitute *poena* (penalty) for *peccatum* (sin) and thus make their interpretation meaningless.

flesh would speak if it reigned over the spirit rebelling against it. Now, since it is the spirit which complains and accuses the flesh, it is evident that the flesh, instead of dominating, is a rebel and irksome to the ruling spirit. None of this is spoken on behalf of the flesh, but rather it is against the flesh. A carnal man standing outside of grace would not do this. Consequently, the grace of God does not allow this work of sin to be imputed to the man, for in reality it is not he who does it. Yet it is in him, and he also really does it, as has been sufficiently stated.

"So I find that when I want to do right, evil lies close at hand" [Rom. 7:21]. The person who wants to do good and who finds evil close at hand is one and the same. The spiritual man wants to do good as a whole [man], but the carnal man adds evil to him so that he is less than a whole [man]. "For I delight in the law of God, in my inmost self, but I see in my members another law at war with the law of my mind and making me captive to the law of sin which dwells in my members" [Rom. 7:22-23]. Paul here explains himself very clearly, for to delight in the law of God is precisely to be a godly and righteous man. He who is not just neither fights nor cares to fight against the law of the members. Further, Paul does not call the law of the mind "natural law," as they term it, but he opposes it to the law of the members. Therefore he is rather giving a name to the will of the spirit which delights in the law of God, and which is opposed to that law of the members which delights in the law of sin. Thus also the law of the members is a will which is contrary to the will of the spirit. He says that it is at war, thus certainly indicating that he is referring to the evil of guilt, not of penalty—for it is certainly evil to war against the law of God. Now he does not only say that it does not obey, but—and this is more serious—that it is "at war." He does this so that you may not underestimate the sin which remains after baptism. It is immense, and it is an immense gift of God which removes it, and it is an immense grace which forgives it for the sake of the spirit which delights in, rather than wars against, the law of God. The last phrase, "making me captive," is [even] more frightening. I want you to observe how great is the power and weight of the words he uses to emphasize the sin which our opponents extenuate and remove. It not only exists, not only lives, not only wills, not only acts, not only is at war—but it even rages and makes captive. I ask you, are these trivialities? And who does not sense that this is what happens in himself? Who does not forever experience the raging thoughts and impulse of anger and of evil desire—and this no matter how unwilling and reluctant one may be? Its fury is untamed—no, on the contrary (and this will astonish you), it does not thus rage in the ungodly, because they do not sustain its onslaught. They yield and obey it, and so never experience how much labor and how much trouble it is to resist and control it. This onslaught requires a strenuous warfare, and so Christ is called "the Lord of hosts" and "the King mighty in battle" [Ps. 24:10, 8], for it is through his gift that these great attacks are not only sustained, but overcome. You therefore see the magnitude of the gift and grace of God which prevents such great evil from damning the godly. The evil thoughts of the godly are stronger than those of the ungodly, and yet they do not pollute and damn, while they truly do pollute and damn the others. Why is this? Isn't it the same sin in both? It is indeed the same sin, but the godly have an antidote, while the others have none. Thus the godly do not sin in the midst of a greater onslaught, while the others do sin in the midst of a lesser one. Sin is in both, so this redounds to the glory of God's grace, not of evil natures. If grace were lacking, sin would truly damn, but now grace prevents it from damning evil nature. Therefore "Not to us, O Lord, but to thy name give glory" [Ps. 115:1]. It is not as the sophists dream that such fury against the law of God is not sin. It is not penalty nor is it weakness, but it is a great sin, of which Ps. 19 [:13] complains, saying: "I shall be innocent of great transgression." We have no right to glory in this our innocence. However, Paul speaks of "making captive," not because what is spiritual is taken captive, but because, from the side of sin, nothing is omitted for the capture of the spiritual man. The same mode of expression is found in Gal. 1 [:13], "I laid waste the church of God." It is impossible to lay waste the church, but he employed all his resources in order to destroy it. Therefore he does not say here that, "It makes war, and I have been captured." Rather, "It makes captive"—but I am not captured. Even if he had said the former, the meaning would compel us to understand that this is in respect to the flesh. Just as he said that he was sold, and that he was carnal according to the flesh, so he here says that he is captive according to the flesh. I prefer this last meaning, for it is simpler.

"Wretched man that I am! Who will deliver me from this body of death?" [Rom. 7:24]. Here he figuratively calls sin death—that is, the greatest burden. In this he imitates Exod. 10 [:17] where Pharaoh asks that the locusts be taken away: "Entreat the Lord your God only to remove this death from me." As in the case of those locusts, he calls sin by the most hateful of names on account of its grievous, monstrous, unceasing, and untamed fury, because of which we are not allowed to have peace in this life but are forced to stand continually in battle array. What Paul fears in this place are the sleeping and quiescent [evil] inclinations of [which] Latomus [speaks]. Nor does Augustine mean what Latomus attributes to him.[98]

It is indeed true that there is no one passion ceaselessly driving us to distraction. Anger does not always burn, evil desire does not always rage, we are not constantly tormented with envy, but one of these succeeds the other. When they all sleep, then languor and sloth do not sleep. If you are strenuously active, then pride awakens. As I have most truly said, just as we are not without the flesh, so we do not work without the flesh. So we are neither free of carnal faults, nor do we act without them. Latomus constructs an extremely stupid syllogism on the basis of a singular or particular premise when he argues thus: Sometimes a passion is quiescent; therefore sin is not in every good work. He ought to have said: Sometimes all are quiescent, and sin is entirely dormant. This is impossible, for sin is a living thing in constant movement, changing as its objects change. That there is indeed no sin in sleep is to be ascribed to the grace of God, not to nature. I mean by this that it is not because of the absence of the use of reason that there is then no sin which is condemned. The fact that we cannot sleep in purity is sin. Why have we not remained in that uprightness in which we could have slumbered purely and done only what is pure? The drunkard is not excused by his drunkenness if he sins because of it. Why did he not remain sober? Thus nothing is for-

---

[98] Latomus cited Augustine's, *Against Julian*, VI, chap. 8. Migne 44, 666.

given us for our own sake, nothing is pure because of us, but only because of the grace and gift of God. What excuses the unbaptized infants who are eternally damned? [99]

"Thanks be to God through Jesus Christ our Lord" [Rom. 7:25]. Paul gives thanks, not to his righteousness, but to the merciful God, and he does this through Jesus Christ our Lord. It is with him that he always shields himself from God, hiding under his wings, and through his grace rejoicing and glorying in the grace and gift of God. He wishes to be freed from this body, for he does not say, "Who will liberate me from the death of this body?", but "From this body of death" [Rom. 7:24]. He says this because he sees that this purity of the Louvainian saints is not possible in this life and, as he chooses to be clean, he therefore chooses to die. The ungodly do not say this, or if they do, they do not say it for this reason. He [Paul] does not thus cry out, pleading for death because of punishment, but because sin troubles him exceedingly. You therefore see that this passage fits the case of those who are most saintly. They suffer from wild and raging sin; and from this we learn not to lessen the grace of God by lessening our evil through denying—because of human interpretations—that it is sin. We underline and emphasize sin as much as we can so as to make clear that this confession and emphasis is the work of God, who is wonderfully present in his saints, doing all his will in them while we yet seem to have sin and, truly, have it. His will is not the sin which is in us, but rather our sanctification from that sin. Therefore Paul concludes his discussion of the condition of life of the godly man in this world by saying, "So then, I of myself serve the law of God with my mind, but with my flesh I serve the law of sin" [Rom. 7:25]. The "I" is here one and the same man. Latomus' quibble does not stand in the way, for he supposes that he can understand this as he did the earlier statement, "Nothing good dwells within me, that is, in my flesh." Paul himself explains what he means when he says, "With my flesh I serve the law of sin." As a choice commentator, you might want to make an addition and say, "My flesh serves the law of sin with the flesh"—but what does this mean?

---

[99] *Ibid.* Luther is following the argument of St. Augustine in his work, *Against Julian,* where he uses the example of the unbaptized children to illustrate his doctrine of original sin.

These words are too clear to suffer from the tricks of the sophists. He says, "I of myself"—not some one else. Next he says, "I serve"—not only do I have sin, but I serve it or (which seems to amount to the same thing) my flesh serves it. But what is it to serve sin? Isn't it to do its will, and to act contrary to the law of God? The flesh does this when it so serves sin as to be at war, when it makes captive, when it rages; but because the spirit is neither obedient to nor vanquished by these ragings, it is not damned. The service of sin becomes empty, for all its impulses are frustrated. Nevertheless, this bondage does not therefore disappear, it does not stop being evil. Although it now serves in vain and its master, sin, does not prevail, the flesh does not cease to sin in this its evil servitude, but rather because of this deserves to be crucified and killed so as to stop serving in this way. "There is therefore no condemnation for those who are in Christ Jesus, who walk not according to the flesh" [Rom. 8:1]. Truly there is no condemnation, but nonetheless there is sin, real sin. Not the sin which Latomus imagines he alone knows, and through which the spirit apart from grace serves sin, but that sin which would be of this sort if that grace and gift which comes through the grace of the one Man did not prevail. The essence of sin is truly in them, but it can no longer do what it could.

Latomus really ought to bring forward a passage of Scripture in which "fighting against the law of God" is not sin, but a penalty or weakness. Enough has been said of how one must take what he cites from Augustine to the effect that man does not sin, viz., that Augustine speaks of sin apart from grace. Yet though I am speaking of sin within grace, this clumsy logician adduces Augustine against me, just as he does everywhere and in everything, begging the question in his accustomed manner as if he had triumphantly shown that there is no sin in men under grace. If he does not produce a text, we shall urge him to stay content with the proper and simple meaning of the statement that to fight against God is most truly sin. He ought to prove that to make captive to the law of sin, and to serve the law of sin, are the same thing as weakness and not sinning. Otherwise we have established that the words are to be taken literally, and that to serve sin or its law—no matter where or by whom it is said—is the same thing as to sin. So speaks Christ in John 8 [:34]: "Everyone who commits sin is a slave to sin." So also in

II Pet. 2 [:19]: "Whatever overcomes a man, to that he is enslaved."
Paul himself says in Rom. 6 [:17, 18]: "You who were once slaves
of sin, having been set free from sin, have become slaves of righteousness." So, in the passage with which we are dealing, Paul is a
servant of sin, but because he adds, "with my flesh," he clearly
distinguishes between serving sin absolutely—which is all that
Latomus wants and pretends to know—and serving sin with the
flesh. What Latomus teaches to the effect that sometimes one is
not enslaved to sin is not true; it is true neither in respect to
absolute servitude to sin, nor in reference to servitude to sin through
the flesh. All the things done by the one who is a servant of sin are
sins. He is handed over to sin. Servitude is not the name of a work
but of a state which includes all the strivings of the entire life. On
the other hand, it is one thing to serve God absolutely, and another
thing to serve him carnally. The righteous serve God absolutely,
for that has to do with the person, but the hypocrites serve him only
with the flesh, because they do so only with works, not with faith
from the heart. Just as the latter are damnable hypocrites, so the
former, as I might say, are saved hypocrites, because they serve sin
with the flesh and are evil in appearance, but in truth are good
Also, as the external works of the hypocrites are not simply nothing,
but are truly useful and good because they are useful creatures of
God, thus also the sins of the righteous are truly evil and harmful
because they are the works of sin. Just as these good works of the
hypocrites are of no benefit [to them], so these sins of the righteous
do no harm [to them]. I asked how it is possible to act without the
flesh, or the will of the flesh, since one cannot exist without them.
Isn't it most inept of Latomus to oppose this with Paul's statement:
"And though we are in the flesh, yet we do not walk according to the
flesh"?—as if to work when the flesh is present were to walk in conformity with the flesh! Such is the blindness of this sort of sophist
that he wants in this way to dispose of the simile of the corroded
instrument which I suggested. Paul, however, serves sin with the
flesh and yet does not walk according to the flesh. Nor does this
weigher of testimonies quote Paul correctly, for Paul says in II
Cor. 10 [:3], "For though we walk in the flesh, yet we do not war
according to the flesh." To be sure, the meaning is the same.

256

Now, what need is there to go through all of Latomus, point by point, since what has been said thoroughly refutes his entire position and confirms mine? I have sufficiently shown that his whole work consists of begging the question, for he does not want to understand my use of "sin" except in his own sense. With deliberate villainy, he distorts both my statements and those of all the fathers, making out that what they say simply of sin is said against sin under grace, or applying what is said of the sin of the whole to, as I might say, the sin of the part. He does this because he, together with his sophists, has never recognized what grace and sin, law and gospel, Christ and man are. He who wishes to discuss sin and grace, law and gospel, Christ and man, in a Christian way, necessarily discourses for the most part on nothing else than God and man in Christ; and in doing this one must pay the most careful attention to predicating both natures, with all their properties, of the whole Person, and yet take heed not to attribute to this what belongs exclusively to God or exclusively to man. For it is one thing to speak of the incarnate God, or of man raised up to God,[100] and another to talk simply of God or of man. So also sin apart from grace is different from sin in grace, so you can picture grace and the gift of God as having become sin in the one case, and sin as having become grace in the other as long as we are in this world, so that because of grace and the gift, sin is no longer sin. However, this is a reflection which needs greater leisure for its development. So I shall stop here until I have more time and can dispose of the rest of Latomus' book.[101]

His discussions of penance and of indulgences are worthless, for he proves everything from human writings. Neither Gregory nor any angel has the right to set forth or teach in the church something which cannot be demonstrated from Scripture. I think I have sufficiently shown from their own writings that scholastic theology is nothing else than ignorance of the truth and a stumbling block in comparison with Scripture. Nor am I moved when Latomus insinuates that I am ungrateful and insulting to St. Thomas,[102]

---

[100] *deificato.*
[101] Cf. p. 135 n. †.
[102] Aquinas (d. 1274).

Alexander[103] and others, for they have deserved ill from me. Neither do I believe that I lack intelligence [to understand them]. This Latomus himself will admit, and it is certainly not difficult to see that I work hard. My advice has been that a young man avoid scholastic philosophy and theology like the very death of his soul. The Gospels aren't so difficult that children are not ready to hear them. How was Christianity taught in the times of the martyrs when this philosophy and theology did not exist? How did Christ himself teach? St. Agnes was a theologian at the age of thirteen, likewise Lucia and Anastasia[104]—from what were they taught? In all these hundreds of years up to the present, the courses at the universities have not produced, out of so many students, a single martyr or saint to prove that their instruction is right and pleasing to God while [the ancients from their] private schools have sent out swarms of saints. Scholastic philosophy and theology are known from their fruits. I have the strongest doubts as to whether Thomas Aquinas is among the damned or the blessed, and would sooner believe that Bonaventure is blessed. Thomas wrote a great deal of heresy, and is responsible for the reign of Aristotle, the destroyer of godly doctrine. What do I care that the bishop of bulls has canonized him? I suppose that my judgment in these matters is not entirely ignorant, for I have been educated in them and have been tested [in debate] by the minds of my most learned contemporaries, and I have studied the best writings of this sort of literature. I am at least partly informed concerning Holy Writ, and besides I have to some extent tested these spiritual matters in experience, but I clearly see that Thomas, and all those who write and teach similarly, have neglected this. Therefore I advise him who would fly to take warning. I do what I must, so with the Apostle I again admonish you: "See to it that no one makes a prey of you by philosophy and empty deceit"—this I confidently and emphatically apply to scholastic theology—"according to human tradition, according to the elemental spirits of the universe"—these are the laws of the bulls and whatever is established in the church apart from Scripture—

---

[103] Alexander of Hales (d. 1245).
[104] According to tradition, all three were martyred under Diocletian (*ca.* 304). Cf. Butler's *Lives of the Saints* (ed. H. Thurston and D. Attwater) for Jan. 21, Dec. 13, and Dec. 25, respectively.

"and not according to Christ" [Col. 2:8]. Here it is clear that Paul wants Christ alone to be taught and heard. Who does not see how the universities read the Bible? Compare what is read and written in the *Sentences*[105] and on philosophy with what they write and teach about the Bible—which ought to flourish and reign as the most important of all—and you will see what place the Word of God has in these seats of higher learning.

But to return to you, my Jonas. I have now expelled this Latomus from me and sent it to you so that it will no longer trouble me. I have already begun to put the Epistles and the Gospels into the vernacular: that is why it has been so bothersome to read and respond to this filth. If it seems good to do so, I shall at some other time respond to all of it; but now, as an exile, I lack books, and I carry the sentence imposed by those judges of heretics—and heretical judges—who wanted to compel the Jews to stick to the bare Bible.[106] For I have only the Bible with me. Not that much depends on my having books, but one should see whether my opponent has correctly cited the statements from the fathers. He cites Dionysius in reference to praying God for the deceased, although I very well remember that Dionysius wrote of "praising." [107]

Why doesn't one of you reply to the rest, either you or Andreas Karlstadt? And what is stopping Amsdorf? Must not all of you equally vindicate the glory of the gospel? I have bruised the head of the serpent, why don't you try to stamp on its body? For example, that verse in Job 9 [:28], "I became afraid of all my works," he explains this way: "I became afraid," that is, I observed. And in Ps. 101 [143:2] where the prophet prays for escape from God's judgment, "Enter not into judgment with thy servant, etc.," his explanation is this: God's entire life is sinless; but no man's entire life is sinless and therefore he will not be judged by comparison with the life of God. Thus he makes the judgment of God, or the presence of God, into the life of God. However, where is this done in Scripture? Is there therefore a part of our lives of which it can be said, "Enter

---

[105] This book, written by Peter Lombard (d. 1160), was the standard theological text of the Middle Ages and the basis for innumerable commentaries.
[106] Cf. above, p. 150 n. 20.
[107] Pseudo-Dionysius. Cf. p. 170 n. 43. On the point at issue here, his *The Ecclesiastical Hierarchy*, VII, 1, 3 supports Luther; but VII, 3, 4 supports Latomus. Cf. WA 8, 128 n. 1.

into judgment"—that is, a part which does not belong to the number of those referred to as "all the living"? Does he not bring forward the fathers? Yet were the fathers not men? Isn't there someone among you who can easily refute this and similar childishness? God's judgment is not the work of God whereby he compares his life to ours, but the work whereby he tests us. How absurd that the Eternal Life should be compared to a momentary one! Much, indeed almost all, of what he says is of this sort. I would like you to do something for the Word so that I could sometime have the leisure to help poor ordinary people. Furthermore, you are young recruits and must be trained, and, in case I perhaps might be able to help, it were best that this happen while I live. However, I ask you to please accept this book. How glad I am that it will tarry with me no longer!

Greetings from my Patmos. June 20, 1521.

THE BURNING
OF BROTHER HENRY

1525

Translated by A. T. W. Steinhäuser

Revised by George W. Forell

INTRODUCTION

Some of the earliest and most devoted followers of Luther outside of Germany were his fellow-Augustinians in the Netherlands. This country was at the time under the regency of Margaret of Savoy, an aunt of Emperor Charles V, who considered it her duty to suppress all tendencies toward the Reformation. The result was that the first martyrs of the Reformation came from the ranks of the Augustinians in the Netherlands. On July 1, 1523, Henry Vos and John van den Esschen were burned at the stake in Brussels. Others escaped a similar fate by recanting their evangelical views or by flight.

Henry of Zütphen, the central figure in this treatise, had been arrested in Antwerp in 1522. But he was almost immediately freed again by supporters of the Reformation, who hid him for a while and later helped him to escape from the Netherlands. It appears that Henry intended to go to Luther in Wittenberg, where he had earlier been a student. But while passing through Bremen he was persuaded to stay and to preach regularly at St. Ansgar's chapel.

His fame as a preacher spread and in the fall of 1524 he was asked by Nicolas Boye, the pastor at Meldorf in Dithmarschen, to conduct a preaching mission in this section of western Holstein. Leaving Bremen, against the advice of his friends, he arrived safely in Meldorf and preached his first sermon on December 4, 1524. But as a result of a great deal of agitation by the prior of the local Dominicans, and with the cooperation of other church leaders and some of the civil authorities, certain peasants of the neighborhood were persuaded to kidnap Henry. After they had accomplished this they drank themselves into a frenzy and lynched him on December 10, 1524.

In addition to his fruitful ministry in Bremen and his courageous death in Dithmarschen little else is known about Henry. Not even his full name has been established, for Zütphen is merely a reference to the town in the Netherlands where he was born about 1488. As a young man he entered the Augustinian order. He

263

studied at Wittenberg, receiving his Bachelor's degree in 1509 and his Master's degree in 1511 at that university. He served as sub-prior of his order at Cologne in 1514 and as prior at Dort in 1515. In 1520 he resumed his studies in Wittenberg and received a Bachelor of Divinity degree in 1521, defending certain theses concerning justification by faith. In 1522 he left Wittenberg to become prior at Antwerp, where our story begins.

After Henry's death in Dithmarschen, Luther wrote this little book in response to a request that he console the Christians in Bremen who grieved about the loss of their pastor. He based the story on letters and oral reports and framed it in the style of a martyrology. It was published in February or March of 1525.

The work appears in *WA* 18, 224-240. It was translated for the Philadelphia Edition by A. T. W. Steinhäuser, who omitted Luther's exposition of the Ninth Psalm. This present translation is based upon the text in *WA* and the earlier translation, but a translation of the psalm has been added.

THE BURNING
OF BROTHER HENRY

The Burning of Brother Henry in Dithmarschen,
Including an Explanation of the Ninth Psalm[1]

Martin Luther, Preacher at Wittenberg to all the elect of God, dear friends in Christ, at Bremen.

Grace and peace from God our Father and our Lord Jesus Christ. Dearly beloved in Christ, I did not want the story of the martyrdom of your evangelist, the sainted Brother Henry of Zütphen, to be hidden in darkness and doubt. Since I know part of it from personal experience and have gathered the rest from trustworthy reports of godly people,[2] I have decided that this story should be made known to the praise and honor of God's grace, so abundantly bestowed in this time upon us condemned, lost, and unworthy people.

For not only do we have, hear, and read the pure Word of God and see it rise like the very sun in its brightness, but we also sense the presence of the Spirit of God and experience how he demonstrates and confirms his Word with great and mighty deeds, as has been his custom from the beginning. Above all, he has given us brave and bold hearts, so that in many places both preachers and hearers are daily being added to the number of the saints. Some have shed their blood, others have suffered imprisonment, others again have been driven from their homes, but all of them endure the shame of the cross of Christ [Heb. 12:2]. In our day the pattern of the true Christian life has reappeared, terrible in the world's eyes, since it means suffering and persecution, but precious and

---

[1] In the title and in the text Luther refers to it erroneously as Psalm 10.
[2] Luther first learned of the martyrdom through a letter from Jacob Propst, Henry's predecessor as prior of the Augustinian monastery in Antwerp. Propst was a student of Luther and pastor at the Church of Our Dear Lady after 1524. WA 18, 216-217; WA, Br 3, 402 (Jacob Propst to Luther, end of December, 1524); PE 4, 182; 187 n. 2.

priceless in God's sight. As the Psalter puts it [Ps. 116:15], "Precious in the sight of the Lord is the death of his saints," and again in Ps. 72 [:14], "Precious is their blood in his sight."

The one who shines most brightly among all these saints is surely your Henry of Zütphen, who suffered such shameful martyrdom in Dithmarschen for the sake of God's Word and who so effectively confirmed the gospel with his blood. However, John and Henry[3] at Brussels, who were the first martyrs, also became two shining lights through their radiant death, being sacrificed to God as a fragrant offering [Eph. 5:2]. Also among these martyrs belong Caspar Tauber, burned to death in Vienna,[4] and George Buchführer, who was put to death in Hungary.[5] More recently I have heard of still another who was burned at the stake in Prague in Bohemia for leaving his monastic order of impure chastity and entering the order of pure chastity, the holy estate of matrimony.

These men and others like them are the ones who, with their own blood, will drown the papacy and its god, the devil. These are the ones too who will preserve the Word of God in its truth and purity against the impure profaners of the Word, the new false prophets, who just now are springing up and spreading everywhere. It is doubtless out of grace that God allows them to die and shed their blood just at this time, when so many falsehoods and factions are arising, so that he may warn us and through them certify that that [doctrine] is the right doctrine wherein the right Spirit is given, which [is the doctrine] they taught, believed, died for, and by their martyrdom confirmed; just as the holy martyrs long ago died for the sake of the gospel and with their blood sealed and certified it for us.

Those who misled the world with their doctrines of works, human righteousness, and free will, have never been able to obtain

---

[3] John van den Esschen and Henry Vos, Augustinian friars from Antwerp, were burned at the stake in Brussels on July 1, 1523, for their loyalty to the evangelical cause. WA 18, 224 n. 1. They were the first Protestant martyrs. PE 4, 181. Luther had commented on this event in a letter of August, 1523, to the Christians in the Netherlands. WA 12, 73-80.

[4] Caspar Tauber, a merchant in Vienna, was beheaded in that city on September 17, 1524. WA 18, 224 n. 2; PE 4, 185 n. 2.

[5] WA, Br 3, 374 (To Nikolaus Hausmann, Nov. 17, 1524) suggests that his name was actually Johannes Cruss and that he was a bookseller. It might have been the sale of Luther's books which led to his execution.

such glory. For that kind of doctrine the devil puts no one to death. He can put up with them all right. Indeed, he gives them the great wealth, honor, and power of this world. They have peace and their life is all sweetness. But even should they die for such doctrines they would not be God's martyrs, but rather their own and the devil's, like the heathen who died for the sake of worldly rights, property, and honor. St. Paul says in Rom. 5 [:7] that perhaps some one might die for a good thing (namely, for all those things the world calls "good," such as riches, honor, and power) but for righteousness' sake one will hardly die. But to die for God's Word and faith is a priceless, precious, and noble death, fit only for the Spirit and children of God. Such a death means to die for the unrighteous and even for those who put us to death, and to intercede for them while dying. This is what Christ did according to the word of Isaiah [Isa. 53:12], "And made intercession for the transgressors." This is why we read of no instance where a Christian died for the doctrine of free will and of works, or for anything but the Word of God.

Since, then, the merciful God has so graciously visited you at Bremen and has been so very close to you, and since he has through Henry attested his Spirit and power in your midst so obviously that you can almost touch it, I have considered it advisable to write down for you and publish the story of his suffering. That way I can admonish your hearts in Christ not to grieve, or to speak ill of his murderers in Dithmarschen, but rather to be glad, and thank and praise God who has made you worthy to see and obtain these his wonders and gifts of grace. His murderers have already been repaid enough and more than enough by staining their hands so terribly with innocent blood and heaping upon themselves such great and awful guilt in the sight of God. There is really far more reason to weep and lament for them than for the sainted Henry, and to pray that not only they, but the whole land of Dithmarschen, may be converted and come to the knowledge of the truth. It is to be expected confidently that this will indeed be the fruit of Henry's martyrdom, especially since many in that region are even now turning eagerly to the gospel and are sorry that such a murder was committed among them. For God, who allowed the sainted Henry to suffer there, surely has it in mind not only to punish the godless if they do not repent, but to use this murder for the benefit of many in that land and by it lead them to eternal life.

For this reason I ask, indeed in this case I command, that you sing and read the Ninth Psalm, which is indeed most appropriate here. It teaches us not to grieve because of the suffering of the martyrs but rather to praise God joyfully for the fruits which he produces on earth through their martyrdom. I certainly do not mind taking the time to explain this psalm briefly to you and to sing it with you, knowing that you are present with me in spirit.

A Short Exposition of the Ninth Psalm[6] Concerning Christ's Martyrs, which begins as follows:

A Psalm of David, to be sung with voice uplifted, about the youth of the son.[7]

This heading indicates the subject of the psalm and the manner in which it is to be sung. It should be sung "with voice uplifted"; that means joyfully and with spirit. And "the youth of the son" refers to the martyrs of Christ, the Son of God. These are his young and strong followers who by faith are made perfect in death.

1. *I will give thanks to the Lord with my whole heart: I will tell of all thy wonderful deeds.*

These wonderful deeds are, as we shall see later, that God overpowers and converts the world, not by force but through the blood and death of his saints. He overcomes the living through the dying and the dead. This is an amazing victory.

---

[6] The English translation follows the RSV as closely as Luther's German translation will permit.

[7] The literal meaning of *Almuth-labben* is, "die for the son" (cf. W. O. E. Oesterley, *The Psalms* (London, 1953), p. 13), which is generally said to mean that the psalm was to be sung according to the melody of a song which began with these words. Luther, following ancient authorities, understood this direction to the choirmaster as a hint to the meaning of this psalm (cf. Moritz Freier, *Luthers Busspsalmen and Psalter* (Leipzig, 1918), p. 14). Although he translates, following Jewish sources, "about the youth of the son," he has in the back of his mind the references to death in Jerome (*Victori super morte filii Canticum*) which explains his interpretation.

2. *I will be glad and exult in thee: I will sing praise to thy name, O Most High.*

His name is as marvelous as his work, for he takes his name from his work. Through death he fosters life and thereby proves himself Lord over both life and death [Rom. 14:9].

3. *Thou hast turned back my enemies. They fell and perished before thy face.*

What a blessed "turning" and "falling" and "perishing" takes place before the face of God. It comes through the recognition of his grace, for then the godless fall in order to rise again and be saved.

4. *For thou hast maintained my just cause; thou hast sat on the throne as a righteous judge.*

The cause is the Word of God, because of which the godless oppose us. But God sees to it that our teaching is vindicated and the enemies are confounded. For he is a righteous judge. We take comfort in the fact that he will not forsake our just cause.

5. *Thou hast rebuked the nations, thou hast destroyed the wicked; thou hast blotted out their name for ever and ever.*

Thou dost perform my cause, by punishing and converting them through thy Word, and thou dost bring to naught all their efforts so that they are utterly of no avail.

6. *The swords of the enemy have failed, their cities thou hast rooted out; the very memory of them has perished.*

That is: The unbelievers stop persecuting and become believers, and no longer praise or even remember their past conduct.

7. *But the Lord sits enthroned for ever, he has established his throne for judgment.*

That is: His Word and kingdom will stand, and all the godless and their deeds are condemned.

8. *And he judges the world with righteousness, he judges the peoples with equity.*

This means that through his Word he leads and teaches the world justly and well.

9. *The Lord is a stronghold for the poor, a stronghold in times of trouble.*

Even if he permits us to be assaulted and some to be killed, he still shields them spiritually and gives the courage so that they do not fear but rather overcome death. Furthermore he makes it evident that we are not all killed, as the godless might wish. His remnant remains forever and even increases.

10. *And those who know thy name put their trust in thee, for thou, O Lord, hast not forsaken those that seek thee.*

God's promise gives us great boldness and comfort, for he assures us that he will not leave those who seek him. These are the people who hold fast to his Word where his name and work are acknowledged and praised, and who do not rely on their own deeds and name as do the work-righteous.

11. *Sing praises to the Lord, who dwells in Zion! Tell among the peoples his deeds!*

That is: Seek and praise his name alone, and preach his Word. He in turn will seek and praise you, as follows.

12. *For he who avenges blood is mindful of them; he does not forget the cry of the afflicted.*

He lets the godless kill and spill blood, and acts as if he had forgotten the afflicted. But he remembers them mightily and sees to it that their blood is avenged. Thus, the more the godless spill blood the greater will become the number of believers and the smaller their own number.

13. *Be gracious to me, O Lord! Behold what I suffer from those who hate me, O thou who liftest me up from the gates of death.*

That is: Carry on as thou hast begun. Continue to help us increase through death. For it is thy way to "lift up from the gates of death," that is, from the power of those who kill, and to put them down.

14. *That I may recount all thy praises, that in the gates of the daughter of Zion I may rejoice in thy deliverance.*

The more I experience thy help, the more I will have to praise thee, and thus thy name and thy honor increase among the believers, as follows.

15. *The nations have sunk in the pit which they made, in the net which they hid has their own foot been caught.*

This means that through their killing and persecuting they kill themselves and bring about their own downfall. For God uses these deeds to strengthen his Word so that it wins more people than it otherwise would.

16. *The Lord has made himself known, he has executed judgment; the wicked are snared in the work of their own hands. Selah.*

The Lord does not forsake his Word but ultimately reveals that it is true; and the godless are caught in their own words and slogans.

17. *The wicked shall depart to hell, all the nations that forget God.*

For this reason we must pray for them, that God may touch their consciences, and through our word so terrify them that they will turn to him.

18. *For the needy shall not always be forgotten, and the hope of the poor shall not perish for ever.*

The godless wish it were otherwise and God makes it appear as if they had it their way. But he comforts us in this passage and tells us not to judge by appearances but rather according to his Word.

19. *Arise, O Lord! Let not man prevail; let the nations be judged before thee!*

That is: Do as thou hast promised and let thy Word be heard among all the heathen so that in conscience they may be judged and terrified.

20. *Appoint a teacher for them, O Lord! Let the nations know that they are but men! Selah.*

He who knows that he is a man knows also that he is nothing and worthless before God. Therefore, he gives up his raving and presumption and is humble and willing to learn from everyone. This insight, however, comes from the public preaching of the Word. For this reason God needs teachers. As Christ says, "Pray therefore

the Lord of the harvest to send out laborers into his harvest"
[Matt. 9:38]. He does not want to deal with us through spirits
without teaching or public word, as some mad prophets nowadays
foolishly assert.

Here you see, my dear sirs and friends, how this psalm comforts
us and bids us hope that, through Henry's precious blood, God will
accomplish much that is good and useful. Comfort yourselves,
therefore, with such divine comfort and pray with the help of this
psalm that God's name be hallowed and his kingdom extended.
Amen.

I ask you, for God's sake, take care of the people of
Dithmarschen. Comfort and help them as friends so that they
may join us. For I hear that many of them are very sorry that
such a tragedy was caused in their land by the monks. God has
kindled a good spark. It will spread and become a great fire if you
act in a spirit of friendship and kindness so that it is not extinguished.
I commend to your care Jacob Propst,[8] your preacher, and also the
other one.[9]

May God strengthen them and all of you and grant you grace
to hold fast to the doctrine sealed by Henry's blood and, if God
should demand it, to follow gladly in his footsteps. Amen. All our
brethren greet you in Christ. Pray for us. The grace of God be
with you. Amen.

THE HISTORY OF BROTHER HENRY OF ZÜTPHEN

Henry came to Bremen in the year A.D. 1522. He had no intention
of preaching there, since he was at the time on his way to
Wittenberg. He had just been expelled for the sake of the gospel
from Antwerp by the tyrants of that city.[10] But while in Bremen,
some godly Christian citizens asked him to preach a sermon. Out
of Christian love he consented, and preached his first sermon on
the Sunday preceding St. Martin's Day [November 9, 1522]. When

---

[8] Cf. p. 265 n. 2. Cf. WA, Br 3, 402 (Jacob Propst to Luther, end of December, 1524); PE 4, 187 n. 2.
[9] John Timann, another preacher of the gospel from Amsterdam who came to Bremen soon after Propst. WA 18, 229 n. 1.
[10] This is a reference to Margaret of Savoy.

the people heard him and realized that he taught the Word of God, the whole congregation earnestly invited and urged him to stay with them in their parish and to preach to them the Word of God. Henry agreed to try it for a while. But as soon as this became known to the so-called "spiritual leaders," namely, the canons,[11] together with the monks and priests, they tried everything to suppress and expel both him and the Word of God. They were, of course, motivated by their greed, as is the case everywhere. Now in order to achieve their purpose they petitioned the honorable and wise city council to expel that wicked heretic, on the grounds that his teaching and preaching were against the holy Christian church. Acting on such a request, the wise city council then summoned the trustees and elders of the parish in which Henry preached and laid before them the accusations of the chapter [of St. Ansgar] and of the other clergy.

To this the trustees of the parish replied that as far as they could tell they had engaged a godly and learned preacher who taught them the Word of God in its truth and purity. If, however, the chapter or anyone else, whoever it might be, could bring proof that Henry had taught or preached anything contrary to God's Word or otherwise heretical, they would not under any circumstances tolerate or keep him, but would rather assist the chapter in prosecuting him. If, however, the lords of the chapter and the other clergy could not prove the charge against Henry that he had taught contrarily to God's Word, and if they were merely trying to drive him out by force and without any fault on his part, the trustees would never tolerate such action. They therefore requested the honorable council, most respectfully, not to expect them to take such action against Henry but rather to protect them in their legal rights. The trustees, on their part, would see to it that their preacher conformed at all times to the law. The honorable council communicated this reply to the chapter through their representatives.

When the "spiritual leaders" perceived that they could accomplish nothing with good words, they resorted to anger and threats.

---

[11] The canons of the chapter of St. Ansgar. The church where Henry preached was a chapel within the parish of St. Ansgar in the city of Bremen. WA 18, 229 n. 3 and 4.

They ran immediately to their bishop[12] and reported to him that the people of Bremen had become heretics and refused obedience to their clergy. They added many complaints about the danger that the whole city would be led astray.

Then the bishop sent two of his councilors[13] to Bremen and instructed them to see to it that the monk was brought to him. When they were asked why Henry was to be surrendered they replied that he was preaching against Holy Church. Asked further to indicate in what way and at which points he had done this, they had no answer. One of the councilors was the suffragan bishop, a Dominican; he did his utmost to apprehend Brother Henry, fearing that he might otherwise find himself without a job.

The honorable council finally answered him. Since the preacher they had engaged had not been refuted from holy Scripture, and since nobody seemed to be able to point out any specific article on which he preached falsely, they saw no way to induce their citizens to let him go. For this reason they respectfully requested their gracious lord bishop to send his foremost theologians to Bremen to hold a disputation with their preacher. If the latter were found to be in error, they would expel him as a fitting punishment; but if not, they could not see their way to dismiss him, etc.

To this statement the suffragan bishop replied, urging them earnestly, for the sake of the peace of the whole land, to surrender the preacher to him. He protested vigorously that he sought nothing but the salvation of their souls. However he accomplished nothing, for the citizens of Bremen held to their original reply.

As a result, the suffragan bishop became very angry and left Bremen. And his anger was so great that he refused afterwards to confirm the children of those heretics. On returning to his lord, he submitted to him the above reply together with the reports he had

---

[12] Bremen was at that time not an imperial city but it was the ecclesiastical and political capital of the archdiocese of Bremen. However, as a member of the Hanseatic League it enjoyed considerable independence from the archbishop, Christopher von Braunschweig, who was also bishop of Verden where he chose to reside. J. Friedrich Iken, "Heinrich von Zütphen" in *Schriften des Vereins für Reformationsgeschichte* (Halle, 1886), VI, 33-34, 43.

[13] Actually he sent the suffragan bishop, who was a Dominican, and two canons of Verden, Michael and Diedrich of Mandelslohe; also the nobleman Alverich Clüver, the magistrate Droste Diedrich of Staphorst, and the chancellor Johann Rapen. *Ibid.*, p. 43.

obtained from the priests and monks. After this, as each day brought fresh news of how the preacher [Henry] was daily delivering ever more powerful sermons against the clergy, they changed their tactics and sent some prominent men to warn the citizens of Bremen of the harm that would come to their city on account of their preacher, for he was violating the decree of his holiness, the pope, and his majesty, the emperor. They also made it known that he was an escaped prisoner of Lady Margaret, which was likely to bring them great harm. They also published writs from Lady Margaret which demanded the surrender of her prisoner. All this was to no avail, for the wise and honorable council always replied to everything in impeccable manner, both in its written and its oral statements.

Then the bishop and his crowd concocted another scheme to suppress the Word of God. They called a provincial synod, not at Bremen, as is customary, but at Buxtehude,[14] where they would be free to deal with Brother Henry as they pleased. To this synod they cited and summoned all the prelates and theologians in the whole diocese, for the announced purpose of discussing matters of faith and practice.

The preacher [Henry] was also cited to this synod, but with the difference that he was to be proceeded against as a heretic, although he had been neither tried nor convicted. Therefore the elders and the whole parish refused to let their preacher attend, for the malice of the enemies was apparent to everybody. Brother Henry, however, prepared a summary of his preaching, that is, of the things he taught and believed, formulated it in brief articles,[15] and sent it to the archbishop with a letter in which he showed his innocence and the truth of his articles. He also offered, if they could show from Scripture where he was in error, to give up and recant such error; only they would have to show it from holy Scripture, for he was prepared to prove the truth of his teaching and preaching from Scripture.

This offer, together with the articles, was [apparently] ignored,

---

[14] March 10, 1523. WA 18, 231 n. 3.
[15] These were his theses on justification which he had submitted at Wittenberg for his Bachelor of Divinity degree (Jan. 12, 1521) and defended before the Augustinian chapter at Grimma (Whitsunday, 1522). WA 18, 231 n. 4.

for he received no answer. What decision the synod reached may be gathered, however, from the fact that immediately afterwards they ordered the bull of Pope Leo X[16] and the imperial edict issued at Worms[17] to be published and posted. Nevertheless the godly preacher continued his sermons without letup, always insisting that he was willing and ready to answer everyone for his doctrine and preaching [I Pet. 3:15].

Meanwhile the papists were not idle but sent their younger clergy every day to his services, in order to entangle him in his words. But God showed his marvelous power and converted some of them, so that a majority of the younger clergy they sent admitted that such doctrine and preaching were the truth and were from God, which no one could oppose. They added that they had never in their lives heard such teaching from any man.

Learning from this experience, his enemies should have abandoned their evil ways, stopped persecuting God's Word, and believed, so that they might have been saved. But their wickedness had blinded them and hardened them like Pharaoh [e.g., Exod. 7:3] and they became even more wicked, as they deserved. Although they daily cried, "Heresy! Heresy!" not one of all these monks has been able to this day to say a single word against Henry's preaching; and they never will be able to.

Now when Almighty God saw that the time had come for the good Henry to bear witness with his blood to the truth he had proclaimed, He sent him into the midst of the murderers whom He had raised up for this purpose. It so happened that in the year A.D. 1524 Henry was called by Pastor Nicolas Boye[18] and other good Christians of the same parish at Meldorf in Dithmarschen to proclaim to them the Word of God and deliver them from the jaws of Antichrist, who was ruling there with great power. Accepting

---

[16] Either the bull, *Exsurge Domine*, of June 15, 1520, which condemned forty-one of Luther's propositions and threatened him with excommunication if he did not recant within sixty days, or the actual bull of excommunication, *Decet Romanum Pontificem*, which had been issued in Rome on January 3, 1521.

[17] The Edict of Worms, written by the papal nuncio, Aleander, dated May 8, 1521.

[18] A member of one of the more prominent families in Dithmarschen, Boye was born about 1500, studied in Wittenberg under Luther, and returned to his homeland in 1523, where he was given charge of the parish of Meldorf. He died in 1542. Iken, *op. cit.*, pp. 76-77; *PE* 4, 91 n. 1.

this as a call from God, Henry promised to come to them. On St. Catherine's eve [November 24, 1524] he invited six good brethren and fellow citizens to his house and told them of his call to Dithmarschen and of his decision to go and see what God would accomplish through him. He added that he was duty bound to preach the Word of God not only to the people of Bremen but to all who desired to hear it. Then he asked them to advise him how he could best proceed to Dithmarschen without telling the whole congregation and having them try to dissuade him, which they would certainly try to do. These good Christians answered by urging him to remain with them and to bear in mind that the gospel had gained only a very loose hold upon the populace in general, especially in the towns surrounding Bremen, and that the persecution was still strong. They also reminded him that he had been called by them to preach the Word of God. If the people of Dithmarschen wanted a preacher, he should send them someone else, for they knew very well what kind of folk these people of Dithmarschen were. Moreover, they told him that they did not know how they could let him go without the consent of the entire parish.

Henry acknowledged that he had indeed been called by them, but he added that they had many godly and learned men to preach to them. Furthermore, the papists were largely discredited, so that even women and children were able to see through and reject their foolishness; besides, he had preached to them for two years, while the people of Dithmarschen had no preacher at all. For this reason he could not with a good conscience refuse their request. As far as their inability to give him leave without the knowledge and consent of the whole congregation was concerned, that was not a conclusive argument to him, for it was not his intention to leave them permanently. His plan was rather to remain in Dithmarschen for only a short time, say one or two months, until he had laid a foundation by his presence and preaching, then he intended to return to Bremen. He therefore requested that after his departure they would make known to the congregation that a call had come to him which he had been unable to decline. He asked them to explain to the congregation the reasons for his secret departure, for he really had to leave secretly on account of his enemies who sought to harm him, lying in wait day and night, as was common knowledge, in order to kill him and get him out of the way. He assured them also that before long he would be back among them again. He convinced them with these words, and they allowed him to leave, for it was their hope that the people of Dithmarschen, who far surpassed other people in their idolatry, might come to a true knowledge of the Word of God.

On Monday of the first week in Advent [November 28, 1524] Henry began his journey through the very center of the diocese of Bremen to Dithmarschen. When he came to Meldorf, the village to which he had been called, he was received with great joy by the pastor of the parish and other good Christians. But as soon as he had arrived, and before he had even preached a sermon, the devil and his followers flew into a rage and stirred up especially a certain Augustine Torneborch, who was the prior of the Black Cloister. (Its monks were called Jacobins[19] or preaching friars.) He ran immediately to his comrade, Master John Snicken,[20] the vicar or commissioner of the legal representative of Hamburg, with whom he consulted about the measures that should be taken to prevent the collapse of their kingdom.

Eventually they decided that above everything they must not let Henry preach. For if he were to preach so that the common man heard him, their deceit would surely be exposed and the game would be up. They knew, of course, what had happened in Bremen. After they had reached this decision, the prior of the Dominicans, not having slept much during the night because of his worries, got up early in the morning—it was the Saturday before the Second Sunday in Advent [December 3, 1524]—journeyed to Heide, and appeared before the forty-eight regents of the whole district. Here he lodged a vigorous complaint, stating that the monk [Henry] had come from Bremen with the purpose of leading the whole land of Dithmarschen astray, just as he had done in Bremen. In these

---

[19] These were Dominicans, who were called Jacobins because their first convent in Paris was in a hospice bearing the name of St. Jacques. *PE* 4, 193 n. 1.

[20] It is interesting to note that John Snicken, who was so active in the persecution of Henry of Zütphen, was eventually converted to the cause of the Reformation and became superintendent in Heide. *WA* 18, 234 n. 1.

accusations the prior was supported by Master Günther,[21] the governmental secretary of the district, and by Peter Hannen,[22] both formidable enemies of the Word of God. Both of them supported the prior most eagerly and told the other forty-six regents, who were uneducated and simple men, that they could gain great fame throughout the Low Countries and earn undying gratitude, especially of the bishop of Bremen, if they would put this heretic monk to death. When they heard this, these poor and ignorant people immediately passed a written resolution to execute him, a man they had never seen, much less tried and convicted.

Finally, the prior obtained a letter or mandate from the forty-eight regents addressed to the pastor of the parish, ordering him, under full penalty of the law, to expel the monk before he ever preached a sermon. Armed with this mandate, the prior sped at once to Meldorf and delivered it to the good pastor during the night, hoping to keep Henry from preaching, for he knew very well how much was at stake. When the pastor read the letter or mandate, its contents puzzled him, for it was not customary for the "forty-eight" to trouble themselves about the churches. According to the ancient custom of this district, the right to manage its own affairs belonged to the duly constituted parish in its entirety. Indeed, it was a standing rule, ever since its adoption by the whole district, that every parish has the right to appoint and dismiss its pastor or preacher according to its own choice.

When the pastor informed Henry of the contents of the letter and told him also of the usage and custom of the district, Henry replied that since he had been called by the whole parish to preach the Word of God, he would abide by this call so long as it was the wish of the whole congregation. For we must obey the Word of God rather than man [Acts 5:29]. Furthermore, if God wished that he should die in Dithmarschen, it was obviously no farther to heaven from there than from any other place. Anyway, he would have to shed his blood some time for the Word of God.

In this mood he mounted the pulpit on the following Sunday [December 4, 1524] and preached his first sermon on Paul's words

---

[21] Günther Werner eventually became a faithful supporter of the evangelical cause. WA 18, 234 n. 3.
[22] The name was actually Nannen. WA 18, 234 n. 4.

in Rom. 1 [:9], "For God is my witness," etc., and on the Gospel for the day [Luke 21:25-36]. At the close of the service the whole congregation was called together and the letter of the forty-eight regents, brought by the above-mentioned prior, was read to them. It stated that under penalty of a thousand Rhenish gulden they were to stop the monk's preaching. In addition they were to send accredited delegates to Heide, where a session of the district council was to be held for disposal of an important matter.

When they heard this letter read, the congregation became very angry that such a mandate had been sent, completely contrary to the custom of the district, which granted each parish the right to elect as its preacher whomever it pleased. They decided unanimously to retain and protect the good Henry as their preacher, for they had been profoundly stirred by the first sermon they had heard him preach. In the afternoon Henry preached again, from Paul's words in Rom. 15 [:1], "We who are strong ought," etc.

On the following Monday [December 5, 1524] the people of Meldorf sent to Heide their delegates, who stated that they were prepared to defend their cause against anyone in the whole district. They also told about what Christian sermons they had heard from Henry. Furthermore, the pastor wrote a letter to the forty-eight regents, informing them that neither he nor Henry had any intention of fomenting trouble. They merely wanted to teach the pure and uncorrupted Word of God. And he offered to defend his and Brother Henry's cause against all accusers. In addition he humbly requested them not to trust the monks who, compelled by hatred and greed, were seeking to suppress the truth, and he asked them not to condemn the Word of God, but first of all to search out the truth very thoroughly and to condemn no one unheard. If they were found to be in the wrong, they were ready to take their punishment.

This offer, together with the testimony, was ignored; they did not even reply to it. Instead, everybody talked, one saying this, another that. Finally, Peter Detlefs,[23] one of the older men, spoke up, "Since there is great dissension everywhere in matters of faith, and since we who are the most unlearned and ignorant people are

---

[23] Peter Detlefs from Delve eventually became a staunch supporter of the Reformation. WA 18, 235 n. 4.

not able to judge such issues, it is our sincere opinion that the matter should be deferred until the forthcoming council. Our district secretary, Master Günther, has reported that such a council is supposed to be held in the near future. We are willing to accept whatever our good friends and neighbors hold and believe at that time. But if, as is claimed, the Word of God is not being taught clearly enough and if anyone is able to teach it more clearly and more purely, we have no intention of forbidding it, for we want no disturbance in our land. Therefore everybody ought to be calm and let the matter rest until next Easter. In the meantime it will perhaps become clear which position is right and which is wrong." This solution satisfied everybody. The delegates from Meldorf returned home and reported this decision to the assembled parish with great joy, hoping that all would turn out well.

On St. Nicholas Day [December 6, 1524] Brother Henry preached two sermons: the first on the Gospel, "A certain nobleman," etc. [Luke 19:12-27], the second on the text, "The priests were many in number," etc. [Heb. 7:23ff.]. He preached with such spirit that everyone was astonished and prayed God earnestly to let them keep such a preacher a long time. On the feast of the Conception of Mary [December 8, 1524] he preached two sermons on the Gospel, "The book of the genealogy" [Matt. 1:1ff.], in which he pointed out the promises concerning Christ which were made to the fathers, and the faith with which they were received. In addition, he showed how we too must be saved by such faith without any merit on our part. All this he taught with such spirit that everyone marveled and thanked God fervently for sending them such a preacher. For they now saw plainly how they had been duped by the monks and priests. They also earnestly urged him to spend Christmas with them and to preach twice a day, for they were afraid he might be called elsewhere.

Meanwhile the prior and Master John Snicken were not idle. For when the prior discovered that his malice had accomplished nothing, he went to Lunden with a Dominican, Doctor William,[24] to seek aid and counsel for accomplishing his purpose, from the

---

[24] William Soltzenhusen from Hamburg. WA 18, 236 n. 6.

gray monks, called barefoot friars or Minorites[25]—monks quite skilled in deceiving poor, naive people with their hypocrisy.

The gray friars at once summoned several of the regents— Peter Nannen, Peter Swin, and Claus Roden—and with their customary loud lamentation showed them how the "heretic" was preaching and misleading the people, some of whom had become his adherents. Unless they [the regents] took action and put the "heretic" to death the praise of Mary would cease and with it the two holy convents. That was the "Scripture" with which they meant to destroy the "heretic," which is precisely what happened. When the poor ignorant people heard the gray friars they became angry, and Peter Swin responded that they had written to the pastor and to Henry on how they were to conduct themselves and if necessary, they would write again. To this the prior replied, "No, you will have to do it some other way. If you begin writing to the heretic, he will reply, and as sure as you live you will be drawn into the same heresy, before you even know it. For when he begins to speak, it is impossible for anyone to hold out against him." Then they decided that he must be captured secretly by night and burned at once at the stake, before it became known to the people and before he could even open his mouth. This plan pleased all of them very much, especially the gray monks.

Now in order to carry out this plan, Peter Nannen, a particular friend of the prior and eager to curry favor, selected several leaders[26] from other villages, with the aid and advice of Master Günther. One should in fairness not mention any names, but since it was fame they were after they ought not to be deprived of it. These are the names of the ringleaders: Peter Nannen, Peter Swin's son, Henning of Lunden, John Holm, Lorenz Hannemann, Ludwig Hannemann, Bostel John Preen, Claus of Weslingburen, Brosi John of Wockenhausen, Marquard Kramer of Henstedt, Ludecke John of Wessling, and Peter Grossvogt of Hemmingstedt. These leaders and the others who were with them were ordered to the parish of Neuenkirchen, where they met at the house of Master Günther, the secretary, to consult on how best to capture the good Henry and

---

[25] Franciscans.
[26] Luther uses the word *Ammeral*, "admirals."

keep him from speaking. For they had already passed sentence upon him to be burned.

They agreed to meet on the second morning after the festival of the Conception of Mary [December 10, 1524] at Hemmingstedt, half a mile[27] from Meldorf, and set up a road block on the streets leading to Meldorf so that no one would be able to warn the people of the village. It was also ordered that at nightfall, at the sound of the Ave Maria bell, the men of all the villages should assemble. As a result, about five hundred peasants gathered. When they were all present, the purpose of the summons was announced to them; for no one but the leaders knew the purpose of the assembly and what they were to do. When the common people heard the plan they wanted to turn back and not commit so wicked a deed. But the leaders commanded them, on pain of life and property, to proceed. It should also be added that they had drunk three barrels of Hamburg beer, which was to put them in a fighting mood. Thus they came fully armed to Meldorf at the stroke of twelve o'clock midnight.

The Jacobins or preaching friars provided them with lights and torches so that they were able to see and to make sure that the good Henry did not escape. They had also a traitor with them, Henning's Hans by name, who had betrayed everything. They broke into the parsonage and, in the manner of drunken, senseless peasants, smashed everything in sight—cans, pots, clothing, cups. But whenever they found something made of silver or gold they took it along. They burst into the pastor's bedroom, smiting and stabbing and shouting, "Kill him! Kill him!" Some drove him naked into the muddy road. There they seized him and ordered him to come along. But others shouted, "Let him go! We have no orders to capture him."

After they had vented their malice upon the pastor they burst in on good Brother Henry, dragged him naked from his bed, beating and stabbing like mad, drunken peasants. Then they tied his hands tightly behind his back and dragged and pushed him until even Peter Nannen—otherwise a venomous foe of the Word of God—was moved with pity, and told them to let Henry walk unmolested; he

---

[27] Approximately 2½ American miles.

would follow all right. They turned him over to a certain John Balke, to lead him, but instead of leading him, he dragged him along.[28]

When they had brought him to Hemmingstedt, they asked him how he had come to their district and what he wanted there. He answered politely and told them the truth, so that even they were moved and shouted, "Away with him! If we keep listening to him we shall become heretics, too." Henry then begged them to put him on a horse, for he was weary and exhausted, and his feet were very sore from having walked and being pulled naked and barefoot through the cold night and over icy roads. But his request produced only mocking laughter; they asked him if they were supposed to maintain a stable for a heretic. Anyway, he would have to walk. Then they continued dragging him through the night as far as Heide, where they took him to the house of a man named Raldenes. They wanted to bind him with iron chains but the owner of the house took pity on him and would not permit it. When he refused to let them have their evil way they took the good Henry to the house of a priest named Reimer Hozek, an assistant of the legal representative of Hamburg, locked him in the cellar, and placed him in the custody of the drunken peasants who spent the whole night deriding and mocking him. Among others, he was visited by Simon, the priest of Altenworden, and Christian, the priest of Neuenkirchen, both most ignorant persecutors of God's Word. They asked him why he had put away the sacred habit. He answered them politely, on the basis of Scripture, but they did not understand what he said.

Master Günther also visited him and asked whether he preferred to be sent to the bishop of Bremen or receive his reward in Dithmarschen. Henry answered, "If I have taught or done anything un-Christian you may indeed punish me for it. God's will be done!" Master Günther replied, "Listen to him, dear friends, he wants to die in Dithmarschen."

However, the crowd in general spent the whole night guzzling. At eight in the morning a council was held in the market place

---

[28] Propst wrote in his letter to Luther that they dragged Henry, tied to the tail of a horse, as far as Heide. WA, Br 3, 402 (Jacob Propst to Luther, December, 1524).

to decide what was to be done. The drunken peasants shouted, "Go ahead, burn him! To the fire with him! Today we shall gain favor with God and man. The longer we let him live the more people he will pervert with his heresy. What's the use of long deliberation? He has to die anyway." Thus the good Henry was condemned to the stake without even a hearing.

Thereupon, an announcement was made that all who had assisted in his capture should march out with their weapons to the fire. The gray or barefoot friars were also on hand, encouraging the wretched creatures. They said, "Now you are doing the thing right," all the time baiting these poor, miserable, drunken people. Then they took Henry and bound him, neck and feet and hands, and led him away with loud shouts to the fire. A woman who was standing in her doorway saw them pass by and began to weep bitterly at this pitiable sight. The good Henry said to her, "Dear woman, do not weep for me!" [Luke 23:28]. When he came to the place where the fire had been prepared, he sat down on the ground completely exhausted. Then came the magistrate, Schoesser Maes,[29] who, as it is credibly reported, was bribed to take this part. He condemned Brother Henry to the fire, pronouncing sentence in these words, "This scoundrel has preached against the Mother of God and against the Christian faith, wherefore, on behalf of my gracious lord, the bishop of Bremen, I condemn him to the fire." Brother Henry replied, "I have not done this, nevertheless, thy will be done, O Lord!" [Luke 22:42]. And lifting his eyes to heaven, he said, "Lord forgive them, for they know not what they do [Luke 23:34]. Thy name alone is holy, O heavenly Father!"

Suddenly Claus Jungen's wife, the sister of Peter Nannen, a resident of Meldorf and a good Christian woman, stepped forward and standing before the fire offered to go to the whipping post and let them take their wrath out on her; besides she would give a thousand gulden, if they would just lock Henry up again until the following Monday so that he could be tried before the court of the whole district. Afterwards he could still be burned. But when

---

[29] It appears that the legitimate local magistrate was not willing to participate in this mockery of legal procedure. Therefore, for ten gulden, the conspirators bribed a former magistrate to add the appearance of legality to their actions. Iken, *op. cit.*, p. 88.

the crowd heard these words they went stark raving mad with fury and struck the woman to the ground and trampled her with their feet. They began beating the good martyr of Christ with all their might. One man beat him over the skull with his rapier, but John Holm of Neuenkirchen struck him with a mace. The rest stabbed him in the sides, the back, the arms, and wherever they could get at him, not just once, but as often as he attempted to speak.

Meanwhile Master Günther egged the crowd on and baited them, shouting to them, "Go to it, my fine fellows! This is God's work!" Then the same Master Günther brought an ignorant gray friar to hear Henry's confession. The martyr of Christ said to him, "Brother, have I ever offended you in any way or provoked you to anger?" "Why, no!" replied the monk. "Then," said good Brother Henry, "what sin should I confess to you that you should forgive me?" The gray monk was ashamed and withdrew.

Now the fire would not burn no matter how often they tried to light it. Nonetheless they gave vent to their malice by beating him with halberds and pikes for about two hours. All that time he stood before the peasants, naked except for his nightshirt, and with eyes lifted to heaven. Finally they got a long ladder, to which they bound him very tightly in order to throw him into the fire. Then the good martyr of Christ began to recite the Creed. But somebody struck him in the mouth with his fist and told him to burn first; he could recite whatever he wanted to afterwards. Then somebody stood with one foot on his chest and tied him by his neck to a rung of the ladder so tightly that his mouth and nose began to bleed. He wanted to strangle him, since he saw that in spite of his many wounds he was unable to die.

Then they raised him up by means of the ladder. Somebody set his halberd against the ladder to help in raising it; for the district has no hangman. The halberd slipped off the ladder and pierced the holy martyr of Christ through the middle. Then they threw him with the ladder on the pile of wood. But the ladder fell off on one side. Finally John Holm pushed forward, took his mace, and struck Henry on the chest until he died, never to move again. Then they roasted him on the coals, for the wood refused to burn.

This, in brief, is the true history of the suffering of the holy martyr, Henry of Zütphen.

INDEXES

INDEX OF NAMES AND SUBJECTS

Absolution (*see also* the Keys)
  by Christ's promise, 47
  as common property, 51, 52, 76
  faith necessary in, 45-50
  role of priests in, 42, 75
Africa, fallen away from pope, 69
Agnes, St., 258
Aleander, Jerome, 5, 103, 123 n. 22, 276 n. 17
  report at Diet of Worms, 123-130
Alexander of Hales, 258
Alexander VI, Pope, 88
Alexandria, theology of, 128 n. 28
Ambrose, St., 9, 194, 221
Amsdorf, Nicholas von, 103, 119, 120, 259
Anastasia, St., 258
Ansgar, St.
  chapel, 263
  chapter, 273
Antioch, theology of, 128 n. 28
Antiochus, King, 96
Antwerp, 263, 264, 265 n. 2, 272
Apostates (*see* Heretics)
Apostles, equality of, 74
Aquinas (*see* Thomas Aquinas)
Arians, 73, 119, 128, 243-244
Aristotle, xviii, 78, 185, 186, 187, 191, 194, 205, 209, 217, 258
  Nichomachean Ethics, 209 n. 75
  Prior Analytics, 215 n. 79
  Topics, 215 n. 79
Arms-bearing, forbidden clergy, 89
Articles of faith
  Latomus' claim, 149
  Luther's denunciation, 83
  pope's power to establish, 76-79
  world drowning in, 154
Attribution, 201, 208
Attrition, 41
Augsburg, bishop of, 116
Augustine, St., 221, 231
  alone in his day, 9
  on canonical books, 118
  and Donatists, 41, 51
  on "fault," 204, 205
  on figurative language, xvii, 167
  on good works, 85, 86
  on the Holy Spirit, 74

  on human writings, 216-217
  on judgment without mercy, 44, 85
  on law
    and forgiveness, 209
    fulfilment of, 156, 157, 189
    and wrath, 154
  and Pelagians, 27
  on sin
    after baptism, 28, 194, 209
    consent to, 238
    apart from grace, 255
    and punishment, 34
  on "tending the sheep," 72
  on test by Scripture, 217
  on the will, 92
  works
    Against Julian, 27 n. 19, 92, 253 n. 98, 254 n. 99
    Against Two Letters of the Pelagians, 194 n. 59
    City of God, 238 n. 80
    Confessions, 44, 85
    Enchiridion ad Laurentium, 98 n. 140
    Letters
      #19 (to Vincentius), 167 n. 39
      #82 (to Jerome), 11, 118 n. 14
      #93 (to Vincentius), 216 n. 80
      #167 (to Jerome), 204 n. 71
    On the Gospel of John, 17 n. 10, 72 n. 85
    On Marriage and Concupiscence, 27 n. 19, 28 n. 20
    On the Spirit and the Letter, 92
    Retractions, 156, 189 n. 55, 209
    Sermons, 34 n. 28
Augustinians, Luther's followers, 263

Balke, John, 284
Ban (*see* Excommunication)
Baptism
  as common property, 51, 52
  Donatists on, 41
  faith necessary in, 14, 16
  and forgiveness of sin, 27, 28, 208, 209
  imperfection after, 191 n. 57
  and "new creation," 27
  and original sin, 21, 27

promise in, 18
and purity, 28
sin remaining after, 19-31, 157-159, 191 n. 57, 194, 203, 206-209, 220-222, 236, 251
withholding by pope, 60, 61
Barefoot friars (see Friars)
Basel
    Council of, 59, 81 n. 98
    Luther's books from, 106
Bede, on unavoidable sins, 183 n. 50
Begging (see Mendicant orders)
Beghards, 129
Belgium, Luther controversy, 135
Bernard, St. 221
Bible translation
    Aramaic, of Old Testament, 193 n. 63
    Luther's, xvi, 135-136, 138 n. 7, 259
Biel, Gabriel, 153 n. 24
Bishops, equality of all, 74
Black Cloister, 278
Bock, Dr., of Strassburg, 116
Bohemians
    "both kinds" in communion, 56, 59
    fallen away from pope, 69
Bonaventure, St., 258
Bondage of the will, 92
Boniface II, Pope, 152 n. 23
Book burning, x, 5, 47, 66, 83, 105, 137 n. 1, 150, 218, 237
Books
    canonical, 118
    Luther's, condemned at Worms, 131
Boye, Nicholas, 263, 276
Brandenburg, Margrave Joachim of, 116, 119
Brandenburg, bishop of, 116
Braunschweig, Christopher von (see Bremen, bishop of)
Bremen, xix, 263-284, passim
Bremen, bishop of, 274 n. 12, 279, 284
Brussels, 263, 266
Bucer, Martin, 103
Buchführer, George, 266
Bulls, papal (see Exsurge Domine and Decet Pontificem)
Bundschuh, 115 n. 10
Burning of books (see Book burning)
Burning of heretics (see Heretics)
Buxtehude, 275

Cajetan, Cardinal, ix
Canon law

ban as medicine, 67 n. 81
    penitential canons, 33 n. 26
Cataphrygians, 211
"Celestial Word," hymn, 57
Cesarini, Cardinal, 90 n. 121
Charity, offenses of, 118
Charles V, Emperor, xiii, xiv, 105-128, passim
    Declaration at Worms, 114
Christ
    in absolution, 47
    benefits in New Testament, 29
    our bishop, 28
    example of, versus doctrine, 33
    freedom from law, 207-208
    merits of, 62
    not preached, 17
    refuge in grace of, 254
    righteousness of, our cover, 28
    signs of, 78
    made sin for us, 200-201, 206
    as teacher only, 154
    to trust instead of works, 235-236, 239-241
Christian of Neuenkirchen, 284
Church councils
    authority, 80-82, 113-114, 127, 159
    "both kinds" decree, 55, 62
    censure by Luther, 117
    on conception of Mary, 79-80
    confidence in by Charles V, 114 n. 9
    contradictions denied, 116
    faith strengthened through, 130
    heresies rejected, 129
    judgment on Luther, 120, 121
Church fathers (see Fathers, church)
Churches, equality of, 82
Classical learning (see Sophists)
Claus of Weslingburen, 282
Cleen, Dietrich von, 116
Clement VI, Pope, 75 n. 89
Clüver, Alverich, 274 n. 13
Cochlaeus, Johann, 119, 120
Cologne, 264
"Commandments of God are impossible" (see Impossible)
Commandments, pope's power to make, 76-79
Communion (see Sacrament of the Altar)
Compostella, St. James of, 41, 96
Condemnation
    and grace, 255
    and involuntary sin, 238-242
Confession, 32-36

faith necessary in, 16
full and complete, 42-44
Henry of Zütphen, 286
Lenten, 36
reliance on at sacrament, 54-55
venial and mortal sins, 42-44, 159
Conradi, Tilemann, 120
Conscience
    examination of, 55
    fear in purgatory, 32
    and grace, 40
    Luther's at Worms, 112, 113, 130
    scars branded on, 36, 37
Constance, Council of, xi, 82, 83 n.
    104, 87, 114 n. 9, 113, 117, 122,
    129 n. 32
Contrition, 32-42, 47-48, 53-54 (see
    also Repentance)
    and death, 54
    faith necessary in, 42
    false, 34-38
    and forgiveness, 47-48
    as fruit of love, 35
    "gallows," 35, 39, 43
    and hypocrisy, 34-38
    "Judas," 35, 36, 39
    and justification, 53
    and the keys, 41
    and meditation on sin, 38
    pope's power in, 41
    prayer for, 35
    not sure, 53-54
    true, 39
    work of, 39-40
Council, church (see Church councils)
Creed
    Athanasian, 159-160
    condemned by pope, 46
    Henry of Zütphen recites, 286
    "life everlasting," 78
    Nicene, 243 n. 92
Crusades (see Turk)
Cruss, Johannes, 266 n. 5
Curia, Roman, ix, xiii
Cyprian, St.
    "sickness unto death," 22
    On Mortality, 22 n. 14

Death
    and contrition, 54
    and forgiveness at, 46
    and perfection, 24
    sin remaining until, 28
    wish for, 22
Debt (see Sin)

Decet Pontificem, xiii, 276 n. 16
Decretalium D. Gregorii Papae IX,
    88 n. 118
Decretals (see Articles of faith)
Decretum Magistri Gratiani, 110 n. 4,
    81 n. 99
Defect (see Sin)
Demodocus, 209
"Desire for the sacrament," 49-50
Desires of the flesh (see Sin in flesh)
Detlef, Peter, 280
Dialectics, Luther's knowledge of,
    184-185
Diedrich, Droste, 274 n. 13
Diet of Worms, xii-xv 101-131
    Luther's speech, 109-113
    reports of
        Aleander, 123-130
        Luther sympathizers, 105-123
Dietrich, Veit, xvi n. 21
Diocletian, 258 n. 104
Dionysius, 170, 259
Dithmarschen, xix, 263-284, passim
Doctrines (see Articles of faith)
Dominicans
    immaculate conception belief, 79
        n. 95
    lynching of Henry Zütphen, 263,
        278
Donatists, and sacraments, 41, 51
Dort, 264
Duns Scotus
    on free will, 153 n. 24
    on immaculate conception, 79 n. 95

Eastern Orthodox church (see Greek
    church)
Eck, Johann (of Ingolstadt), ix, x, 5,
    67 n. 83, 98, 99
Eck, Johann (secretary to archbishop
    of Trier), 104-124, passim
Eckhart, Meister, 95 n. 132
Edict of Worms, 123-130, 276
Ephesus, Council of, 128 n. 28
Erasmus, 135, 137 n. 5
Esschen, John van den, 263, 266
Eternal life compared to earthly, 260
Eucharist (see Sacrament of the
    Altar)
Eutychians, 128
Excommunication
    attitude toward ban, 67
    of bishops or presbyters, 87 n. 113
    Luther's, ix, 5, 115, 125, 234

Decet Pontificem, xiii, 276 n. 16
external penalty, 66-67
Waldenses, 129 n. 30
Exsurge Domine, ix, 5, 83 n. 105, 109,
    137 n. 1, 187 n. 52a, 276 n. 16
    German translation, 15 n. 8, 45

Fabri, Johann, x
Faith
    articles of (*see* Articles of faith)
    "built on history," xvii-xviii
    dispute forbidden, 130
    as hidden gift, 227-232
        purges sin, 229, 232-233
    infusion of, 49
    and the law, 178
    offenses of, 118
    and sacraments (*see* Sacraments)
    and salvation, 15
    and trust in Christ, 235-236, 239-
        241
    unity of, 74, 82
Fasting, 21
Fathers, church
    erring, 151, 189
    tested by Scripture, 217
    wilderness, sacrament, 61
Fault (*see* Sin)
Fear
    erased by pope, 44
    in death, 31-32
Felix V, Pope, 81 n. 98
Fifth Lateran Council, 78 n. 91
Figurative language
    Augustine on, xvii, 167
    use in Scripture, 195-201
Flesh, "nothing good in," 249
Forgiveness
    in baptism, 27, 28, 208, 209
    and contrition, 47-48
    at death, 46
    faith necessary in, 44-47, 50
    and law, 209
    and mercy of God, 44, 48
    and remission of penalties, 76
    sin against Holy Spirit, 95-96
Franciscans
    on immaculate conception, 79 n. 95
    Minorites, 282 n. 25
    Frederick II, xiii n. 13
Frederick the Wise, Elector, xiii
Free will, 136
    and law, 153
    in "modern" theology, 153-154
    and original sin, 92-94

and sophists, 94
Friars
    gray, barefoot, 282, 285
    preaching, 278, 283
Fruit of the sacrament, 60

"Gallows contrition" (*see* Contrition)
General councils (*see* Church
    councils)
George of Wertheim, Count, 116
George of Saxony, Duke, 116
Gerson, John, 160
Gift (*see* Faith)
Glapion, 103
"God commands the impossible" (*see*
    Impossible)
God
    man cannot do, 35
    none in flesh, 249
Good works
    "actual performance," 155-156
    church hidden by, 7
    exalting of, 182
    and grace, 86, 154, 225, 226
    and indulgences, xi, 64
    judgment on, 172-176
    and justification, 84-85, 191-192
    and love, 38
    and peace, 193
    pope's power in, 76-79
    pride in, 91
    reliance on, 44, 54-55
        God's mercy, 83, 91, 172, 175,
            209
    sin in, 83-87, 91, 94, 136, 160-217,
        234-235, 253-254
    testing on last day, 95
Gospel, the
    and children, 258
    and freedom from sin, 226-229
    and law, 136, 177, 257
Gospel writings, dispute prohibited,
    148, 149
Grace (*see also* Mercy of God)
    and belief, 45
    and condemnation, 255
    and conscience, 40
    desire for, 13
    as gift of God, 251
    and good works, 86, 154, 225, 226
    as outward good, 178, 227-232
    infusion of, 49
    and justification, 208, 209
    and law, fulfilment of, 153, 157,
        177

in New Testament, 28
and refuge in Christ, 254
and sin, 23, 38, 136, 257
as the spirit, 177
in "modern" theology, 153-154
and virtues, 225-226
Gray friars (see Friars)
Greek church
and communion, 59
and the pope, 68, 69
as schismatic, 60
and Scripture, 96
Gregory, St., 221
on authority of Scripture, 257
on contending with God, 85
on good works, 85, 86, 91
on sin after baptism, 158-159
on sin against Holy Spirit, 95-96
validity of, xviii
on voluntary sin, 242
works
Dialogorum Libri, 95 n. 133
Epistles, 158 n. 29
Moralia, 85 n. 109, 91
Works, 242 n. 90
Grossvogt, Peter of Hemmingstedt, 282
Guilt
remission of, 50-53
and repentance, 27

Half-sacrament, 56, 58, 59
Hannemann, Lorenz and Ludwig, 282
Hanseatic League, 274 n. 12
Healing through sacraments, 24
Heaven
pope's "heaven," 30
and "tinder" of sin, 29-31
Heide, 278, 280, 284
Hell, pains of, 31
Hemmingstedt, 283, 284
Henning of Lunden, 282
Henning's Hans, 283
Henry of Zütphen, xviii, 261-286
Henry VIII, 122 n. 21
Henstedt, Marquard Kramer of, 282
Heretics
burning, 87-89, 128
punishment of empire, xiii n. 13
Hilary
and defending truth, 144
"heavenly precepts," 194
on sin as penalty, 244
works
On the Trinity, 144 n. 12, 194

n. 60
Against Constantius, 244 n. 94
Holland, Luther controversy, 135
Holm, John, 282, 286
Holy Communion (see Sacrament of the Altar)
Holy Spirit
and blasphemy, 163, 164
and freedom from law, 79
"inpouring" of, 35-36
and the Jews, 164
nature of, 73-74
and pseudorighteousness, 173, 175
sin against, 95-96
work against sin, 23
work in Lord's Prayer, 24
Homoousion, 243, 244
Hope, erased by pope, 44
Horace
"Epicurean swine," 141
new words from old, 195 n. 61
works
The Art of Poetry, 195 n. 61
Epistles, 141 n. 10
Hozek, Reimer, 284
Human writings
freedom of use, 216 217
use by Latomus, 257
not lucid, 236-238
not sacred, 243-245
sophists exalt, 148
Humanism, 135
Hungary, 266
Huss, John, xi, xii, 56 n. 59, 71, 74, 75, 82-83, 83 n. 104, 87, 117, 127, 129
Hutten, Ulrich von, xii
Hypocrisy, and contrition, 34-38
Hypocrites, "saved" and "damned," 256

Idolatry, 136
Immaculate conception of Mary, 79-80
Immortality
papal decree, 77-78
philosophical ideas, 78 n. 92
Imperfection
after baptism, 191 n. 57
sin as (see Sin)
Impossible, God commands the, 151-157, 180, 209-210, 215
Imputation (see Sin)
Indulgences
antichristian fraud, 64-66
bell-ringing, 51 n. 54

Eck's support of, 103
and good works, xi, 64
Latomus on, 136, 257
pious fraud, xi, 64-66
satisfaction remitted by, 32-34
treasures of the church, 62-64
and the Turks, 88, 90
validity of, 33-34
Infants, unbaptized, 54
Infusion of faith and grace, 49
Innocent III, Pope, 61
Intercession, souls in purgatory, 97-98

Jacobins, 278, 283
Jacques, St., hospice, 278 n. 19
Jerome of Prague, 87
Jerome, St., 221
  alone in his day, 9
  on death, 268 n. 7
  on false contrition, 36
  "God commands the impossible,"
    152, 156
  invented words, 243, 244 n. 93
  on Isa. 64:6, 161
  on justification, 192
  man as sinner, 188
  method in commentaries, 161 n. 37
  on sin after baptism, 21
  on will of God, 189
  works
    Commentary on Isaiah, 36 n. 32
    Dialogue Against the Pelagians,
      152 n. 22, 188 n. 53, 189 n.
      54; 56
    Jerome to Augustine, 161 n. 37
    Preface to the Books of Samuel
      and Malachi, 96 n. 135
Jerusalem, rebuilding, 162, 163
Jewish works (see Reuchlin controversy)
Jonas Justus, xvi, 103, 120, 137, 259
Jonathan, targumist, 196
"Judas contrition" (see Contrition)
Judas Maccabeus, 96
Judgment (see also Wrath)
  God's accuracy, 86
  "eating and drinking," 54-55, 57
  on good life, 44
  on good works, 172-176
  man cannot face, 84, 85
  without mercy, 44, 45
  God's purpose in, 259-260
Jungen, wife of Claus, 285
Justification, 136
  and contrition, 53

and good works, 84, 85, 191-192
and grace, 208, 209
Henry of Zütphen's theses on, 275-
  276
and law, 155-156
prevention of, 43

Kalkoff, Paul, 103
Karlstadt, Andreas, 259
Keys, the (see also Absolution)
  and contrition, 41
  faith necessary in, 42, 76
  priest's power, 50-51
  remission of guilt, 52
  remission of penalty, 75-76
  right of possession, 51, 52
Knights of Rhodes, house of, 105, 106
Knowledge in the sinner, 136

Ladislas, King, 90
Laity
  "both kinds" at sacrament, 55-62
  Christian understanding, 7
  value of opinion, 81
Lambert of Beghe, 129 n. 29
Languages, ancient, Latomus on, 135
Lateran Council, Fifth, 78 n. 91
Latomus, works
  Articulorum doctrinae fratis
    M. Lutheri per theologos Lovanien-
      sis . . ., 135, 140 n. 9
  Condemnatio doctrinalis librorum
    Martini Lutheri . . . Lovaniensis
    et Coloniensis facta, 142 n. 11
  Dialogue on Three Languages, 135,
    153, 186, 205
  Works, 185 n. 51
Law (see also Canon law)
  ceremonial, 178
  and faith, 178
  and forgiveness, 209
  and free will, 153
  freedom from, 79, 207-208, 223-226
  fulfilment of, 155-157, 177, 189
  and gospel, 136, 177, 257
  and justification, 155-156
  and the letter, 177
  and sin, 20-22, 223-224, 246-247
  understanding by high priests, 10
  and wrath, 154, 224-226
Laws, human
  church hidden by, 7
  Luther's obedience to, 118
Leipzig Debate, 137 n. 2
Leo I, Pope, 148-149

Leo X, Pope, x, 5, 122 n. 21, 187 n. 52a, 276
Logic, Luther's knowledge of, 184-185
Lombard, Peter, *Sentences*, 26, 259
Lord's Prayer
  forgiveness of sin, 25
  work of Holy Spirit, 24
  pope's attitude, 56
Lord's Supper (*see* Sacrament of the Altar)
Louvain, xvi, 135-260, *passim*
Love
  and contrition, 35
  and fear, 31-32
  in good works, 38
  and repentance, 29
  and sin, 29
  in "tending sheep," 72-73
Lucia, St., 258
Lucifer, 30, 51, 81
Lunden, 281
Luther, works
  Adversus execrabilem Antichristi bullam, 5
  Assertio omnium articulorum . . . damnatorum, 5
  Babylonian Captivity of the Church, 33 n. 27, 56 n. 62, 59 n. 68
  Commentary on the Lord's Prayer, 106
  Commentaries on the Psalms, 106
  Concerning Confession and the Pope's Power to Order It, 159 n. 30
  Confitendi ratio, 44 n. 41
  Defense Against the Malignant Judgment of Johann Eck, 67 n. 83
  Disputation Against Scholastic Theology, 151 n. 21, 154 n. 25
  Disputation of Johann Eck and Martin Luther, 64 n. 73, 65 n. 74, 82 n. 101, 95 n. 130, 97 n. 136; 138
  Explanation of the Articles Debated at Leipzig, 80 n. 97, 83 n. 106, 176 n. 46
  Explanations of the Ninety-Five Theses, 65 n. 75, 76, 77; 97
    Thesis 4, 89 n. 119
    Thesis 5, 74 n. 87
    Thesis 7, 12 n. 5; 45 n. 44
    Thesis 13, 91 n. 122
    Thesis 18, 97 n. 137
    Thesis 24, 29 n. 21
    Thesis 26, 79 n. 94

    Thesis 58, 86 n. 111, 151 n. 21
    Thesis 80, 87 n. 112
  The Freedom of a Christian, 117
  Grund und Ursach aller Artikel . . . unrechtlich verdammt sind, 5
  Heidelberg Disputation, 92 n. 125, 159 n. 32
  Larger Treatise on Usury, 98 n. 141
  Leipzig Debate, Thesis 2, 19 n. 12, 158 n. 29
  Ninety-Five Theses
    Thesis 14, 31 n. 23
    Theses 56 & 58, 62 n. 70
  Of Threefold Justice, 117
  On Good Works, 106
  Open Letter to the Christian Nobility, 82 n. 102
  Proceedings at Augsburg, 81 n. 99
  Responsio Lutheriana ad condemnationem doctrinalem . . ., 135, 142 n. 11, 149 n. 18
  Sermon on Excommunication, 66 n. 79
  Sermon on Indulgence and Grace, 32 n. 24
  Sermon on Repentance, 35 n. 30, 38 n. 35, 42 n. 40, 44 n. 42, 47 n. 48, 49 n. 50, 53 n. 56
  Sermon on the Sacrament of Penance, 50 n. 53
  Sermon on the Worthy Preparation . . . the Eucharist, 54 n. 57
  Treatise Concerning the Ban, 66, 67 n. 82
  Treatise on the Blessed Sacrament, 56 n. 60
  Unterricht auf etlich Artikel, 95 n. 131
  Wider die Bulle des Endchrists, 5
  Why the Books of the Pope . . . Were Burned, 137 n. 1
Lyra, Nicholas of, 161

Maes, Schoesser, 285
Manasseh, King, 48
Mandelslohe, Michael and Diedrich, 274 n. 13
Margaret of Savoy, 263, 272 n. 10, 275
Marriage, and sin, 211-212
Martin, St., 116-117
Martyrs
  Henry of Zütphen, 261-286
  Reformation, xviii, 263, 266, 267
Mary (*see* Virgin Mary)

Masses, equality of all, 51-53
Masson, Jacobus (see Latomus)
Maximilian I, 150 n. 20
Meditation on sin (see Sin)
Melanchthon, Philip, xvi
Meldorf, 263-285, *passim*
Mendicant orders, 98-99
Mercy of God (see also Grace)
  and forgiveness, 44, 48
  and good works, 83, 91, 172, 175, 209
  and justification, 209
Merits
  Christ's and saints', 62-64
  in purgatory, 97
Minorites, 282
"Modern" theology, 153-154
Monckedamis, Rudolph de, 140 n. 9
Montanists, 128, 211 n. 78
Morals, pope's power over, 76-79

Nannen, Peter, 279, 282, 283, 285
Nestorians, 128
Netherlands, Luther controversy, 263
Neuenkirchen, parish of, 282
"New creation"
  in baptism, 27
  and free will, 94
  and sin, 39-40
New Testament
  benefits of Christ, 29
  grace in, 28
  sacraments and symbols in, 17-19
Nicaea, Council of, 128 n. 25, 243 n. 92
Nicholas of Lyra, 161
Nicholas of Tudesco, 81
Nicholas, St., 116-117
Ninth Psalm, exposition, 264, 265, 268-272

Obstacle, put in the way an (see Sacraments)
Occam, William, 153 n. 24
Offenses of charity and faith, 118
Old Testament
  Aramaic translations, 196 n. 63
  sacraments and symbols in, 18-19
Onkelos, 196
Oppenheim, 123
Orange, Synod of, 152, n. 23
Orient, fallen away from pope, 69
Origen, 194, 217
Original sin
  and baptism, 21, 27

and free will, 92-94
and repentance, 21
"tinder" of (see Tinder of sin)

Palatine, Count, quarters, 106
Panormitanus, 81
Papacy, human invention, 68-74, 82
Pappenheim, Ulrich von, 105, 106
Peace, and good works, 193
Pelagians, 27
Penalty (see also Punishment)
  remission of, 33-34, 52, 63, 75-76
  sin as (see Sin)
  on hardened sinners, 37
Penance, 32-34, 136, 257
  as common property, 51
  "gallows contrition," 43
  pope's duty in, 61
  power to give, 50-53
  priest's power in, 59-60
  remission of guilt, 52
  source of, 16
Persius, *Satires*, 196 n. 62
Peter, St.
  belief in Rome burial, 96
  pope's claims about, 68-74
  power of, 76, 82
Peutinger, Konrad, 116, 120
Pfefferkorn, Johann, 150 n. 20
Photinians, 128
"Pious fraud" (see Indulgences)
Pius IX, Pope, 79 n. 95
"Pledge of the Nobles," 115 n. 10
Poor Men of Lyons, 129
Pope
  "binding and loosing," 74-76
  Latomus on reproving, 143
    Luther's reply, 143-148
  called murderer, 89
  power in handling sins, 52
  not vicar of Christ, 67-74
Power of the keys (see Keys)
Prayer
  bed-time, of pope, 88
  for contrition, 35
  desire for grace, 13
  of the Jews, 163
  the Lord's Prayer (see Lord's Prayer)
  for pope, 143-144
  before sacrament, 54-55
  and secret sins, 43, 44
Preaching, papacy's lack, 73
Preen, Bostel John, 282
Prierias, Sylvester Cardinal, ix

Priesthood of all believers, 50-53, 73
Prophetic writings, dispute prohibited, 148, 149
Prophets
  low status, xi, 9
  rarity, 8, 9
Propst, Jacob, 265 n. 2, 272, 284, n. 28
Pseudorighteousness, 173, 175
Punishment (*see also* Penalty)
  attribution of, 201
  rule of pope as, 61
  and salvation, 65
  self-punishment, 33, 34, 65
Purgatory, 136, 143
  fear in, 32
  intercession for souls in, 97-98
  as imperfect love for God, 31
  Luther's belief in, 95-98
  merits in, 97
  pope's captive, 75
  and sin, 97
"Put an obstacle in the Way" (*see* Sacraments)

Quintilian, 202, 234

Rapen, Johann, 274 n. 13
Recantation, Luther urged to make, xi, xii-xvi, 108, 120, 124, 125, 127-128
Remission of guilt, 50-53
Remission of penalty (*see* Penalty)
Repentance (*see also* Contrition)
  canons, 33
  compulsory, 37
  as cure, 24
  faith necessary in, 49
  and forgiveness of sins, 28
  "gallows," 35, 39, 43
  and guilt, 27
  highest form of, 38-42
  hypocritical, 40
  "Judas," 35, 36, 39
  source in love, 29
  and meditation on sin, 38
  and original sin, 21
  and purity, 28
  required in sacrament, 13
Reuchlin controversy, 150, 176, 186 n. 52
Righteousness
  of Christ, our cover, 28
  judgment on, 172-176
Ritual, church hidden by, 7
"Rock, the," conflicting claims, 68-74

Roden, Claus, 282
"*Roma locuta, causa finita,* xiii

Sacrament of the Altar (*see also* Sacraments)
  "both kinds" to laity, 52-62
  and confession, 54-55
  Donatists on, 41, 51
  faith necessary in, 16-17, 54-55, 60, 62
  fruit of, 60
  Greek church, 59
  prayer before, 54-55
  preparation, reliance on, 54-55
  unworthy reception of, 58
Sacraments (*see also* Baptism, Penance, Sacrament of the Altar)
  authority of pope, 41-42, 50-53
  benefits, 49-50
  "desire for," 49-50
  faith necessary in, 13-17, 42, 49-50
  healing through, 24
  in New Testament, 17-19
  in Old Testament, 18-19
  "put an obstacle in the way," 12-18, 41
  and repentance, 13
  as signs, 15
  worthy reception of, 13
Safe-conduct, Diet of Worms, xiv, 115, 120, 121, 122
St. James of Compostella, 41, 96
Saints
  and Christ's word, 71
  doubt of sainthood, 96
  merits of, 62
  perfect in heaven, 31
  rebuke of, xi-xii, 9
  not scholastics, 258
  sin remaining in, 19-29, 37, 38, 43, 44, 53, 84, 93, 151, 159-160, 176, 180-181, 188, 210-211, 216, 254
  and work-righteousness, 83
Salvation
  and the Bible, 217
  and the law, 156
  and punishment, 65
  and sin, 28
Sanctification, 23, 136, 254
Santiago de Compostella (*see* St. James of Compostella)
Saracens, 129
Satisfaction for sin
  merits of Christ and saints, 62-64
  remission by indulgences, 32-34

Savonarola, Girolamo, 88
Schnaidpeck, Johann, 122 n. 19
Scholastic theology (*see also* Sophists) xviii, 257-259
Schurff, Jerome, 103, 106, 119, 120, 123
Scriptures (*see also* Bible translation)
  authority, 11-12, 81, 96, 159, 257
  and human interpretation, 223, 236-238, 243-245
  meaning of sin, 247-256
  and salvation, 217
Scultetus, Jerome, 116
Second Coming, 139-140, 203
Sedition, Luther on, 147-148
Self-punishment, 33, 34, 65
Sentences (*see* Peter Lombard)
Shrove Tuesday carnival, 31
"Sickness unto death," 22
Signs
  recording of Christ's, 78
  Word and sacraments, 15
Simon of Altenworden, 284
Sin
  attribution of, 201, 208
  after baptism (*see* Baptism)
  Christ made sin, 200-201, 206
  confession of, 42-44
  debt as, 231
  defect as, 25-31, 84-85
  devil as, 194
  dormant, 253-254
  fault as, 194, 203-217
  fighting of, 212-213
  in flesh, 19-29, 249, 252-256
    not ruling, 250-251
  forgiveness of (*see* Forgiveness)
  freedom from through
    gospel, 226-229
    law, 223-226
  in good works, 83-87, 91, 94, 136, 160-217, 234-235, 253-254
  and grace, 23, 38, 136, 255, 257
  imperfection as, 194, 203-217, 219, 220
  imputation of 249, 251
  involuntary, 238-242
  and law, 20-22, 223-224, 246-247
  and love, 29
  Luther's definition, 195
  in marriage, 211-212
  meditation on, 34-38
  motions of, 194, 214
  original (*see* Original sin)
  penalty as, 25, 194-195, 203-217,

230, 232, 244, 246, 249-251, 255
  and purgatory, 97
  reigning, 213-214
  and salvation, 28
  in Scripture, 247-256
  secret, 43, 44
  servant of, 256
  substance of, 201-202
  as "tinder" (*see* Tinder of sin)
  unavoidable, 183 n. 50
  in ungodly, 23, 252, 254
  voluntary, 242
  weakness as, 158, 203-220, 230-232, 246, 255
"Sin-grace," 221
Sixtus IV, Pope, 79 n. 95
Snicken, John 278, 281
Soltzenhusen, William, 281
Sophists (*see also* Scholastic theology)
  classical learning, ix
  "Epicurean swine," 141
  exalting words of men, 148
  and free will, 94
  at Louvain, 135-260, *passim*
  Luther not understood by, xviii
Spalatin, Georg, xii, xiv, xv, 103, 121, n. 18
Spaniards at Worms, 114
Spirit, the (*see* Holy Spirit)
Stadion, Christopher von, 116
Strassburg, 95
Sturm, Caspar, 106, 123
Swin, Peter, 282
Symbols, in Bible, 18-19
Synechdoche, 165-172, 179, 189, 190, 195, 249

Titian, 211
Tauber, Caspar, 260
Tauler, Johann, 95
"Tending the sheep," 71-73, 87, 88
Tertullian, 128 n. 26
Theology, "modern," 153-154
Thomas Aquinas, 257-258
  accused of heresy, xviii
  on immaculate conception, 79 n. 95
Timann, John, 272
"Tinder" of sin, 29-31, 214, 233
"To do what is in one," 153 n. 24, 154
Torneborch, Augustine, 278
Treasures of the church, 62-63
Trier, archbishop of, 116, 120-122
Truth, Luther on, 149
Turks, 10, 60, 72, 88, 89-91, 129, 149

Unbaptized infants, 254
Ungodly, the
    defending truth against, 144
    sin in (*see* Sin)
Unity
    churches, 82
    faith, 74, 82

Van den Esschen, John, 263, 266
Varna, Battle of, 90
Vehus, Dr., Chancellor of Baden, 118, 120
    Declaration at Worms, 116-117
Verbum Supernum Prodiens, hymn, 57 n. 64
Verden, 274 n. 13
Vestments
    church hidden by, 7
    as symbols, 18
Vienna, 266
Vienne, Council of, 129 n. 29
Virgil, *Aeneid,* 167 n. 40, 168 n. 41
Virgin Mary, the
    annunciation, 40
    controversy over conception, 79-80
    fulfilment of the law, 157
    lineage, 172
    Nestorian heresy, 128 n. 28
    praise of threatened, 282
Virtue in the sinner, 136
Virtues, not meriting grace, 225-226
Vos, Henry, 263, 266

Votum sacramenti, 49 n. 51

Waldenses, 129
Waldo, Peter, 129 n. 30
Wartburg, xvi, 135, 138
Weakness (*see* Sin)
Werner, Günther, 279-286, *passim*
Wessling, Ludecke John, 282
Will, bondage of, 92
Wittenberg, 263-265, 272, 276 n. 18
    burning papal bull at, 5, 105
    University of, 106 n. 1
Wockenhausen, Brosi John, 282
Word, the
    dissension over, 111
    power of, xii, xv, xvi, xviii, xix
    in universities, 259
Words of men (*see* Human writings)
Works (*see* Good works)
Worms, Diet of (*see* Diet of Worms)
Wrath (*see also* Judgment)
    and good works, 172-176
    and law, 154, 224-226
    wholly under, 228
Writings, human (*see* Human writings)
Wycliffe, John, 83, 129

Zevenberghen, Maximilian von, 122 n. 20
Zütphen, Henry of (*see* Henry of Zütphen)

INDEX TO SCRIPTURE PASSAGES

Genesis
3:15 — 20
4:4 — 84
4:4-5 — 199
4:7 — 213
6:3 — 93, 182
6:4 — 146
6:5 — 93, 225
8:21 — 93, 182, 225
10:9 — 64
11:1-9 — 89
15:6 — 15
17:14 — 183
23:13 — 146
32:28 — 193
49:7 — 197

Exodus
6:20 — 200
7:3 — 276
10:17 — 253
12:15 — 183
13:18 — 30
32:25 — 198
33:8 — 176

Numbers
11:5 — 223
22.1ff. — 150
22:28 — 10
23:19 — 26
25:3 — 140

Deuteronomy
4:19 — 196
6:7 — 197
28:65 — 31

Joshua
7:1-26 — 90
15:63 — 249
23:13 — 249

Judges
1 — 203
1:21 — 249
14:6 — 146
20:12-48 — 90

I Samuel
16:6-13 — 10

II Samuel
21:16-17 — 137

I Kings
8:46 — 181, 183
15:5 — 188

II Kings
1:2 — 140
19:28 — 161
20:3 — 191

Nehemiah
13:24 — 245

Job
1:21 — 122
5:13 — 112
9 — 173
9:3 — 85
9:5 — 112
9:15 — 86
9:21 — 91
9:22 — 172
9:28 — 91, 182, 259
32ff. — 218
41:1 — 146
41:14 — 146
42:1 — 146

Psalms
1:3 — 165
2:5 — 31
2:10 — 145
2:11 — 165
3:3 — 181
5:6 — 165, 226
5:9 — 197
6:2f. — 31
6:10 — 139
7:6 — x
7:8 — 192
9 — 268-272
10:5 — 213
14:3 — 169
14:6 — 10
15:2 — 173
16:4 — 163
16:11 — 168
18:37 — 219
19:1 — 195, 196

19:12 — 23, 43, 44, 53, 55, 91
19:13 — 252
24:8 — 252
24:10 — 252
25:11 — 47
28:5 — 169
32:1-2 — 169
44:17-18 — 173
45:3 — 168
45:7 — 190
51:5 — 211
51:10 — 23
58:4 — 215
66:12 — 95
68:18 — 206
69:4 — 200
69:5 — 200
69:9 — 200
72:14 — 266
73:2f. — 226
74:22 — x
78:18 — 171
80:12-13 — x
82:7 — 182
88:2 — x
89:17 — 181
89:32 — 33, 64
89:48 — 186
91:5-6 — 117
105:37 — 30
105:40 — 171
109:7 — 163
111:7 — 26
112:3 — 236
112:7 — 32
115:1 — 252
116:15 — 266
119:15 — 198
119:23 — 198
119:46 — 145
119:70 — 226
119:86 — 26
119:121 — 173
138:6 — 9
143:2 — 43, 53, 84, 172, 190, 193, 259
144:5 — 146
146:3 — 120

Proverbs
1:26 – 147
1:30 – 148
3:5 – 141
8:30-31 – 199
26:28 – 31
28:1 – 67
28:23 – 142

Ecclesiastes
7:20 – 83
7:29 – 212
10:10 – 198

Song of Solomon
2:14 – 240
2:15 – x

Isaiah
1:5 – 170, 179
1:6 – 170
2:4 – 88
2:8 – 181
2:10 – 240
5:14 – 139
6:10 – 199
7:14 – 140
8:14-15 – 118
10:8f. – 164
11:5 – 206
11:6 – 88
13:15 – 170
14:13 – 164
16:6 – 216
17:7-8 – 199
26:20 – 235
36:4f. – 164
37:29 – 161
41:3 – 40
48:9 – 48
48:11 – 48
53:4 – 63
53:12 – 267
56:10 – 146
57:1 – 166
59:2 – 85
63:3 – x
63:17 – 177
63:19 – 177
64:5 – 173, 174
64:5-12 – 162
64:6 – 83, 161, 169
64:7 – 166
64:8 – 164
64:9 – 164
66:12 – 198

Jeremiah
5:4f. – 10
6:14 – 12
8:11 – 12
9:1 – 139
9:23 – 181, 226
15:20 – 139
17:5 – 120
17:16 – 191, 192
18:18 – 9
23:5 – 173
30:11 – 173
49:12 – 173

Lamentations
1:4 – 237
2:2 – 169

Ezekiel
4:12 – 223
13:10 – 12
13:16 – 12
20:25 – 177, 178
29:3 – 164

Daniel
9:27 – 16, 163
11:31 – 16
12:11 – 16, 163

Hosea
1:9 – 164
5:12 – 178
5:14 – 178

Amos
1:1 – 9

Micah
2:9 – 91

Nahum
1:3 – 40

Habakkuk
2:4 – 14

Haggai
2:9 – 163

Malachi
4:2 – 236

Matthew
1:1ff. – 281

1:25 – 119
3:2 – 232
3:8 – 232
4:17 – 232
5:15 – 11
5:17 – 33
5:18 – 32
7:17 – 84
7:20 – 193
7:26 – 83
8:5-13 – 116
8:8 – 48
8:13 – 49
9:2 – 13, 32, 46
9:38 – 272
10:28 – 108
10:33 – 107
12:32 – 95, 96
12:33 – 116
12:40 – 171
13:33 – 24, 227, 232
13:43 – 30
13:58 – 13
16:18 – 68, 69
16:19 – 39, 42, 45
19:24 – 156
19:25 – 156
19:26 – 156
19:29 – 141, 168
21:31 – 37
23:10 – 77
23:16 – 142
23:33 – 141
24:5 – 64
24:15 – 16, 77, 92
24:24 – 77
26:26 – 16, 56
26:27 – 56
27:44 – 171
27:45 – 170

Mark
3:29 – 95
9:23 – 49
11:24 – 13
14:22f. – 56
16:15 – 145
16:16 – 16, 50
16:18 – 245

Luke
1:26-37 – 40
2:1 – 170
2:34 – 141
3:7 – 141

301

7:50 — 46
9:54-56 — 88
10:29-37 — 24
10:30ff. — 232
11:27 — 108
11:36-50 — 33
12:11-12 — 108
19:2-11 — 116
19:12-27 — 281
21:25-26 — 280
22:17f. — 56
22:38 — 168
22:42 — 285
23:28 — 285
23:34 — 285
24:47 — 231

John
1:8 — 248
1:14 — 228
1:16 — 228
1:17 — 228
3:10 — 146
4:21 — 163
4:23 — 163
4:44 — 13
6:51 — 63
7:19 — 221
7:20 — 141
8:11 — 32
8:33-36 — 92
8:43 — 255
8:44 — 141
8:55 — 141
10:12 — 146
13:10 — 158, 232
13:14 — 158
14:28 — 119
15:1ff. — 23
15:2 — 232
15:3 — 23
16:8 — 206
16:11 — 206
18:19-23 — 111
18:30 — 159
20:27 — 11
21:15-19 — 71
21:25 — 78

Acts
1:15-26 — 74
4:32 — 117
5:29 — 118, 146, 279
5:38-39 — 121
7:52 — 89

8:14 — 73
8:36f.— 14
9:6 — 40
10:34 — 145
13:10 — 142
13:38-39 — 155
15:5 — 156
15:9 — 54
15:10 — 155
15:11 — 18, 156
17:5 — 12
17:18 — 12
18:12 — 12
19:19 — 150
19:23-41 — 12

Romans
1:9 — 280
1:17 — 14
2:6 — 172
3:5 — 182
3:9 — 177
3:11-12 — 169
3:19-20 — 91
3:20 — 195, 223
3:21 — 227
3:23 — 171
3:24 — 47
3:24-26 — 28
3:25 — 239
3:28 — 227
4:7 — 169
4:15 — 154, 224
5:1 — 54, 227, 235
5:2 — 228, 236
5:7 — 267
5:12 — 224
5:13 — 37, 224
5:15 — 227, 239
5:20 — 154
6 — 194, 248
6:6 — 208, 214, 233
6:12 — 20, 208, 210, 212, 214, 231, 233
6:14 — 208, 211, 233
6:17 — 256
6:18 — 256
6:23 — 224, 229
7 — 158, 218, 248
7:7 — 19, 26, 194, 195, 223
7:12 — 178
7:13 — 233
7:14 — 237, 242, 246
7:15 — 246

7:15-25 — 242, 243
7:16 — 248, 250
7:17 — 248
7:18 — 19, 158, 249
7:19 — 246
7:19-20 — 250
7:20 — 25
7:21 — 251
7:22 — 20, 22, 237, 251
7:23 — 233
7:24 — 253, 254
7:25 — 21, 25, 233, 237, 246, 254
8 — 194, 248
8:1 — 27, 239, 255
8:2 — 79, 207, 233
8:3 — 200, 206
8:3-4 — 155
8:10 — 21
8:13 — 21, 207
8:26 — 164
8:28 — 66
8:34 — 28
9:29 — 170
9:32-33 — 118
10:10 — 15
11:32 — 91
14:23 — 14, 35, 55, 92
15:1 — 280
15:31 — 139

I Corinthians
1:31 — 181
3:4 — 182
3:13-15 — 95
4:3 — 182, 191
4:4 — 53, 55, 191, 235
5:7ff. — 248
5:8 — 233
7:3 — 211
7:5 — 211, 233, 248
7:28 — 188, 210
9:26 — 193
9:27 — 21
10:3f. — 18
10:4 — 70, 200
10:17 — 57
10:31 — 189
11:23-26 — 57
11:26 — 58
11:27 — 58
11:28 — 55, 58
11:31 — 33, 64
14:29 — 217
15:56 — 37

II Corinthians
3 — 178
3:6 — 79, 178
3:10 — 177
3:13 — 177
4:13 — 18, 140, 176
5:21 — 206
6:15 — 63
9:15 — 240
10:3 — 256
10:18 — 53

Galatians
1:8 — 56, 81, 119, 141
1:13 — 252
3:1 — 26
3:10 — 224
3:21 — 37
3:22 — 177, 224
5:4 — 198
5:11 — 198
5:16ff. — 248
5:17 — 20, 93, 231
5:19 — 22
5:22 — 193
5:24 — 20
6:13 — 198
6:15 — 39

Ephesians
1:6 — 139
2:2 — 11
4:4-16 — 74
4:5 — 51, 52
4:14 — 26
4:19 — 23
4:22 — 233, 248
5:2 — 266
5:26 — 30
5:27 — 30

Philippians
1:6 — 8
1:15-18 — 49
2:7 — 145
2:21 — 171, 165

3:2 — 142

Colossians
1:19-20 — 236
2:4 — 142
2:8 — 77, 142, 259
3:5 — 21, 207, 248, 233
3:8 — 233
3:17 — 189
4:3 — 139

I Thessalonians
5:21 — 11, 119, 217

II Thessalonians
2:3 — 63, 92
2:4 — 46, 66, 139
2:9 — 71
2:10 — 94
3:2 — 139

I Timothy
3:2ff. — 143
4:1 — 36, 77
6:20 — 223

II Timothy
2:9 — 145
2:24-26 — 92
4:2 — 197
4:7ff. — 192
4:13 — 189

Titus
1:9 — 149, 194
1:10 — 142
2:13 — 192

Hebrews
4:15 — 200
7 — 156
7:23ff. — 281
7:26 — 28
10:38 — 14
12:1 — 23, 233, 248
12:2 — 265

James
1:5ff. — 13
1:18 — 24
3:1 — 77

I Peter
2:5 — 70
2:8 — 118
2:11 — 20, 214, 231
3:15 — 276
5:8 — 188
5:9 — 70

II Peter
2:1 — 77, 93
2:19 — 256
3:13 — 29

I John
1:8 — 23
1:10 — 25
3:9 — 211
4:18 — 31

Revelation
3:20 — 40
8:3 — 139
13:1-18 — 82
17:8 — 66

APOCRYPHA

Wisdom of Solomon
4:16 — 71
19:7 — 74

Ecclesiasticus
34:11-13 — 94

Prayer of Manasseh
14 — 48

II Maccabees
12:43 — 96

Type used in this book
Body, 10 on 13 Caledonia
Display, Bulmer and Caledonia
Paper: Standard White Antique

303